The Princeton Review®

W0114364

# AP®
## ECONOMICS
## MICRO & MACRO
## PREMIUM PREP

**22nd Edition**

The Staff of The Princeton Review

PrincetonReview.com

Penguin
Random
House

The Princeton Review
110 East 42nd Street, 7th Floor
New York, NY 10017
princetonreview.com
penguinrandomhouse.com

Published in the United States by Penguin Random House LLC, New York.

ISBN: 978-0-593-51825-0
ISSN: 2690-5353

The material in this book is up-to-date at the time of publication. However, changes may have been instituted by the testing body in the test after this book was published.

If there are any important late-breaking developments, changes, or corrections to the materials in this book, we will post that information online in the Student Tools. Register your book and check your Student Tools to see if there are any updates posted there.

Editor: Orion McBean
Production Editors: Liz Dacey and Ali Landreau
Production Artist: Jennifer Chapman
Content Developer: Corinne Dolci

Manufactured in the United States of America

10  9  8  7  6  5  4  3  2  1

22nd Edition

EU Contact:
Penguin Random House Ireland
32 Nassau Street
Dublin D02 YH68
https://eu-contact.penguin.ie

**The Princeton Review Publishing Team**
Rob Franek, Editor-in-Chief
David Soto, Senior Director, Data Operations
Stephen Koch, Senior Manager, Data Operations
Deborah Weber, Director of Production
Jason Ullmeyer, Production Design Manager
Jennifer Chapman, Senior Production Artist
Selena Coppock, Director of Editorial
Aaron Riccio, Director, Editorial Admissions Content
Orion McBean, Senior Editor
Meave Shelton, Senior Editor
Chris Chimera, Editor
Patricia Murphy, Editor
Laura Rose, Editor
Isabelle Appleton, Editorial Assistant

**Penguin Random House Publishing Team**
Tom Russell, VP, Publisher
Alison Stoltzfus, Senior Director, Publishing
Emily Hoffman, Managing Editor
Mary Ellen Owens, Assistant Director of Production
Suzanne Lee, Senior Designer
Eugenia Lo, Publishing Assistant

For customer service, please contact **editorialsupport@review.com**, and be sure to include:

- full title of the book
- ISBN
- page number

# Acknowledgments

The Princeton Review would like to give a tremendous thanks to Corinne Dolci for her hard work in contributing to the 22nd Edition. We'd also like to thank our devoted production team for making this book the best it can be.

# Contents

Get More (Free) Content ........................................................................................ viii

**Part I: Using This Book to Improve Your AP Score** ........................................ 1

Preview: Your Knowledge, Your Expectations ........................................... 2

Your Guide to Using This Book ................................................................... 2

How to Begin .............................................................................................. 3

**Part II: About the AP Economics Exams** .......................................................... 5

The Structure of the AP Economics Exams ................................................ 6

The AP Micro and Macro Exams are Hybrid Digital .................................. 6

How the AP Economics Exams Are Scored ................................................. 7

Overview of Course Units and Big Ideas ................................................... 8

How AP Exams Are Used ............................................................................ 9

Other Resources ........................................................................................ 9

Designing Your Study Plan ........................................................................ 10

**Part III: Test-Taking Strategies for the AP Economics Exams** ....................... 11

1    **How to Approach Multiple-Choice Questions** ..................................... 13

2    **How to Approach Free-Response Questions** ........................................ 23

3    **Using Time Effectively to Maximize Points** ......................................... 29

4    **Pacing Drills** ......................................................................................... 33

**Part IV: Content Review for the AP Economics Exams** ................................... 53

## REVIEW OF MICROECONOMICS CONCEPTS

5    **Micro Unit 1: Basic Economics Concepts** ............................................. 57

Scarcity ....................................................................................................... 58

Resource Allocation and Economic Systems ............................................. 58

The Production Possibilities Curve ............................................................. 59

Comparative Advantage and Gains from Trade ......................................... 62

Cost-Benefit Analysis ................................................................................. 64

Marginal Analysis and Consumer Choice .................................................. 64

Chapter 5 Key Terms .................................................................................. 66

Chapter 5 Drill Questions ........................................................................... 67

Chapter 5 Summary .................................................................................... 70

6    **Micro Unit 2: Supply and Demand** ....................................................... 73

Demand ....................................................................................................... 74

Supply ......................................................................................................... 76

Elasticity ..................................................................................................... 82

Market Equilibrium, Disequilibrium, and Changes in Equilibrium ............. 92

The Effects of Government Intervention in Markets ................................... 93

International Trade and Public Policy .......................................................... 97

Chapter 6 Key Terms .................................................................................. 99

Chapter 6 Drill Questions ........................................................................... 100

Chapter 6 Summary .................................................................................... 104

**7**    **Micro Unit 3: Production, Cost, and the Perfect Competition Model** ........................... 109

    The Production Function ........................................................ 110

    Short- and Long-Run Production Costs ........................................ 116

    Types of Profit ..................................................................... 117

    Profit Maximization ............................................................... 118

    Perfect Competition .............................................................. 120

    Chapter 7 Key Terms ............................................................ 124

    Chapter 7 Drill Questions ....................................................... 125

    Chapter 7 Summary .............................................................. 127

**8**    **Micro Unit 4: Imperfect Competition** ............................................... 129

    Monopoly .......................................................................... 130

    Price Discrimination .............................................................. 132

    Monopolistic Competition ....................................................... 133

    Oligopoly and Game Theory .................................................... 135

    Chapter 8 Key Terms ............................................................ 140

    Chapter 8 Drill Questions ....................................................... 141

    Chapter 8 Summary .............................................................. 144

**9**    **Micro Units 5 and 6: Factor Markets, Market Failure,**
    **and the Role of Government** ....................................................... 145

    Factor Markets .................................................................... 146

    Changes in Factor Demand and Factor Supply .............................. 148

    Profit-Maximizing Behavior in Perfectly Competitive Factor Markets ...... 155

    Monopsonistic Markets .......................................................... 157

    Socially Efficient and Inefficient Market Outcomes ........................ 159

    Externalities ....................................................................... 160

    Public and Private Goods ........................................................ 162

    Income and Wealth Inequality ................................................. 163

    Chapter 9 Key Terms ............................................................ 166

    Chapter 9 Drill Questions ....................................................... 167

    Chapter 9 Summary .............................................................. 170

**10**   **Microeconomics Drill Questions: Answers and Explanations** ..................... 173

### REVIEW OF MACROECONOMICS CONCEPTS

**11**   **Macro Units 1 and 2: Basic Economics Concepts, Economic Indicators,**
    **and the Business Cycle** ............................................................ 187

    The Circular Flow and GDP ..................................................... 188

    Unemployment ................................................................... 191

    Price Indices and Inflation ...................................................... 192

    Real vs. Nominal GDP ........................................................... 193

    Business Cycles ................................................................... 195

    Chapter 11 Key Terms .......................................................... 199

    Chapter 11 Drill Questions ...................................................... 200

    Chapter 11 Summary ............................................................ 202

**12**   **Macro Unit 3: National Income and Price Determination** .......................... 205

    Aggregate Demand .............................................................. 206

    Short-Run and Long-Run Aggregate Supply ................................. 208

    Equilibrium and Changes in the Aggregate Demand-Aggregate Supply Model ........................ 213

    Fiscal Policy ....................................................................... 217

Chapter 12 Key Terms .................................................................... 221
Chapter 12 Drill Questions ............................................................. 222
Chapter 12 Summary ..................................................................... 225

**13  Macro Unit 4: Financial Sector** ................................................. 229
Financial Assets ........................................................................... 230
Definition, Measurement, and Functions of Money ........................ 230
Banking and the Expansion of the Money Supply .......................... 231
Monetary Policy ........................................................................... 236
Chapter 13 Key Terms .................................................................... 242
Chapter 13 Drill Questions ............................................................. 243
Chapter 13 Summary ..................................................................... 245

**14  Macro Unit 5: Long-Run Consequences of Stabilization Polices** ...... 247
The Phillips Curve ........................................................................ 248
Money, Growth, and Inflation ........................................................ 251
Government Deficits and National Debt .......................................... 251
Crowding Out ............................................................................... 252
Economic Growth .......................................................................... 253
Chapter 14 Key Terms .................................................................... 254
Chapter 14 Drill Questions ............................................................. 255
Chapter 14 Summary ..................................................................... 257

**15  Macro Unit 6: Open Economy, International Trade, and Finance** ....... 259
Balance of Payments Accounts ..................................................... 260
Exchange Rates and the Foreign Exchange Market ......................... 261
Effects of Changes in Policies and Economic Conditions on the Foreign Exchange Market ....... 264
Changes in the Foreign Exchange Market and Net Exports ............. 265
Real Interest Rates and International Capital Flows ......................... 266
Chapter 15 Key Terms .................................................................... 271
Chapter 15 Drill Questions ............................................................. 272
Chapter 15 Summary ..................................................................... 274

**16  Macroeconomics Drill Questions: Answers and Explanations** ......... 277

**Part V: Practice Tests** ................................................................. 285

**17  Microeconomics Practice Test 1** ............................................. 287
**18  Microeconomics Practice Test 1: Answers and Explanations** ......... 307
**19  Macroeconomics Practice Test 1** ............................................ 319
**20  Macroeconomics Practice Test 1: Answers and Explanations** ........ 345

Appendix: Formula Sheets ............................................................. 361

**Online Practice Tests**

Microeconomics Practice Test 2 ..................................................... online
Microeconomics Practice Test 2: Answers and Explanations ............ online
Macroeconomics Practice Test 2 .................................................... online
Macroeconomics Practice Test 2: Answers and Explanations ........... online

# at **PrincetonReview.com/prep**

## As easy as **1·2·3**

**1** Go to PrincetonReview.com/prep or scan the **QR code** and enter the following ISBN to register your book: **9780593518250**

**2** Answer a few simple questions to set up an exclusive Princeton Review account. *(If you already have one, you can just log in.)*

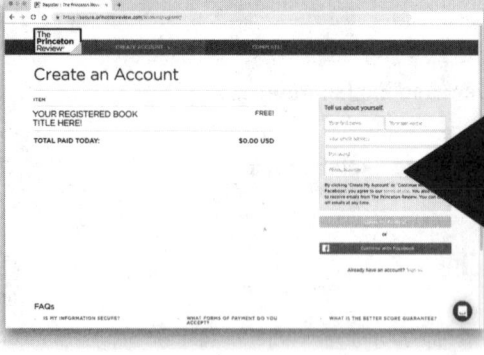

**3** Enjoy access to your **FREE** content!

# Access Your Online Test Practice

Your AP Prep book comes with new interactive practice exams to help you prepare for digital test-taking! Find these tests in your online Student Tools, provided in two different formats:

- Fully digital versions with a timer option to simulate the exam experience
- Downloadable interactive PDFs with digital features like clicking your answer in Section I

Check back often as we continue to update the included AP Student Tools.

## PLUS, IN YOUR ACCOUNT YOU CAN:

- Get valuable advice about the college application process, tips for essay writing, and financial aid info
- Use our searchable rankings to learn more about your dream school

- Access comprehensive study guides, vocab list, and formula sheet
- Check whether there have been any updates or corrections to this edition

## Need to report a potential **content** issue?

Contact **EditorialSupport@review.com** and include:

- full title of the book
- ISBN
- page number

## Need to report a **technical** issue?

Contact **TPRStudentTech@review.com** and provide:

- your full name
- email address used to register the book
- full book title and ISBN
- Operating system (Mac/PC) and browser (Chrome, Firefox, Safari, etc.)

## Look For These Icons Throughout The Book

 **PROVEN TECHNIQUES**

 **APPLIED STRATEGIES**

 **ONLINE ARTICLES**

 **ONLINE VIDEO TUTORIALS**

 **WATCH OUT**

 **OTHER REFERENCES**

 **STUDY BREAK**

# Part I
# Using This Book to Improve Your AP Score

- Preview: Your Knowledge, Your Expectations
- Your Guide to Using This Book
- How to Begin

## PREVIEW: YOUR KNOWLEDGE, YOUR EXPECTATIONS

Welcome to your *AP Economics Micro & Macro Premium Prep* book. Your route to a high score on the AP Microeconomics or Macroeconomics Exam depends a lot on how you plan to use this book. To help you make that determination, please respond to the following questions.

1. Rate your level of confidence about your knowledge of the content tested by the AP Microeconomics or Macroeconomics Exam:

    A.   Very confident—I know it all (99%)

    B.   I'm pretty confident, but there are topics for which I could use help (75%)

    C.   Not confident—I need quite a bit of support (25%)

    D.   I'm not sure (1%)

2. Circle your goal score for the exam.

    5   4   3   2   1

3. What do you expect to learn from this book? Circle all that apply to you.

    A.   A general overview of the test and what to expect

    B.   Strategies for how to approach the test

    C.   The content tested by this exam

    D.   I'm not sure yet

## YOUR GUIDE TO USING THIS BOOK

This book is organized to provide as much—or as little—support as you need. Use this book to benefit your knowledge base and your learning curve in whatever way will be most helpful to improving and targeting your score on the AP Microeconomics or Macroeconomics Exam.

Once you register your book online, you can download and print the second practice tests and free-response booklets.

- The remainder of **Part I** provides guidance on how to use this book and will help you determine your strengths and weaknesses.

- **Part II** of this book provides information on the following topics:
    o the structure, scoring, and content of the Economics Exams
    o making a study plan
    o finding additional resources

- **Part III** of this book explores the following strategies:
    o how to tackle multiple-choice questions
    o how to approach free-response questions
    o how to manage your time to maximize the number of points available to you

- **Part IV** of this book covers the content you need for the AP Economics Exams.

- **Part V** contains the first practice tests, answers and explanations, bubble sheets that you can tear out, and a handy formula sheet for your reference.

# HOW TO BEGIN

1. **Measure Your Confidence**

   Before you can decide how to use this book, you need to get a sense for how well you already understand the material. Doing so will give you insight into your strengths and weaknesses, and help you make an effective study plan. Depending on whether you're taking the Micro or Macro Exam, turn to the corresponding Pacing Drill that begins on page 34 or page 39 and work through each question. If you're feeling anxious about completing these drills, remind yourself that this practice is a tool for diagnosing yourself—it's not how well you do that matters, but how you use information gleaned from your performance to guide your preparation.

2. **Check Your Answers**

   Using the answers that begin on page 43 or page 49, count the number of multiple-choice questions you answered correctly and the number you missed. We'll get to analyzing your answers soon.

3. **Reflect on the Pacing Drills**

   After checking your answers, respond to the following questions:
   - How much time did you spend on the multiple-choice questions?
   - How many multiple-choice questions did you miss?
   - Which questions did you feel most and least comfortable solving?

4. **Read Part II of this Book and Design Your Study Plan**

   Part II provides information on how the test is structured and scored. It also outlines areas of content that are tested.

   As you read Part II, reevaluate your answers to the questions above. At the end of Part II, you will revisit and refine your answers to these questions. You will then be able to make a study plan, based on your needs and time available, that will allow you to use this book most effectively.

If you focus on improving your overall accuracy, keeping in mind that getting correct answers is the most important for your score, you'll find that speed improves with practice!

5. **Engage with Parts III and IV as Needed**

Notice the word *engage*. You'll get more out of this book if you use it intentionally than if you read it passively, hoping for an improved score through osmosis. Application and active learning will be the key to your success.

The strategy chapters in Part III will help you think about your approach to the question types on this exam. This part opens with a reminder to think about how you approach questions now, and then closes with a reflection section asking you to think about how/whether you will change your approach in the future.

The content chapters in Part IV are designed to provide a review of the content tested on the AP Economics Exams, including the level of detail you need to know and how the content is tested. You will have the opportunity to assess your knowledge of the content of each chapter through test-appropriate questions and a reflection section.

6. **Tackle More Practice in Part V and Assess Your Test Performance**

Once you feel you have developed the strategies and knowledge needed to do well on the exam, you should test that theory by taking Practice Test 1 in Part V of this book.

Assess your performance by checking your answers. On which topics did you hit and on which did you miss? Reflect on what areas you still need to work on, and revisit the chapters in this book that address those deficiencies.

Finally, download Practice Test 2 online by registering your book via Student Tools (follow the instructions on the Get More Free Content page). Repeat the process above. Through this type of reflection and engagement, you will continue to improve.

7. **Keep Working**

As discussed before, there are other resources available to you, including a wealth of information on the AP Students website, such as AP Classroom Resources. You can continue to explore areas in which you can improve and engage in those areas right up to the day of the test.

**Looking for More Help with Your APs?**

We now offer specialized AP tutoring and course packages. To see which courses are offered and available, and to learn more about the course guarantee, visit PrincetonReview.com/ college/ap-test-prep

# Part II
# About the AP Economics Exams

- The Structure of the AP Economics Exams
- The AP Micro and Macro Exams are Hybrid Digital
- How the AP Economics Exams Are Scored
- Overview of Course Units and Big Ideas
- How AP Exams Are Used
- Other Resources
- Designing Your Study Plan

## THE STRUCTURE OF THE AP ECONOMICS EXAMS

Whether you are planning to take the AP Microeconomics or AP Macroeconomics Exam, your exam will include 60 multiple-choice questions and 3 free-response questions.

Let's break that down in handy chart format:

| Question Type | Time | Score | More Score Info |
|---|---|---|---|
| 60 multiple-choice questions | 70 minutes | Section accounts for 66% of AP Exam score | No guessing penalty for any incorrect multiple-choice questions |
| 3 free-response questions (FRQs): 1 long, 2 short | 60 minutes: 10 minutes reading/planning time, 50 minutes writing time | Section accounts for 33% of AP Exam score | Within section, 1 long FRQ accounts for 50% of total section score (10 points); 2 shorter FRQs each account for 25% total section score (5 points each) |

**Calculator Policy**

Per the AP Exam Calculator Policy, a basic four-function calculator is **permitted** on the exam for both Microeconomics and Macroeconomics. For the digital section of the exam, you can use either the built in Desmos graphing calculator in the Bluebook app or your own approved calculator.

## THE AP MICRO AND MACRO EXAMS ARE HYBRID DIGITAL

While the multiple-choice section of both the AP Microeconomics and Macroeconomics Exams are administered digitally via the College Board's Bluebook testing app, the free-response questions are viewed digitally, but your answers must be written in the paper exam booklet given to you and returned for scoring.

For the digital portion of the Micro and Macro Exams, access to the Bluebook app is available via Windows, Mac laptops/desktops, iPads, tablets, and Chromebooks. If your computer or tablet is owned or managed by your school, your school official will likely already have this installed. The test cannot be taken on a smartphone.

The Bluebook app allows you to annotate and highlight texts, eliminate answers, and flag questions for review later. You will also have access to scratch paper to plan responses to essay questions. Unlike other digital exams like the SAT, the hybrid digital AP Exam will NOT be adaptive: this means that the difficulty of questions will not change depending on how well you do on earlier sections of the test.

It is important to note that the hybrid digital AP Micro and Macro Exams include the same number of sections, types of questions, and timing as the previous paper exams. This means the strategies used for success on paper versions of the exam are just as applicable to the digital version. So don't worry, the practice tests in this book will still prepare you for test day and the digital practice tests are available via your Student Tools to give you the full online experience.

# HOW THE AP ECONOMICS EXAMS ARE SCORED

Each AP Exam receives a numerical score of 1 to 5 with each score meaning the following:

5 = Extremely Well Qualified
4 = Very Well Qualified
3 = Qualified
2 = Possibly Qualified
1 = No Recommendation

Colleges decide for themselves the minimum score they will accept for college credit and/or advanced placement. The American Council on Education recommends the acceptance of scores of 3 or above, and many colleges adhere to these standards. Check the website of the college(s) of your choice to learn each school's policy on granting credit or advanced placement.

Each year, the College Board creates a formula that converts the raw score on an exam into a composite score, which is then used to determine what score (from 1 to 5) each test-taker receives.

For your reference, here is the College Board's score distribution data from the 2024 AP Micro and Macro Economics, the latest exam administration prior to the publication of this book.

| AP Microeconomics—Score Distributions | | | |
| --- | --- | --- | --- |
| Score | 2024* Percentage | Credit Recommendation | College Grade Equivalent |
| 5 | 22.9% | Extremely Well Qualified | A+, A |
| 4 | 23.9% | Very Well Qualified | A–, B+, B |
| 3 | 20.8% | Qualified | B–, C+, C |
| 2 | 19.2% | Possibly Qualified | – |
| 1 | 13.2% | No Recommendation | – |

| AP Macroeconomics—Score Distributions | | | |
| --- | --- | --- | --- |
| Score | 2024* Percentage | Credit Recommendation | College Grade Equivalent |
| 5 | 20.7% | Extremely Well Qualified | A+, A |
| 4 | 20.7% | Very Well Qualified | A–, B+, B |
| 3 | 23.8% | Qualified | B–, C+, C |
| 2 | 20.8% | Possibly Qualified | – |
| 1 | 14.1% | No Recommendation | – |

*Data from The College Board, May 2024 AP Exam administrations

# OVERVIEW OF COURSE UNITS AND BIG IDEAS

The College Board organizes the AP Economics courses into six units each. There are also topics within each unit your AP teacher will review during the school year, and we'll discuss those starting on page 19. Take a look at the table below and familiarize yourself with the units that are weighted the most and the least on the exam. This will help you prioritize which areas you most need to study for test day.

| Course Units | |
| --- | --- |
| **Microeconomics** | **Macroeconomics** |
| Unit 1: Basic Economic Concepts (12–15% of exam) | Unit 1: Basic Economic Concepts (5–10% of exam) |
| Unit 2: Supply and Demand (20–25% of exam) | Unit 2: Economic Indicators and the Business Cycle (12–17% of exam) |
| Unit 3: Production, Cost, and the Perfect Competition Model (22–25% of exam) | Unit 3: National Income and Price Determination (17–27% of exam) |
| Unit 4: Imperfect Competition (15–22% of exam) | Unit 4: Financial Sector (18–23% of exam) |
| Unit 5: Factor Markets (10–13% of exam) | Unit 5: Long-Run Consequences of Stabilization Policies (20–30% of exam) |
| Unit 6: Market Failure and the Role of Government (8–13% of exam) | Unit 6: Open Economy-International Trade and Finance (10–13% of exam) |

In addition to the course units, the College Board also emphasizes four Big Ideas and Skill Categories connecting the many topics you will learn throughout each unit. These are listed in the following table.

| **Microeconomics** | **Macroeconomics** |
| --- | --- |
| **BIG IDEA 1:** Scarcity and Markets | **BIG IDEA 1:** Economic Measurements |
| **BIG IDEA 2:** Costs, Benefits, and Marginal Analysis | **BIG IDEA 2:** Markets |
| **BIG IDEA 3:** Production Choices and Behavior | **BIG IDEA 3:** Macroeconomic Models |
| **BIG IDEA 4:** Market Inefficiency and Public Policy | **BIG IDEA 4:** Macroeconomic Policies |
| **Skills for Both AP Courses** | |

1. *Principles and Models:* Define economic principles and models.
2. *Interpretation:* Explain given economic outcomes.
3. *Manipulation:* Define outcomes of specific economic situations.
4. *Graphing and Visuals:* Model economic situations using graphs or visual representations.

As you go through your economics course during the school year, make sure you are paying very close attention to how your AP teacher ties in each topic with the Big Ideas and Skill Categories.

# HOW AP EXAMS ARE USED

Different colleges use AP Exam scores in different ways, so it is important that you go to a particular college's website to determine how it uses AP Exam scores. The three items below represent the main ways in which AP Exam scores can be used.

- **College Credit.** Some colleges will give you college credit if you score well on an AP Exam. These credits count toward your graduation requirements, meaning that you can take fewer courses while in college. Given the cost of college, this could be quite a benefit indeed.

- **Satisfy Requirements.** Some colleges will allow you to "place out" of certain requirements if you do well on an AP Exam, even if they do not give you actual college credits. For example, you might not need to take an introductory-level course, or perhaps you might not need to take a class in a certain discipline at all.

- **Admissions Plus.** Even if your AP Exam will not result in college credit or allow you to place out of certain courses, most colleges will respect your decision to push yourself by taking an AP Course or even an AP Exam outside of a course. A high score on an AP Exam shows knowledge of content that is more difficult than what is taught in many high school courses, and colleges may take that into account during the admissions process.

**More Great Books**

Check out The Princeton Review's college guide books, including *The Best 391 Colleges*, *The Complete Book of Colleges*, *Paying for College*, and many more!

# OTHER RESOURCES

There are many resources available to help you improve your score on the AP Economics Exams, not the least of which are your teachers. If you are taking an AP class, you may be able to get extra attention from your teacher, such as obtaining feedback on your practice free-response answers. If you are not in an AP course, reach out to a teacher who teaches Economics, and ask whether the teacher will review your writing or otherwise help you with content.

Another wonderful resource is **AP Students**, the official site of the AP Exams. The most recent updates of the following items can be found at AP Students:

- course description, which includes detailed information about what content is covered

- sample multiple-choice questions for both AP Microeconomics and AP Macroeconomics via the AP Classroom Resource tab

- sample free-response questions for both AP Microeconomics and AP Macroeconomics

- exam practice tips

- information about exam fees and accommodations

**Got a Question?**

For answers to test-prep questions for all your tests and additional test-taking tips, subscribe to our YouTube channel at youtube.com/ThePrincetonReview

The AP Students home page address is <u>apstudents.collegeboard.org</u>.

The AP Microeconomics Course home page address is <u>apstudents.collegeboard.org/courses/ap-microeconomics</u>.

The AP Macroeconomics Course home page is <u>apstudents.collegeboard.org/courses/ap-macroeconomics</u>.

Finally, The Princeton Review offers tutoring for the AP Economics Exams. Our expert instructors and programs can help you add to your content knowledge and provide strategic analysis of concepts. For more information, call **1-800-2REVIEW.**

## DESIGNING YOUR STUDY PLAN

Review your diagnostic reflection from page 2 and the Overview of Course Units and Big Ideas on page 8. Next to each one, indicate your rank of the topic as follows: "1" means "I need a lot of work on this," "2" means "I need to beef up my knowledge," and "3" means "I know this topic well." Then answer the following questions.

Break up your review into manageable portions. Download our helpful study guide for this book once you register online.

- How many days/weeks/months away is your AP Economics Exam?

- What time of day is your best, most focused study time?

- How much time per day/week/month will you devote to preparing for your AP Economics Exam?

- When will you do this preparation? (Be as specific as possible: Mondays and Wednesdays from 3:00 to 4:00 P.M., for example.)

- Based on the answers above, will you focus on strategy (Part III) or content (Part IV) or both?

- What are your overall goals in using this book?

Based on your answers to these questions, you should now have a better understanding of how to study for the exam. Use your answers to customize a study plan that meets your specific needs based on the amount of time you have until test day. It is important to tailor your study plan to your schedule and topics you need to further review.

# Part III
# Test-Taking Strategies for the AP Economics Exams

1  How to Approach Multiple-Choice Questions
2  How to Approach Free-Response Questions
3  Using Time Effectively to Maximize Points
4  Pacing Drills

# Chapter 1
# How to Approach
# Multiple-Choice
# Questions

# CRACKING THE MULTIPLE-CHOICE QUESTIONS

Multiple-choice questions account for two-thirds of your total examination grade (66.65%). During the multiple-choice section of each exam, you will have 70 minutes to answer 60 questions, or 70 seconds per question. On the exam, you may encounter several types of multiple-choice questions. One type may deal with economic policy, asking for examples of how an expansionary monetary policy is likely to affect interest rates, investment, and aggregate demand. Another question type may ask you to interpret a graph. For example, you might be asked which labeled section of a graph represents consumer surplus. A third type of question may ask you to distinguish true from false statements. These questions may seem more difficult than a standard true/false question because you will be given three or four statements (labeled with roman numerals) and asked, for example, whether the truth is represented by I, II, III; I and III; or II and IV. Because the questions vary, you will have an opportunity to practice each of these types of questions both in the practice tests and in the drills that you'll find later in this chapter.

**Reminder!**

The multiple-choice sections for both the AP Micro and AP Macro Exams are completed digitally via the Bluebook app.

**Proven Techniques**

Use POE and the Two-Pass System to help boost your score.

**Digital Functions for the Multiple-Choice Section**

Digital AP Exams allow you to highlight and annotate exam stimuli and questions, mark questions to revisit, and eliminate answer choices for the multiple-choice section. So be sure to use these functions on your MC section.

## Process of Elimination

For questions that stump you, try using a technique we call Process of Elimination, or POE, to help you guess more accurately. Oftentimes it is easier to spot incorrect answer choices than to know the correct answer. To use this technique, first read *all* of the possible responses, even if you think you know the answer right away, just to make sure you aren't missing something. If no answer choice is clearly correct, eliminate as many as you can by actually marking them off on your screen. After you have eliminated as many as you can, select an answer from the remaining choices. Every time you get rid of one answer choice, the odds of selecting the correct answer go up significantly. Here's an example:

What is the name for the idea that governments should actively regulate trade in order to maintain a positive balance of trade?

(A)   Free trade
(B)   Mercantilism
(C)   Elasticity
(D)   Monopoly
(E)   Laissez-faire

If you tried to just answer this question from your own knowledge, you'd probably be stumped. Instead, let's use POE!

Well, it can't be free trade or laissez-faire because they were all about removing government restrictions on economic activity, so get rid of (A) and (E). Elasticity refers to the sensitivity of quantities demanded or supplied to changes in prices, which has nothing to do with trade, so get rid of (C). Monopoly refers to one company controlling all of the supply of a good or service, which isn't really about trade, so get rid of (D). This means the answer must be (B)! POE can be a really powerful way to give you a fighting chance on even the toughest questions.

Based on our experience grading practice test questions, we have determined that students who fill in one response and then change to another most often change from the correct answer to an incorrect answer. If you're considering changing an answer and you feel fifty-fifty about which choice is correct, consider the time it will take to erase the first answer and fill in the second. Time is always a factor to consider on the AP Exam, so you might be better off just leaving the answer as is. If your test-taking history has proven that your initial response is not as reliable as your second thought, however, go with your gut, sacrifice the time, and make the change.

## Use the Two-Pass System

Go through the multiple-choice section twice. The first time, do all the questions that you can get answers to immediately. In other words, first answer questions that require little or no analysis and any questions dealing with economics topics in which you are well-versed.

To put it another way, the first time through, skip the questions in the topics about which you are least confident. Also, you might want to skip the ones that look like number crunchers. Although calculators are permitted on the exam, don't waste time using them if they don't actually save you time. Mark the questions that you skip on your screen so you can find them easily during the second pass. Once you've answered all the questions that come easily to you, go back and answer the tough ones that you have the best shot of getting right. And, because you don't lose points for wrong answers on AP Exams, make sure you do not leave any questions blank. When you get to questions that are too time-consuming, or you don't know the answer to (and can't eliminate any options), use what we call your letter of the day (LOTD). Selecting the same answer choice each time you guess will increase your odds of getting a few of those skipped questions right.

That's why the two-pass system is so handy. By using it, you make sure that you see all the questions that you can get right, instead of running out of time because you became bogged down on time-consuming questions.

Which brings us to another important point. . . .

> **Remember this for the MC section!**
> While you can go back within a section or part to review or complete previous questions, you may not return to parts within a section that have already been completed.

## Don't Turn a Question into a Marathon!

Most people don't run out of time on standardized tests because they work too slowly. Instead, they need more time because they spend half the test wrestling with two or three difficult-seeming questions or get stuck between two answer choices. The goal is to keep up your accuracy and pacing; remember, you have approximately 70 seconds per question.

You should never spend more than a minute or two on any question. If a question doesn't involve a straightforward calculation, then take an educated guess at the answer. Figure out where you stand on a question, make a decision, and move on.

Any question that requires more than two minutes' worth of calculations probably isn't worth doing. Keep in mind that questions you find easy are worth the same as questions that might stump you. If you're low on time, or just don't know the answer, LOTD and move on!

> **Remember!**
> The Bluebook testing app provides a countdown clock that you can view or hide while taking the multiple-choice section of the exam. We recommend to hide the countdown and look at the clock in the testing room or your watch every few questions to pace your timing.

# DRILLS

Below are examples of each of the types of multiple-choice questions already mentioned. In each of these examples, the use of graphs and the Process of Elimination will help you to hone in on the correct answer. Be sure to use these techniques and the two-pass system to maximize your score.

## Economic Policy Questions

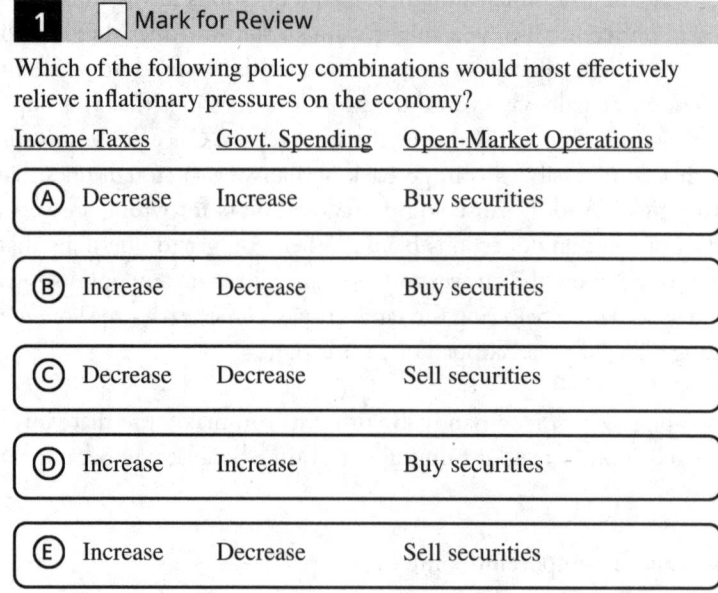

**1** ☐ Mark for Review

Which of the following policy combinations would most effectively relieve inflationary pressures on the economy?

| Income Taxes | Govt. Spending | Open-Market Operations |
|---|---|---|
| (A) Decrease | Increase | Buy securities |
| (B) Increase | Decrease | Buy securities |
| (C) Decrease | Decrease | Sell securities |
| (D) Increase | Increase | Buy securities |
| (E) Increase | Decrease | Sell securities |

**Apply Strategy**
Use POE to crack this question.

### Here's How to Crack It

Question 1 asks which policies would most effectively relieve inflationary pressures on the economy. You might begin by drawing an aggregate demand/aggregate supply (AD/AS) graph to help you visualize what needs to happen to decrease the price level.

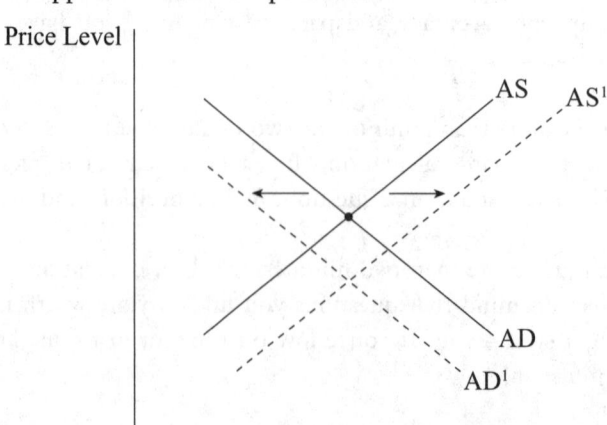

As you look at the AD/AS graph, you should be able to see that the price level will decrease when aggregate demand decreases (shifts left) or aggregate supply increases (shifts right). This information alone allows you to begin the Process of Elimination. Start with government spending. Since government spending is part of aggregate demand (AD), any increase in government spending will increase AD, thus shifting it to the right, which would *increase* prices. Therefore, you can eliminate (A) and (D). Now keep going! If income taxes decrease, then people would have more money in their pockets, which has the same effect as an increase in income, which increases AD. Thus, since increasing AD leads to higher prices, you can eliminate (C). Finally, you know that buying securities increases the money supply, lowers the interest rate, increases investment, and thus increases AD and the price level. Therefore, you can rule out (B), and you are left with (E) as the correct answer.

## Interpret Graph Questions

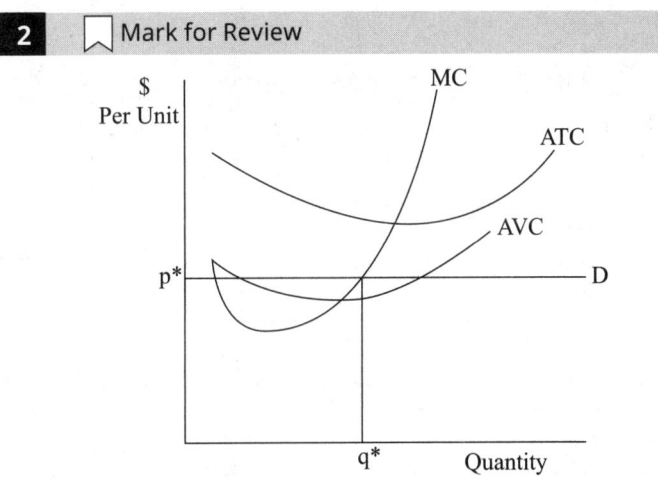

**2**  ☐ Mark for Review

A firm is in a perfectly competitive industry. Given the cost and demand schedules depicted in the graph above, what should the firm do in the short run?

(A) Shut down

(B) Stay open and produce q*

(C) Stay open and produce more than q*

(D) Stay open and produce less than q*

(E) Stay open but produce zero units

### Here's How to Crack It

Question 2 asks you to interpret a graph and determine the optimal behavior for a firm in the short run. Since the price for this firm's product is below its average total cost (ATC), it is losing money. However, if you read carefully, you'll see that the question is asking what the firm should do in the short run, in which the current price exceeds average variable cost (AVC) and covers some of the fixed costs (average fixed costs are the difference between ATC and AVC). The firm should therefore stay open, as it will lose less than if it shuts down. Get rid of (A). In a perfectly competitive industry, marginal revenue (MR) = demand. When the price is less than ATC but greater than AVC, a firm should engage in loss minimization and produce at the level at which marginal cost (MC) = MR. This means that $q^*$ is the optimal quantity to produce, making (B) the correct answer. If a firm produces more than $q^*$, then the cost of making each additional unit is more than the revenue the firm would receive. Eliminate (C). If the firm produces less than $q^*$, then revenue would exceed the cost and the firm would keep producing. Eliminate (D). If a firm produced 0 units, it would not cover its fixed costs, so you can eliminate (E).

---

# Distinguishing True from False Statements Questions

---

**3** ⬜ Mark for Review

Which of the following characterize a non-price-discriminating monopoly?

I.     Large barriers to entry
II.    MR = P
III.   Perfectly elastic demand
IV.    A unique product

(A) I and II only

(B) III and IV only

(C) I and IV only

(D) IV only

(E) I, II, and IV only

### Here's How to Crack It

Question 3 asks you to identify characteristics of a non-price-discriminating monopoly. Price-discrimination means that a firm charges different prices to different clients. If a firm is non-price-discriminating, it charges the same price to all its clients. By drawing a typical monopoly graph, you immediately see that demand is not perfectly elastic (horizontal) and that price is above marginal revenue. This rules out items II and III and (A), (B), and (E). The distinguishing question between (C) and (D) is whether or not there are large barriers to entry in a monopoly. Because a monopoly by definition has no successful competitors, the barriers to entry must be large and the correct answer must be (C).

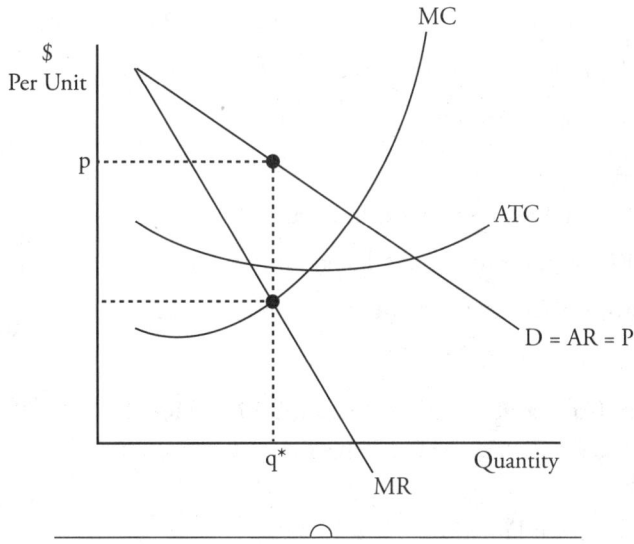

## THE EMPHASIS OF MULTIPLE-CHOICE QUESTIONS

The percentages below indicate how the College Board weighs the multiple-choice questions on the current AP Microeconomics and AP Macroeconomics Exams. Each course is now divided into 6 units with various economics topics within each unit. This book has been divided along the same lines to better prepare you for the exam.

## AP Microeconomics Concepts

### Unit 1: Basic Economic Concepts (12–15% of the exam)

You'll study the foundations of microeconomic thinking, including how to evaluate decisions based on constraints and trade-offs and make rational economic choices.

1.1 Scarcity

1.2 Resource Allocation and Economic Systems

1.3 Production Possibilities Curve

1.4 Comparative Advantage and Trade

1.5 Cost-Benefit Analysis

1.6 Marginal Analysis and Consumer Choice

**Bonus Tips and Tricks . . .**
Check us out on YouTube for additional test-taking tips and must-know strategies at youtube.com/ThePrincetonReview

### Unit 2: Supply and Demand (20–25% of the exam)

You'll learn the basis for understanding how markets work with an introduction to the supply and demand model.

2.1 Demand

2.2 Supply

2.3 Price Elasticity of Demand

2.4 Price Elasticity of Supply

2.5 Other Elasticities

2.6 Market Equilibrium and Consumer and Producer Surplus

2.7 Market Disequilibrium and Changes in Equilibrium

2.8 The Effects of Government Intervention in Markets

2.9 International Trade and Public Policy

### Unit 3: Production, Cost, and the Perfect Competition Model (22–25% of the exam)

You'll explore the factors that drive the behavior of companies and learn about the perfect competition model.

3.1 The Production Function

3.2 Short-Run Production Costs

3.3 Long-Run Production Costs

3.4 Types of Profit

3.5 Profit Maximization

3.6 Firms' Short-Run Decisions to Produce and Long-Run Decisions to Enter or Exit a Market

3.7 Perfect Competition

### Unit 4: Imperfect Competition (15–22% of the exam)

You'll learn how imperfectly competitive markets work and how game theory comes into play in economic models.

4.1 Introduction to Imperfectly Competitive Markets

4.2 Monopoly

4.3 Price Discrimination

4.4 Monopolistic Competition

4.5 Oligopoly and Game Theory

### Unit 5: Factor Markets (10–13% of the exam)

You'll learn how concepts such as supply and demand and marginal decision-making apply in the context of factor markets.

5.1 Introduction to Factor Markets

5.2 Changes in Factor Demand and Factor Supply

5.3 Profit-Maximizing Behavior in Perfectly Competitive Factor Markets

5.4 Monopsonistic Markets

**Unit 6: Market Failure and the Role of Government (8–13% of the exam)**

You'll examine the conditions under which markets may fail and the effects of government intervention in markets.

6.1 Socially Efficient and Inefficient Market Outcomes

6.2 Externalities

6.3 Public and Private Goods

6.4 The Effects of Government Intervention in Different Market Structures

6.5 Inequality

# AP Macroeconomics Concepts

**Unit 1: Basic Economic Concepts (5–10% of the exam)**

You'll start the course with an introduction to economic concepts, principles, and models that will serve as a foundation for studying macroeconomics.

1.1 Scarcity

1.2 Opportunity Cost and the Production Possibilities Curve (PPC)

1.3 Comparative Advantage and Gains from Trade

1.4 Demand

1.5 Supply

1.6 Market Equilibrium, Disequilibrium, and Changes in Equilibrium

**Unit 2: Economic Indicators and the Business Cycle (12–17% of the exam)**

You'll look at how economic phenomena such as employment and inflation are measured.

2.1 The Circular Flow and GDP

2.2 Limitations of GDP

2.3 Unemployment

2.4 Price Indices and Inflation

2.5 Costs of Inflation

2.6 Real vs. Nominal GDP

2.7 Business Cycles

**Unit 3: National Income and Price Determination (17–27% of the exam)**

You'll explore how changes in aggregate spending and production, economic fluctuations, and policy actions affect national income, unemployment, and inflation.

3.1 Aggregate Demand (AD)

3.2 Multipliers

3.3 Short-Run Aggregate Supply (SRAS)

3.4 Long-Run Aggregate Supply (LRAS)

3.5 Equilibrium in the Aggregate Demand-Aggregate Supply (AD-AS) Model

3.6 Changes in the AD-AS Model in the Short Run

3.7 Long-Run Self-Adjustment

3.8 Fiscal Policy

3.9 Automatic Stabilizers

**Unit 4: Financial Sector (18–23% of the exam)**

You'll examine the financial sector and explain how monetary policy is implemented and transmitted through the banking system.

    4.1 Financial Assets

    4.2 Nominal vs. Real Interest Rates

    4.3 Definition, Measurement, and Functions of Money

    4.4 Banking and the Expansion of the Money Supply

    4.5 The Money Market

    4.6 Monetary Policy

    4.7 The Loanable Funds Market

**Unit 5: Long-Run Consequences of Stabilization Policies (20–30% of the exam)**

You'll spend more time exploring the effects of fiscal and monetary policy actions and examine the concept of economic growth.

    5.1 Fiscal and Monetary Policy Actions in the Short Run

    5.2 The Phillips Curve

    5.3 Money Growth and Inflation

    5.4 Government Deficits and the National Debt

    5.5 Crowding Out

    5.6 Economic Growth

    5.7 Public Policy and Economic Growth

**Unit 6: Open Economy—International Trade and Finance (10–13% of the exam)**

You'll examine the concept of an open economy in which a country interacts with the rest of the world through product and financial markets.

    6.1 Balance of Payments Accounts

    6.2 Exchange Rates

    6.3 The Foreign Exchange Market

    6.4 Effect of Changes in Policies and Economic Conditions on the Foreign Exchange Market

    6.5 Changes in the Foreign Exchange Market and Net Exports

    6.6 Real Interest Rates and International Capital Flows

# Chapter 2
# How to Approach
# Free-Response
# Questions

# CRACKING THE FREE-RESPONSE QUESTIONS

The free-response questions account for one-third of the total score for each of the exams (33.35%). There are three free-response questions on each exam. The first is worth about 50 percent of your free-response score. The second and third questions are each worth about 25 percent of your free-response score. The main purpose of these questions is to test your content knowledge, analytical skills, and organizational skills. You will likely be asked to apply your understanding of economic graphs and tables. You will be allowed 10 minutes to read over the questions and think about your answers, and then 50 minutes to answer the questions. It is recommended that you allocate 25 minutes to the long question and 12.5 minutes to each of the two short questions. All topics are fair game on the free-response section, so be prepared!

Avoid rambling blindly into inaccuracy. Your first task after reading a free-response question is to determine which of your economic tools to apply to its solution. The use of graphs, equations, and structured reasoning will guide you to correct answers and allow you to check for potentially incorrect statements (if you are unsure of where to start).

Experimenting with possible approaches to the problem is not a bad idea. Apply the graphs, equations, or tables that seem the most relevant; if they don't lead to an answer, try another approach.

## How to Approach the Questions—Work Your Graphs

Drawing graphs is not only the key to earning points on graph questions, but it is also the secret to solving problems that may not even require a graph. Have you noticed that economists seem compulsive about drawing graphs? It's not that they are repressed artists. Rather, they know this secret: economics may seem very hard to sort out in your head, but it can be relatively easy with a few illustrations. Invest the time necessary to learn to draw the graphs. Resist the temptation to interpret the question with words alone. Although the graders often permit a high point allocation for good prose (word-only) responses, the most successful prose responses are typically explanations of graphs that show that the students understood the graphs and visualized them in their minds.

Consider the following question:

**4**    ☐ Mark for Review

Suppose there is a drought and a successful advertising campaign for parsley in the same year.

A.    Draw a correctly labeled supply and demand diagram to represent this scenario.

B.    Explain how the shift identified in part A will affect the equilibrium and quantity of parsley.

The first part of a free-response question often involves sketching the situation, but even when it doesn't, or if you are dealing with a tricky multiple-choice question, you still want to be able to quickly draw the basic situation. The only difference is that because you're handing in this chart, you should make sure you clearly label everything.

A.

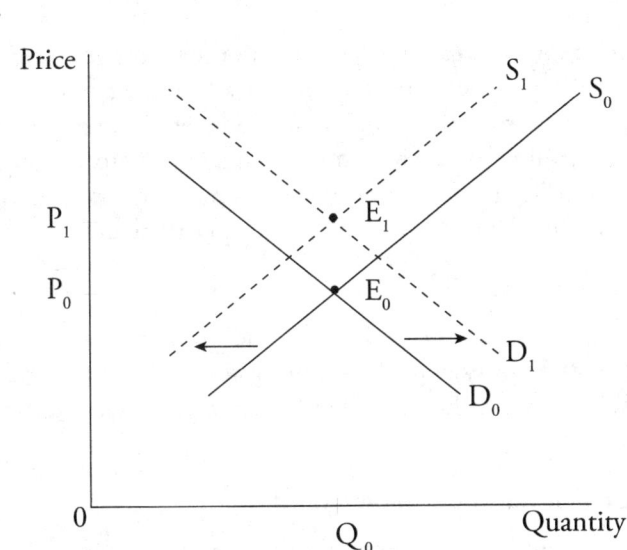

B.   Because a drought decreases supply from $S_0$ to $S_1$ and successful advertising increases demand from $D_0$ to $D_1$, the new equilibrium price will be higher, and the quantity may increase or decrease depending on the size of the supply and demand curve shifts.

## Common Mistakes and Careless Errors

Don't lose points by making the following common mistakes:

- **Mislabeled or Unlabeled Graphs**

  Labels matter. Just because you drew lines shaped like supply and demand curves when the question clearly is looking for them doesn't mean the graders will assume you knew what you were doing. Label every line and every axis.

- **Skipped Steps in the Story**

  Don't hold back information that is part of the answer even if it seems obvious. The graders want to read about every step between cause and effect. Don't just say, for example, that expansionary monetary policy increases aggregate demand. Explain how the Fed's expansionary action shifts the money supply curve to the right, thus lowering interest rates. Explain how the lower interest rates attract more investment, shifting the aggregate expenditure function upward. Explain how the autonomous shift in aggregate expenditures results in an ultimate increase in aggregate demand equal to the change in investment times the multiplier.

- **Illegible Graphs or Writing**

  Don't be in such a hurry that your brilliant answers turn into wasted ink.

- **Saying Too Much**

  Don't stray into unquestioned territory. You won't get points for the right answer to the wrong question and your reader might think you don't know what you're talking about!

- **The Punt**

  Even if you don't think you can answer a question or a part of a question, first answer the parts about which you are more confident, and then use any spare time to make your best attempt at writing something logical and coherent. Some questions might not be asking for as much complexity as you think. You might pick up a point or two if you show enough signs of intelligent life. Unfortunately, some students give up and write down jokes instead. Not even the best joke will earn any partial credit.

- **Examples Without Explanations**

  Too often, questions that seek definitions or conditions are answered merely with examples. If a question asks, for example, "What is distinct about public goods?" explain how they are nonrival and nonexcludable. Don't just say, "National defense is an example of one."

- **Breaking the Golden Rule of Economics: MC = MB**

  One of the primary lessons in economics is that we should do whatever we do until the marginal cost (MC) equals the marginal benefit (MB). Marginal cost is the cost of one more and marginal benefit is the benefit from one more. The answers to many questions have to do with equating marginal cost and marginal benefit, after adapting these terms to the situation. For firms, the marginal "benefit" is generally assumed to be marginal revenue, and every type of firm maximizes profits or minimizes losses by producing when marginal cost equals marginal revenue (if they should operate at all). Likewise, we assume that individuals seek to maximize utility, which is accomplished by consuming goods until the marginal cost to individuals (the price) equals the marginal utility (measured in dollars). We should also continue until MC = MB when renting pizza ovens, searching for a job, studying, eating, shopping, etc.

  The reasoning behind this rule is straightforward. Regardless of what we are buying, selling, making, or doing, if one more unit costs less than the benefit it adds, there is a net benefit from proceeding with it. If one more unit costs more than the benefit it adds, we should not proceed with it. So in terms of the AP Economics Exam, if you're struggling with a question that has to do with how much of something should happen, try to identify the marginal cost and marginal benefit for the decision maker and suggest that they be equated.

  For example, suppose you are asked how a competitive firm should decide how many workers to hire in the short run. The MC of hiring a worker is the worker's wage. The MB is the worker's marginal product (MP)—how many widgets that worker will produce—times the price per widget.

  Even if you don't remember the jargon that MC = MB = MP × P, you should earn worthwhile partial credit for explaining that the firm should hire workers until the last worker's wage equals the last worker's contribution to output times the price.

  At the same time, the rule that MC = MB applies to you too! If you've been writing for 25 minutes on the long question, even if you feel you have more to say, ask yourself "Does the marginal benefit of writing an extra few sentences on this question equal the marginal cost of maybe not finishing the short questions because I run out of time?" Probably not.

# GRAPH DRILL

Now use the advice above to help you answer the following sample of a free-response question.

---

**1**  ☐ Mark for Review

The formula for the price elasticity of demand is

$$\frac{\dfrac{\text{change in } Q_d}{Q_d}}{\dfrac{\text{change in } P}{P}}$$

(i)   Explain why price elasticity of demand values is typically negative.
(ii)  Explain the relationship between the price elasticity of demand and the slope of a demand curve.
(iii) Explain why a monopoly should never operate on the inelastic portion of its demand curve.

## Here's How to Crack It

Although the question does not ask for a graph, the use of graphs will lead you to the correct answer and help convey that answer to the graders.

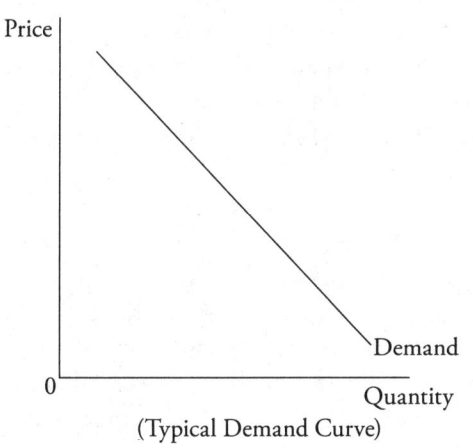
(Typical Demand Curve)

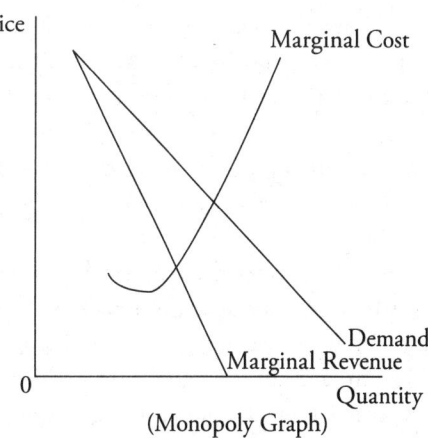
(Monopoly Graph)

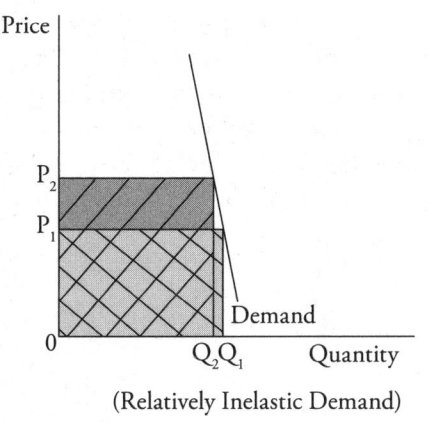
(Relatively Inelastic Demand)

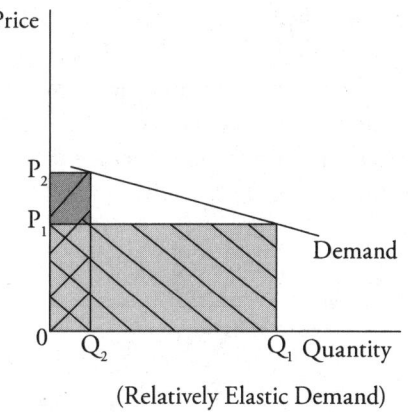
(Relatively Elastic Demand)

For part (i), draw a typical demand curve graph and remember the law of demand: when the price goes up, the quantity demanded goes down, and vice versa. In the elasticity formula, price (P) and quantity (Q) will always be positive. According to the law of demand, if the change in the price demanded is positive, the change in quantity demanded will be negative. If the change in the price demanded is negative, the change in quantity demanded will be positive. Either way, there will be a single negative value on the top or bottom of the formula, resulting in a negative elasticity value. After drawing the graph, you can explain this answer to the grader just as it is explained above.

For part (ii), you should gather your thoughts on the two items in question before venturing into a comparison. You probably remember that slope is "rise" over "run." Draw a complete demand curve graph including the axes. You will note that the vertical change, or "rise," in the demand curve represents a change in the price and the horizontal change, or "run," is a change in quantity. Thus,

$$\frac{\text{rise}}{\text{run}} = \frac{\text{change in P}}{\text{change in Q}}$$

A comparison of this formula with the elasticity formula clearly shows that slope and elasticity are not the same. Slope is the inverse of the elasticity formula without the P and Q. Thus, as slope increases, elasticity decreases (and vice versa), but elasticity also changes when P and Q change regardless of the slope. Use of the graph, the slope equation, and this explanation of the nature of the inverse relationship should yield a high score.

Part (iii) might seem difficult until you construct some visual cues. Because the question is about a monopoly, draw a complete monopoly graph including D, MR, and MC. Perhaps you remember the relationship between demand elasticity and MR: demand is elastic when MR is positive, is elastic when MR is zero, and is inelastic when MR is negative. Putting this information together with what is on the graph will tell you the answer. Because MC is always positive and firms operate when MR = MC (if at all), the firm must operate when MR is positive. Producing on the inelastic portion of the demand curve is equivalent to producing when MR is *negative,* meaning that total revenue would increase by producing less.

If you don't remember the relationship between MR and elasticity, there is still hope. Because the question asks about elasticity, draw a very inelastic (steep) and very elastic (almost flat) demand curve to exaggerate the characteristics of these two types of demand. On the relatively inelastic demand curve, if the monopoly raises prices and correspondingly lowers production, total revenue (the rectangle on the graph representing price times quantity of output) increases. With revenues increasing and output (and therefore costs) decreasing at the same time, profits must be rising. Thus, the monopoly should keep increasing prices as long as it is operating on the inelastic portion of the demand curve. It is clear from the elasticity formula that as price increases and quantity decreases, demand becomes more and more elastic. On the exaggerated elastic demand curve, since price increases result in lower revenues, before a monopolist raises prices, they should determine whether the loss in revenues is less than the decrease in costs. If we lower P to sell one more unit, $Q_d$ will change by a smaller percent so that $P \times Q = TR$ will fall.

# Chapter 3
# Using Time
# Effectively
# to Maximize
# Points

Very few students stop to think about how to improve their test-taking skills. Most assume that if they study hard, they will test well, and if they do not study, they will do poorly. Most students continue to believe this even after experience teaches them otherwise. Have you ever studied really hard for an exam and then blown it on test day? Have you ever aced an exam for which you thought you weren't well prepared? Most students have had one, if not both, of these experiences. The lesson should be clear: factors other than your level of preparation influence your final test score. This chapter will provide you with some insights that will help you perform better on the AP Economics Exams and on other exams as well.

## PACING AND TIMING

A big part of scoring well on an exam is working at a consistent pace. The worst mistake made by inexperienced or unsavvy test-takers is that they come to a question that stumps them, and rather than just skip it, they panic and stall. Time stands still when you're working on a question you cannot answer, and it is not unusual for students to waste five minutes on a single question. It is important to be aware of how much time you have spent on a given question and on the section you are working on. There are several ways to improve your pacing and timing for the test.

- **Know your average pace.** While you prepare for your test, try to gauge how long you take on 5, 10, or 20 questions. Knowing how long you spend on average per question will help you identify how many questions you can answer effectively and how best to pace yourself for the test.

- **Have a clock-checking strategy.** The Bluebook testing app provides a countdown clock that you can view or hide. We recommend that you keep it hidden as your default, because constantly checking the clock is, in itself, a waste of time and can be distracting. Devise a plan. Try checking the clock after every 15 or 20 questions to see whether you are keeping the correct pace or whether you need to speed up; this will ensure that you're cognizant of the time but will not permit you to fall into the trap of dwelling on it.

- **Know when to move on.** Since all multiple-choice questions are scored equally, investing appreciable amounts of time on a single question is inefficient and can potentially deprive you of the chance to answer easier questions later on. If you are able to eliminate answer choices, do so, but don't worry about picking a random answer and moving on if you cannot find the correct answer. Remember, tests are like marathons; you do best when you work through them at a steady pace. You can always come back to a question you don't know. When you do, very often you will find that your previous mental block is gone, and you will wonder why the question perplexed you the first time around (as you gleefully move on to the next question). Even if you still don't know the answer, you will not have wasted valuable time you could have spent on easier questions.

- **Be selective.** You don't have to do any of the questions in a given section in order. If you are stumped by a free-response or multiple-choice question, skip it or choose a different one. In the section below, you will see that you may not have to answer every question correctly to achieve your desired score. Select the multiple-choice questions or FRQs that you can answer and work on them first. This will make you more efficient and give you the greatest chance of getting the most questions correct.

- **Use Process of Elimination on multiple-choice questions.** Many times, one or more answer choices can be eliminated. Every answer choice that can be eliminated increases the odds that you will answer the question correctly. Review the section on this strategy in Chapter 1 to find these incorrect answer choices and increase your odds of getting the question correct.

Remember, because all the multiple-choice questions on this test are of equal value, no one question is that important. Your overall goal for pacing is to get the most questions correct. Finally, you should set a realistic goal for your final score. In the next section, we will break down how to achieve your desired score and provide ways of pacing yourself to do so.

## GETTING THE SCORE YOU WANT

Depending on the score you need, it may be in your best interest *not* to try to work through every multiple-choice question. If you're aiming for credit hours and need to score a 5, it's best to find out as early in your preparation as possible. On the other hand, if you're simply aiming for placement and you find out your first choice of college sets the cut-off point at a score of 3, some of the pressure is off and you can prepare without feeling crushed by anxiety.

It's important to remember that AP Exams in all subjects no longer include a "guessing penalty" for incorrect answers. Instead, students are assessed only on their total number of correct answers. A lot of AP materials, even those you receive in your AP class, may not include this information. So, if you find yourself running out of time, you should click an answer for every question before the time for the multiple-choice section is up. Even if you don't plan to spend a lot of time on every question and even if you have no idea what the correct answer is, it's to your advantage to fill something in.

> **The Letter Of The Day**
>
> Remember your Letter of the Day (LOTD); when it's down to the buzzer, just fill it in for any remaining choices to maximize your chances for more points.

## TEST ANXIETY

Most people experience anxiety before and during an exam. To a certain extent, test anxiety can be helpful. Some people find that they perform more quickly and efficiently under stress. If you have ever pulled an all-nighter to write a paper and ended up doing good work, you know the feeling.

However, too much stress is definitely a bad thing. Hyperventilating during the test, for example, almost always leads to a lower score. If you find that you stress out during exams, here are a few preemptive actions you can take.

- **Take a reality check.** Evaluate your situation before the test begins. If you have studied hard, remind yourself that you are well prepared. Remember that many others taking the test are not as well prepared, and (in your classes, at least) you are being graded against them, so you have an advantage. If you didn't study, accept the fact that you will probably not ace the test. Make sure you get to every question you know something about. Don't stress out or fixate on how much you don't know. Your job is to score as high as you can by maximizing the benefits of what you do know. In either scenario, it is best to think of a test as if it were a game. How can you get the most points in the time allotted to you? Always answer questions you can answer easily and quickly before you answer those that will take more time.

- **Try to relax.** Slow, deep breathing works for almost everyone. Close your eyes, take a few slow, deep breaths, and concentrate on nothing but your inhalation and exhalation for a few seconds. This is a basic form of meditation, and it should help you to clear your mind of stress and, as a result, concentrate better on the test. If you have ever taken yoga classes, you probably know some other good relaxation techniques. Use them when you can (obviously, anything that requires leaving your seat and, say, assuming a handstand position won't be allowed by any but the most free-spirited proctors).

- **Eliminate as many surprises as you can.** Make sure you know where the test will be given, when it starts, what type of questions are going to be asked, and how long the test will take. You don't want to be worrying about any of these things on test day or, even worse, after the test has already begun.

The best way to avoid stress is to study both the test material and the test itself. Congratulations! By buying and reading this book, you are taking a major step toward a stress-free AP Economics Exam.

# Chapter 4
# Pacing Drills

Use the following multiple-choice drills to practice the pacing techniques and strategies you've learned. Then check your answers at the end of the chapter.

# MICROECONOMICS DRILL

**1**  ⚑ Mark for Review

Which of the following accurately describes the law of diminishing marginal utility?

(A) Utility increases as per-unit consumption increases.

(B) Utility decreases as per-unit consumption increases.

(C) Utility is unrelated to per-unit consumption.

(D) Utility increases as total consumption increases.

(E) Utility decreases as total consumption increases.

**2**  ⚑ Mark for Review

Which of the following would cause a decrease in the supply of soccer balls?

(A) The rubber used to make soccer balls becomes less expensive

(B) A new pump is introduced that inflates soccer balls twice as fast

(C) Soccer balls are expected to become less expensive as soccer becomes more popular

(D) Sporting goods stores begin to go out of business

(E) The government wants a more competitive Olympic soccer team, so it subsidizes the production of soccer balls

**3**  ⚑ Mark for Review

Imagine you own a business that sells a product with inelastic demand. What would be the best way for you to bring in more revenue while selling fewer units?

(A) Decrease the price

(B) Hold the price constant

(C) Increase the price

(D) Open a second storefront

(E) Increase production

**4**  ⚑ Mark for Review

Setting a minimum wage is an example of

(A) a price floor.

(B) a price ceiling.

(C) free market capitalism.

(D) an excess burden.

(E) efficiency loss.

**5**  ☐ Mark for Review

If a firm wants to maximize profits, it should produce at a quantity for which

(A)  total costs exceed total revenue by a large margin.

(B)  total costs exceed total revenue by a modest margin.

(C)  total costs equal total revenue.

(D)  total revenue exceeds total cost by a large margin.

(E)  total revenue exceeds total cost by a modest margin.

**6**  ☐ Mark for Review

During a pandemic, there may be a shortage of goods. If the price of water increased from $2.00 per liter to $2.50 per liter, mainly due to the U.S. government instituting a $0.50 increase in plastic tax, what effect would this have on consumers?

(A)  Consumers would be responsible for all taxes.

(B)  Consumers would have a significant tax burden.

(C)  Producers would be responsible for all taxes.

(D)  Producers would not have a significant tax burden.

(E)  There would be no effect.

**7**  ☐ Mark for Review

Suppose that there are only two goods: x and y. Which of the following is NOT correct?

(A)  One can have a comparative advantage in producing both goods.

(B)  One can have both an absolute advantage and a comparative advantage in producing x.

(C)  One can have an absolute advantage and no comparative advantage in producing x.

(D)  One can have a comparative advantage and no absolute advantage in producing x.

(E)  All the statements above are true.

**8**  ☐ Mark for Review

A change in which of the following will NOT cause a shift in the demand curve for hamburgers?

(A)  The price of hot dogs

(B)  The price of hamburgers

(C)  The price of hamburger buns

(D)  Income levels of hamburger consumers

(E)  The price of ketchup

**9** ☐ Mark for Review

The ability of firms to enter and exit a market over time means that

Ⓐ the marginal cost is zero

Ⓑ the marginal revenue is zero

Ⓒ the long-run supply curve is more elastic

Ⓓ the long-run supply curve is more inelastic

Ⓔ the firms make positive economic profit

**10** ☐ Mark for Review

When a good is taxed, the tax burden falls mainly on the consumer if

Ⓐ the demand is inelastic and the supply is inelastic

Ⓑ the demand is inelastic and the supply is elastic

Ⓒ the demand is elastic and the supply is inelastic

Ⓓ the demand is elastic and the supply is elastic

Ⓔ the tax is levied on the consumers

**11** ☐ Mark for Review

Elsa values her time at $50 per hour, and tutors David for two hours. David is willing to pay $175 for two hours of tutoring, but they negotiate a price of $125 for the entire two hours. Which of the following statements is true about the transaction above?

Ⓐ Consumer surplus is greater than producer surplus by between $50 and $75.

Ⓑ Producer surplus is greater than consumer surplus by between $50 and $75.

Ⓒ Consumer surplus is greater than producer surplus by more than $75.

Ⓓ Producer surplus is greater than consumer surplus by more than $75.

Ⓔ The difference between consumer and producer surplus is $25.

# MICROECONOMICS FREE-RESPONSE QUESTIONS

**1**   🔖 Mark for Review

Imagine that tablets are produced in a perfectly competitive market without externalities. The graph below shows the market supply and demand curves for tablets in Eduland.

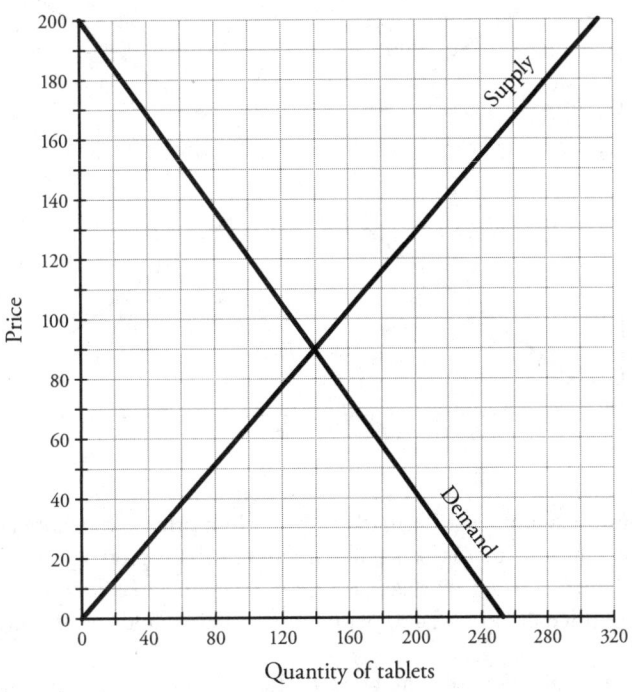

A.   What is the total economic surplus at the market equilibrium? Show your calculations.

B.   To make tablets more affordable, the president of Eduland sets a price ceiling at $50 per tablet. How will the quantity of tablets sold change as a result? Use data to explain your response.

C.   After the price ceiling proves unpopular, the president removes the price ceiling and offers a $30 subsidy to tablet stores instead.
   (i)    How much will consumers pay per tablet after the subsidy goes into effect?
   (ii)   What will be the total cost of the subsidy to the government of Eduland?
   (iii)  How does the subsidy affect the deadweight loss, as compared to the market equilibrium in part (A)? Explain.

**2**  ▢ Mark for Review

The graph below shows the rental market for 1-bedroom apartments in Beach City. The city government is considering intervening in this rental market.

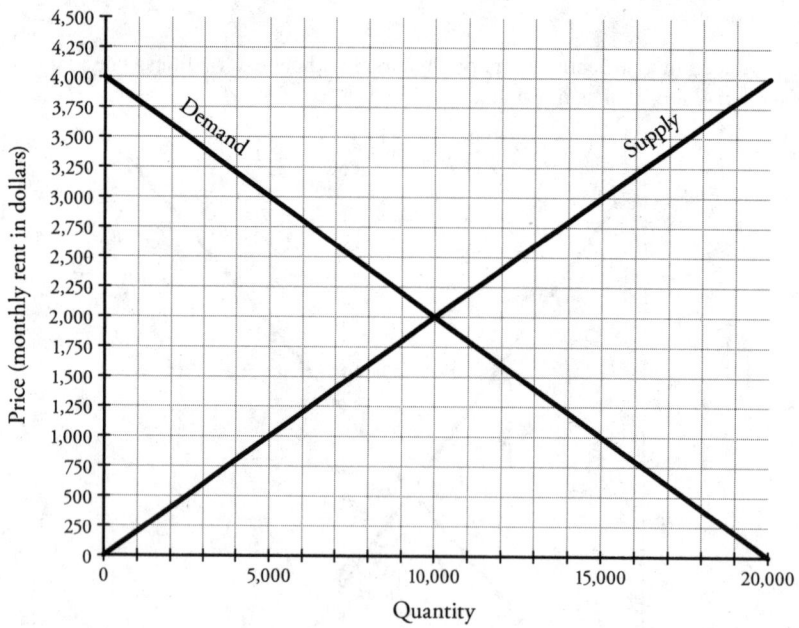

A.   Calculate the total consumer surplus at the market equilibrium price and quantity. Show your work.
B.   If the city imposes rent control—that is, sets a maximum price that property owners can charge for rent—at $1,500 per month, is there a housing shortage, a surplus, or neither? Explain.
C.   If instead the city sets a price floor of $2,400 per month, is there a housing shortage, a surplus, or neither? Explain.
D.   If instead the city tries to limit overcrowding by restricting the number of 1-bedroom apartments that can be put up for rent to 6,000 apartments, calculate the deadweight loss. Show your work.

# MACROECONOMICS DRILL

**1**  📑 Mark for Review

If an economy is currently in an inflationary gap, which of the following changes would result in a decrease in real GDP in the short run?

(A) Increase in the labor supply

(B) New developments in technology

(C) Fewer government regulations

(D) Increased taxes

(E) Decreased wages

**2**  📑 Mark for Review

Which of the following would lead to a decrease in nominal interest rates?

(A) Increase in anticipated inflation

(B) Decrease in money supply through open operations

(C) Increase in the supply of loanable funds

(D) Increase in demand for loanable funds

(E) Decrease in taxes

**3**  📑 Mark for Review

Expansionary fiscal policy is associated with all of the following EXCEPT:

(A) depreciation of domestic currency relative to foreign currencies

(B) increased interest rates

(C) increased demand for domestic currency

(D) exports decrease

(E) imports increase

**4**  📑 Mark for Review

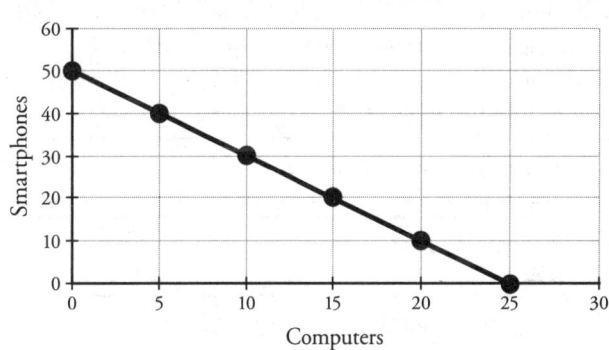

The graph above shows the production-possibilities frontier for a nation in Europe that exports computers and smartphones. Which of the following combinations of computers and smartphones is impossible given the nation's available resources?

(A) 10 computers, 35 smartphones

(B) 5 computers, 40 smartphones

(C) 15 computers, 10 smartphones

(D) 25 computers, 0 smartphones

(E) 0 computers, 40 smartphones

**5** ☐ Mark for Review

Which of the following statements is true regarding an economy with ample reserves?

(A) A central bank can increase the reserve ratio to increase the money supply.

(B) A central bank can decrease the reserve ratio to increase the money supply.

(C) A central bank can increase the reserve ratio to decrease the money supply.

(D) A central bank can decrease the reserve ratio to decrease the money supply.

(E) The reserve ratio will have no impact on the money supply.

**6** ☐ Mark for Review

An American buys an entertainment system that was manufactured in China. How do the U.S. national income accounts treat this transaction?

(A) Net exports and GDP both rise.

(B) Net exports and GDP both fall.

(C) Net exports and GDP go in opposite directions.

(D) Net exports fall, and there is no change in GDP.

(E) There is no change in net exports, and GDP falls.

**7** ☐ Mark for Review

Which of the following would be included in U.S. GDP calculations?

(A) An auto mechanic fixing his dentist's car for a filling

(B) A stay-at-home dad providing childcare for his children

(C) A worker donating $200 to the Red Cross

(D) High school students spending their Saturdays building homes for the homeless

(E) A college student paying another student $50 in cash for a used laptop

**8** ☐ Mark for Review

Suppose a country produces only crude oil. Which of the following statements is true based on the production and price data below?

|  | Production (millions of barrels) | Price (per barrel) |
|---|---|---|
| 2014 | 300 | $25.00 |
| 2015 | 250 | $30.00 |

(A) Real GDP decreased and nominal GDP increased.

(B) Both real and nominal GDP increased.

(C) Both real and nominal GDP decreased.

(D) Real GDP decreased and nominal GDP remained unchanged.

(E) Real GDP remained unchanged and nominal GDP increased.

**9** ⬚ Mark for Review

A financial planner on a popular TV show convinces more Americans to save for retirement. What is the result on the supply and demand for loanable funds?

Ⓐ The supply curve would shift up, increasing the equilibrium interest rate.

Ⓑ The demand curve would shift up, increasing the equilibrium interest rate.

Ⓒ The supply curve would shift down, decreasing the equilibrium interest rate.

Ⓓ The demand curve would shift down, decreasing the equilibrium interest rate.

Ⓔ Both the supply and demand curves would shift.

**10** ⬚ Mark for Review

Suppose the reserve ratio is 0.1. If a bank gets $200 in deposits, what is the maximum amount it can lend?

Ⓐ $20

Ⓑ $180

Ⓒ $2,000

Ⓓ Greater than $200 but less than $500

Ⓔ None of the above

# MACROECONOMICS FREE-RESPONSE QUESTIONS

**1** ☐ Mark for Review

The table below provides economic data for the fictional nation of Zoolandia. Assume Year 1 is the base year, and the GDP deflator in Year 2 is 125.

|                | Year 1     | Year 2     |
| -------------- | ---------- | ---------- |
| Population     | 1,000      | 1,500      |
| Nominal GDP    | $500,000   | $800,000   |

A. What is Zoolandia's real GDP in Year 2?
B. How does real GDP change from Year 1 to Year 2? How does this impact the demand for money and the nominal interest rate?
C. What is the inflation rate between Year 1 and Year 2?
D. Using the data, explain how the standard of living changed from Year 1 to Year 2.
E. If there is a 20% increase in nominal wages between Year 1 and Year 2, how did the real wages of workers in Zoolandia change during this period? Explain.

**2** ☐ Mark for Review

The following is a simplified balance sheet for Java Bank in the United States. For the purpose of this question, assume that the United States is operating with limited reserves.

| Assets                      | Liabilities              |
| --------------------------- | ------------------------ |
| Required Reserves  $5,000   | Demand Deposits  $50,000 |
| Excess Reserves       $3,000 |                          |
| Government Bonds $7,000      |                          |
| Loans                   $35,000 |                        |

A. What is the reserve requirement?
B. Assume that Kingston deposits $10,000 in his checking account.
   (i) By how much will Java Bank's required reserves change based on Kingston's deposit?
   (ii) As a result of the deposit, what is the new value of excess reserves based on the reserve requirement?
C. Suppose that the Federal Reserve Bank purchases $6,000 worth of bonds from Java Bank. What will be the immediate change in dollar value of each of the following after the purchase?
   (i) excess reserves
   (ii) the M1 measure of the money supply

# MICROECONOMICS DRILL: ANSWERS AND EXPLANATIONS

1. **B** The law of diminishing marginal utility states that utility decreases as additional units of a good are consumed. The only answer to accurately state this is (B).

2. **D** Choice (A) reflects a decrease in input costs. Choice (B) reflects an improvement in technology. Choice (C) reflects that there are expectations of lower prices in the future. Choice (E) reflects a subsidy. All of these would cause an increase in the supply of soccer balls. The only answer that would cause a decrease in the supply of soccer balls is (D), a reduction in the number of sellers.

3. **C** When businesses face inelastic demand, the best way to bring in more revenue while selling fewer units is to raise the price of the product, (C). Decreasing the price would raise total revenue if the product in question were elastic. Without any other changes, holding the price constant wouldn't affect the total revenue. Opening a second storefront would increase costs and reduce total revenue. Increasing production would shift the supply curve outward, causing the price to decrease.

4. **A** A price floor is an artificially imposed minimum price. The government sets a minimum price on labor using a minimum wage, so (A) is the correct answer. A price ceiling, (B), occurs when the government limits the maximum price of a good. A minimum wage is an example of a government intervention in the economy, and would not be considered an example of free market capitalism, (C). An excess burden, (D), and an efficiency loss, (E), are the same, the losses to consumer and producer surplus that come as the result of a tax.

5. **D** To maximize total profits, a firm will want to produce when total revenue exceeds total cost by a large margin. When costs exceed revenue, a firm is operating at a loss. When costs equal revenue, a firm breaks even. The greater the positive distance between revenue and cost, the greater the profits will be. As a result, (D) is the best answer.

6. **B** Consumers would be responsible for paying for the increased cost per liter on water. Choices (A) and (C) can be eliminated because consumers and producers wouldn't be responsible for *all* taxes; the only mentioned tax increase is to that on plastic. Eliminate (D) because the only tax mentioned is on plastic, and no information is given that is relevant to producers' tax burden. Lastly, eliminate (E) since there would be an effect on consumers, especially during a pandemic shortage. The answer is (B).

7. **A** Application-of-definition questions can be very tricky. The best approach is to see whether the answer choice "fits" the definition or not. Given past classical examples, (B), (C), and (D) can be quickly eliminated. (See the Comparative Advantage and Gains from Trade section in Chapter 5 for more discussion on this.) Choice (A) forces test-takers to think about the possibility of having a comparative advantage in producing both goods (which cannot be possible). It is possible to have absolute advantage in producing both goods, but impossible to have comparative advantage in producing both goods (as one can have a comparative advantage in only one good). Therefore, the answer is (A).

8. **B** A shift in the demand curve comes about due to changes in the price of substitutes, changes in the price of complementary goods, or changes in income (this last point is sometimes forgotten on the AP Exam). Thus, (A), (C), and (E) can be eliminated, as hot dogs and hamburger buns count as substitutes and complementary goods, respectively, and ketchup also counts as a complementary good (to both hamburgers and hot dogs, but here the only focus is hamburgers). Changes in income level will cause the demand curve for hamburgers to shift, so (D) can also be eliminated. As the price of hamburgers changes, the demand curve does not shift, but there is movement along the (existing) demand curve. Therefore, the answer is (B).

9. **C** As companies can enter and exit the market over time, only those suppliers who can efficiently supply will choose to remain in the market. This would make the long-run supply curve more elastic, so the answer is (C).

10. **B** The tax burden falls primarily on those who have the greatest relative inelasticity. As the question is asking for conditions for which the consumer bears most of the tax burden, eliminate (C) and (D). For the consumers to bear most of the burden, the supply needs to be elastic; therefore, eliminate (A). Choice (E) is tricky. Even though consumers are charged a tax, suppliers may still bear the tax burden through the shift in demand curve. Eliminate (E), and you're left with (B) as the answer.

11. **E** The best way to approach numerical questions that give answer choices in ranges is to do the math. In this case, Elsa is willing to provide her services for $100, but she received $125. Therefore, the producer surplus is $25. David is willing to pay $175 for the services he receives, but he pays $125 for them. Therefore, consumer surplus is $50. The difference between consumer and producer surplus is $25, so the answer is (E).

# MICROECONOMICS FREE-RESPONSE ANSWERS AND EXPLANATIONS

1.

    A. Remember that economic surplus equals consumer surplus plus producer surplus. Graphically, this is represented by the triangle created by points (0,0), (0,200), and (140,90). The equation is $(0.5)(200 \times 140) = \$14,000$.

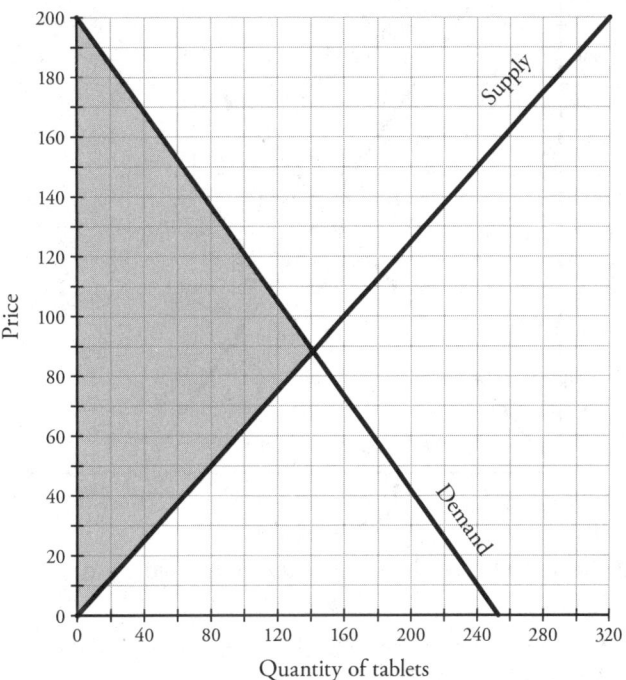

    B. Lowering the price to $50 will restrict the supply to 80 tablets. As a result, fewer tablets (80) will be sold with the price ceiling than at the equilibrium price ($140).

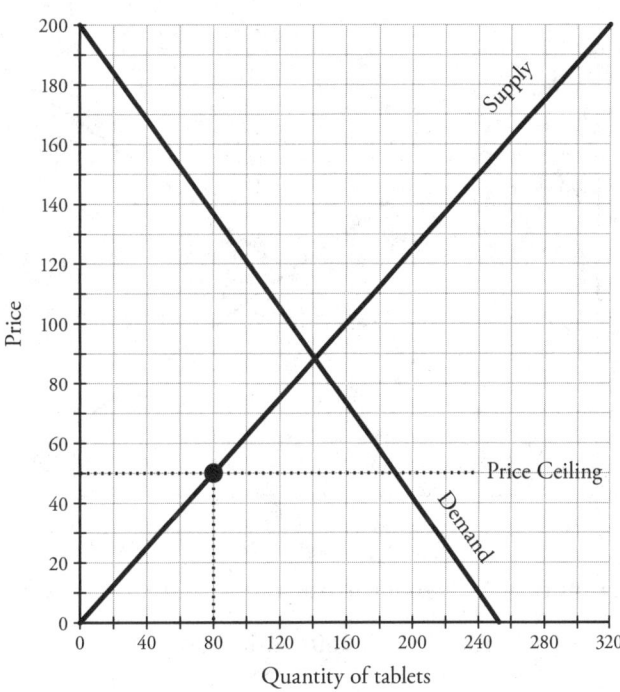

C. (i) For a per-unit subsidy, the equilibrium occurs when the vertical distance between the supply and demand curves equals the value of the subsidy. In other words, the equilibrium point with the subsidy occurs at the quantity for which the price to the producer equals the price the consumer pays plus the subsidy. In this case, the quantity is 160, at which suppliers will charge and consumers will pay $100.

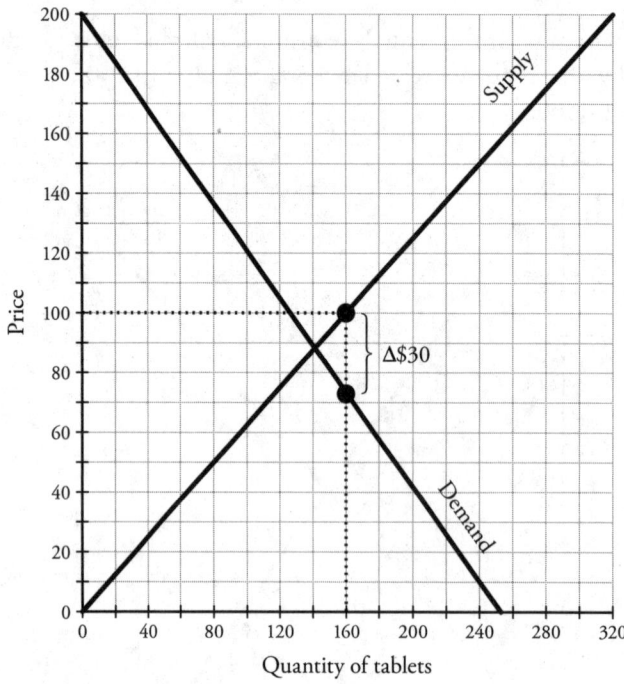

(ii) The total cost of the subsidy equals the subsidy multiplied by the quantity of tablets sold. In this case, $30 × 160 = $4,800.

(iii) The deadweight loss increases as the equilibrium quantity of tablets with the subsidies (160) exceeds that at the efficient quantity (100).

2.

A.

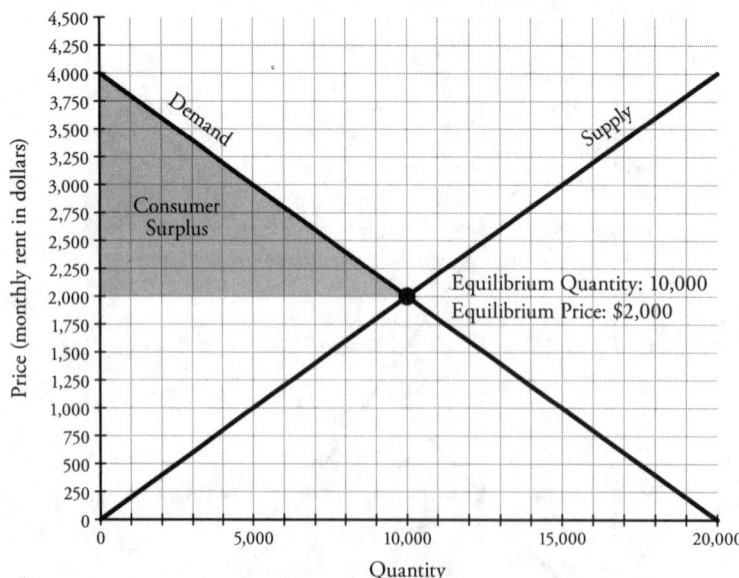

At equilibrium, the quantity of 1-bedroom apartments is 10,000 and the price is $2,000. Therefore, the total consumer surplus is ($\frac{1}{2}$ × 10,000 × $2,000) = $10,000,000.

B.

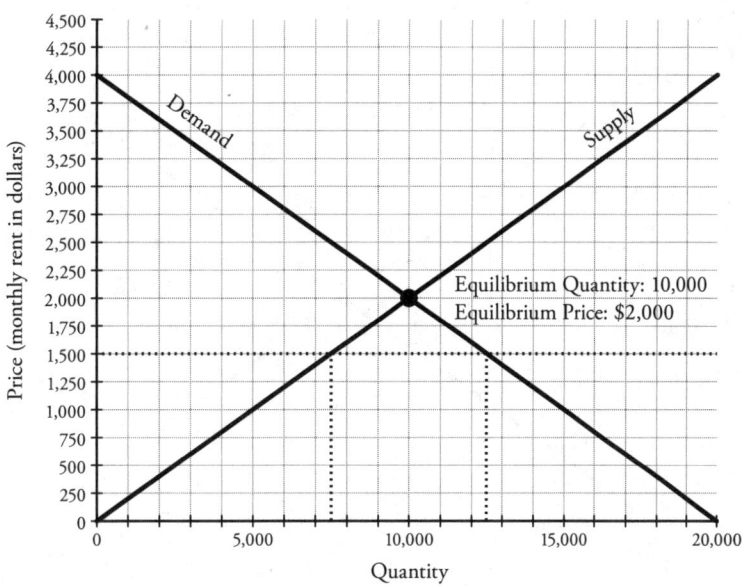

If the government sets a price ceiling of $1,500, then 12,500 apartments will be demanded, but only 7,500 apartments will be supplied. This means that there will be a shortage of 5,000 apartments.

C.

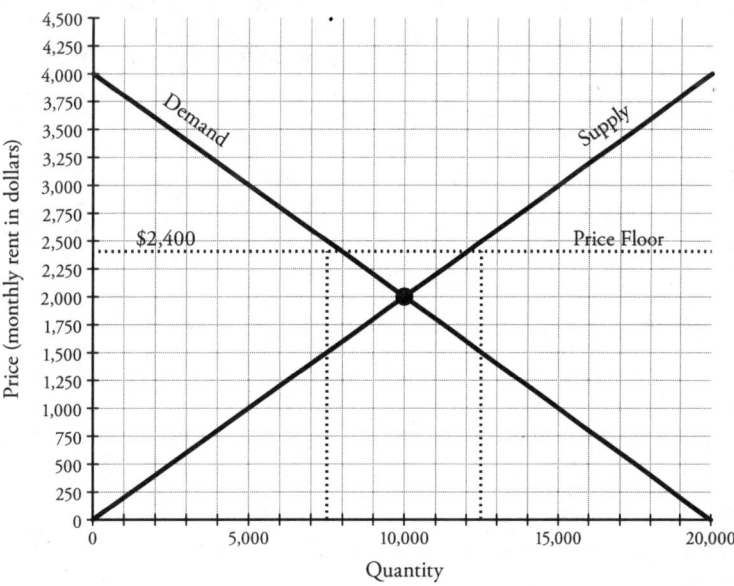

If the government sets a price floor of $2,400, then 12,000 apartments will be supplied, but only 8,000 apartments will be demanded. This means that there will be a surplus of 4,000 apartments.

D.

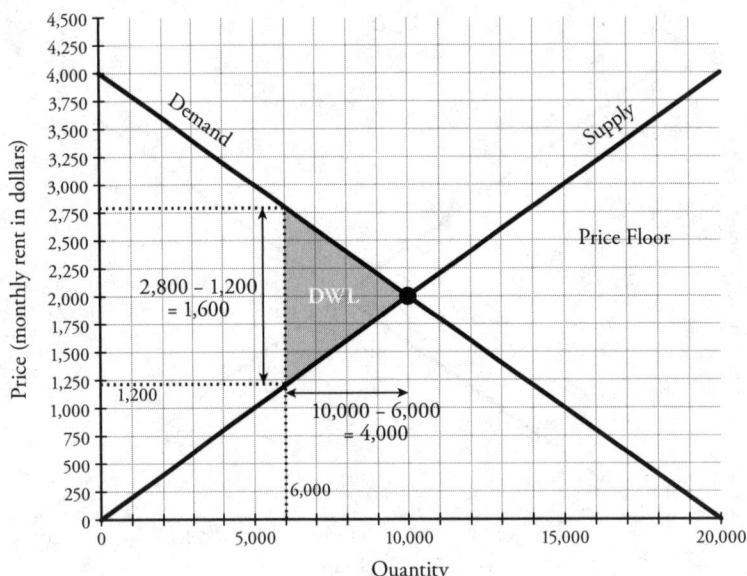

To calculate the deadweight loss (DWL), first figure that 6,000 apartments would be supplied at a price of $1,200 and demanded at a price of $2,800. This means that the difference between the price supplied and the price demanded is $1,600. The difference between the equilibrium quantity and the imposed quantity is 10,000 − 6,000 = 4,000. Calculate DWL as follows: ($\frac{1}{2}$ × $1,600 × 4,000) = $3,200,000.

# MACROECONOMICS DRILL: ANSWERS AND EXPLANATIONS

1. **D** This question is testing your knowledge of factors that impact the aggregate supply curve. Of the options provided, only increased taxes will shift the curve inward and thus reduce real GDP, so (D) is the best answer. Increases in the labor supply, new developments in technology, fewer government regulations, and decreased wages would all cause an increase in aggregate supply, which would increase real GDP and make the inflationary gap more pronounced.

2. **C** The nominal interest rate equals the real interest rate plus anticipated inflation, so any decreases in the real interest rate or anticipated inflation will cause the nominal interest rate to decrease. An increase in anticipated inflation would increase nominal interest rates, so (A) can be eliminated. Decreasing the money supply through open operations would also cause the interest rate to rise, so (B) can be eliminated. If the demand for loanable funds increases, the interest rate will increase, so (D) can be eliminated. Decreasing taxes can have various effects on the nominal interest rate depending on the context, so eliminate (E). An increase in the supply of loanable funds would lower the real interest rate, thus lowering the nominal interest rate, so (C) is the best answer.

3. **A** Expansionary fiscal policy is associated with higher interest rates, increased demand for domestic currency, appreciation of domestic currency relative to foreign currencies, decreased exports, and increased imports. Choice (A) is the best answer.

4. **A** As with all production possibilities curves, points that fall on or below the curve are possible, but points that fall outside of the curve are impossible. Of the options provided, (A) is the only answer that falls outside of the curve.

5. **E** In nations with ample reserves, adjusting the reserve ratio will have no impact on the money supply. Instead, central banks with ample reserves use administered interest rates to manage the money supply.

6. **B** GDP is the sum of consumption, investment, government spending, and net exports (in equation form: GDP = C + I + G + X). In this case, as the American is buying something made in China, net exports would fall, causing GDP to fall. The answer is (B).

7. **C** For a transaction to be captured in GDP calculations, it needs to be recorded and reported to the government. The answer is (C) because while a charitable donation would be reported to the government, all the other transactions would not. On a side note, other countries (United Kingdom and Germany) are looking at ways to include parallel market transactions as part of their GDP.

8. **D** Real GDP is a measure of a country's actual production. In this case, the production fell, so eliminate (B) and (E). Nominal GDP is the price of total production. In this case, the price for 2014 is 300 × $25 = $7,500 and the price for 2015 is 250 × $30 = $7,500. Therefore, the answer is (D).

9. **C** As there is more money available to invest, the supply curve would shift down (from S to S′ in the figure below). This would decrease the equilibrium interest rate (from I to I′). The answer is (C).

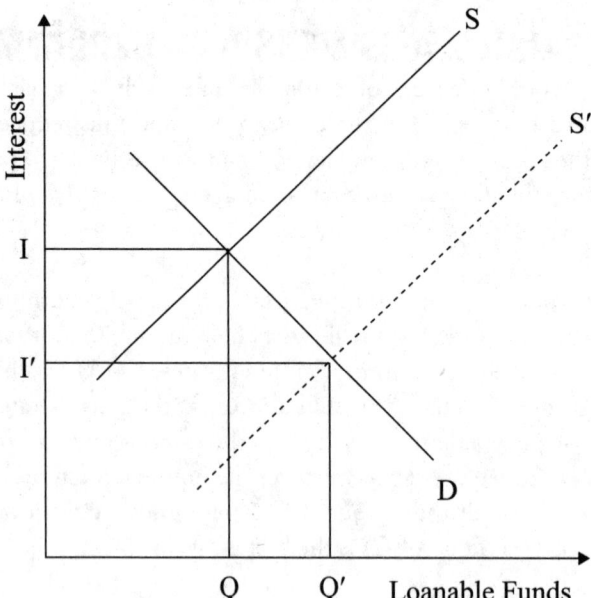

10. **C**  The reserve ratio is defined as follows: Reserve Ratio = $\dfrac{\text{Bank Reserves}}{\text{Total Deposits}}$. If the bank holds the $200 in reserve, it can lend $\dfrac{\$200}{0.1}$ = $2,000. Therefore, the answer is (C).

# MACROECONOMICS FREE-RESPONSE ANSWERS AND EXPLANATIONS

1.  A.  Real GDP equals the nominal GDP divided by the GDP deflator and multiplied by 100. In this case:
    $$\left( \frac{800,000}{125} \right) \times 100 = \$640,000.$$

    B.  In Year 1, real GDP equals $400,000, so real GDP increases between Year 1 and Year 2. As the real GDP increases, the demand for money and nominal interest rates would also increase.

    C.  To calculate the inflation rate from this data, divide the nominal GDP by the real GDP. In this case, $800,000 divided by $640,000 equals 1.25, so inflation is 25%.

    D.  The best way to approach this question is to consider real GDP per capita. In Year 1, real GDP is $400,000, so per capita real GDP is $400. In Year 2, real GDP per capita equals $462.67. As a result, one can reasonably infer there was a slight increase in the standard of living during this time.

    E.  As inflation was 25%, and nominal wages only increased 20%, then wages have not kept up with inflation. The real wages of workers in Zoolandia decreased during this period.

2.  A.  Since the required reserves are $5,000 and demand deposits are $50,000, the reserve requirement is $5,000 divided by $50,000, or 10 percent.

    B.  (i)   If Kingston deposits $10,000, then the demand deposits will now equal $60,000 and required reserves will now have to increase to $6,000.

        (ii)  Since required reserves increased to $6,000, then $1,000 of Kingston's deposit will go to required reserves. The remaining $9,000 will go to excess reserves, increasing it to $12,000.

    C.  (i)   If the Federal Reserve Bank purchases $6,000 worth of bonds, then the excess reserves increase by $6,000. Since the excess reserves were at $12,000, they are now at $18,000.

        (ii)  This is a bit of a trick. The M1 money supply does not immediately change at all. While the bank is now able to loan out more money based on the increase in its excess reserves, which would increase the money supply, until it makes a loan, M1 remains the same.

# REFLECT

Think about what you've learned in Part III, and respond to the following questions:

- How long will you spend on multiple-choice questions?

- How will you change your approach to multiple-choice questions?

- What is your multiple-choice guessing strategy?

- What will you do before you begin answering a free-response question?

- How will you change your approach to the free-response questions?

- Will you seek further help, outside of this book (such as from a teacher, tutor, or AP Students), on how to approach multiple-choice questions, the free-response questions, or a pacing strategy?

# Part IV
# Content Review for the AP Economics Exams

**Review of Microeconomics Concepts**

5    Micro Unit 1: Basic Economics Concepts
6    Micro Unit 2: Supply and Demand
7    Micro Unit 3: Production, Cost, and the Perfect Competition Model
8    Micro Unit 4: Imperfect Competition
9    Micro Units 5 and 6: Factor Markets, Market Failure, and the Role of Government
10   Microeconomics Drill Questions: Answers and Explanations

**Review of Macroeconomics Concepts**

11   Macro Units 1 and 2: Basic Economics Concepts, Economic Indicators, and the Business Cycle
12   Macro Unit 3: National Income and Price Determination
13   Macro Unit 4: Financial Sector
14   Macro Unit 5: Long-Run Consequences of Stabilization Polices
15   Macro Unit 6: Open Economy, International Trade, and Finance
16   Macroeconomics Drill Questions: Answers and Explanations

# Review of Microeconomics Concepts

# Chapter 5
# Micro Unit 1:
# Basic Economics
# Concepts

## 5.1 SCARCITY

**Scarcity** occurs because our unlimited desire for goods and services exceeds our limited ability to produce them due to constraints on time and resources. The **resources** used in the production process are sometimes called **inputs**, or **factors of production**. They include:

- **capital**—manufactured goods that can be used in the production process, including tools, equipment, buildings, and machinery (this is often referred to as **physical capital**)

- **labor**—the physical and mental effort of people, including **human capital**, the knowledge and skill acquired through training and experience

- **entrepreneurship**—the ability to identify opportunities and organize production, and the willingness to accept risk in the pursuit of rewards

- **natural resources/land**—either term can refer to any productive resource existing in nature, including wild plants, mineral deposits, wind, and water

> **Fierce Actors of Production**
>
> Memorable acronyms, initialisms, or acrostic mnemonics can be a good way to keep track of concepts. Here's an acrostic mnemonic the factors of production:
>
> **C**razy—Capital
> **L**eopards—Labor
> **E**nvy—Entrepreneurship
> **N**arwhals—Natural resources/land

Energy and technology are also important contributors to the production process, but they can be treated as by-products of the four factors of production listed above. Because economists like to work with two-dimensional graphs, the production model is often simplified to include just two inputs: labor and capital.

Consider the factors of production needed for a bagel shop. The shop building, mixers, and ovens are examples of capital. Natural resources, including land and rain, will help provide the wheat for the dough. Labor will form the dough into bagels, place them into the ovens, and sell them. The bagel chef uses her skill and experience—human capital—to make the bagels smooth on the outside and soft on the inside. How did this shop come about? An entrepreneur risked a large amount of money and poured his ideas and organizational talents into the success of the shop. Thus, our bagel shop requires all four factors of production. In contrast, a soda-pop vending machine is an example of a capital-intensive business that requires little beyond canned drinks and the machine itself to produce soft drink sales.

## 5.2 RESOURCE ALLOCATION AND ECONOMIC SYSTEMS

**Economics** is the study of how societies allocate scarce resources among competing ends. Although some think economics is only about business and money, in truth, the field is as broad as the list of scarce resources, and deals with everything from air to concert tickets. Few things have an infinite supply or zero demand, meaning that the need to make choices in response to scarcity—economics—can apply to almost everything and everyone. Even the world's 1,800-plus billionaires must struggle with constraints in time and resources. That brings us to reason number 493 why economics is great: almost any topic is within its domain. Economists are currently studying war, crime, endangered species, marriage, systems of government, child care, legal rules, death, birth . . . the sky's the limit.

Economists view the world in terms of positive economics and normative economics. **Positive economics** *describes* the way things are, whereas **normative economics** addresses the way things *should* be. For example, "The unemployment rate hit a three-year high" is a positive statement, while "The Fed should lower the federal funds rate" is a normative statement.

# 5.3 THE PRODUCTION POSSIBILITIES CURVE

Because economics is the study of the distribution of scarce goods, economists are always looking for ways to analyze human choices. For example, the fact that you are reading this book right now means that you cannot simultaneously be doing a number of other things, like reading the newspaper, swimming, or horseback riding. If the best alternative to reading this book is swimming, then the opportunity cost of reading this book is not being able to go swimming. **Opportunity cost** is the value of the best alternative sacrificed as compared to what actually takes place. The opportunity cost of going to the prom with Pat may be that you can't go with Chris. The opportunity cost of going to college may be that you can't spend the same time working at McDonald's.

When we use resources to produce one good or service, the opportunity cost is that we cannot produce another good or service. When we make birdcages, we cannot use the same resources to make chairs. The choices an economy faces and the opportunity cost of making one good rather than another can be illustrated with a **production possibilities curve** (PPC). Figure 1 illustrates a production-possibilities frontier for a simplified economy that can use its resources to produce either birdcages or chairs.

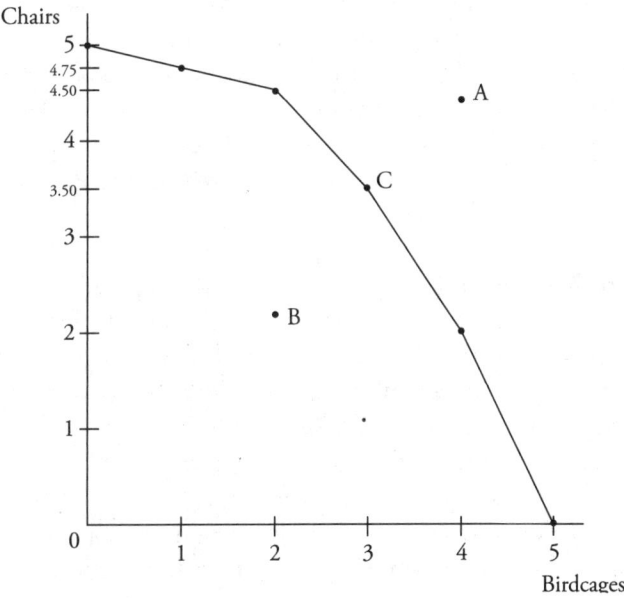

**Figure 1: Production Possibilities Curve**

The curve or "frontier" itself represents all of the combinations of the two goods that could be produced using all of the available resources and technology. For example, the economy could produce 5 birdcages and 0 chairs, or 5 chairs and 0 birdcages, or 3 birdcages and 3.5 chairs, and so on.

Birdcage-chair combinations outside the frontier, such as point A on the figure, require more resources than the economy has, and are therefore unobtainable. Points inside the frontier are obtainable, but inefficient. **Efficiency** in this context means that the economy is using all of its resources productively, as is true at every point on the PPC. Producing a birdcage-chair combination that lies inside the PPC, such as point B, results in some resources going to waste.

Rather than producing at B, more of both products could be produced by moving to a point such as C on the frontier. Only those points on the frontier itself correspond with the use of all of the available resources.

Resources are often specialized for making one thing rather than another. For example, wood may be ideal for producing chairs, but troublesome as a source of birdcage walls because drilling or carving is necessary to make the birds visible. On the other hand, metal may be simple to weave into a wire birdcage but less than ideal for chairs, because a solid-feeling chair becomes heavy and expensive when made of metal.

When the economy is producing only one good, say chairs, all of the available resources are devoted to that good, including resources that are not especially useful for chair production. Starting from the production of chairs only, the opportunity cost of birdcages—the number of chairs that must be given up to make another birdcage—is initially small because the resources used will be those specialized for making birdcages (metal, plastic, wire-bending machines) and not so useful for making chairs.

Notice that opportunity costs can be read directly off the PPC in Figure 1. Start from the point at which 5 chairs and 0 birdcages are made and stay on the PPC. Making 1 birdcage necessitates a decrease in chair production of 0.25 (from 5 to 4.75). That is, the opportunity cost of the first birdcage is a quarter of a chair. Likewise, the opportunity costs of the second through fifth birdcages are 0.25, 1, 1.5, and 2 chairs, respectively. Why does the opportunity cost of making birdcages increase? Because as more birdcages are produced, the resources that must be used to make birdcages are those less and less specialized for birdcage production and more and more specialized for chair production. The economy must therefore give up an increasing number of chairs for each additional birdcage.

The **slope** of a line between two points is "the rise over the run," meaning the vertical change divided by the horizontal change between the two points. The **absolute value**, the value after removing the negative sign, of the slope of the PPC between two points also indicates the average opportunity cost of the horizontal axis good (birdcages) between those two points. This is because the movement from left to right along the horizontal axis, the "run," indicates an increase in birdcages, while the movement along the vertical axis, "the rise," indicates the corresponding decrease in the number of chairs. To summarize, the decrease in chairs per increase in birdcages defines both the opportunity cost of birdcages and the slope of the PPC. The slope of the PPC increases in absolute value from left to right, reflecting the increasing opportunity cost of birdcages.

In the special case in which an economy must allocate its resources between two goods that involve no specialization of resources, the PPC will be a straight line. Consider an economy that allocates its resources between radishes and carrots. It may be that the skills, tools, fertilizer, and other resources needed to produce the two goods are virtually identical, and thus the opportunity cost of each good and the PPC slope would not change at different production levels, as in Figure 2.

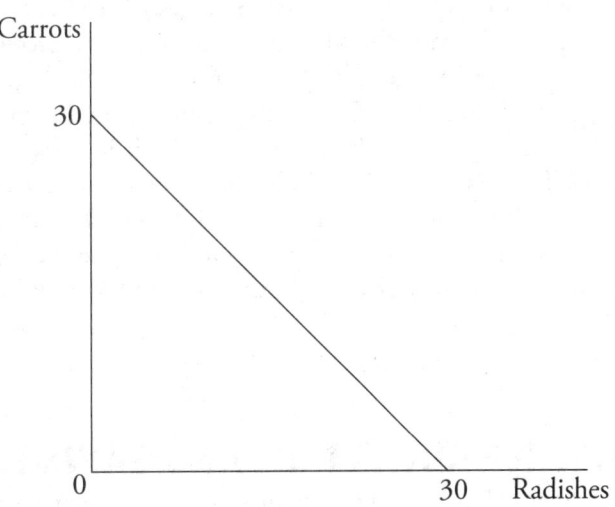

**Figure 2**

The production-possibilities frontier apparatus is also useful for analyzing production decisions between consumer goods and capital goods. **Consumer goods** are products that are for sale in any typical retail or consumer market and used directly by consumers. Anything purchased in a supermarket or shopping mall would be a consumer good. **Capital goods** are things purchased to produce other goods. If a baker decides to invest in an industrial mixer, that mixer would be a capital good. We could use all available resources to produce food, clothing, and other items to be consumed in the present, but that would contribute nothing to our ability to produce goods in the future. Alternatively, we could forgo some current consumption to produce tractors, looms, and other capital goods that add to the ability to produce both capital and consumer goods later on.

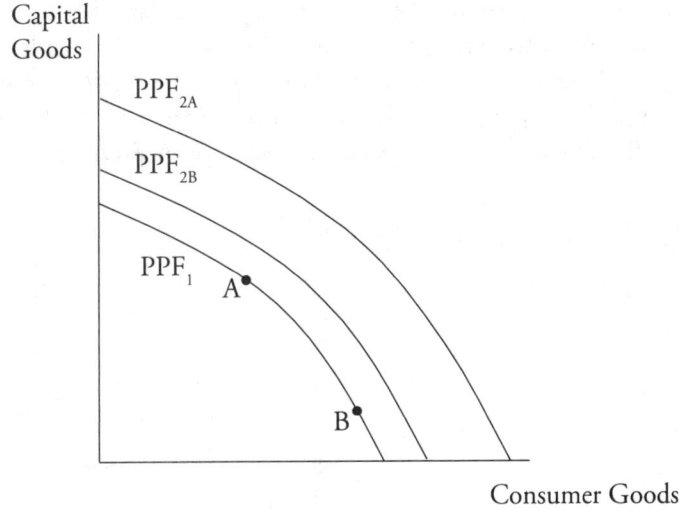

**Figure 3**

Let PPC$_1$ in Figure 3 represent the production possibilities in Period 1. Point A represents a combination of capital and consumer goods that includes a relatively large investment in capital. The substantial investment in capital comes at the expense of current consumption but allows for considerable growth in future production possibilities as represented by the Period 2 production-possibilities frontier labeled PPC$_{2A}$. Point B represents a production combination that caters to current consumers at the expense of future production. The relatively low level of investment in capital goods results in limited growth in Period 2 as represented by PPC$_{2B}$. If no capital goods were produced at all, the inability to replace worn-out capital would decrease production possibilities and lead to a Period 2 PPC that fell below the current PPC$_1$. In summary, current investment in capital leads to future growth, so there are important **trade-offs** between consumption and growth that can be captured with the PPC diagram.

## 5.4   COMPARATIVE ADVANTAGE AND GAINS FROM TRADE

When people have different abilities, having them specialize in what they are relatively good at enhances **productivity**. **Specialization** is more efficient than having each person contribute equally to every task. It is better for LeBron James to be a full-time basketball player and Brad Pitt to be a full-time actor than to have them both divide their time equally between the court and the stage. Even if every person were identical, efficiency would be improved by a division of necessary tasks among those carrying out the tasks. This is because such a **division of labor** permits people to develop expertise in the task(s) that they concentrate on—practice improves performance. If different members of your family specialize in shopping, car repair, cooking, or child care, your family exhibits a division of labor not unlike what occurs in businesses and governmental agencies.

Just as individuals benefit from specialization, so too do larger groups. There are two types of advantages that economists focus on when comparing countries (or other groups of individuals). A country is said to have an **absolute advantage** in the production of a good when it can produce that good using fewer resources per unit of output than another country. A country is said to have a **comparative advantage** in the production of a good when it can produce that good at a lower opportunity cost (a smaller loss in terms of the production of another good) than another country. The opportunity for two countries to benefit from specialization and trade rests only on the existence of a *comparative* advantage in production between the two countries.

Consider Brazil and Mexico and the production of coffee and broccoli. Figure 4 illustrates fictional production-possibilities frontiers for the two countries, simplified to be straight lines.

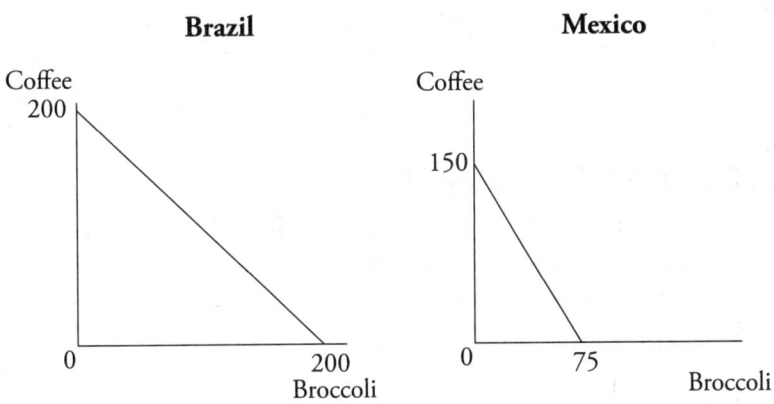

**Figure 4**

If we assume that the two countries have identical resources, the PPCs indicate that Brazil has an absolute advantage in both coffee and broccoli, because it can produce more of each good with the same resources. In order to examine comparative advantages, we need to look at the opportunity costs facing each country. When Brazil goes from producing 200 units of broccoli to producing 200 units of coffee, it gives up one unit of broccoli for each unit of coffee, so the opportunity cost of coffee in terms of broccoli is 1. (Because the PPC is a straight line, the opportunity cost is the same for each increment of production.) When Mexico goes from producing 75 units of broccoli to producing 150 units of coffee, it gives up one-half as much broccoli as it increases in coffee, so the opportunity cost of coffee in terms of broccoli is 0.5. Mexico has a comparative advantage in the production of coffee because each unit of coffee costs Mexico 0.5 unit of broccoli, which is less than the opportunity cost of 1 in Brazil. Likewise, Brazil has a comparative advantage in the production of broccoli because each unit of broccoli costs Brazil 1 unit of coffee, which is less than the opportunity cost of 2 units of coffee per unit of broccoli in Mexico.

Because relative production costs differ, these two countries can each benefit from trade. Suppose that in the absence of trade, each country divides its resources equally between the two goods—Brazil produces and consumes 100 units of each, and Mexico produces and consumes 75 units of coffee and 37.5 units of broccoli. A beneficial trade agreement will have each country specialize in the good for which it has a comparative advantage. Mexico should satisfy the two countries' needs for coffee up to the first 150 units, and Brazil should satisfy the countries' needs for broccoli up to the first 200 units. As an example of a mutually beneficial trade situation, Mexico could produce 150 units of coffee, and Brazil could produce 150 units of broccoli and 50 units of coffee. Mexico could then trade 60 units of coffee for 40 units of broccoli—representing an exchange price of 1.5 units of coffee per unit of broccoli. Because Brazil and Mexico have opportunity costs for broccoli of 1 and 2, respectively, any exchange price for broccoli between 1 and 2 will give Brazil more than its production cost and allow Mexico to purchase at less than its private production cost. After the trade, Brazil can consume 110 units of broccoli and 110 units of coffee, while Mexico can consume 40 units of broccoli and 90 units of coffee. In the end, *each* country can enjoy more of *each* good than if it did not trade because, remember, we supposed that in the *absence* of trade Brazil produced and consumed

100 units of each, and Mexico produced and consumed 75 units of coffee and 37.5 units of broccoli. In other words, with trade, each country enjoys a **consumption possibilities frontier** that exceeds its production-possibilities frontier. The slope of the consumption possibilities frontier is determined by the **terms of trade**.

## 5.5    COST-BENEFIT ANALYSIS

Each business project involves two factors: the cost of implementing the project and the resulting benefits. For all such projects, the economists and financial experts must compare the values of the cost and benefits using tables, mathematical principles, graphs, and other decision-making tools.

Imagine that you are elected as a member of the city council. The city manager comes to you with a plan to put a large-scale traffic light at every city intersection. The necessary funds are $10,000. The benefit of lighting is to increase driver safety. Engineering research confirms that the installation of the traffic lights will reduce the risk of accidents during operation by 1.6% to 1.1%. At this point the final decision is made based on the **cost-benefit analysis**.

## 5.6    MARGINAL ANALYSIS AND CONSUMER CHOICE

An efficient allocation of inputs requires that the output of one good cannot be increased without decreasing the output of another good. This is true when firms satisfy the cost-minimizing production condition, which says that the ratio of input prices equals the ratio of marginal products (MP) of the inputs. (The proof of this is beyond the scope of introductory economics, but previous AP Exams have tested for an understanding of this condition, so we will explain it and provide a bit of insight.)

### Who Will Receive the Final Products?

When an economy asks who will receive the final products, it is seeking **distributive efficiency** or **efficiency in exchange**. This type of efficiency requires that those who place the highest relative value on goods receive them. Auctions, for example, distribute goods to those who value them the most, while lotteries do not. Suppose Pat loves chocolate and has a mild interest in football, while Chris loves football and dislikes chocolate. If Chris receives chocolate for Valentine's Day and Pat receives football tickets through a lottery, distributive efficiency would not be achieved. An exchange of Chris's chocolates for Pat's tickets would benefit both parties.

An economy achieves distributive efficiency when consumers make purchases that maximize their satisfaction, or **utility**, given their budgetary constraints. Just as firms achieve productive efficiency by maximizing their "bang for the buck" in terms of inputs, consumers should do the same for their purchases. Consumers get the most utility for a given budget by equating the **marginal utility** or **MU** (the additional utility from the last unit) per dollar in the **price** (P) of each good they purchase. That is, if consumers purchase food (F) and clothing (C), utility is maximized when

$$\frac{MU_F}{P_F} = \frac{MU_C}{P_C}$$

By multiplying both sides by $P_C$ and dividing both sides by $MU_F$, this equation becomes

$$\frac{P_C}{P_F} = \frac{MU_C}{MU_F}$$

The ratio of marginal utilities on the right-hand side of this equation is called the **marginal rate of substitution** (MRS). The formal condition for distributive efficiency is that the marginal rate of substitution be equal for every consumer; for example, $MRS_{PAT} = MRS_{CHRIS}$. With consumers facing the same prices, $\frac{P_C}{P_F}$ will be the same for every consumer; if all consumers maximize utility by equating their MRS to $\frac{P_C}{P_F}$, then everyone will have the same MRS and distributive efficiency will be achieved.

A long-run competitive equilibrium implies that P = MC. With firms minimizing their costs and consumers maximizing their profits, economic theory holds that all three types of efficiency are achieved when a perfectly competitive market is in long-run equilibrium.

# CHAPTER 5 KEY TERMS

## 5.1

scarcity
resources
inputs (factors of production)
capital
physical capital
labor
human capital
entrepreneurship
natural resources/land

## 5.2

economics
positive economics
normative economics

## 5.3

opportunity cost
production-possibilities curve
efficiency
slope
absolute value
consumer goods
capital goods
trade-offs

## 5.4

productivity
specialization
division of labor
absolute advantage
comparative advantage
consumption possibilities frontier
terms of trade

## 5.5

cost-benefit analysis

## 5.6

distributive efficiency (efficiency in exchange)
utility
marginal utility (MU)
price
marginal rate of substitution

# CHAPTER 5 DRILL QUESTIONS

See Chapter 10 for answers and explanations.

**Question 1 refers to the following.**

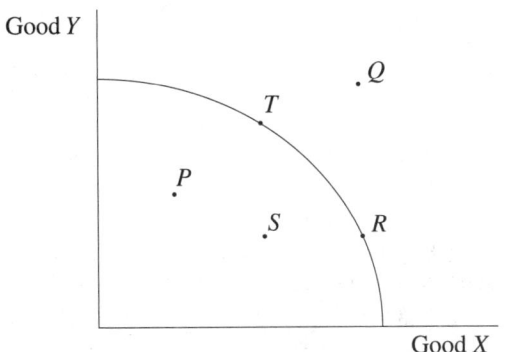

☐ Mark for Review

Lauren spends her total budget on 3 burgers and 4 milkshakes. At her current level of consumption, Lauren's current marginal utility for burgers is $18 and her current marginal utility for milkshakes is $12. What should Lauren do in order to maximize her total utility?

(A) Consume more burgers and fewer milkshakes regardless of the prices

(B) Consume fewer burgers and more milkshakes regardless of the prices

(C) Maintain her current level of consumption regardless of the prices

(D) Maintain her current level of consumption if the price of a burger is $6 and the price of a milkshake is $4

(E) Maintain her current level of consumption if the price of a burger is $3 and the price of a milkshake is $3

**1** ☐ Mark for Review

Which of the following points is impossible to produce on the given production possibilities curve?

(A) Point P

(B) Point Q

(C) Point R

(D) Point S

(E) Point T

**2** ☐ Mark for Review

Which of the following would NOT be considered a capital good?

(A) An expensive necktie

(B) A screwdriver

(C) Industrial machinery for factory assembly lines

(D) A truck that transports milk

(E) A large baking oven

**4** ☐ Mark for Review

The table below shows Diego's marginal utilities for buying posters and figurines for his anime collection.

| Quantity of Posters | Marginal Utility of Posters (in dollars) | Quantity of Figurines | Marginal Utility of Figurines (in dollars) |
|---|---|---|---|
| 1 | 30 | 1 | 72 |
| 2 | 27 | 2 | 60 |
| 3 | 24 | 3 | 48 |
| 4 | 21 | 4 | 36 |
| 5 | 18 | 5 | 24 |
| 6 | 15 | 6 | 12 |

Assume that the price of a poster is $3 and the price of a figurine is $6. If Diego's total budget is $36, which of the following combinations maximizes Diego's utility for buying posters and figurines?

(A) 2 posters and 5 figurines

(B) 3 posters and 4 figurines

(C) 4 posters and 4 figurines

(D) 5 posters and 3 figurines

(E) 6 posters and 3 figurines

**5** ☐ Mark for Review

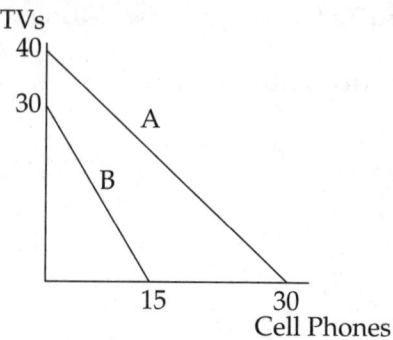

The above diagram represents the production possibilities of Country A and Country B, with the use of the same resources. Which of the following would be true for both Country A and Country B?

(A) Countries A and B CANNOT benefit from trade with each other.

(B) Country A has a comparative advantage in TVs and Country B has a comparative advantage in cell phones.

(C) Country A has a comparative advantage in cell phones and Country B has a comparative advantage in TVs.

(D) Country A has an opportunity cost of $1\frac{1}{4}$ cell phones when it produces 1 TV.

(E) Country B has an opportunity cost of $\frac{1}{2}$ TV when it produces 1 cell phone.

**6** 🔖 Mark for Review

Which of the following would NOT be considered a factor of production for a car company?

(A) The cost of the car designer's studio

(B) The car designer's time

(C) The car designer's creativity

(D) The car designer's preference for designing homes instead of cars

(E) The steel and rubber used in car production

**7** 🔖 Mark for Review

Which of the following components are associated with analyzing the cost-benefit relationship?

(A) Cost of a decision and variable costs

(B) Cost of a decision and opportunity cost

(C) Cost of a decision and production of a commodity

(D) Cost and effectiveness of a decision

(E) Cost and potential rewards of a decision

# Chapter 5 Summary:
# Basic Microeconomics Concepts

## 5.1 Scarcity

o The **resources** used in the production process are called **inputs**, or **factors of production**. They include the following factors:
- capital
- labor (human capital)
- entrepreneurship
- natural resources/land

## 5.2 Resource Allocation and Economic Systems

o **Economics** is the study of how to allocate scarce resources among competing ends.

o **Positive economics** describes the way things are; **normative economics** describes the way things should be.

## 5.3 The Production Possibilities Curve

o **Opportunity cost** is the value of the best alternative sacrificed as compared to what actually takes place.

o A **production-possibilities frontier** is a curve that represents all of the combinations of the two goods that could be produced using all of the available resources and technology.

o **Efficiency** in this context means that the economy is using all of its resources productively, as is true at every point on the PPF.

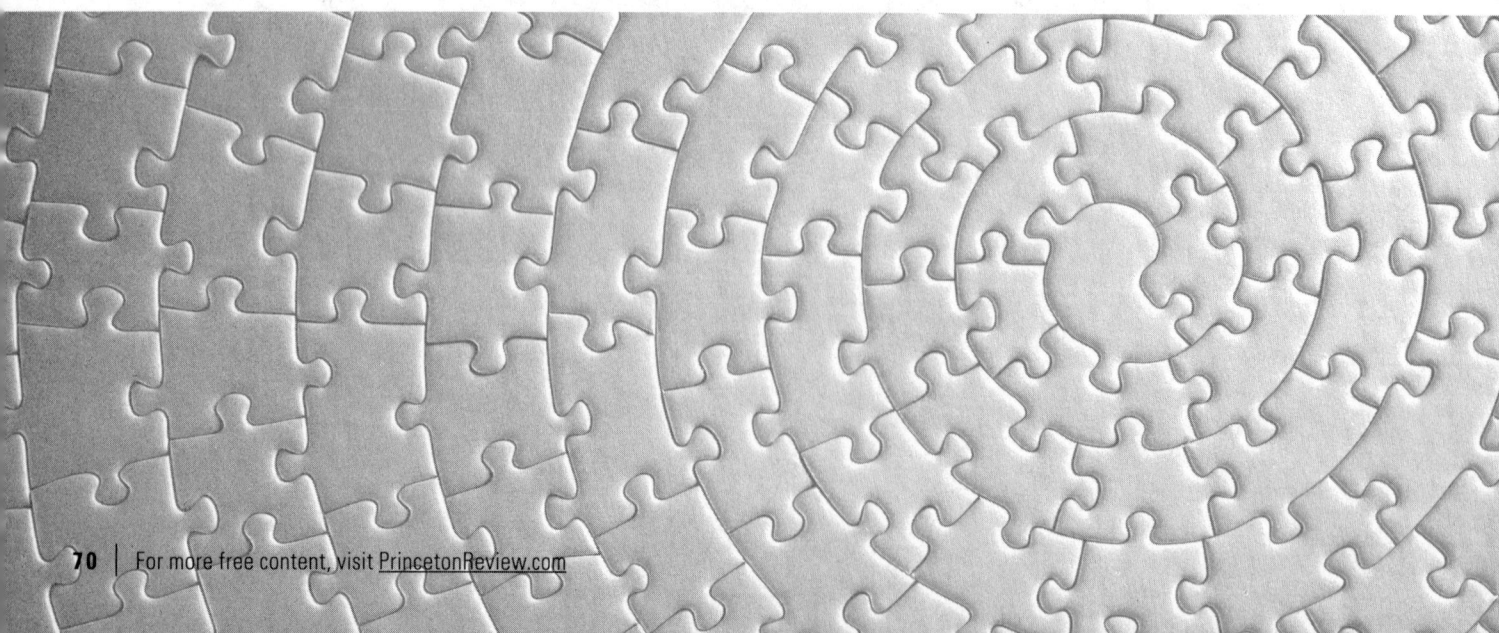

## 5.4    Comparative Advantage and Gains from Trade

o    The **division of labor** permits people to develop expertise in the task(s) that they concentrate on.

o    A country is said to have an **absolute advantage** in the production of a good when it can produce that good using fewer resources per unit of output than another country.

o    A country is said to have a **comparative advantage** in the production of a good when it can produce that good at a lower opportunity cost than another country.

## 5.5    Cost-Benefit Analysis

o    Cost-benefit analysis is a process by which all the expected benefits are compared to the expected costs in an economic activity.

o    Each business project involves two factors: the cost of implementing the project and the resulting benefits. For all such projects, the economists and financial experts must compare the values of the cost and benefits using tables, mathematical principles, graphs, and other decision-making tools.

## 5.6    Marginal Analysis and Consumer Choice

o    An economy reaches **distributive efficiency**, or **efficiency in exchange**, when those who place the highest relative value on goods receive them; distributive efficiency occurs when the **marginal rate of substitution** (the ratio of marginal utility for two given goods) is equal for every consumer.

# Chapter 6
# Micro Unit 2: Supply and Demand

## 6.1   DEMAND

### Price and Quantity Determination

The **demand curve** displays the relationship between price and the quantity demanded of a good within a given period. For example, Figure 1 indicates that Davon would purchase 6 avocados at a price of 25 cents each and 3 avocados at a price of 95 cents each.

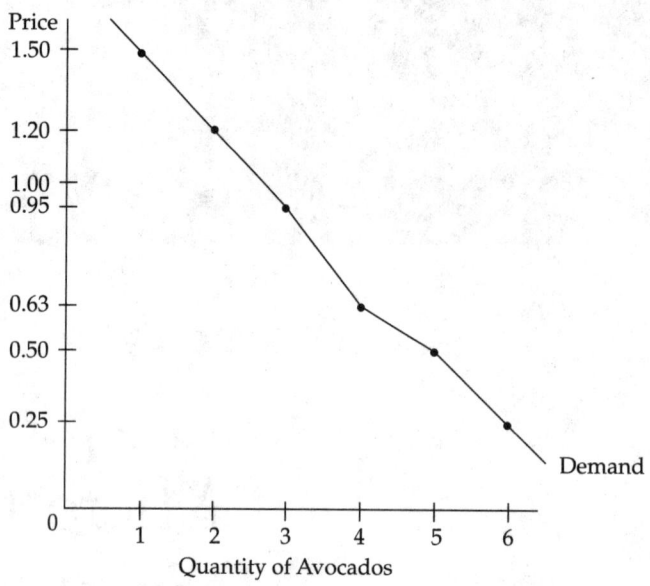

**Figure 1: The Demand Curve**

An individual's demand curve for a good reflects the additional benefit or "marginal utility" (measured in dollars) received from each incremental unit of the good. Davon values the first avocado at $1.50, the second at $1.20, the third at $0.95, and so on. A line through the points on this graph makes a demand curve. The same information is represented in Table 1, which is known as a **demand schedule.**

| Price (dollars per avocado) | Quantity of avocados demanded |
|---|---|
| 1.50 | 1 |
| 1.20 | 2 |
| 0.95 | 3 |
| 0.63 | 4 |
| 0.50 | 5 |
| 0.25 | 6 |

**Table 1**

Notice that Davon receives less and less additional benefit—his marginal utility decreases—as he gets more and more avocados. That first avocado will go toward his greatest need, perhaps extreme hunger. However, as he consumes more avocados, he becomes less hungry, and his avocados are used to satisfy less and less important needs (e.g., feeding the cat, batting practice).

The decreasing satisfaction gained from additional units of a good consumed in a given period is called the **law of diminishing marginal utility**.

The law of diminishing marginal utility corresponds with the **law of demand**, which states that as the price of a good rises, the quantity of that good demanded by consumers falls. Similarly, as the price of a good falls, the quantity demanded of that good rises. Davon would buy three avocados at a price of 75 cents because each of the first three is worth more than 75 cents to him, but the fourth and subsequent units are worth less than 75 cents to him, so he wouldn't buy them. If the price fell to 35 cents, the quantity he demanded would increase, because then the fourth and fifth avocados (in addition to the first, second, and third as before) would be worth more to him than the price. This explains the inverse relationship between prices and the quantity demanded suggested by the law of demand.

The market demand curve is found by simply adding up the demands of all the individual demanders in the market. For simplicity, assume that Davon and Mary are the only two purchasers of avocados (perhaps they share a tropical island). Figure 2 exhibits the individual demand curves for Davon and Mary and the associated market demand curve.

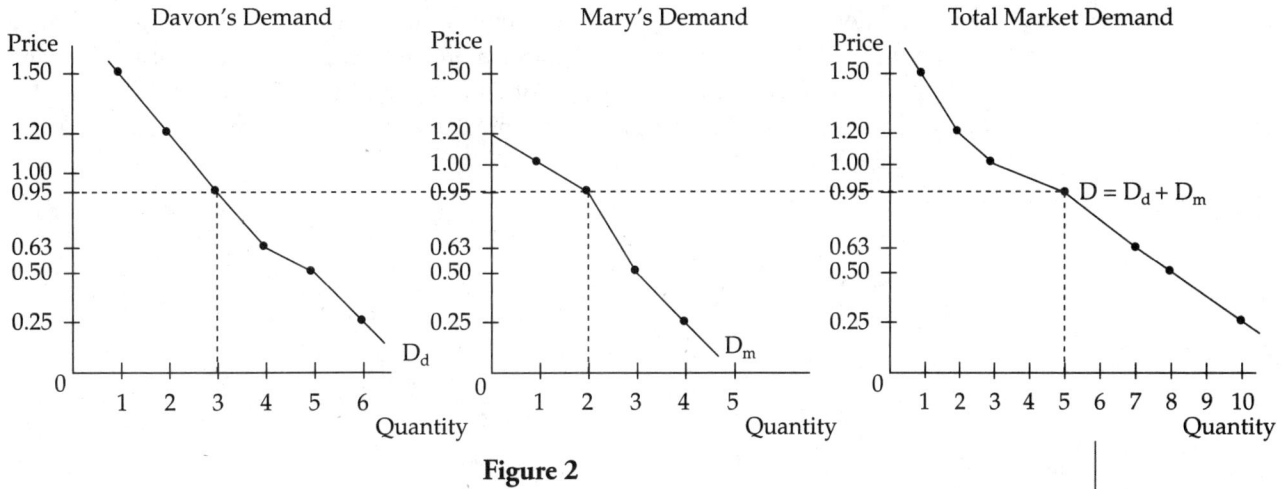

**Figure 2**

At each price, the market demand curve combines the demand curves of the two consumers. At $1.50, Davon purchases one and Mary purchases zero so the market demand is one. At $0.95, Davon purchases three and Mary purchases two, so the market demand is five, and so on.

The standard supply and demand model is built upon the assumption of a perfectly competitive market, meaning that many small firms sell the same product and can enter or leave the market without cost.

## 6.2 SUPPLY

The **supply curve** (Figure 3) for a perfectly competitive firm and the corresponding **supply schedule** (Table 2) show the relationship between price and quantity supplied by that firm within a given period.

The **law of supply** says that as the price increases, the quantity of a good supplied in a given period will increase, other things being equal. Think about how many avocados you would be willing to supply at different prices. At a price of $0.25, you probably wouldn't be very enthused about the prospects, but perhaps you would be willing to give up some of your least valuable time—the time you spend watching *The Simpsons* reruns—to grow 100 avocados as a hobby. With such a low return, you might not want to give up your second-least-favorite pastime of picking on your sibling. However, if the price rose to $0.50 per avocado, forget picking on your sibling; you might be willing to spend more time and invest more money into growing 200 avocados.

Although efficiencies may come about in the beginning, eventually the additional cost of producing another unit—the **marginal cost**—will increase for several reasons. The opportunity cost of your time will increase as you have to give up more and more valuable alternatives in order to grow more avocados. You will start by hiring the best and cheapest inputs (avocado pickers, tractors, land) and then resort to inferior inputs as necessary. You might get less and less out of each additional unit of an input as opportunities for efficient specialization are exploited and you run into redundancy and congestion (for more on this, see the Marginal Product and Diminishing Returns section in Chapter 7). For all of these reasons, higher prices are needed to induce more avocado production, and the supply curve and schedule might look something like Figure 3 and Table 2, respectively.

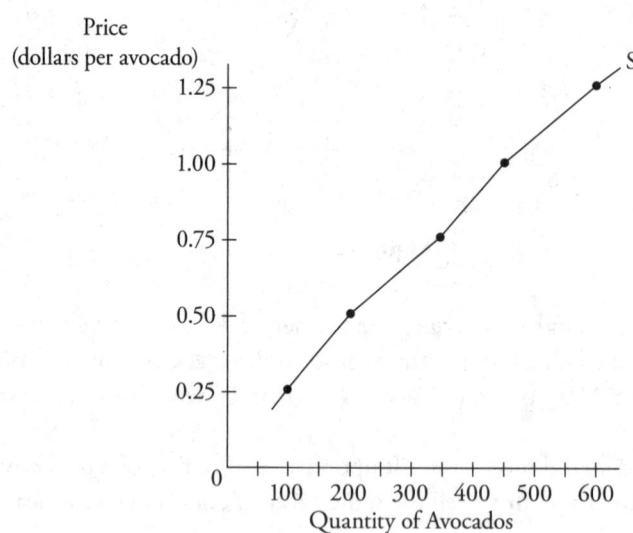

**Figure 3: The Supply Curve**

| Price (dollars per avocado) | Quantity of avocados supplied |
|---|---|
| 1.25 | 600 |
| 1.00 | 450 |
| 0.75 | 350 |
| 0.50 | 200 |
| 0.25 | 100 |

**Table 2**

The **market supply curve** indicates the total quantities of a good that suppliers are willing and able to provide at various prices during a given period of time. It is the horizontal summation of all of the firm's supply curves. Figure 4 illustrates how the supply curves of two firms are added to find the market supply.

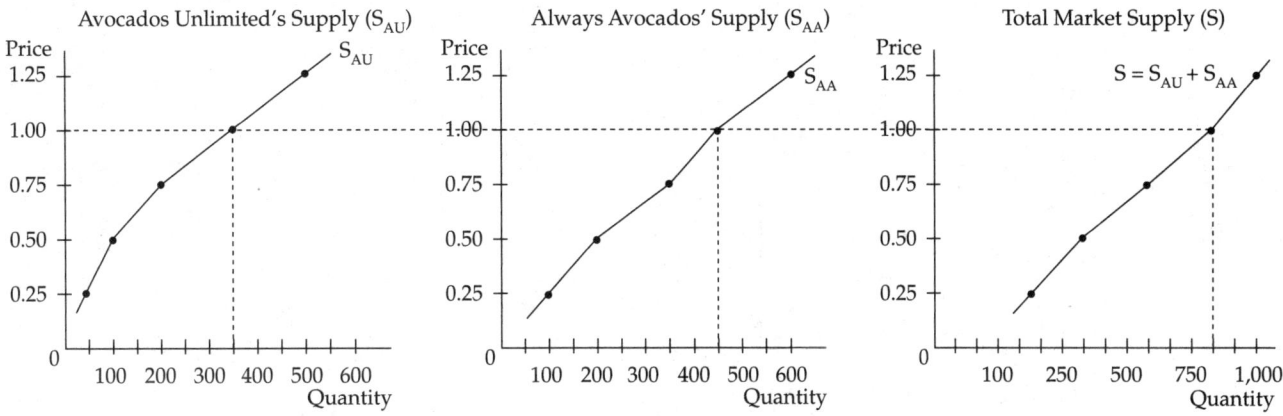

**Figure 4**

For example, if Avocados Unlimited is willing to produce 350 avocados for $1 each, and Always Avocados is willing to produce 450 at $1 each, and these are the only two producers in the market, then the market supply is 350 + 450 = 800 at a price of $1. The market supply curve reflects the marginal cost (MC) of producing various quantities of a good and the size and number of firms in the market (see Chapter 7 for a discussion of when a firm will shut down and supply zero).

## Understanding and Manipulating Supply

Remember that the law of supply says that as the price increases, the quantity of a good supplied in a given period will increase, other things being held equal. In this section, you will study how supply changes with different economic factors.

It is important to distinguish between a **change in quantity supplied** and a **change in supply**. A movement of the equilibrium along a stationary supply curve represents a change in the quantity supplied. In other words, there has been a change in price, and sellers adjust the quantity they are willing to sell accordingly. Because the supply curve shows the relationship between quantity supplied and price, changes in price simply bring us to different points on the same supply curve, thereby causing changes in the quantity supplied.

In contrast, a shift in the supply curve represents a change in the overall supply, meaning that at each price point along the curve, there is an increase in the quantity supplied. In other words, sellers are willing to sell more of a good at any given price than they were previously.

An increase in supply (a rightward shift in the supply curve) can result from anything that leads to more units of the good being produced at any given price, as illustrated in Figure 5.

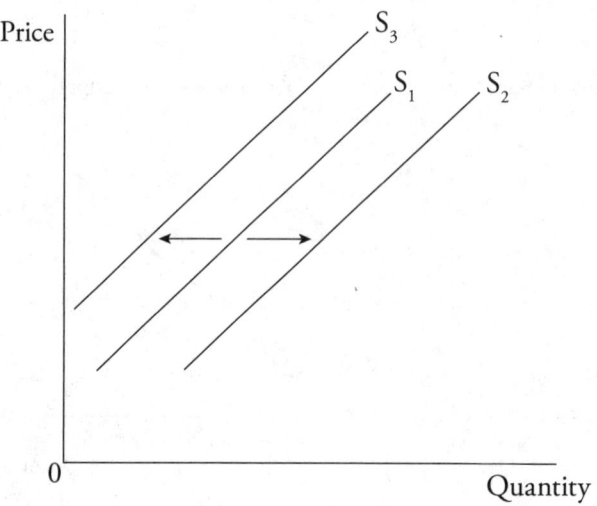

**Figure 5: Shifts in Supply**

Specifically, an increase in supply is expected to follow these events:

- **A decrease in input costs**. If wages, rents, or other costs associated with the provision of the good go down, more will be provided for a given price.

- **An improvement in technology**. For example, the advent of the airplane increased the supply of cross-country package delivery.

- **Expectations of lower prices in the future**. Think of ticket scalpers at a ballgame. As the game approaches, they know they will soon be unable to charge much, if anything, for their tickets, so they become increasingly willing to sell at lower prices.

- **An increase in the number of sellers**. More sellers mean more supply curves have to be added horizontally to find the market supply curve.

- **A decrease in the price of a substitute in production.** Paper and lumber are substitutes in production, as are milk and cheese. If the price of cheese goes down, then more milk will be supplied because less will be used for the production of cheese, because the producer stands to make more money selling it alone. Imagine you're a farmer with 100 gallons of milk. You sell some of it as milk and make the rest into cheese. If the price you can fetch for cheese falls, what are you going to do? Sell more as milk. Similarly, as the price of lumber goes up, more dead trees are devoted to lumber rather than paper.

- **An increase in the price of a joint product.** Lumber and wood mulch are **joint products,** as are leather and beef—the production of one makes the other available. If the price of leather increases, more cows will be slaughtered, and the supply of beef will increase.

- **Lower taxes or higher subsidies.** For example, the government subsidizes the creation of roads into the national forests. This decreases the cost of cutting down trees and increases the supply of lumber.

- **Less restrictive regulations.** For example, if the government allowed companies to pollute more, the cost of toxic waste disposal would go down and the supply of the associated goods would increase.

The opposite of each of these changes would result in a **decrease in supply** (a leftward shift in the supply curve).

You can remember the primary reasons for a **shift in supply** with the acronym ROTTEN.

**R** – **R**esource costs

**O** – **O**ther goods' prices (substitutes in production and joint products)

**T** – **T**axes and subsidies

**T** – **T**echnology changes

**E** – **E**xpectations of suppliers

**N** – **N**umber of suppliers

## Important Distinctions Between Similar Terms

> There is often confusion over a set of similar terms that describe the relationship between costs and output. AP Exam questions often test students' understanding of the distinctions among these terms. Read on!

The relationships between costs and output are defined in close proximity below, so that you can compare and contrast their meanings.

**Economies of scale** are enjoyed over the range of output for which the long-run average cost curve slopes downward (has a negative slope), meaning that the cost per unit is falling. This can result from increasing returns to scale as described below. It can also result from the use of equipment, such as combines, robots, and assembly lines, that becomes economically efficient only when handling large volumes of output. And it can result from the cost of inputs like copyrights to a book that need not increase whenever output increases and thus are spread over larger and larger output levels. (This is a long-run phenomenon.)

**Good to Note!**

**Long-run average cost** (LRAC) is the cost function that represents the average cost per unit of producing some good.

**Diseconomies of scale** exist over the range of output when LRAC is increasing.

**Increasing returns (to scale)** exist when output increases (proportionately) more than increases in *all* inputs—for example, when doubling all of the inputs would result in more than double the amount of output. This is frequently confused with increasing *marginal* returns, which involve an increase in only one input, holding all of the other inputs constant. Here is an example of increasing returns to scale: suppose a storage container consists of a box with six $1' \times 1'$ cardboard sides. Thus, 6 square feet of cardboard (the input) creates 1 cubic foot of storage space (the output). If instead the storage company uses six $2' \times 2'$ sides, the input increases to $6 \times 2' \times 2' = 24$ square feet of cardboard and the output increases to $2' \times 2' \times 2' = 8$ cubic feet of storage space. Because the input increased fourfold (from 6 to 24 sq. ft.) and the output increased eightfold (from 1 to 8 cu. ft.), increasing returns to scale are in place. (This is a long-run phenomenon.)

**Decreasing returns (to scale)** exist when output increases (proportionately) less than increases in all inputs. For example, doubling all of the inputs would result in less than double the amount of output.

**Constant returns (to scale)** exist when output increases in proportion to increases in all inputs. For example, doubling all inputs would result in double the amount of output.

**Diminishing (marginal) returns** exist when an additional unit of an input increases total output by less than the previous unit of the input, *holding all other inputs constant.* (This is a short-run phenomenon.)

An **increasing cost firm** is a firm facing decreasing returns to scale, meaning that output increases less than in proportion to all inputs.

A **decreasing cost firm** is a firm facing increasing returns to scale, meaning that output increases more than in proportion to all inputs.

An **increasing cost industry** experiences increases in average production costs as industry output increases, perhaps because input prices are bid upward by increasing demand. This is more likely to occur in large industries such as automobile production that use a large proportion of an input such as steel. The result is a positively sloped, long-run supply curve.

A **constant cost industry** is one that does not experience increased production costs as output grows. This might be the case for industries that use a small proportion of the inputs they employ. For example, an expansion in the marble industry would probably not bid up the price of glass, because marble manufacturers make up a small fraction of the world demand for glass. The result is a horizontal long-run supply curve.

A **decreasing cost industry** experiences decreasing average production costs as industry output increases, perhaps because mass production of inputs becomes feasible with increased input demand. This might be the case for solar panels and electric cars. The result is a negatively sloped, long-run supply curve.

Figure 6 illustrates the decreasing cost scenario. Short-run industry supply and demand, $S_1$ and $D_1$, intersect at quantity $Q_1$ and determine the market price $P_1$. The representative firm produces $q_1$ and receives zero economic profits. With an increase in demand from $D_1$ to $D_2$, price will initially rise to $P_2$, leading the existing firms to produce $q_2$ and raising the quantity supplied by the market to $Q_2$. Notice that with a price of $P_2$, the representative firm is earning economic profits, because its price (which is also its average revenue and marginal revenue) is above its average cost. The availability of profits in this market will attract new firms, causing the market supply curve to shift to the right. As a decreasing cost industry expands, the average and marginal costs paid by each firm decrease. When market supply has increased far enough to bring the market price back down to $P_1$, firms will still receive economic profits because their costs will be lower than in the beginning when a price of $P_1$ corresponded with zero economic profits. Thus, the supply curve will continue to increase, until falling prices catch up to falling average and marginal costs, and zero economic profits are earned by the firms. This occurs at the intersection of $S_2$ and $D_2$ with a market price of $P_3$ and a market quantity of $Q_3$. At this price, the representative firm will select the quantity $q_3$ at which marginal revenue (the price) equals marginal cost on the new, lower $MC_2$. The elimination of economic profits will discourage any additional firms from entering, and the market will have arrived at a new point on its long-run supply curve at $Q_3$, $P_3$.

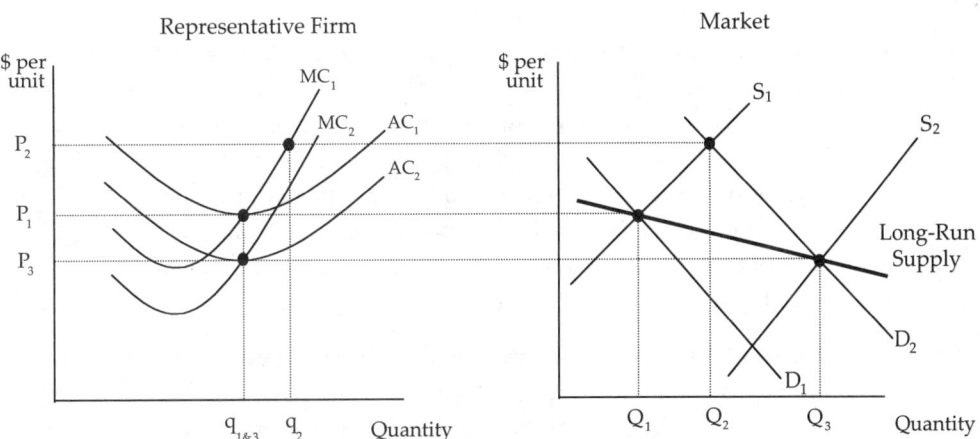

**Figure 6: Decreasing Cost Industry**

**Productive efficiency** occurs when a firm produces at the lowest unit cost, when MC = AC.

**Economies of scope** exist when a firm's average production costs decrease because multiple products are being produced. This occurs when the production of two or more products—such as juice and fruit, or pork and pigskin—is complementary. It also occurs when several products can share research and development costs or distribution networks.

## 6.3 ELASTICITY

**Elasticity** indicates how responsive consumer behavior is to changes in the product or service they want. In this section, we will discuss such changes in products and services.

## Price Elasticity of Demand

Suppliers often consider how changes in the price of a good or service will affect demand for that good or service. If the price of gum increased by 50 percent from 4 cents to 6 cents, by what percent would the quantity demanded decrease? How many fewer people would buy a ticket for a vacation cruise if the cost increased by 50 percent from $1,000 to $1,500? The **price elasticity of demand** indicates how responsive the quantity demanded of a good is to price changes. In other words, when economists think about the price elasticity of demand, they're thinking about how sensitive consumer behavior is to changes in the price of a good. Generally speaking, when consumer behavior is affected by price, the good is elastic; when consumer behavior is unaffected by changes in price, the good is inelastic.

The elasticity (responsiveness to price changes) of a good's demand tends to relate to the following factors:

> You can remember the factors that impact the price elasticity of demand using the acronym PAID:
> - the **P**roportion of the consumer's income spent on the good
> - the **A**vailability of close substitutes
> - the **I**mportance of a good
> - the ability to **D**elay the purchase of a good

- **The proportion of income spent on the good**. If a good represents a high proportion of a consumer's income, the demand for the good will likely be elastic. Consider the gum and cruise price-change scenarios mentioned above. The quantity of cruises purchased will probably be more affected by a 50 percent price increase than the quantity of gum, because an extra 2 cents is not a big deal, but an extra $500 is more likely to be prohibitive. In other words, consumers are more sensitive to a particular percent change in price at higher price levels.

- **The availability of close substitutes**. If there are many substitutes available, the demand for the good will likely be elastic. For example, if there are 10 brands of bicycles available and the price of one of them increases, the quantity of that brand demanded is likely to fall a lot. On the other hand, the demand for bicycles as a whole is less elastic than the demand for a particular brand because the substitutes for bikes in general—cars, skateboards, walking—are not as close.

- **The importance of the good**. The less essential a good is, the more likely consumers are to forego the good when it becomes more expensive. If a good is very important to the consumer, the consumer will continue to purchase it even if the price changes, and demand for that good will be inelastic.

- **The ability to delay the purchase of the good**. When time is short, it is more difficult to change purchasing patterns in response to price changes; therefore, when less time is available, demand for a given good is less elastic. The more time consumers have to adapt, the more they are able to find substitutes or learn to do without goods whose prices have increased.

When thinking about elasticity, economists divide goods into three groups: elastic, unit elastic, and inelastic. If the percentage change in quantity demanded exceeds the percentage change in price for a particular good—meaning, for example, that a 50 percent price increase results in more than a 50 percent decrease in quantity demanded—the demand for that good is on the more price-sensitive side and is labeled **elastic**. Goods with an elastic demand are categorized as **luxuries**. If the percentage change in quantity demanded equals the percentage change in price, demand for the good is labeled **unit elastic**. If the percentage change in quantity demanded is less than the percentage change in price, the demand is labeled **inelastic** and the good is categorized as a **necessity**.

Allowing $\Delta$ to represent change and $Q_d$ to represent the quantity demanded, the formula for price elasticity is the percentage change in quantity demanded divided by the percentage change in price:

$$\frac{\%\Delta Q_d}{\%\Delta P} = \frac{\dfrac{\Delta Q_d}{Q}}{\dfrac{\Delta P}{P}} = \frac{\dfrac{Q_{new} - Q_{old}}{Q_{old}}}{\dfrac{P_{new} - P_{old}}{P_{old}}}$$

The above formula uses the initial price and quantity as the basis for calculating the percentage change. Although this is the simplest way to do it, the following formula is more precise, especially when the changes in price or quantity are large:

$$\frac{\dfrac{\text{Change in quantity}}{\text{Average quantity}}}{\dfrac{\text{Change in price}}{\text{Average price}}} = \frac{\dfrac{Q_{new} - Q_{old}}{\left(\dfrac{Q_{new} + Q_{old}}{2}\right)}}{\dfrac{P_{new} - P_{old}}{\left(\dfrac{P_{new} + P_{old}}{2}\right)}}$$

This formula is more precise because a percent increase in price or quantity is different from a percent decrease in price or quantity over the same range. Here's an example: a percent increase from $4 to $5 = 25 percent, whereas a percent decrease from $5 to $4 = 20 percent.

Conveniently, the second formula produces the same elasticity measure between two points on a demand curve, regardless of which point you consider the "old" point and which you consider the "new" point. Finding the elasticity measure is simply a matter of plugging in the new and old prices and quantities.

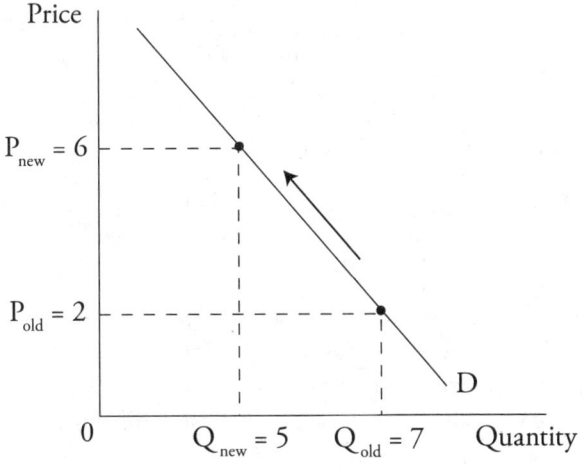

**Figure 7**

For example, the price elasticity of demand in the range shown in Figure 7 is

$$\frac{\dfrac{5-7}{\left(\dfrac{5+7}{2}\right)}}{\dfrac{6-2}{\dfrac{6+2}{2}}} = \frac{\dfrac{-2}{6}}{\dfrac{4}{4}} = \frac{-1}{3} = -0.\overline{3}$$

Keep in mind that the results for the equation to determine elasticity will always be negative given the law of demand. As the law of demand says, an increase in price should result in a decrease in the quantity demanded, and a decrease in price should result in an increase in the quantity demanded. Because price and quantity demanded are always going in opposite directions, either the top or the bottom of the elasticity formula will always be negative, and the other half will be positive. Either way, the elasticity of demand (Figure 8) will come out negative. This being the case, it is conventional to drop the negative sign (take the *absolute value*) and refer to price elasticities in positive terms. The above elasticity would thus be $\frac{1}{3}$.

Because the elasticity quotient is less than one, the demand is inelastic. In this equation, 1 is the critical number in determining elasticity. If the quotient is less than 1, as is the case here, then the denominator ($\%\Delta P$) is greater than the numerator ($\%\Delta Q_d$), and the good is therefore inelastic. If the numerator and the denominator are equal, the result is 1, and the good is unit elastic. If the result is greater than 1, then the numerator is greater than the denominator, and the good is elastic.

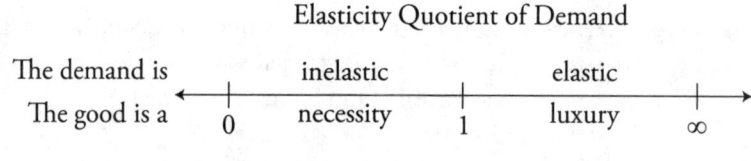

Elasticity Quotient of Demand

**Figure 8**

The elasticity of demand relates to the slope of the demand curve, but it *does not equal the slope of the demand curve*. Note the difference:

$$\text{slope} = \frac{\text{rise}}{\text{run}} = \frac{\Delta P}{\Delta Q_d}$$

$$\text{elasticity} = \frac{\dfrac{\Delta Q_d}{Q_d}}{\dfrac{\Delta P}{P}} = \frac{\Delta Q_d}{\Delta P}\left(\frac{P}{Q_d}\right)$$

Looking at the last part of each equation, you can see that elasticity is the inverse of the slope multiplied by price over quantity. The relationship between slope and elasticity is such that for a given P and Q, a steeper demand curve (one with a greater slope) is less elastic than a flatter demand curve (one with a smaller slope). A vertical demand curve as in Figure 9 is called **perfectly inelastic** because price has no influence on the quantity demanded and the elasticity value is 0.

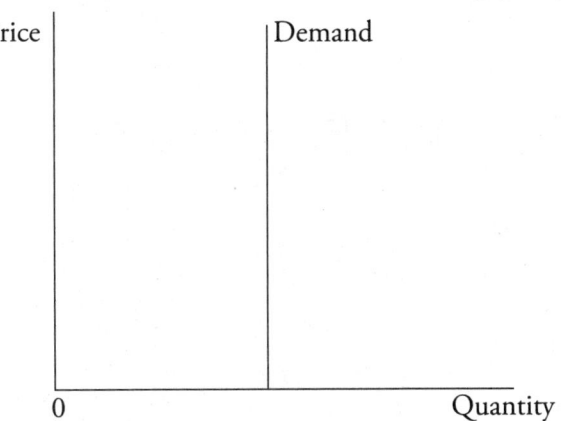

**Figure 9: Perfectly Inelastic Demand**

This approximates the demand for a lifesaving operation, insulin for a diabetic person, or a drug to which the user is addicted.

A horizontal demand curve, as in Figure 10, is called **perfectly elastic** because any increase in price will result in a quantity demanded of zero and the elasticity value is infinite.

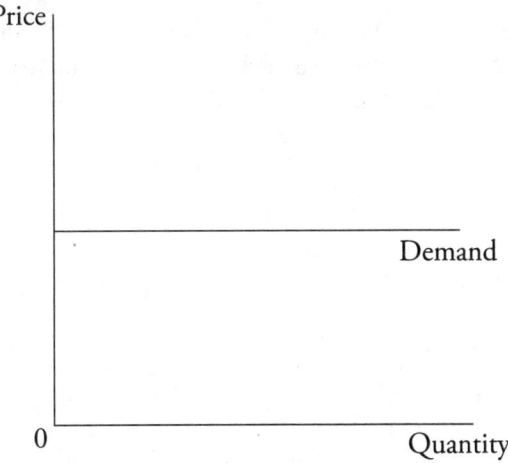

**Figure 10: Perfectly Elastic Demand**

This approximates the demand curve facing a corn farmer. As one of thousands of sellers of an identical product, she can sell all she wants at the price set by the market, but if she raises her price even one cent, no one will buy from her, because there are thousands of others selling the same product for the lower price. Because of price regulations, she is unable to lower her price.

A straight line demand curve, as in Figure 11, will have different elasticities at different points along the curve.

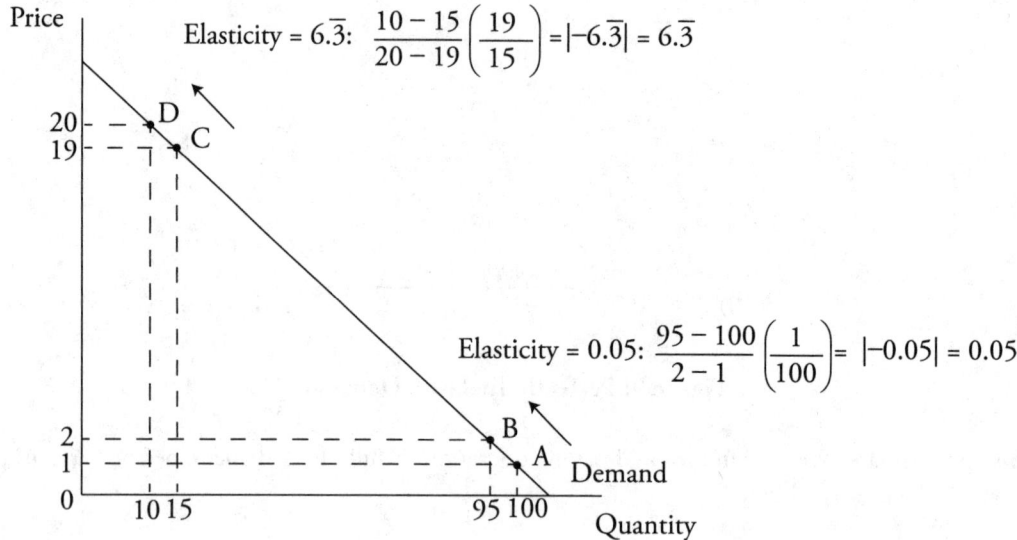

$$\text{Elasticity} = 6.\overline{3}: \quad \frac{10-15}{20-19}\left(\frac{19}{15}\right) = |{-6.\overline{3}}| = 6.\overline{3}$$

$$\text{Elasticity} = 0.05: \quad \frac{95-100}{2-1}\left(\frac{1}{100}\right) = |{-0.05}| = 0.05$$

**Figure 11**

Note that the elasticity moving from point A to point B is 0.05 while the elasticity moving from point C to point D is $6.\overline{3}$, even though the price and quantity changes are of the same size. More generally, the elasticity along a straight line demand curve will go from infinity to 0 moving left to right as illustrated in Figure 12.

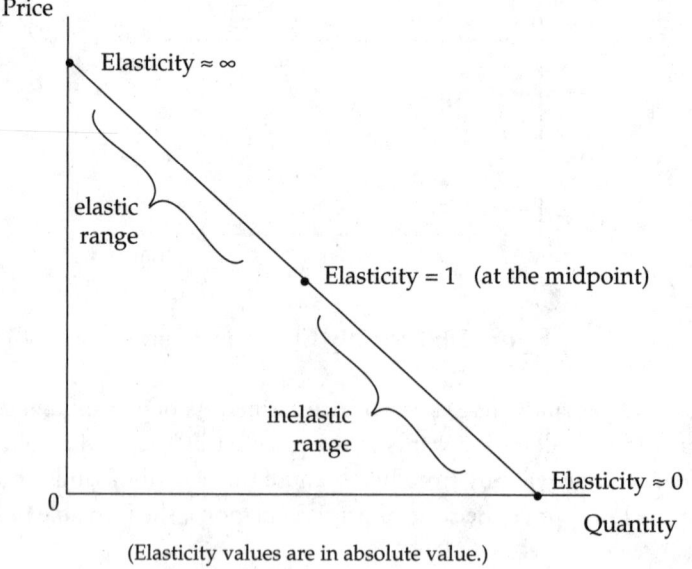

(Elasticity values are in absolute value.)

**Figure 12**

Why should a business care about the elasticity of demand? One reason is that the elasticity determines what happens to revenue when price changes. Note that total revenue (TR) equals price times quantity, which can be graphically related to the area of a rectangle that has a length equal to the price and a width equal to the quantity (length × width equals the area of a rectangle). Figure 13 illustrates three demand curves: one relatively inelastic, one unit elastic, and one relatively elastic.

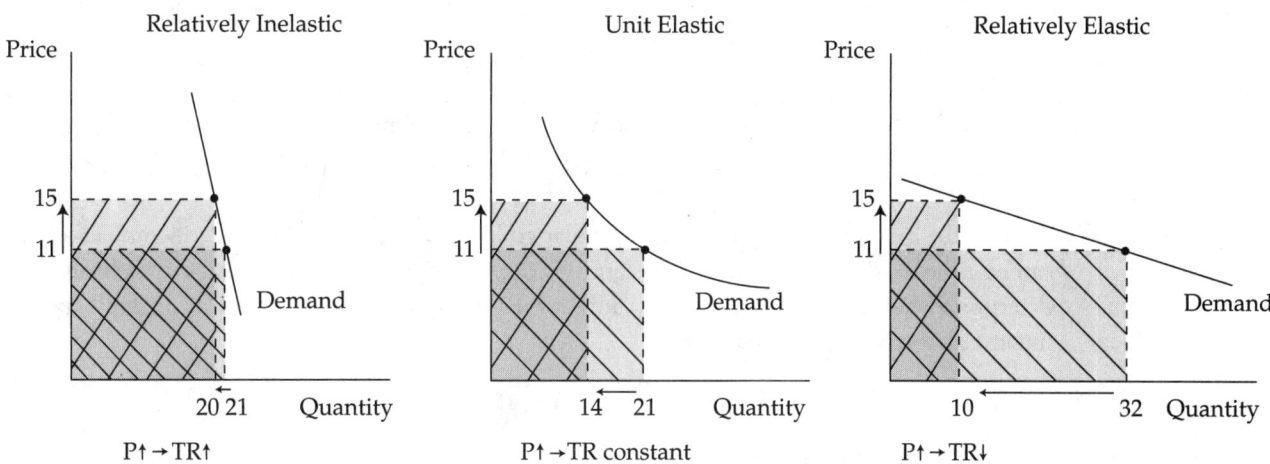

**Figure 13**

The price in each case has risen by the same amount. Nonetheless, it's clear when you compare the change in revenue (represented graphically by the shaded boxes in the figures above) that revenue has increased in the inelastic case, stayed the same in the unit elastic case, and decreased in the elastic case. Thus, businesses should remember this rule: when facing an inelastic demand, the best way to bring in more revenue (while selling fewer units) is to raise the price of the good. Use Figure 14 to help you remember all that.

### Price and Total Revenue

| | | |
|---|---|---|
| Elastic | Price ↑ | TR ↓ |
| | Price ↓ | TR ↑ |
| Inelastic | Price ↑ | TR ↑ |
| | Price ↓ | TR ↓ |

**Figure 14**

# Income Elasticity of Demand

Because income is a large factor in an individual's purchasing patterns, changes in income typically result in shifts in the demand curves for particular goods, thus changing the quantities of those goods demanded at any given price. The **income elasticity of demand** measures the responsiveness of the quantity demanded to changes in income. Goods that an individual purchases more of when her income increases and less of when her income decreases are called **normal goods** for that individual. Examples might include steak, designer clothing, and diamonds. Goods that an individual purchases less of when her income increases and more of when her income decreases are called **inferior goods**. Examples might include hot dogs, generic products, and fake pearls.

The formula for income elasticity of demand is

$$\frac{\text{Percentage Change in Quantity Demanded}}{\text{Percentage Change in Income}}$$

Because the quantity demanded of a particular good can change with income, income elasticity can be either positive or negative. The sign (positive/negative) on income elasticity can be used to determine whether a good is normal or inferior. Figure 15 summarizes the relationship between income elasticity and product type.

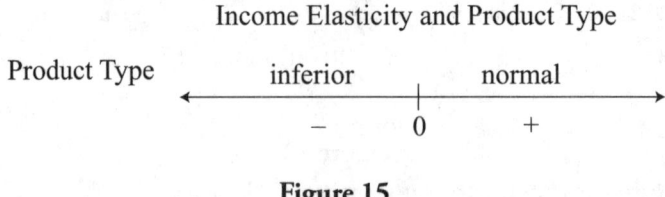

Income Elasticity and Product Type

**Figure 15**

If the quantity demanded changes in the same direction as income—increasing as income increases and vice versa—the income elasticity of the good is positive and the good is normal. If quantity demanded changes in the opposite direction as income, the income elasticity of the good is negative and the good is inferior.

## Cross-Price Elasticity of Demand

Elasticity is also used to describe the relationships between associated goods. The **cross-price elasticity of demand** measures the responsiveness of the quantity demanded of one good to the price of another good. For example, as the entrance fee for ski resorts drops, more vacationers go to these resorts, increasing the demand for rental skis. This *inverse* relationship between the price of entry and the demand for rental skis makes them **complements**. Other examples are coffee and cream, peanut butter and jelly, and gasoline and large cars. On the other hand, if the price of burgers goes up, then people will probably buy more hot dogs. If the price of one good and the quantity demanded of another good move in the *same* direction, they are called **substitutes**.

> The formula for cross-price elasticity of demand is
>
> $$\frac{\text{Percentage Change in Quantity Demanded of Good X}}{\text{Percentage Change in Price of Good Y}}$$

The elasticity value will be positive for substitutes and negative for complements. This relationship is summarized in Figure 16.

Cross-Price Elasticity and Product Relationship

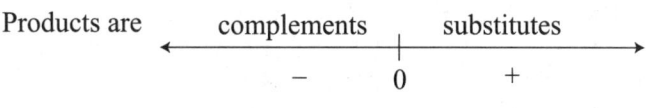

**Figure 16**

## Elasticity of Supply

The **elasticity of supply** measures the responsiveness of the quantity supplied to price changes. The law of supply tells us that higher prices lead to larger quantities being supplied (supply curves slope upward), so the elasticity of supply should be positive. The formula for this elasticity is identical to that for demand elasticity, except that "quantity demanded" is replaced with "quantity supplied."

$$\frac{\text{Percentage Change in Quantity Supplied}}{\text{Percentage Change in Price}}$$

As with demand elasticity, when supply elasticity is greater than 1, supply is elastic, and if it is less than 1, supply is inelastic. In many cases, the elasticity of supply will increase over time as producers are able to adjust their production processes to respond to changes in prices. If the price of radishes increases, there may be little that can be done to increase supply within a few weeks, but within a few months farmland that was used to produce carrots can be replanted with radishes and the supply will become more responsive to price. The supply curve for particular entertainers like Taylor Swift is perfectly inelastic (vertical), because there is only one Taylor Swift to supply, regardless of the price.

## A Case Study in Elasticity

Let's consider how the concepts of supply, demand, elasticity, and surplus work together in real life. Imagine a product with relatively elastic demand, such as over-the-counter painkillers. There are many substitute brands producing them, and they aren't absolutely necessary (minor aches and pains usually fade with time). As a result, demand for over-the-counter painkillers is relatively elastic, as illustrated by Figure 17.

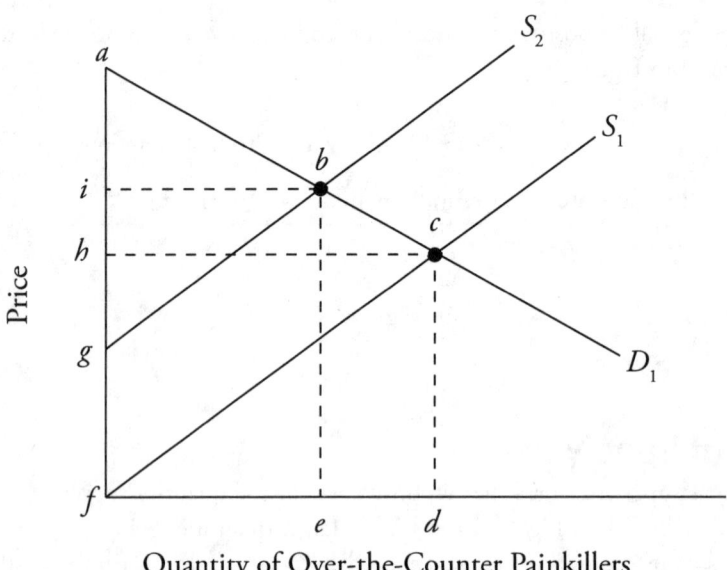

**Figure 17**

The initial supply and demand for over-the-counter painkillers are illustrated by $S_1$ and $D_1$. Suppose there is an environmental catastrophe, and one of the ingredients for over-the-counter pain killers becomes more expensive, causing the supply curve to shift inward. This shift is illustrated by $S_2$. As a result, the equilibrium price increases from $h$ to $i$, and the quantity demanded decreases from $d$ to $e$. The change in total revenue is reflected by the difference between areas *hcdf* and *ibef*. Consumer surplus shifts from areas *ach* to *abi*. Producer surplus shifts from areas *hcf* to *ibg*. Note that the changes in both consumer and producer surplus are relatively proportionate to the change in supply.

Now consider a product with relatively inelastic demand, such as opioid painkillers. There are few substitutes, and opioids are highly addictive, causing people to feel as though their lives depend on these drugs. As a result, the demand curve for opioids is relatively inelastic, as illustrated by Figure 18.

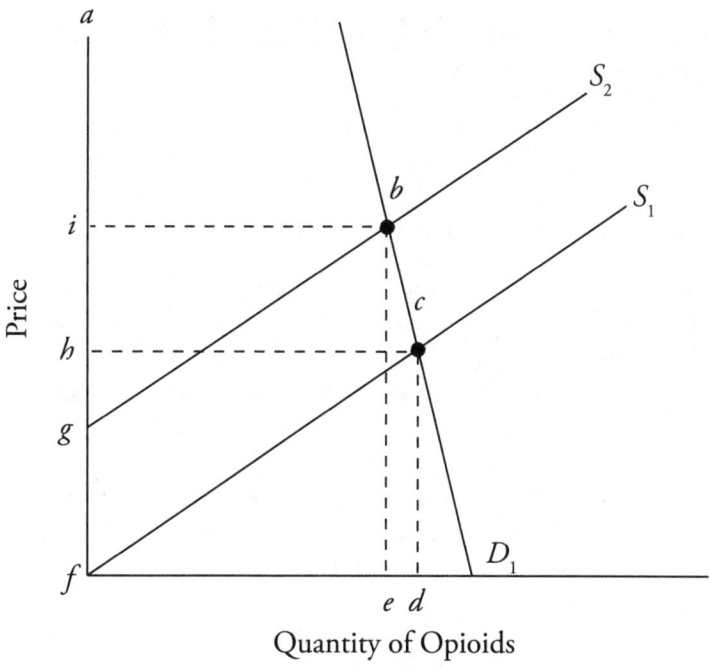

**Figure 18**

The initial supply and demand for opioids are illustrated by $S_1$ and $D_1$. Suppose another environmental catastrophe strikes, this time limiting opioid production. As a result, the supply curve shifts inward to $S_2$. Notice the change in price, from $h$ to $i$, and the adjusted total revenue *ibef*.

Due to the inelasticity of the demand curve, the change in supply affects opioids differently than it affects over-the-counter painkillers. For opioids, the reduction in quantity, from $d$ to $e$, is less than that for over-the-counter painkillers, and the increase in price, from $h$ to $i$, is greater than that for over-the-counter painkillers. Due to the inelasticity of the demand curve, there is a greater change in price and total revenue for opioids per percent change in supply than that for over-the-counter painkillers.

The effect of elasticity can also be seen in consumer surplus. While consumer surplus is illustrated by area *abi* in Figure 17, the corresponding point $A$ for opioids can't be captured within the confines of Figure 18 because the demand curve is so steep. While consumer surplus is restricted in Figure 17, one can imagine that in a situation of perfect inelasticity, consumer surplus approaches infinity because the demand curve never intersects with the *y*-axis. In this way, both elasticity and consumer surplus model consumer behavior. The slope of the demand curve models consumer sensitivity to price, and consumer surplus models the utility buyers' experience beyond the cost they paid for the good.

## 6.4 MARKET EQUILIBRIUM, DISEQUILIBRIUM, AND CHANGES IN EQUILIBRIUM

**Market equilibrium** is the result of a certain relationship between supply and demand. This relationship is established when the quantity demanded is equal to the quantity supplied. There is no out of range for any of these quantities in the market. That is, the expectations of both customers and suppliers are met without any external interruption.

When external factors impact both or either of the supply and demand quantities, it results in market **disequilibrium**. During such conditions, the demand and supply quantities mismatch, and the market goes out of balance. Various elements such as subsidies, government interventions and regulations, changes in consumers' behaviors, and so forth can result in market disequilibrium.

Contributing factors to the market equilibrium are not always stable. Many variables can impact the quantities of supply and demand. When there are changes in both demand and supply quantities, the equilibrium price and quantity will shift.

The demand curve and the supply curve for a particular good live on the same graph, with price on the vertical axis and quantity on the horizontal axis. Because the consumer's marginal utility (additional benefit) from the first few units of a good is often relatively high and the supplier's marginal (additional) cost of producing the first few units is often relatively low, the demand curve begins above the supply curve as in Figure 19.

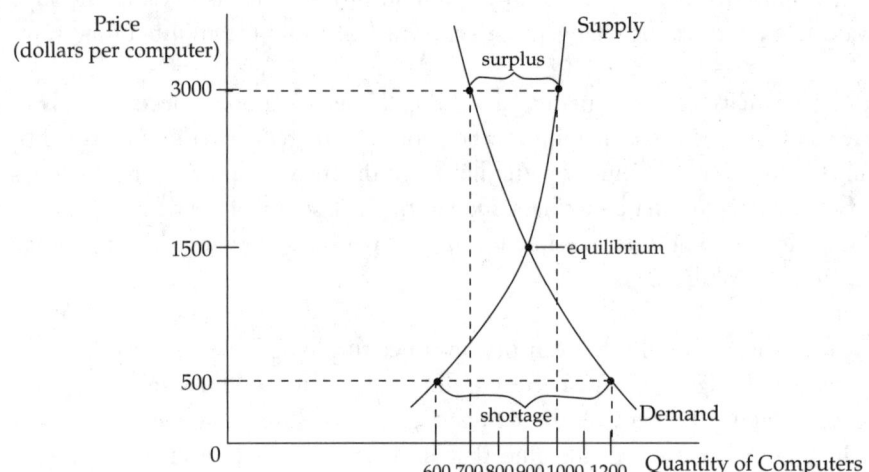

**Figure 19**

The point of intersection between the two curves is called the **equilibrium** point. It is only at the equilibrium price of $1,500 that the quantity of computers demanded equals the quantity supplied (900). For that reason, the equilibrium price is also called the **market clearing price**. If the price were above $1,500—say, $3,000—the 1,000 computers supplied would exceed the 700 demanded. The resulting **surplus** of 300 computers would lead sellers to lower their prices until equilibrium is reached. Likewise, if the price were below $1,500, say $500, a **shortage** of 600 computers would exist because the 1,200 demanded would exceed the 600 supplied. With lines out their doors for computers, the computer sellers would raise their prices until equilibrium was reached. Economic theory predicts that in the long run, the market price and quantity will equal the equilibrium price and quantity.

## 6.5 THE EFFECTS OF GOVERNMENT INTERVENTION IN MARKETS

The allocation of scarce resources can be largely influenced by the system of government in a country or region. This section provides a brief thumbnail of three forms of government and the prominent decision-making mechanisms they entail.

**Communism** is a system in which the government owns all the resources in society and answers the three economic questions: what, how, and for whom goods are produced. Communism is designed to minimize imbalance in wealth via the collective ownership of property. Legislators from a single political party—the communist party—divide the available wealth for equal advantage among citizens. The problems with communism include a lack of incentives for extra effort, risk taking, and innovation. The critical role of the central government in allocating resources and setting production levels makes this system particularly vulnerable to corruption.

**Socialism** is a system in which the government maintains control of sectors of the economy that are particularly prone to market failure, such as energy, education, and health care. Socialism shares with communism the goal of fair distribution and the pitfall of inadequate incentives. Rather than the government controlling wages as under a communist system, wages are determined by negotiations between trade unions and managers. Another difference between socialism and communism is that under socialism, a single political party does not rule the economy.

**Capitalism** is a system in which individuals and private firms own the resources in society and answer the three economic questions: what, how, and for whom goods are produced. Under a capitalist system, private individuals control the factors of production and operate them in the pursuit of profit. Wages are determined by negotiations between managers and employees or their unions. The market forces of supply and demand largely determine the allocation of scarce resources. Government may regulate businesses and provide tax-supported social benefits.

## Basic Government Interventions

This section studies three basic steps governments can take to manage their economies: a price ceiling, a price floor, and a tax.

## Price Ceiling

A **price ceiling** is an artificial cap on the price of a good. Examples include **rent controls** in many U.S. cities and limits on the price of bread in some parts of Europe. In order for a price ceiling to have any effect, the ceiling must be *below* the equilibrium price as in Figure 20.

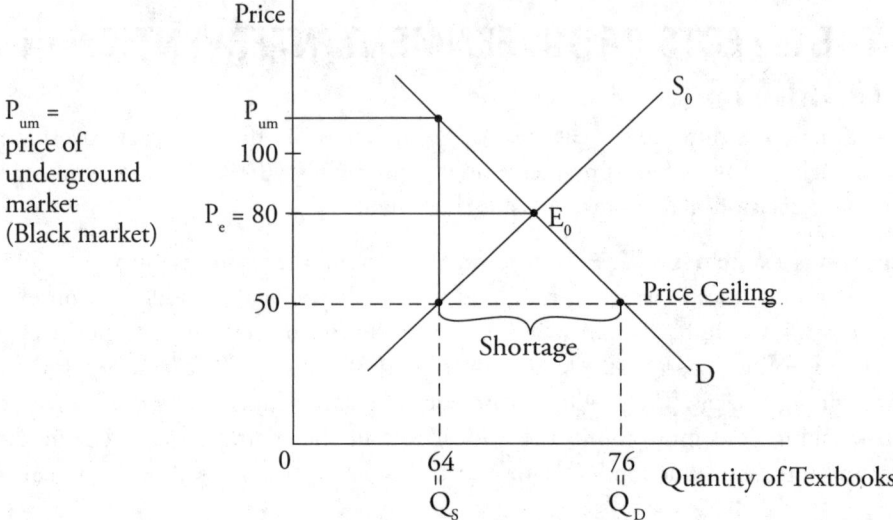

**Figure 20: Price Ceiling**

If the equilibrium price for textbooks was $80 and a price ceiling of $100 was imposed, it would have no effect because the price would not be that high anyway. A price ceiling of $50, however, means that 76 would be demanded and 64 would be supplied, resulting in a shortage of 12 textbooks.

Although price ceilings provide lower prices for those who are able to purchase the good, negative repercussions are common. To purchase the good, buyers may need to wait in line for long periods of time. Because the price of Duke basketball tickets is below the equilibrium price (perhaps due to a self-imposed price ceiling), students wait in line for as long as a week to purchase tickets to individual games. The time they lose waiting in line constitutes a **queuing cost** and would be unnecessary if the price were able to reach equilibrium at which the number of buyers equaled the number of tickets available at that price.

Price ceilings can also result in black market activity. Again looking at Figure 20, because the potential buyers of the 65th and subsequent textbooks value them at close to $100 and the seller(s) could provide them for just over $50, there is an opportunity for mutually beneficial but illegal transactions, called **black market** transactions. For example, if the 65th book was sold illegally for $80 by a seller with a marginal cost of $55 to a buyer who values it at $99, the seller nets $25 and the buyer would get $19 worth of value in excess of what she paid for the textbook. (This assumes they do not get caught.) There are black markets for such goods as tickets to sporting events and concerts, foreign currencies that have a fixed official price (exchange rate), and human organs.

## Price Floor

A **price floor** is an artificially imposed minimum price. Since 1938, the government has placed such a floor on the price of labor—the **minimum wage**. In order to have any effect, a price floor must be *above* the equilibrium price as in Figure 21.

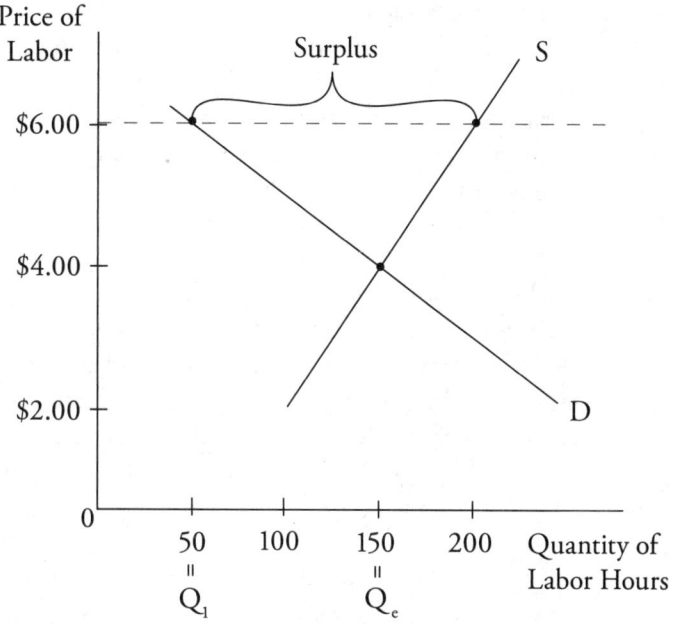

**Figure 21: Price Floor**

A minimum wage of $2 per hour would be meaningless because even without any intervention, the higher equilibrium wage of $4 would be attained. With a minimum wage of $6 per hour, 200 workers will be supplied, 50 will be demanded, and a surplus of 150 will be unemployed. Notice that this is more than the 100 workers ($Q_e - Q_1$) that would be employed at $4 but not at $6. The other 50 are from new entrants into the workforce who did not want to work for $4 an hour but do want to work for $6. Clearly the minimum wage helps the 50 workers who are still employed at the higher wage, but hurts those who lost their jobs due to the decreased quantity of labor demanded at $6 an hour.

## Tax

Let's examine how a tax on a consumer good interplays with the concepts of supply, demand, elasticity, and surplus. Consider the effect of a tax on the use of hotel rooms. Fictional demand and supply curves for hotel rooms are illustrated in Figure 22.

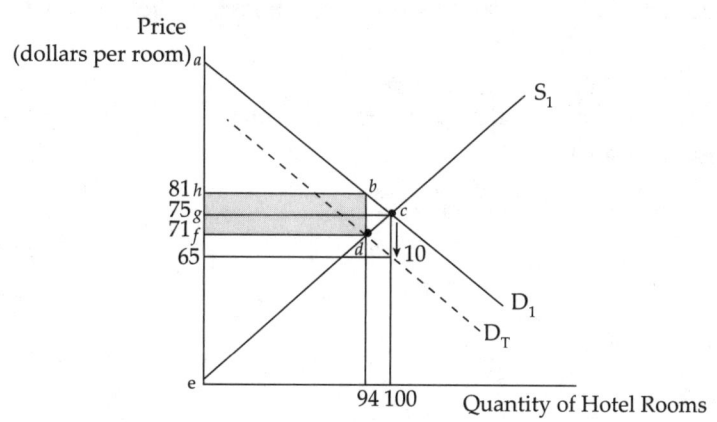

**Figure 22**

In the absence of a tax, supply is $S_1$, demand is $D_1$, and the equilibrium price is $75 per night. Now suppose that a city tax of $10 per night is imposed on hotel guests. The original demand curve ($D_1$) indicates the quantity of hotel rooms that will be demanded at a given price. Because consumers now have to pay $10 per room to the city, the amount they are willing to pay the hotels goes down by $10 per room, so the demand curve shifts down. The dotted line indicates the new demand curve ($D_T$) facing hotels, and the new equilibrium is at a price of $71 and a quantity of 94 rooms. Of course, the total amount that consumers pay is $71 *plus the $10 tax*, or $81.

It is important to note that the total payment by the consumers has gone up by only $6—less than the amount of the tax. The amount received by the hotels has gone down by the other $4 of the tax. Thus, the burden of the tax does not depend on who has to pay for it. Rather, it depends on the relative elasticities of supply and demand. If you illustrate this same story with a perfectly inelastic (vertical) supply curve, you will find that the entire burden of the tax would be paid by hotels. That is, the total payment by consumers will be $75 per room just as before the tax, and hotels will receive only $65 per room.

Tax burden can be a difficult topic for many students. Keep in mind that a tax creates a gap (or a wedge) between what consumers pay and what firms receive. The amount of the gap is exactly equal to the tax. Note that the new price paid minus the original equilibrium price (before the tax) is the consumer tax burden. The original equilibrium price (before the tax) minus the new amount collected (net of the tax) is the share borne by the producer, or the producer tax burden.

In Figure 22, consumer surplus and producer surplus before the tax are represented by the areas *acg* and *gce*, respectively. The shaded area *hbdf* represents the tax revenue of $10 × 94 rooms = $940, which is carved partially out of the pre-tax consumer surplus and partially out of the pre-tax producer surplus. The areas *abh* and *fde* represent the post-tax consumer and producer surpluses, respectively. Notice that the post-tax consumer surplus goes all the way up to the original demand curve ($D_1$). This is because $D_1$ still indicates the most that consumers would pay for various numbers of hotel rooms. $D_T$ illustrates what the consumers would pay minus the portion of that payment that must go to the city.

The area *bcd* is called the **deadweight loss**, the **efficiency loss**, and the **excess burden** of the tax, because it represents the loss to former consumer and producer surplus in excess of the total revenue of the tax. That is, deadweight loss ultimately stems from the fact that fewer hotel rooms are consumed now than before a tax was imposed. In other words, every portion of the pre-tax consumer and producer surplus either remains as surplus or is captured as tax revenues *except* that triangle, which is lost to everyone. With experimentation, you will find that, like the distribution of the tax burden, the size of the deadweight loss is also determined by the elasticity of the supply and demand curves.

Figure 23 illustrates the fact that the outcome is the same if the tax is imposed on the hotels rather than on the consumers.

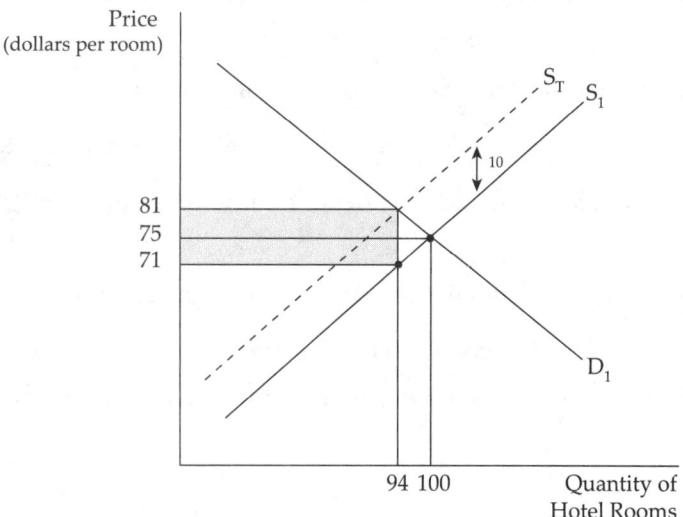

**Figure 23: A Tax on Suppliers**

A $10 room tax collected from hotels shifts the supply curve facing consumers up by $10. In addition to the minimum the hotels must receive to provide a given number of rooms as indicated by $S_1$, they now must receive an additional $10 per room to give to the city. Note that the resulting total price that consumers pay, the price that hotels receive after paying the tax, the tax revenue, the quantity, and the deadweight loss are identical to the case in which the consumers paid the tax.

## 6.6   INTERNATIONAL TRADE AND PUBLIC POLICY

The United States has an **open economy**, meaning it trades with other nations to acquire goods that cannot be supplied within its borders and sells goods in international markets. By contrast, countries that don't engage in foreign trade are considered to have **closed economies**. In open economies, the effects of fiscal policy on interest rates can have additional implications on international trade. For example, **expansionary fiscal policy** can cause the following chains of events, leading to a decline in net exports:

Government (G) spending increases or Taxes (T) decrease $\Rightarrow$

Higher interest rates (the crowding-out effect) $\Rightarrow$

Increased demand for the domestic currency for investment purposes (e.g., Treasury bonds) $\Rightarrow$

Appreciation of the domestic currency relative to foreign currencies $\Rightarrow$

Exports (X) decrease and Imports (M) increase

- Net Exports (X – M) decrease, partially offsetting the effects of the expansionary policy

Likewise, **contractionary fiscal policy** can cause the following events leading to an increase in net exports:

Government (G) spending decreases or Taxes (T) increase ⟹

Lower interest rates (due to the government demanding fewer loanable funds) ⟹

Decreased demand for the domestic currency for investment purposes (e.g., Treasury bonds) ⟹

Depreciation of the domestic currency relative to foreign currencies ⟹

Exports (X) increase and Imports (M) decrease ⟹

- Net Exports (X – M) increase, partially offsetting the effects of the contractionary policy

# CHAPTER 6 KEY TERMS

## 6.1

demand
demand curve
demand schedule
law of diminishing marginal utility
law of demand

## 6.2

supply
supply curve
supply schedule
law of supply
marginal cost
market supply curve
change in quantity supplied
change in supply
joint products
decrease in supply
shift in supply (ROTTEN)
economies of scale
long-run average cost
diseconomies of scale
increasing returns (to scale)
decreasing returns (to scale)
constant returns (to scale)
diminishing (marginal) returns
increasing cost firm
decreasing cost firm
increasing cost industry
constant cost industry
decreasing cost industry
productive efficiency
economies of scope

## 6.3

elasticity
price elasticity of demand
elastic
luxury
unit elastic
inelastic

necessity
perfectly inelastic
perfectly elastic
income elasticity of demand
normal goods
inferior goods
cross-price elasticity of demand
complements
substitutes
elasticity of supply

## 6.4

market equilibrium
disequilibrium
equilibrium
market clearing price
surplus
shortage

## 6.5

communism
socialism
capitalism
price ceiling
rent controls
queuing cost
black market
price floor
minimum wage
deadweight loss
efficiency loss
excess burden

## 6.6

open economy
closed economy
expansionary fiscal policy
contractionary fiscal policy

# CHAPTER 6 DRILL QUESTIONS

See Chapter 10 for answers and explanations.

**1** ☐ Mark for Review

A demand curve slopes downward for an individual as the result of

(A) diminishing marginal utility

(B) diminishing marginal returns

(C) the Fisher effect

(D) diminishing returns to scale

(E) increasing marginal cost

**2** ☐ Mark for Review

The supply curve for lawn-mowing services is likely to slope upward because of

(A) decreasing marginal costs

(B) increasing opportunity cost of time

(C) diminishing marginal utility

(D) increasing returns to scale

(E) economies of scope

**3** ☐ Mark for Review

If both supply and demand increase, the result is

(A) a definite increase in price and an indeterminate change in quantity

(B) a definite increase in quantity and an indeterminate change in price

(C) a definite decrease in quantity and an indeterminate change in price

(D) a definite decrease in price and a definite increase in quantity

(E) a definite increase in price and a definite increase in quantity

**4** ☐ Mark for Review

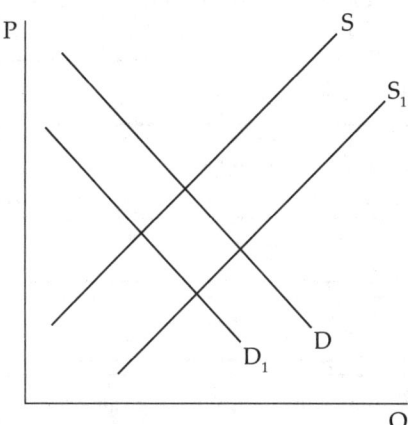

For the market supply and demand graph above, when the demand curve shifts from D to $D_1$ and the supply curve shifts from S to $S_1$, then

(A) the equilibrium price falls and the equilibrium quantity is undetermined

(B) the equilibrium price falls and the equilibrium quantity is unchanged

(C) the equilibrium price is unchanged and the equilibrium quantity rises

(D) the equilibrium price is undetermined and the equilibrium quantity falls

(E) None of the above

**5** ☐ Mark for Review

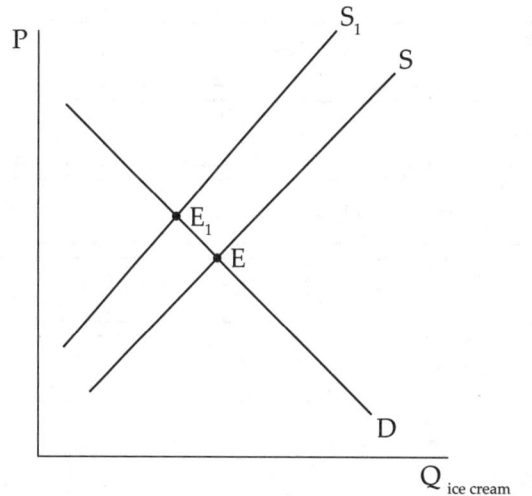

In the graph above, the shift in the supply curve from S to $S_1$ for ice cream could occur because

(A) consumer incomes declined and ice cream is an inferior good

(B) the price of ice cream rose

(C) chocolate sauce production increased

(D) the cost of milk, which is used in the production of ice cream, fell

(E) the cost of milk, which is used in the production of ice cream, rose

**6** ☐ Mark for Review

If a 3 percent increase in price leads to a 5 percent increase in the quantity supplied,

(A) supply is unit elastic

(B) demand is inelastic

(C) demand is elastic

(D) supply is elastic

(E) supply is inelastic

**7** ☐ Mark for Review

Normal goods always have

(A) an elastic demand curve

(B) an inelastic demand curve

(C) an elastic supply curve

(D) a negative income elasticity

(E) a positive income elasticity

**8** ☐ Mark for Review

When the cross-price elasticity of demand is negative, the goods in question are necessarily

(A) normal

(B) inferior

(C) complements

(D) substitutes

(E) luxuries

**9** ☐ Mark for Review

If a business wants to increase its revenue and it knows that the elasticity quotient of demand of its product is equal to 0.78, it should

(A) decrease price because demand is elastic

(B) decrease price because demand is unit elastic

(C) decrease price because demand is inelastic

(D) increase price because demand is inelastic

(E) increase price because demand is elastic

**10** ☐ Mark for Review

Which of the following elements results in market disequilibrium?

(A) Externalities

(B) More firms going bankrupt

(C) More banks going bankrupt

(D) Imposing a price ceiling

(E) Low supply and demand at the same time

**11** ☐ Mark for Review

When the labor demand curve is downward-sloping, an increase in the minimum wage is

(A) beneficial to some workers and harmful to other workers

(B) beneficial to all workers and harmful to some employers

(C) harmful to all workers and employers

(D) beneficial to all workers and employers

(E) none of the above

**12** ☐ Mark for Review

Which of the following examples would result in consumers paying for the largest burden of an excise tax placed on a producer?

(A) If the demand curve is price elastic and the supply curve is price inelastic

(B) If the demand curve is price elastic and the supply curve is perfectly elastic

(C) If the demand curve is price inelastic and the supply curve is price elastic

(D) If the demand curve is price inelastic and the supply curve is price inelastic

(E) If the demand curve is perfectly inelastic and the supply curve is price elastic

**13** ☐ Mark for Review

Which of the following would be considered contractionary monetary policy?

(A) The purchase of bonds

(B) The sale of bonds

(C) An increase in taxes

(D) An increase in government spending

(E) A decrease in the discount rate

**14** ☐ Mark for Review

In what ways is contractionary fiscal policy in the United States likely to affect domestic interest rates and the international value of the dollar?

(A) Interest rates increase and the dollar depreciates.

(B) Interest rates decrease and the dollar appreciates.

(C) Interest rates increase and the dollar appreciates.

(D) Interest rates decrease and the dollar is not affected.

(E) Interest rates decrease and the dollar depreciates.

# Chapter 6 Summary

## 6.1  Demand

o  The **demand curve** displays the relationship between price and the quantity demanded of a good within a given period.

o  The decreasing satisfaction gained from additional units of a good consumed in a given period is called the **law of diminishing marginal utility**.

o  The law of diminishing marginal utility corresponds with the **law of demand**, which states that as the price of a good rises, the quantity of that good demanded by consumers falls.

## 6.2  Supply

o  The supply curve shifts with
  - **R**esource costs
  - **O**ther goods' prices
  - **T**axes and subsidies
  - **T**echnology changes
  - **E**xpectations of suppliers
  - **N**umber of suppliers

o  **Diseconomies of scale** exist over the range of output for which LRAC is increasing.

o  **Increasing returns (to scale)** exist when output increases proportionately more than increases in all inputs, as compared to **decreasing returns** and **constant returns**.

o  **Diminishing (marginal) returns** exist when an additional unit of an input increases total output by less than the previous unit of input.

o  An **increasing cost firm** faces decreasing returns to scale; a **decreasing cost firm** faces increasing returns to scale.

o   An **increasing cost industry** experiences increases in average production costs as industry output increases; a **constant cost industry** does not experience increased production costs as output grows; a **decreasing cost industry** experiences decreasing average production costs as industry output increases.

o   **Productive efficiency** occurs when a firm produces at the lowest unit cost, when MC = AC.

o   **Economies of scope** exist when a firm's average production costs decrease because multiple products are being produced.

## 6.3 Elasticity

o   The **price elasticity of demand** for a given good describes the extent to which consumer behavior will change as the price of the good changes.

o   The elasticity of a good relates to
   - the **P**roportion of the consumer's income spent on the good
   - the **A**vailability of close substitutes
   - the **I**mportance of a good
   - the ability to **D**elay the purchase of a good

o   A good is **elastic** (a **luxury**) if $\%\Delta Q_d > \%\Delta P$.

o   A good is **unit elastic** if $\%\Delta Q_d = \%\Delta P$.

o   A good is **inelastic** (a **necessity**) if $\%\Delta Q_d < \%\Delta P$.

o   Knowing the elasticity of a demand curve tells sellers how much their total revenue will change with a change in price:
   - elastic goods: P↑→TR↓
   - unit elastic goods: P↑→TR constant
   - inelastic goods: P↑→TR↑

o   **Income elasticity of demand** measures the responsiveness of the quantity demanded to changes in income.
   - Income elasticity is calculated by $\dfrac{\%\Delta Q_d}{\%\Delta \text{Income}}$.

o Individuals buy more **normal goods** (positive income elasticity) when their income increases; they buy more **inferior goods** (negative elasticity) when their income decreases.

o The **cross-price elasticity of demand** measures the responsiveness of the quantity demanded of one good to the price of another.

- Cross-price elasticity of good $X$ in relation to good $Y$ is calculated by $\dfrac{\%\Delta Q_d(X)}{\%\Delta P(Y)}$.

o When cross-price elasticity is negative, then goods $X$ and $Y$ are **complements**; when cross-price elasticity is positive, then goods $X$ and $Y$ are **substitutes**.

o The **elasticity of supply** measures the responsiveness of the quantity supplied to price changes.

- Elasticity of supply is calculated by $\dfrac{\%\Delta Q_s}{\%\Delta P}$.

## 6.4 Market Equilibrium, Disequilibrium, and Changes in Equilibrium

o **Market equilibrium** is the result of a certain relationship between supply and demand. This relationship is established when the quantity demanded is equal to the quantity supplied.

o When external factors impact both or either of the supply and demand quantities, it results in **market disequilibrium.** During such conditions, the demand and supply quantities mismatch, and the market goes out of balance. Various elements such as subsidies, government interventions and regulations, changes in consumers' behaviors, and so forth can result in market disequilibrium.

## 6.5 The Effects of Government Intervention in Markets

o **Communism** is a system in which the government owns all the resources in society and answers the three economic questions: what, how, and for whom are goods produced.

o **Socialism** is a system in which the government maintains control of some resources in society, such as energy distribution, education, and health care.

- o **Capitalism** is a system in which individuals and private firms own the resources in society and answer the three economic questions: what, how, and for whom are goods produced.

- o A **price ceiling** is an artificial cap on the price of a good.

- o A **price floor** is an artificially imposed minimum price.

- o **Deadweight loss** (also known as **efficiency loss** or **excess burden**) is the loss to former consumer and producer surplus in excess of total revenue of a tax.

- o Calculating the effects of a new tax is tricky: the burden of the tax does not depend on who has to pay for it. Rather, the weight of the tax burden depends on the relative elasticity of the supply and demand curves for the good in question.

## 6.6 International Trade and Public Policy

- o **Expansionary fiscal policy** involves increasing government purchases, increasing transfers, or decreasing taxes in order to shift aggregate demand to the right and boost real GDP. To summarize the effects:

$$G \uparrow \text{ or } T \downarrow \Rightarrow AD \uparrow \Rightarrow Y \uparrow \Rightarrow Md \uparrow \Rightarrow r \uparrow \Rightarrow I \downarrow \Rightarrow Y \downarrow$$

- o **Contractionary fiscal policy** involves decreasing purchases, decreasing transfers, or increasing taxes, thus shifting aggregate demand to the left, which will lower the price level and decrease real GDP:

$$G \downarrow \text{ or } T \uparrow \Rightarrow AD \downarrow \Rightarrow Y \downarrow \Rightarrow Md \downarrow \Rightarrow r \downarrow \Rightarrow I \uparrow \Rightarrow Y \uparrow$$

# Chapter 7
# Micro Unit 3: Production, Cost, and the Perfect Competition Model

## 7.1    THE PRODUCTION FUNCTION

### The Functions of an Economic System—What, How, and for Whom to Produce

Every economy must make three important decisions: what goods and services will be produced, how much of each input will be used in the production of each good, and who will receive the final products. How these questions are answered determines a society's economic structure and standard of living and involves various types of efficiency.

### What Goods and Services Will Be Produced?

When an economy asks what to produce, it is seeking **allocative efficiency** or **efficiency in output**. Allocative efficiency requires that national output reflect the needs and wants of consumers. More precisely, resources are allocated efficiently if each good is produced until the **marginal cost** (the cost of producing one more unit) equals the **marginal value** (the value of one more unit). Because the equilibrium price represents the marginal value of output, the condition for allocative efficiency is that price equals marginal cost (**P = MC**) for each type of output.

### How Much of Each Input Will Be Used in the Production of Each Good?

When an automaker makes a car, it could do so using many different combinations of labor and machinery (capital). The manufacturer could assemble the car using mostly hand assemblers, robots, or a balance of these two inputs. When an economy asks how much of each input to use in the production process, it is seeking **efficiency in production** or **technical efficiency**.

Imagine a simplified firm in which labor and capital are the only two inputs needed to produce a particular good. The price of labor is the **wage**, and the price of capital is called the **rental rate**. The cost-minimizing production condition requires that the wage (w) divided by the rental rate (r) of capital equal the **marginal product of labor** ($MP_L$) (the additional output produced by one more unit of labor) divided by the **marginal product of capital** ($MP_K$) (the additional output produced by one more unit of capital). Note that the marginal product of an input is sometimes referred to as the **marginal physical product**. The equation looks like this:

$$\frac{\text{labor cost}}{\text{capital cost}} = \frac{\text{wage}}{\text{rental rate}} = \frac{w}{r} = \frac{MP_L}{MP_K}$$

If you simply multiply both sides of the first equation by $MP_K$ and divide both sides by w, you get this equivalent:

$$\frac{MP_K}{r} = \frac{MP_L}{w}$$

The second equation makes more sense intuitively, indicating that cost minimization means equating the additional output gained for each dollar of input cost—the "bang per buck." If the marginal product of labor per dollar of wages (the right side of the second equation) is larger than the marginal product of capital per dollar of rental costs (the left side), the firm should hire more labor and less capital because labor is a better value (and vice versa). As more labor is hired, its marginal product will decrease; and as less capital is used, its marginal product will increase. Thus, as the firm alters its input mix to favor the input with the largest "bang per buck," the two sides of the efficiency equation will come closer and closer to equality. When they are equal, the firm has achieved efficiency in production.

## Marginal Product and Diminishing Returns

In order to efficiently produce goods, business owners compare the quantity of goods produced—output—to the amount of investment required in production—input. **Marginal product** is the additional output produced per period when one more unit of an input is added, *holding the quantities of other inputs constant.* If we are producing bagels, the marginal product of labor is the additional number of bagels produced per hour when one more worker is hired. Using $\Delta$ to represent change, TP to represent total product, and L to represent the number of units of labor hired per hour, the formula for the marginal product of labor is

$$MP_L = \frac{\Delta TP}{\Delta L}$$

This is sometimes called the marginal *physical* product of labor ($MPP_L$) to clarify the fact that dollars are not involved—it is simply a measure of physical output. The marginal products of other inputs are found the same way, substituting the appropriate letters (K for capital, etc.) for L.

Figure 1 on the next page illustrates a **marginal product curve** for labor and the corresponding average and total product curves.

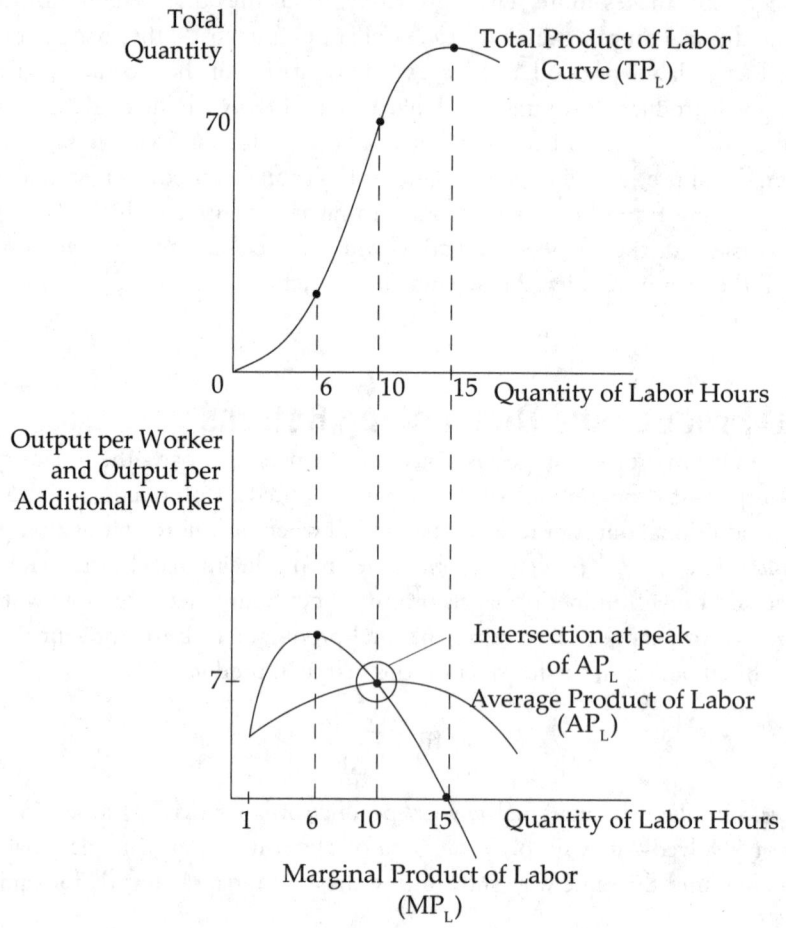

**Figure 1**

Marginal product often increases with the first few workers because they are able to take advantage of specialization. When operating a bagel shop with only one worker, that worker must do everything—work the ovens, mix the dough, service customers, answer the phone, and so on. As additional workers are hired, each can become better at a particular task than the smaller number of less specialized workers were, so for a while each additional worker will contribute more to total output than the one before her. This is why the marginal product curve increases for the first few workers.

The **law of diminishing marginal returns** states that as the amount of one input is increased, *holding the amounts of all other inputs constant*, the incremental gains in output ("marginal returns") will eventually decrease. In the bagel example, after so many workers have been hired, opportunities to take advantage of specialization will dwindle. Remember that we are increasing only the number of workers; the amounts of the other inputs remain the same. Additional workers will become redundant—they may not have enough ovens, counter space, or phones to work with, and congestion will eventually take a toll. Added workers who become bored might even start distracting the original workers or create a party atmosphere. When additional workers contribute less to total output than the workers before them, **diminishing marginal returns** have set in and the marginal product curve starts falling. In Figure 1, that occurs after six workers are hired.

# Average Product and Total Product

While businesses are always exploring ways to enhance marginal production, they remain interested in monitoring production costs as averaged across all units produced. By monitoring average costs, businesses are able to determine the selling price that is most efficient and profitable for them.

> The formula for **average product** is
> $$AP = \frac{\text{Total Product}}{\text{Quantity of Input}}$$

Can you identify how this differs from the marginal product formula? Note that the average product of labor rises when marginal product is above it, falls when marginal product is below it, and reaches its maximum at its intersection with the marginal product curve. It makes sense that the marginal product pulls the average up or down. Think of a baseball player's batting average. If the player's last (or "marginal") at-bat produced a hit, his batting average will go up. If the last at-bat was a strikeout, the player's average will go down.

The **total product curve** shows the relationship between the total amount of output produced and the number of units of an input used, holding the amounts of other inputs constant. The *slope* of the total product curve is

$$\frac{\text{Rise}}{\text{Run}} = \frac{\text{Change in Total Product}}{\text{Change in the Number of Units of Input}} = \text{Marginal Product}$$

Knowing this simple trick—that the slope of the total product curve equals marginal product—makes it easier to tell what the total product curve looks like when you have a marginal product curve, and vice versa. When marginal product is positive, the total product curve has a positive slope (it rises from left to right). When the marginal product is increasing or decreasing, the slope of the total product curve is increasing or decreasing respectively. And when the marginal product is zero, the slope of the total product curve has zero slope (it is flat). In Figure 1, we see the marginal product and the slope of the total product increase, decrease, go to zero, and then become negative.

There is a similar trick for relating the average product curve and the total product curve. The average product for a given quantity of an input is the slope of a line from the origin—the lower left corner with coordinates (0, 0)—to the point on the total product curve corresponding to that quantity of the input. For example, in Figure 2 the average product when 10 workers are employed is the slope of a line (not shown) from the origin to the total product curve when 10 workers are employed. The line has a rise of 70 and a run of 10, so the slope and average product are $\frac{70}{10} = 7$. Using these tricks, if you remember or are given what a total product curve looks like, you can draw the corresponding marginal and average product curves, or vice versa.

## Average and Marginal Costs and Revenues

When economists talk about costs, they mean all costs including opportunity costs. Even if the bagel maker owns her ovens, she could sell or rent them to someone else if she were not using them, so there is a clear opportunity cost of their use. Similarly, if the bagel maker spends time in the shop that could be spent earning money elsewhere, the value of that time is included in the cost, whether she explicitly pays herself for it or not. Thus, the costs discussed below are not necessarily actual expenditures by the firm as accountants would measure them. Instead, these costs tell a more complete story and permit more appropriate decision-making.

Production costs are divided into two types, fixed and variable, which are added together to find total costs. **Fixed costs** *do not change* when more output is produced. In a bagel shop, these might include rent and payments for ovens, mixers, display cases, and the like. Whether the shop makes one bagel or 1,000, it has to pay the rent and purchase a minimal amount of equipment. **Variable costs** are those that *do change* as more output is produced. For example, as more bagels are made, the shop will hire more workers and purchase more ingredients. When you put all the costs together, you have total costs.

$$\text{Total Costs} = \text{Total Fixed Costs} + \text{Total Variable Costs}$$
$$\text{or}$$
$$\text{TC} = \text{TFC} + \text{TVC}$$

An example of this calculation is provided in Table 1, where for each level of output, the fixed cost of 10 plus the variable cost in the third column equals the total cost in the fourth column.

| Number of Bagels | Fixed Cost | Total Variable Cost | Total Cost | Marginal Cost | Average Fixed Cost | Average Variable Cost | Average Total Cost |
|---|---|---|---|---|---|---|---|
| 0 | 10 | 0 | 10 | — | — | — | — |
| 1 | 10 | 5 | 15 | 5 | 10 | 5 | 15 |
| 2 | 10 | 8 | 18 | 3 | 5 | 4 | 9 |
| 3 | 10 | 9 | 19 | 1 | 3.3 | 3 | 6.3 |
| 4 | 10 | 11 | 21 | 2 | 2.5 | 2.75 | 5.25 |
| 5 | 10 | 15 | 25 | 4 | 2 | 3 | 5 |

**Table 1**

An exam question might provide a table with total cost levels for each quantity of output and ask you to determine the fixed cost, among other things. You can identify the fixed cost as the total cost when quantity is zero, because when no output is produced, there is no variable cost, and the total cost equals the fixed cost.

Figure 2 on the next page illustrates typical TC, TFC, and TVC curves.

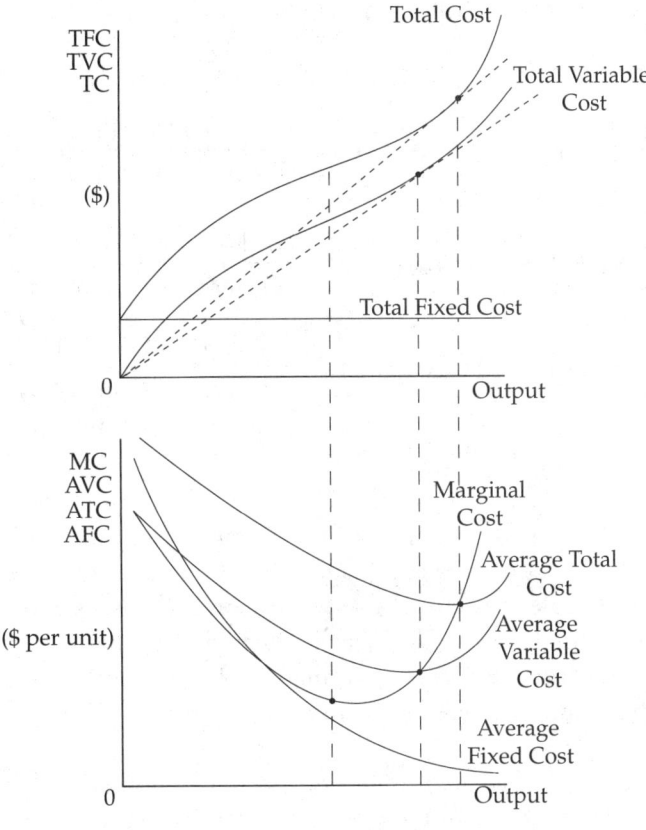

**Figure 2**

The total fixed cost curve is horizontal because, by definition, fixed costs do not change as output increases. The slope of the total cost (TC) and total variable cost (TVC) curves—the amount by which costs increase when one more unit of output is produced—is called the **marginal cost** (MC). Because the only part of total cost that changes is variable cost, total cost and total variable cost change by the same amount when output is increased, and they have the same slope at any given level of output:

$$MC = \frac{\Delta TC}{\Delta Q} = \frac{\Delta TVC}{\Delta Q}$$

Marginal cost and equivalently the slope of TC and TVC decrease in the beginning because the first few units of *input* produce more additional output than the units before them (refer back to the discussion on marginal product to review). Getting more output from each additional worker translates into lower costs for each additional unit of output. The law of diminishing marginal returns indicates that additional units of an input will eventually yield less and less additional output. This causes the marginal cost and equivalently the slope of the total and variable cost curves to increase.

The fifth column of Table 1 illustrates the calculation of marginal cost. For example, going from an output of zero bagels to an output of one bagel, the variable cost increases by five. Five is thus the marginal cost of the first bagel. Likewise, the marginal cost of the fifth bagel is four because total and variable cost each increase by four when output increases from four to five bagels. A typical marginal cost curve is illustrated in the lower half of Figure 2. Note that it decreases and then increases, just as the slope of the total and variable cost curves decreases and then increases.

**Average total costs**, **average variable costs**, and **average fixed costs** are found by simply dividing the total cost values by the quantity of output.

$$\text{Average Total Cost (ATC)} = \frac{\text{Total Cost (TC)}}{\text{Quantity of Output (Q)}}$$

$$\text{Average Variable Cost (AVC)} = \frac{\text{Total Variable Cost (TVC)}}{\text{Quantity of Output (Q)}}$$

$$\text{Average Fixed Cost (AFC)} = \frac{\text{Total Fixed Cost (TFC)}}{\text{Quantity of Output (Q)}}$$

Do not just look at these graphs—practice drawing them yourself!

Look at Table 1 for examples of the average cost values and look at the lower half of Figure 2 for typical average cost curves. Note that the average total and average variable cost curves rise when marginal cost is above them, fall when marginal cost is below them, and intersect marginal cost at their minimum points. Average fixed cost continually falls as quantity increases because the same fixed cost is divided by a larger and larger quantity.

The tricks described in the previous section for finding average and marginal product from the total product curve also work for finding average and marginal cost from the total cost curve. That is, the AFC, AVC, and ATC values when a particular quantity is produced are equal to the slopes of the lines from the origin to the corresponding points on the TFC, TVC, and TC curves, respectively. And as mentioned, the marginal cost when a given quantity is produced is the slope of the total cost curve (and equivalently the slope of the total variable cost curve).

## 7.2   SHORT- AND LONG-RUN PRODUCTION COSTS

There are two primary distinctions between the **long run** and the **short run.** One is that in the short run, the amount of at least one input (also known as a "factor of production") cannot change. In a simple model with only capital and labor as inputs, it is usually assumed that in the short run, the amount of labor can change but the amount of capital is fixed. For example, in the short run you can't get out of your lease, and you don't have time to build, so you are stuck with your present building. The other distinction is that for similar reasons, firms can neither enter nor leave an industry in the short run.

The ability to change the amount of capital and other inputs in the long run has repercussions on the long-run and short-run cost curves. Because everything is variable in the long run, there are no fixed costs. Total, average, and marginal costs will be higher in the short run than in the long run if the fixed amount of capital held in the short run is more or less than the cost-minimizing amount for producing the desired quantity of output.

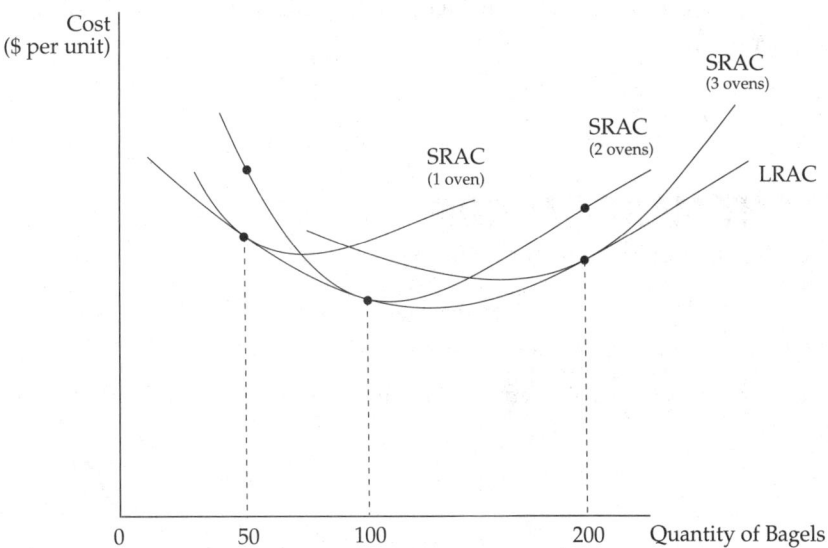

**Figure 3: Long-Run and Short-Run Average Cost**

Figure 3 illustrates a **long-run average cost (LRAC)** curve and the **short-run average cost (SRAC)** curve supposing that the number of bagel ovens (capital) held in the short run is the cost-minimizing number for producing 100 bagels. To produce 200 bagels in the short run, only the amount of labor and not the number of ovens can be increased. This permits an expansion of output, but the average cost per bagel will be higher than if both the ovens and labor could be increased by the proportions that minimize costs. Likewise, if the shop wishes to produce 50 bagels, it cannot decrease the number of ovens in the short run; it can release only workers, so the average cost will again be higher than in the long run when it can adjust the amount of capital to its ideal level.

If the current amount of capital were the cost-minimizing amount for producing 150 or 250 bagels, the short-run average cost curve would share a point with the long-run average cost curve at which quantity equals 150 or 250. A different short-run average cost curve could be drawn corresponding to every possible amount of capital, touching the long-run average cost curve at the quantity for which that amount of capital is the cost-minimizing amount.

## 7.3   TYPES OF PROFIT

In general, the value remaining after paying all costs and financial obligations of a company is called **profit**.

$$\text{Profit} = \text{TR} - \text{TC}$$

Profit is one of the major aspects of any business, and is used as an indicator of performance.

The most common type of profit is gross profit, which is equivalent to the difference between the total sales and the total cost of goods or services. For example, if the total income of a company from sales and services is $3,000,000 per year and the total cost of the company is $1,200,000, then the gross profit of the company is $3,000,000 – $1,200,000 = $1,800,000.

Subtracting the operating expenses from the gross profit produces another level of profit called operating profit. The amount left after deducting all other expenses such as taxes and loan interests is called net profit.

## 7.4    PROFIT MAXIMIZATION

**Profit** is the difference between total revenue and total cost.

$$\text{Profit} = \text{TR} - \text{TC}$$

Figure 4 illustrates the relationship between total revenue, total cost, and profit.

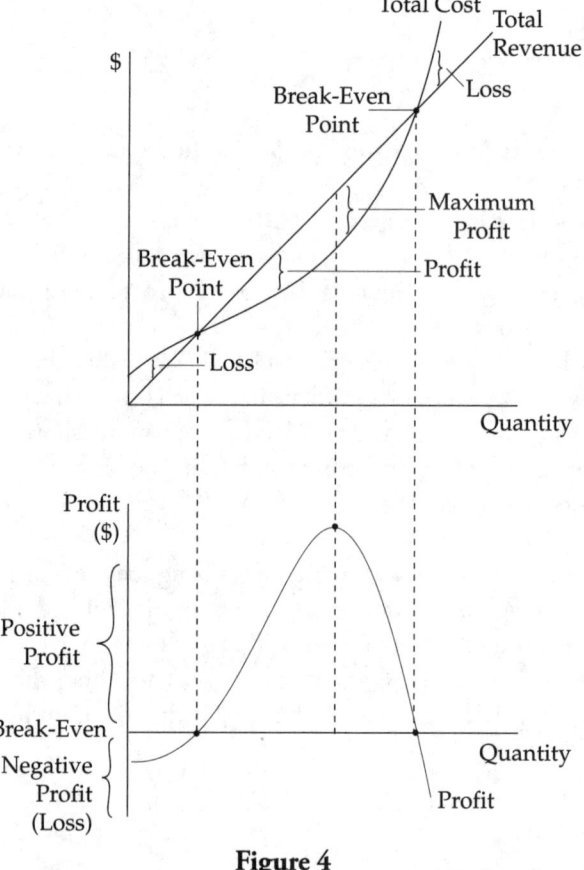

**Figure 4**

The points on the upper graph at which total revenue equals total cost are called **break-even points**. When total revenue exceeds total cost, the vertical distance between the two curves represents profits. When total revenue is less than total cost, the vertical distance between the two represents losses. The lower graph illustrates the profits or losses resulting from each level of output in the upper graph. You can use a graph like this one to determine the point of **profit maximization**, also known as **loss minimization**.

A profit-maximizing firm wants to produce when TR > TC and when the distance between the total revenue curve and the total cost curve is as large as possible. In the range for which positive profits are being made, if the slope of the total revenue curve is larger than the slope of the total cost curve, the gap between them is widening, and it pays to produce more. If the slope of the total revenue curve is less than that of the total cost curve, then the two curves are coming together, and the gap would be wider at a lower quantity. It is at the point at which the two slopes are equal that the gap between them is the widest and profits are maximized. Because marginal revenue is the slope of the total revenue curve and marginal cost is the slope of the total cost curve, equating the slopes of these two curves is equivalent to following the golden rule of economics and setting marginal revenue equal to marginal cost. Thus, the firm will maximize profits by producing when MR = MC (read on for a discussion of when a firm should not operate at all).

Figure 5 illustrates the profit-maximizing point for the representative firm. Note that some teachers and books refer to the AC curve as the ATC for Average Total Cost.

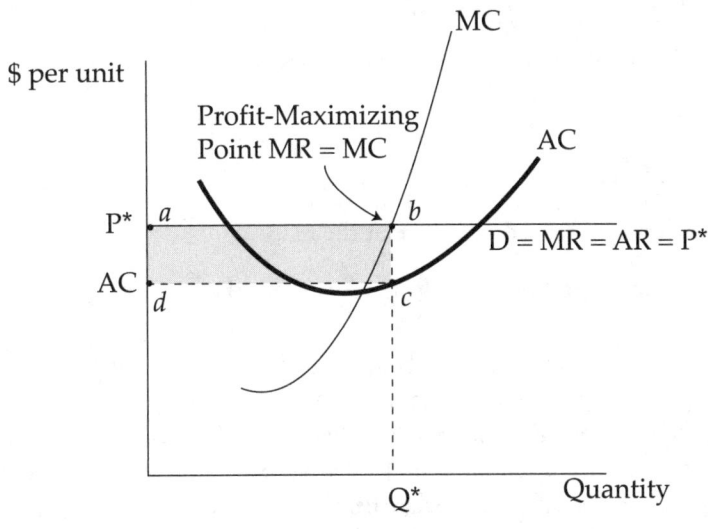

**Figure 5**

> The individual firm graph is often used in practice and on AP Exams to illustrate the profit or loss story.

Unlike the graph with total cost and total revenue, the firm graph measures dollars per unit of output rather than total dollars. To find profit, note that the **average profit** is the difference between average revenue and average cost. Average profit is positive if AR > AC and negative if AR < AC. Given that

$$\text{Average Profit} = \frac{\text{Total Profit}}{\text{Quantity}}$$

it follows, by multiplying both sides by the quantity of output, that

$$\text{Average Profit} \times \text{Quantity} = \text{Total Profit}$$

In Figure 5, the area of the rectangle *abcd* represents total profit—its length *ab* is quantity, its width *bc* is average profit, and its area is length times width, which is average profit times quantity, or total profit. Remember that if the price (which is average revenue) is less than average cost, the analogous rectangle represents total losses.

## 7.5 PERFECT COMPETITION

**Perfect competition** describes a theoretical market structure in which supply and demand determine the market price and quantity of a good sold. Though perfect competition is extremely rare in reality, considering perfect competition provides economists with a benchmark to assess the efficiency and efficacy of any given marketplace.

These are the characteristics of perfect competition:

- many sellers, each seller representing a small market share

- identical products

- firms are "price takers"

- sellers and buyers can freely enter and exit the market

- buyers have complete and perfect information about the product

A perfectly competitive industry involves a large number of sellers selling an identical good to a large number of buyers. Each buyer and seller is too small to have a noticeable effect on the market price or quantity, making the sellers **price takers**—they accept the market price as given and can sell all that they want at that price. Each buyer and seller has perfect information about prices and the availability of goods. Thus, if a seller were to raise her price at all above the market price, all the buyers would purchase their goods from the many other sellers offering the same item at the lower market price. At the same time, there is no incentive for a firm in a perfectly competitive industry to lower its price below the market price, because any amount can be sold at the market price. Agricultural goods such as corn and rice have market structures that approximate perfect competition, with their thousands of buyers and sellers, homogeneous products, and ease of entry and exit. (Note: Market failure occurs anytime marketplaces don't meet the criteria for perfect competition and resources are allocated inefficiently. See Chapter 9 for further discussion of market failure.)

In a perfectly competitive industry there are no barriers to entry or exit. Anyone can become a seller in this market at relatively little expense. It follows that there are zero economic profits in the long run, because firms will enter the market and compete away any existing profits, and firms will leave until output prices and input costs adjust to eliminate any losses. Do not think that earning zero economic profits is a bad thing. **Economic profits** are total revenues minus total costs, with opportunity costs included among the costs. If the entrepreneur could be making $100,000 per year doing something else, that opportunity cost is included in the total cost. Thus, making zero economic profit means you couldn't make any more doing anything different.

Entrepreneurs earning zero economic profits are often described as earning **normal profits**, or **breaking even**, because they are earning a return equivalent to the opportunity cost of their time. The calculation of **accounting profits** yields more attractive-sounding results. Accountants determine profits by subtracting from revenues only the explicit (monetary) cost of production, not such implicit costs as the opportunity cost of entrepreneurs' time. If a coffee shop owner took in revenues of \$250,000, paid \$150,000 in expenses, and could be earning \$100,000 per year as a computer programmer, her accounting profit is \$250,000 – \$150,000 = \$100,000, while her economic profit is \$250,000 – \$150,000 – \$100,000 = 0. In economics books such as this one, the term *profit* refers to economic profit.

Figure 6 illustrates the relationship between the firm and market.

Note that the price for any given good produced by the representative firm is set by the industry market, meaning that anything affecting the equilibrium price in the industry market will also affect the factor market. When it comes to demand, that relationship is direct. Anything that increases demand for a product will also increase demand for the factors of production for that product.

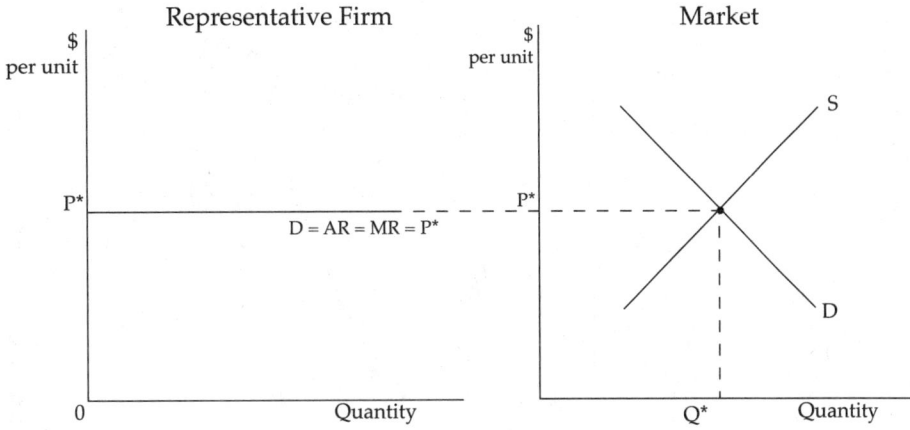

**Figure 6**

The graph in Figure 6 shows the industry demand and supply curves found by adding all the individual demand curves and firm supply curves horizontally as described earlier in this review. The market price (P*) is established by the equilibrium between the industry supply and demand curves. This price is dictated to the individual firms, which face a horizontal demand curve as illustrated for a representative firm on the left graph. The vertical axis on each graph measures the price per unit of output. The horizontal axis on the left measures the output of an individual firm and that on the right measures the total industry output.

To examine decisions about firm production levels, we must first consider revenue and the associated curves. **Total revenue** (TR) is the amount of money taken in from the sale of a good, calculated by multiplying price (P) by the quantity of output sold (Q): TR = P × Q. As you might expect, **marginal revenue** (MR) is the addition to revenue gained when one more unit is sold, and **average revenue** (AR) is the total revenue divided by quantity.

$$MR = \frac{\Delta TR}{\Delta Q}$$

$$AR = \frac{TR}{Q}$$

Because a competitive firm can sell as much as it wants at the market price, that price is both the additional amount gained from selling one more unit and the average amount gained per unit sold. That is, for a competitive firm, price equals marginal revenue and average revenue.

$$P = MR = AR$$

## Product Pricing and Outputs

The **shutdown decision** for a firm in a perfectly competitive industry hinges on whether or not the price covers average variable cost. Consider the three price ranges in Figure 7, keeping in mind that purely competitive firms maximize profits by producing the quantity that equates marginal revenue (the price per unit for a competitive firm) and marginal cost. If price is *above* minimum average total cost, the average revenue (price) exceeds the average total cost at the profit maximizing quantity.

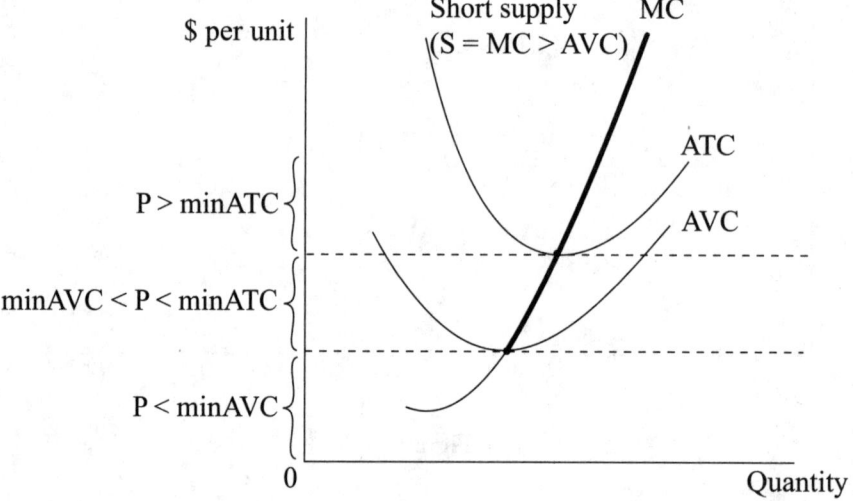

**Figure 7**

Use your pencil to represent the perfectly elastic (horizontal) demand for the purely competitive firm at a price level above ATC on Figure 7. Because P = MR = AR at the demand price for a purely competitive firm, the point at which your pencil intersects the MC curve is the point at which MR = MC, and the profit maximizing quantity is shown on the Quantity axis directly below this point. Note that AR (again represented by the height of your pencil) exceeds ATC at this quantity. The firm is making more than enough to cover all of its costs, and economic profits are positive. This is an enviable situation that will lead other firms to enter the market and compete for some of these economic profits in the long run.

For the range of prices between minimum average total cost and minimum average variable cost (minAVC < P < minATC), losses are being incurred. However, it is important to examine the two choices the firm faces in the short run.

1. The firm can shut down and not incur any variable costs, but not obtain any revenues to help pay for fixed costs.

2. The firm can remain open, cover all of its variable costs (because P > AVC), and pay off some of its fixed costs with the difference between price and average variable cost.

The lesser of these two evils is to stay open and recover some of the fixed costs in addition to paying all of the variable costs.

As an example, suppose that at the market price of $0.25 per bagel the bagel shop minimizes its losses by producing 500 bagels per day (it is at this quantity that MR = MC). The fixed cost per day for shop and equipment rental, utilities, and insurance is $50, meaning an average fixed cost of $\frac{\$50}{500}$ = $0.10. The total variable cost for labor and ingredients is $100 when 500 bagels are produced, giving an average variable cost per bagel of $\frac{\$100}{500}$ = $0.20. By producing the 500 bagels for $0.25 each, the shop covers its variable cost of $0.20 per bagel and collects an additional $0.05 per bagel—a total of $25 per day—to pay half of the fixed costs. The alternative is to shut down and lose the entire $50 per day of fixed costs. In the long run, however, when the shop owner has a choice of canceling or renewing her rental, utility, and insurance contracts, these costs will no longer be fixed, and it would be wise to shut down if losses are still being incurred.

If the price is below average variable cost, the firm is spending more on the average for each unit sold than it costs to supply the labor and ingredients for those units. It would lose less by shutting down immediately than it would by staying open. To continue the bagel shop example, suppose the market price is $0.20 per unit and that MR = $0.20 = MC at a quantity of 300. The average fixed cost for this quantity will be $\frac{\$50}{300}$ ≈ $0.17. Suppose that the total variable cost is $66, meaning an average variable cost of $0.22 per bagel. If the shop stays open and produces 300 at $0.20, it will lose the entire fixed cost, plus an average of $0.22 – $0.20 = $0.02 per unit on variable costs, for a grand total of $56. (It would lose even more by producing any other nonzero quantity.) Its best strategy is to shut down immediately and limit losses to only $50.

# CHAPTER 7 KEY TERMS

## 7.1

functions of an economic system
allocative efficiency (efficiency in output)
 P = MC
marginal cost
marginal value
efficiency in production (technical efficiency)
 P = min ATC
wage
rental rate
marginal product of labor
marginal product of capital
marginal physical product
marginal product
marginal product curve
law of diminishing marginal returns
diminishing marginal returns
average product
total product curve
fixed cost
variable cost
marginal cost
average total cost
average variable cost
average fixed cost

## 7.2

long run
short run
long-run average (total) cost (LRAC)
short-run average (total) cost (SRAC)

## 7.3

types of profit

## 7.4

profit
break-even points
profit maximization (loss minimization)
average profit

## 7.5

perfect competition
price takers
economic profits
normal profits (breaking even)
accounting profits
total revenue
marginal revenue
average revenue
shutdown decision

# CHAPTER 7 DRILL QUESTIONS
See Chapter 10 for answers and explanations.

**1** ☐ Mark for Review

The long-run average cost curve

(A) is always below the short-run average cost curve

(B) is always above the short-run average cost curve

(C) always intersects the short-run average cost curve at the minimum of short-run average cost

(D) is above the short-run average cost except at one point

(E) is below the short-run average cost except at one point

**2** ☐ Mark for Review

Marginal cost always intersects average variable cost at

(A) the profit-maximizing quantity

(B) the minimum of marginal cost

(C) the maximum of average variable cost

(D) the minimum of average variable cost

(E) the maximum of marginal cost

**3** ☐ Mark for Review

Consider a profit-maximizing firm in a perfectly competitive market with several sellers and several buyers (i.e., the firm is a "price taker" of the goods it sells and a "price taker" of the hourly wages it pays its workers). If a technological innovation made by someone in this firm were to significantly raise the firm's marginal physical product (but not that of any other firm's), then this innovation would

(A) reduce the firm's employment level, because fewer workers are now needed

(B) raise the workers' hourly wage as they now contribute more marginal revenue

(C) lead the firm to hire more workers but not to raise their wages

(D) lead the firm to hire more workers and to pay them higher wages

(E) None of the above

**4** ☐ Mark for Review

A competitive firm's demand for labor is determined directly by

(A) profits

(B) the opportunity cost of workers' time

(C) the wage and the average (physical) product of labor

(D) the marginal (physical) product of labor and the output price

(E) marginal utility and marginal cost

**5** ☐ Mark for Review

Assume a firm hires labor at a $15/hr rate and sells its products for $3 each. If the MP of the third worker is 10, which of the following statements would be the most true?

Ⓐ The firm should hire more labor so that the $MRP_L$ will increase.

Ⓑ The firm should hire more labor so that the $MRP_L$ will decrease.

Ⓒ The firm should hire less labor so that the $MRP_L$ will increase.

Ⓓ The firm should hire less labor so that the $MRP_L$ will decrease.

Ⓔ The firm should do nothing because it is currently maximizing profit.

**6** ☐ Mark for Review

Marginal revenue equals marginal cost at the point for which

Ⓐ total revenue is greater than total cost at its greatest distance

Ⓑ total revenue is equal to total cost

Ⓒ marginal product is at its highest point

Ⓓ total product is at its highest point

Ⓔ average total cost is at its minimum

**7** ☐ Mark for Review

Which variables are involved in defining the gross profit?

Ⓐ Total revenue from sales and the total cost of labor

Ⓑ Total revenue from sales and the total cost of production

Ⓒ Total benefit from sales and the total cost of labor

Ⓓ Total revenue from sales

Ⓔ Total revenue and fixed costs

**8** ☐ Mark for Review

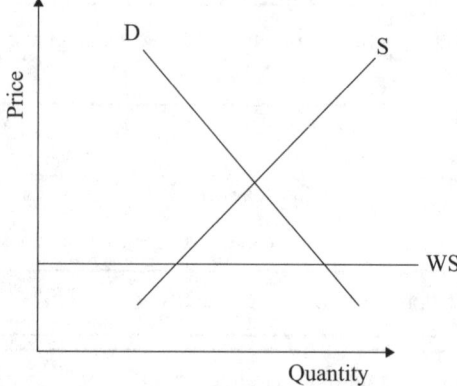

Suppose the supply and demand for cotton in the United States are represented by curves S and D, respectively in the figure above. Also assume that the world supply for cotton is so large that the United States would be a "price taker" in the world market (as represented by WS). If the United States were to open its cotton market to free trade with the world, then

Ⓐ the domestic price of cotton would rise, and the United States would export cotton

Ⓑ the domestic price of cotton would fall, and the United States would export cotton

Ⓒ the domestic price of cotton would rise, and the United States would import cotton

Ⓓ the domestic price of cotton would fall, and the United States would import cotton

Ⓔ there would be no change in the price of cotton in the United States

# Chapter 7 Summary

## 7.1 The Production Function

o An economy reaches **allocative efficiency**, or **efficiency in output**, when the **marginal cost** (the cost of producing one more unit) equals the **marginal value** (the value of one more unit).

   • Allocative efficiency is reached when **P = MC**.

o An economy reaches **efficiency in production**, or **technical efficiency**, when factors of supply are used to maximize production.

   • The cost-minimizing production condition requires that the **wage** (w) divided by the **rental rate** (r) equal the **marginal product of labor** ($MP_L$) divided by the **marginal product of capital** ($MP_K$), the additional output produced by one more unit of capital.

   • Efficiency in production is calculated by the following formula: $\dfrac{MP_K}{r} = \dfrac{MP_L}{w}$

o **Marginal product** is the additional output produced per period when one more unit of an input is added, holding the quantities of other inputs constant.

o Using $\Delta$ to represent change, TP to represent total product, and L to represent the number of units of labor hired per hour, the marginal product of labor is calculated as follows:

$$MP_L = \frac{\Delta TP}{\Delta L}$$

o The **law of diminishing marginal returns** states that as the amount of one input is increased, holding the amounts of all other inputs constant, the incremental gains in output ("marginal returns") will eventually decrease.

o **Average product** is calculated as follows:

$$AP = \frac{\text{Total Product}}{\text{Quantity of Input}}$$

o The **total product curve** shows the relationship between the total amount of output produced and the number of units of an input used, holding the amounts of other inputs constant.

- ○ **Fixed costs** do not change when more output is produced; **variable costs** are those that do change as more output is produced.

- ○ **Total Costs** (TC) = Total Fixed Costs (TFC) + Total Variable Costs (TVC)

- ○ The **marginal cost** is the amount by which costs increase when one more unit of output is produced.

## 7.2   Short- and Long-Run Production Costs

- ○ The **short run** is a time frame of analysis in which at least one factor of production is held constant, and firms can neither enter nor exit the market; in the **long-run** view, all factors of production are variable and there are no fixed costs.

## 7.3 & 7.4   Types of Profit and Profit Maximization

- ○ **Profit** is the difference between total revenue and total cost.

## 7.5   Perfect Competition

- ○ Perfect competition is characterized by
  - many sellers
  - standardized products
  - firms that are **price takers:** they accept the market price
  - firms that can enter and exit the market freely
  - buyers have complete and perfect information about the product

- ○ **Economic profits** are total revenues minus total costs (as opposed to **accounting profits**).

- ○ Firm production levels are related to **total revenue**, the amount of money taken in from the sale of a good; **marginal revenue**, the addition to revenue gained when one more unit is sold; and **average revenue**, total revenue divided by quantity.

$$MR = \frac{\Delta TR}{\Delta Q} \qquad\qquad AR = \frac{TR}{Q}$$

# Chapter 8
# Micro Unit 4:
# Imperfect
# Competition

## 8.1 MONOPOLY

Table 1 summarizes the characteristics of the major market structures.

| | Perfect Competition | Monopolistic Competition | Oligopoly | Monopoly |
|---|---|---|---|---|
| **Firms** | very many | many | few | one |
| **Barriers** | none | low | high | prohibitive |
| **Market Power** | none | some | substantial | complete |
| **Product** | homogenous | differentiated | homogenous or differentiated | unique |
| **Long-Run Economic Profit** | zero | zero | positive or zero | positive or zero |

**Table 1**

# Monopoly

A **monopoly** is the sole provider of a unique product. Local monopolies are common. For example, many towns have only one movie theater or supermarket. Utility companies often have a regional monopoly. At the national and international level, absolute monopolies are rare, although individual companies often control large shares of markets, as does De Beers with diamonds and Microsoft with operating systems. Barriers to the entry of competitors allow successful monopoly firms to sustain economic profits even in the long run. These barriers include:

- patents (for example, on new drugs)

- control of resources (for example, diamond mines or the mind of Bill Gates)

- economies of scale and other cost advantages (for example, small towns could not support a second movie theater)

- exclusive licenses (for example, intellectual property rights granted by the patent office to an inventor for their invention)

- network externalities (for example, social media networks are more valuable as more people join one specific site and old sites die off)

The demand curve for a monopoly is the entire downward-sloping market demand curve. Unless the monopoly can price discriminate by charging different prices to different customers (as discussed further below), a lower price must be charged for all units to sell more. This means that the additional revenue from selling one more unit of output, the **marginal revenue**, is not simply the price as it is for a perfectly competitive firm that can sell as much as it wants at the market price. Rather, the marginal revenue for a firm facing a downward-sloping demand curve is the price minus the decrease in revenues resulting from the lower prices on all the units previously sold at a higher price. For example, suppose that Monopoly Ale Company sells 10 bottles a day for $1.00 per bottle and that in order to increase sales to 11 bottles per day, it must decrease its price to $0.95 per bottle. The marginal revenue from the 11th bottle sold is the $0.95 price, minus the decrease in revenue from the 10 bottles previously sold for $1.00: $0.95 − (10 × $0.05) = $0.45. Another way to find the marginal revenue from the 11th bottle is to subtract the total revenue from selling 10 bottles at $1.00 each from the total revenue from selling 11 bottles at $0.95 each: $10.45 − $10.00 = $0.45. Similarly, any firm that charges every customer the same price and faces a downward-sloping demand curve will earn a marginal revenue that is below its price.

A typical monopoly graph appears in Figure 1.

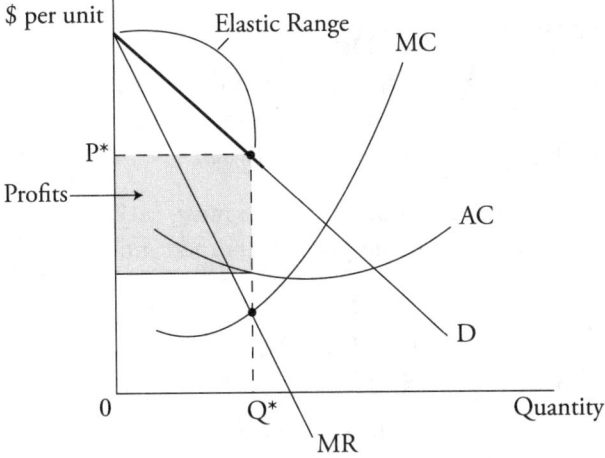

**Figure 1: The Monopoly Graph**

As a rule, if the downward-sloping demand curve is a straight line, the marginal revenue curve is a straight line with twice the slope of the demand curve and located halfway between the demand curve and the vertical axis. The relationship between elasticity and revenue provides a useful way of determining the elasticity of demand at various points along the demand curve. The elasticity of demand is 1 at the quantity for which marginal revenue equals 0, demand is elastic (greater than 1 in absolute value) at quantities for which marginal revenue is positive, and demand is inelastic (less than 1 in absolute value) at quantities for which marginal revenue is negative. Like a competitive firm, the monopoly maximizes profits by producing the quantity that equates marginal cost and marginal revenue. Because marginal cost is positive, it must equal marginal revenue when marginal revenue is positive, meaning that demand is elastic. Thus, when maximizing profits, a monopoly always operates on the elastic portion of its demand curve. We repeat:

> When maximizing profits, a monopoly always operates on the elastic portion of its demand curve.

Having found the profit-maximizing quantity at which MR = MC, the monopolist will go straight up from that quantity to the demand curve, and then over to the price axis to determine the most that consumers will pay for that quantity. It is a common misconception that monopolies can charge whatever price they want and remain in business. Of course, they would love to be able to charge an infinite amount, but nobody would buy their product if the price level were higher than the demand curve. In order to sell Q* in Figure 1, the monopoly can't charge more than P*. As with a competitive firm, profits are represented by the area of a box from average cost to the demand curve (above Q*) in height and from 0 to Q* in width. If average cost is above price at the quantity for which marginal revenue equals marginal cost, the firm experiences losses rather than profits.

## 8.2 PRICE DISCRIMINATION

Some businesses are able to charge different customers different prices that do not reflect differences in production costs. Airlines and car dealers are good examples. This practice is called **price discrimination**. There are three general requirements for price discrimination.

1. The firm must have market power. That is, it must face a downward-sloping demand curve. Perfectly competitive firms are price takers and cannot price discriminate.

2. Buyers with differing demand elasticities must be separable. This is the case for consumers of different ages, from different locations, and so on.

3. The firm must be able to prevent the resale of its goods so that those paying the lower price cannot resell their goods to those who should pay the higher price.

The ideal for the firm is to charge every customer the most they will pay, thus capturing their consumer surplus and avoiding the need to lower prices on more than one unit in order to sell one more. This practice is called **perfect price discrimination**, and it results in a marginal revenue curve that coincides with the demand curve.

> **Remember This!**
>
> You can remember the three general requirements for price discrimination with the following acrostic mnemonic:
>
> **M**any–Market power
>
> **S**neaky–Separable buyers
>
> **P**rices–Prevent resale
>
> If it helps, know that MSP also refers to the Manufacturer's Sales Price, which reflects the differing cost charged by a manufacturer to wholesalers, retailers, and direct consumers.

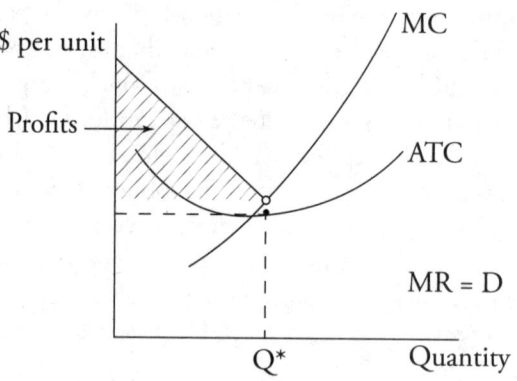

**Figure 2: Perfect Price Discrimination**

As illustrated in Figure 2, because marginal revenue equals demand, a perfectly discriminating monopolist will maximize profits by producing the quantity that equates marginal cost and demand. This results in the allocatively efficient output level at which P = MC. The downside for consumers is that the monopoly receives among its profits everything that consumers would have received as consumer surplus if the market were perfectly competitive.

Another possibility is that the firm can charge different prices to different groups, as airlines do for business and leisure travelers by charging more for those not staying over a Saturday night. Figure 3 illustrates the case of a firm selling to two separate markets with differing demand elasticities.

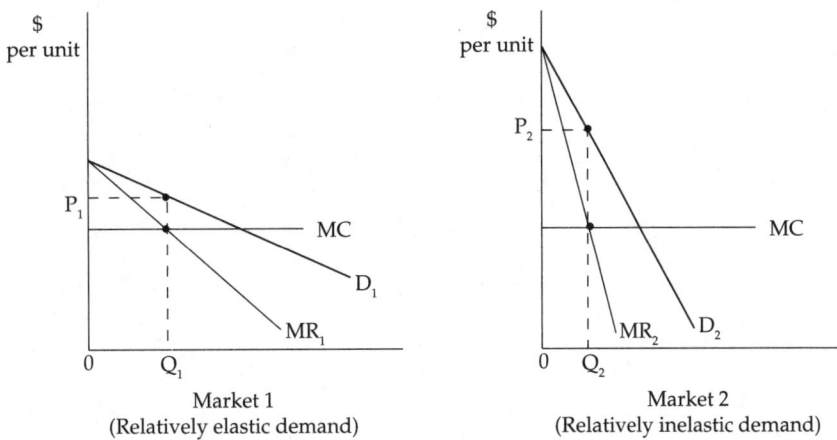

Market 1
(Relatively elastic demand)

Market 2
(Relatively inelastic demand)

**Figure 3: Price Discrimination**

For simplicity, the marginal cost is assumed to be constant. In each market, the firm equates marginal revenue and marginal cost to find its profit-maximizing quantity and then goes up to the demand curve to find the most it can charge for that quantity. As one would expect, the market segment on the right with the relatively inelastic demand (meaning that it is less sensitive to price increases) pays a higher price than the segment with the relatively elastic demand.

# 8.3 MONOPOLISTIC COMPETITION

A **monopolistically competitive** firm faces more competition than an oligopoly or monopoly but maintains some market power due to product differentiation. Examples include restaurants, gas stations, radio stations, and clothing stores. Like any type of firm, monopolistically competitive firms can enjoy economic profits in the short run. As with perfectly competitive firms, due to low barriers to entry, new firms will enter in the long run until economic profits are reduced to zero.

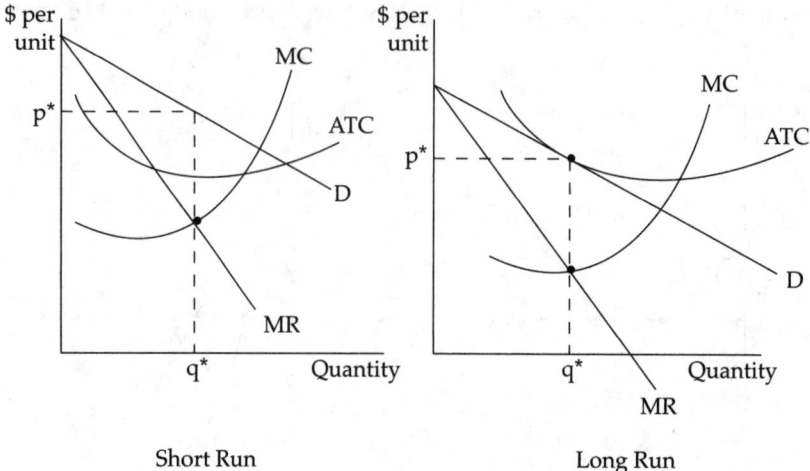

**Figure 4: Monopolistic Competition**

The left side of Figure 4 illustrates a monopolistically competitive firm making short-run profits. As new firms enter seeking a share of the profits, they take customers away from existing firms, thus shifting the existing firms' demand curves to the left. This process continues until every firm earns zero economic profits and their graphs resemble the right side of Figure 4.

# Bilateral Monopoly

A monopoly exists when there is only one seller and a monopsony exists when there is only one buyer. A situation in which there is just one seller and one buyer in the same market is called a **bilateral monopoly**. Because a union acts as a single seller of labor, and there are many industries dominated by a small number of employers that hire labor, situations resembling bilateral monopolies are not uncommon. Unlike the simple monopoly and monopsony situations, theory cannot predict the final wage in a bilateral monopoly. This will depend on the relative bargaining skills and strengths of the union and employer involved.

## 8.4   OLIGOPOLY AND GAME THEORY

An **oligopoly** is an industry with a small number of firms selling a standardized or differentiated product. Barriers to entry are high, and **market power** (the ability of an individual firm to influence price) is substantial. Examples include the airline, automobile, cereal, and soft drink industries. Unlike perfectly competitive firms that are so small that they have no significant effect on one another and unlike monopolies that face an entire market, oligopolistic firms must consider the reactions of their rivals to marketing decisions. The mutual interdependence among oligopolistic firms complicates decisions regarding price, quantity, advertising, and product offerings. Nonetheless, economists have developed tools that address the uncertainties of strategic behavior, as you will see in the section on game theory below.

Don't let the various types of market structures intimidate you. In each type of market that doesn't involve price discrimination, firms follow these steps to maximize profits.

1. Locate where marginal revenue equals marginal cost.

2. Draw a line straight down to the quantity axis to determine the optimal quantity to produce, $q^*$.

3. Draw a line straight up from that quantity to the firm demand curve to determine the highest price that can be charged for that quantity, $p^*$.

4. If that price is below average variable cost, they shut down. Otherwise they produce $q^*$ and sell it for $p^*$.

5. $p^*$ – average total cost = profit (if positive) or loss (if negative) per unit sold. The total profit or loss is $(p^* - ATC) \times q^*$.

Practice that process on graphs for each type of firm and you'll get the hang of it.

## Game Theory

When studying single-firm behavior, perfect competition, and monopoly, graphs serve to illustrate relevant economic theory. In oligopoly, firms must engage in strategic decision-making. **Strategic decision-making** occurs anytime one individual must make a choice, but the consequences of that choice depend on factors unknown to the decision maker. In other words, one firm's profits are affected by the unpredictable choices of other firms. For example, if Sally's Sportswear is across the street from Samantha's Sportswear, Sally needs to consider her factors of production, consumer demand, and the prices at Samantha's Sportswear when trying to maximize her profits. Sally cannot necessarily predict when Samantha will put her sportswear on sale, so Sally needs to make strategic decisions about when to put her sportswear on sale to maximize profits. Because oligopoly forces firms into strategic decision-making, economists use game theory to illustrate theoretical relationships therein.

**Game theory** considers the strategic decisions of "players" (including interdependent oligopolistic firms and consumers) in anticipation of their rivals' reactions. Figure 5 illustrates what is called a **payoff matrix** for a simple game between car dealerships.

Seda

| | High | Low |
|---|---|---|
| **High** | B: 400<br>S: 300 | B: −800<br>S: 500 |
| **Low** | B: 600<br>S: −800 | B: −500<br>S: −500 |

Bob (on left side, rows)

**Figure 5**

The players, Bob and Seda, each must decide whether to follow a strategy of high prices or low prices. Suppose that each must submit an advertisement to the newspaper a week in advance for the upcoming Labor Day sales. They must commit to a strategy before knowing the other side's strategy. The profits for Bob and Seda under each possible set of strategies appear in the boxes corresponding to the sets of strategies. Bob's profits are listed first, followed by Seda's. For example, if Bob sets his prices high and Seda sets her prices low, Seda will attract the lion's share of the customers; Bob will lose $800 and Seda will gain $500. If they both set high prices, Bob will make $400 and Seda will make $300.

To analyze the likely outcome, isolate one strategy and one player at a time and circle the best choice for the other player. The order does not matter; let's start with Seda choosing the high price strategy. Looking at the payoffs in the left column, which represents Seda going high, we see that Bob will make $400 going high and $600 going low, so Bob would prefer to go low in that situation (Figure 6).

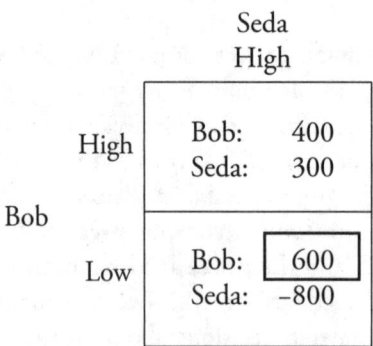

**Figure 6**

If Seda goes low, Bob will lose $800 going high and $500 going low, so he prefers to go low (Figure 7).

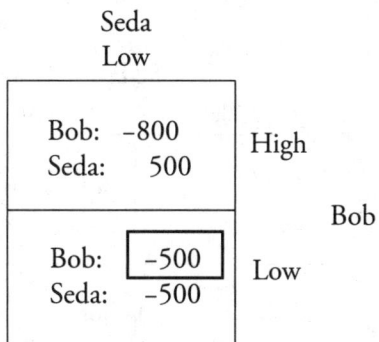

**Figure 7**

Now consider Seda's outlook depending on Bob's strategy. If Bob goes high, Seda will make $300 going high and $500 going low, so she prefers to go low (Figure 8).

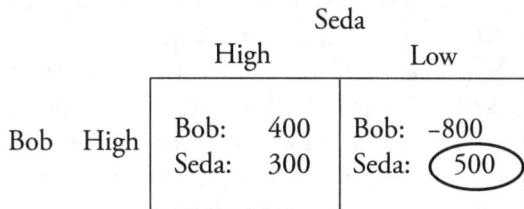

**Figure 8**

If Bob goes low, Seda will lose $800 going high and $500 going low, so she prefers to go low (Figure 9).

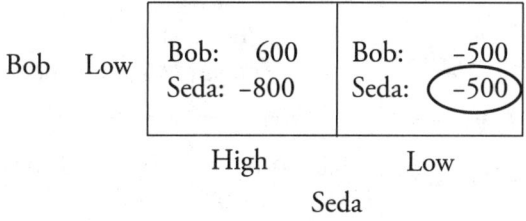

**Figure 9**

As you can see in Figure 10, because both of Bob's boxes are in the "low" row, we can conclude that Bob has a **dominant strategy** of going low, meaning that he prefers to go low regardless of what Seda does. Seda also has a dominant strategy of going low, indicated by the two circles in her "low" column.

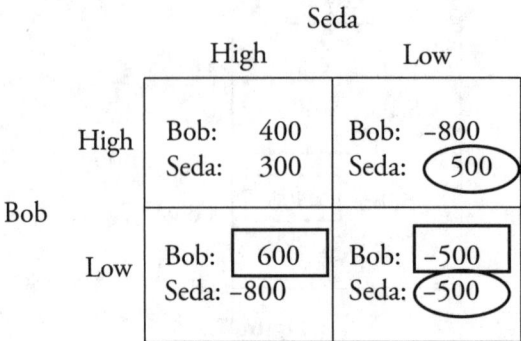

**Figure 10**

It is generally assumed that when each player has a dominant strategy, those strategies will be followed, and the resulting collection of actions (Bob low, Seda low) is called a **dominant strategy equilibrium**. A **Nash equilibrium** occurs whenever two circles appear in the same square. When this happens, neither party has an incentive to deviate from their strategy given the strategy of the other side. When a player's outcomes are the same regardless of which course of action they take, they are said to be indifferent. Every dominant strategy equilibrium is a Nash equilibrium, but not every Nash equilibrium is a dominant strategy equilibrium.

Take a look at the game in Figure 11.

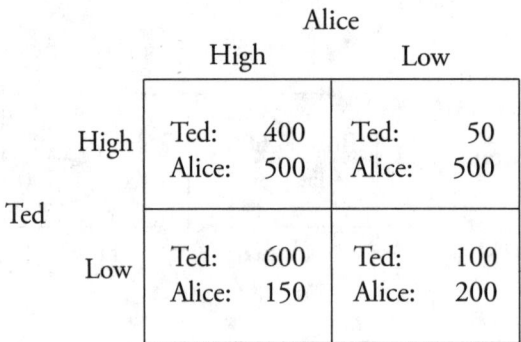

**Figure 11**

As you can see in Figure 12, this is an example of a game that has a Nash equilibrium that is not a dominant strategy equilibrium (Alice does not have a dominant strategy—she prefers high when Ted is high and low when Ted is low).

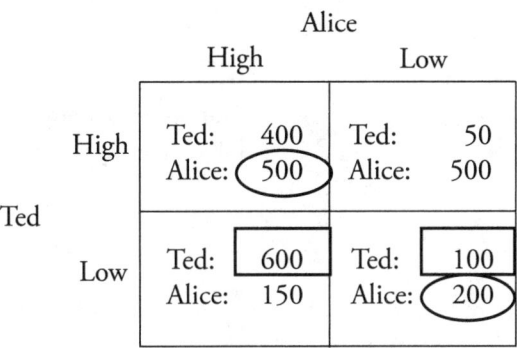

**Figure 12**

The irony of the first game is that both sides would be better off if they switched to the alternative strategy.

The classic version of this game is played by two people accused of collaborating on a crime. In separate rooms, they must choose to confess or deny, and as illustrated in Figure 13, the "payoffs," the length of their prison terms, might be such that they both confess even though they would be better off if they both denied committing the crime.

X

|  | Confess | Deny |
|---|---|---|
| **Confess** | X: 5<br>Y: 5 | X: 1<br>Y: 10 |
| **Deny** | X: 10<br>Y: 1 | X: 2<br>Y: 2 |

Y (labeled on left side)

**Figure 13**

This type of game is called a **prisoner's dilemma**. Prisoner's dilemmas help to explain arms races (purchasing arms is a dominant strategy even though both sides are better with peace), the failure of cartels (cheating on the cartel is a dominant strategy), and excessive spending on advertising expenditures, among other interesting applications in economics and the social sciences.

# CHAPTER 8 KEY TERMS

**8.1**

monopoly
marginal revenue

**8.2**

price discrimination
perfect price discrimination

**8.3**

monopolistic competition
bilateral monopoly

**8.4**

oligopoly
market power
strategic decision-making
game theory
payoff matrix
dominant strategy
dominant strategy equilibrium
Nash equilibrium
prisoner's dilemma

# CHAPTER 8 DRILL QUESTIONS

See Chapter 10 for answers and explanations.

**1** ☐ Mark for Review

Company A

| | | Expand | Don't Expand |
|---|---|---|---|
| **Company B** | Expand | 200 · 300 | 100 · 800 |
| | Don't Expand | 800 · 100 | 200 · 200 |

Company A and Company B are competing firms that are deciding whether or not to expand their operations. The payoff matrix provided shows the profit to be earned (expressed in thousands) from any decision that is made. Based on the data provided

(A) Company A has a dominant strategy and Company B does not

(B) Company B has a dominant strategy and Company A does not

(C) neither company has a dominant strategy and a Nash equilibrium exists

(D) both companies have a dominant strategy and a Nash equilibrium exists

(E) Company A and Company B should expand their operations

**2** ☐ Mark for Review

A monopoly with a straight, downward-sloping demand curve has a marginal revenue curve that is

(A) upward sloping

(B) halfway between the demand curve and the vertical axis

(C) initially downward sloping and then upward sloping

(D) parallel to the demand curve

(E) parallel to the vertical axis

**3** ☐ Mark for Review

In an oligopoly market, firms

(A) CANNOT earn economic profits

(B) are interdependent

(C) are not subject to antitrust legislation

(D) are large in number

(E) have no market power

**4**  Mark for Review

Relative to a competitive product market with the same costs, a monopoly can be expected to involve

(A)  more deadweight loss

(B)  lower prices

(C)  higher production levels

(D)  more firms

(E)  higher-quality products

**5**  Mark for Review

### Company A

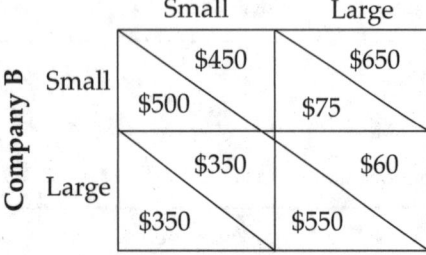

Company A and Company B above operate in a non-collusive oligopolistic market. Each needs to decide whether to have a large or small advertising strategy. According to the data, the dominant strategies for Company A and Company B would be

(A)  Company A small, Company B small

(B)  Company A small, Company B large

(C)  Company A large, Company B small

(D)  Company A large, Company B large

(E)  There is no dominant strategy for A or B.

**6**  Mark for Review

A monopoly is less efficient than a perfect competitor because

(A)  a monopoly produces more output and sells for a higher price

(B)  a monopoly produces less output and sells for a higher price

(C)  a monopoly can make profit in the short run but not in the long run

(D)  a perfect competitor breaks even in the short run and the monopoly does not

(E)  a monopoly is allocatively efficient, whereas the perfect competitor is productively efficient

**7**  Mark for Review

A price discriminating monopoly differs from a non-discriminating monopoly because a discriminating monopoly

(A)  has a demand curve that is more elastic than a non-discriminating monopoly

(B)  earns less revenue than a non-discriminating monopoly

(C)  earns more revenue than a non-discriminating monopoly

(D)  will produce less than a non-discriminating monopoly

(E)  has a marginal revenue curve that is less than a non-discriminating monopoly

**8**  📖 Mark for Review

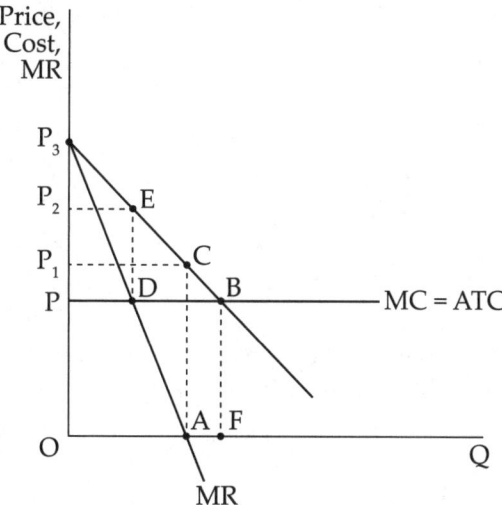

For this monopolist, profit is the area represented by

- Ⓐ $P_1$OAC
- Ⓑ triangle $P_3$PD
- Ⓒ triangle DBE
- Ⓓ POFB
- Ⓔ PDEP$_2$

**9**  📖 Mark for Review

A bilateral monopoly exists when

- Ⓐ a monopsony buys from a monopoly
- Ⓑ a monopoly sells to two different types of consumers
- Ⓒ a monopoly buys from a monopsony
- Ⓓ a monopolist sells two different types of goods
- Ⓔ a monopoly sells at two different prices

# Chapter 8 Summary

## 8.1 Monopoly

o   A **monopoly** is the sole provider of a unique good.

## 8.2 Price Discrimination

o   **Price discrimination** occurs when a seller can provide the same good to different buyers at different prices; **perfect price discrimination** occurs when a seller can charge each buyer the most they are willing to pay.

## 8.3 Monopolistic Competition

o   A **bilateral monopoly** occurs when there is only one buyer and one seller in the market.

## 8.4 Oligopoly and Game Theory

o   An **oligopoly** is an industry in which a few firms sell a standardized or differentiated product.

o   **Market power** is the ability of an individual firm to influence price.

o   **Strategic decision-making** occurs anytime one individual must make a choice, but the consequences of that choice depend on factors unknown to the decision maker.

o   **Game theory** considers strategic decisions individuals in a game (or in a marketplace) will make in anticipation of their rivals' actions.

o   The **prisoner's dilemma** identifies a situation in which distrust leads two individual actors to choose a less-than-optimal result.

# Chapter 9
# Units 5 and 6: Factor Markets, Market Failure, and the Role of Government

## 9.1 FACTOR MARKETS

## Deriving Demand for Factors of Production

The demand for factors of production such as land, labor, and capital is derived from the demand for the products they produce. For example, if the demand for ice cream increases, the demand for ice cream ingredients will also increase.

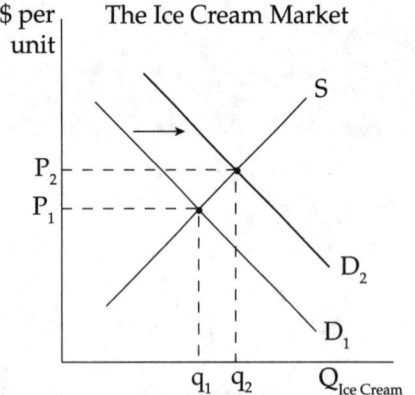
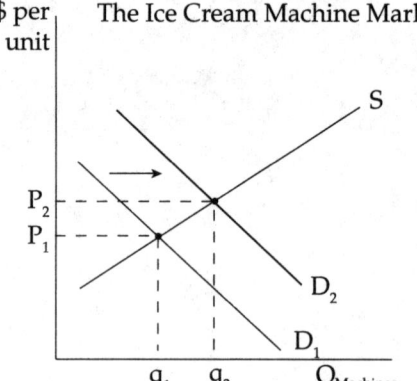

**Figure 1**

If the demand for ice cream increases as illustrated on the left side of Figure 1, the price of ice cream—the value of the output of ice cream machines—will increase. Thus, the demand for such machines (a form of capital) will increase as illustrated on the right side of Figure 1.

The most that firms would be willing to pay for additional factors of production is determined by the value of each factor's contribution to the production process. If a fourth bagel baker in a price-taking bagel shop would increase bagel production by 10 bagels per hour and bagels sell for $0.50 each, the most the bagel shop would pay for another baker is $10 \times \$0.50 = \$5.00$ per hour. In the language of economics, the marginal product of labor here is 10, the marginal revenue is $0.50, and the **marginal revenue product of labor** ($MRP_L$) is $5.00. More generally,

$$MRP_L = MP_L \times P_{output}$$

The fourth baker will be hired if the wage is less than $5.00 per hour. (If the wage is exactly $5.00 per hour, the shop is indifferent toward hiring the worker or not.)

Firms with market power face downward-sloping demand curves and are not price takers. In order to sell the additional output produced by additional units of an input, firms with downward-sloping demand curves must lower their prices on all units sold (assuming they cannot price-discriminate). Thus, the marginal revenue from each additional unit of output is not the price, but the price minus the losses on units previously sold at a higher price. The most such a firm would be willing to pay for another worker in the short run is again the $MRP_L$.

The "L" for labor in the $MRP_L$ equation could be replaced with any other factor of production to establish the marginal revenue product formula for that factor. The $MRP_L$ curve represents the demand curve for either type of firm when only one factor of production is variable. In the long run, when capital (for example) is variable in addition to labor, changes in the amounts of capital among other factors of production can affect the $MP_L$ and thus the $MRP_L$ and result in a labor demand curve that differs from the $MRP_L$ curve.

The $MRP_L$ curve slopes downward due to diminishing marginal returns, as explained above.

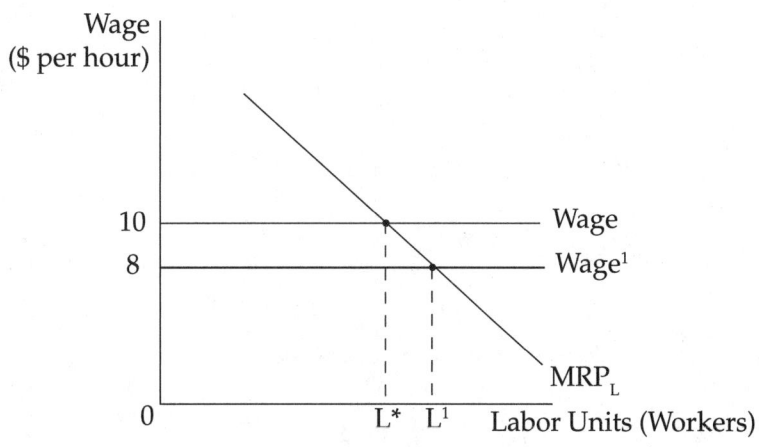

**Figure 2**

If the wage is $10 per hour as illustrated in Figure 2, the optimal quantity of labor to hire (L*) is found on the labor axis directly below the intersection, between the wage line and the $MRP_L$ line. If fewer than L* workers are hired, there is an opportunity to hire more workers and pay them less than the value of their contribution to revenues. If more than L* workers are hired, those in excess of L* are paid more than the value of their contribution to revenues and the firm would increase profits or decrease losses by cutting labor back to L*.

If the wage fell to $8, it would then be beneficial to hire those workers with marginal revenue products between $8 and $10; a total of $L^1$ workers should be hired. If $MRP_L$ increased, as it would if the price of output increased or the marginal product of workers increased (for example, due to better training or technology), the demand for labor would shift to the right and more workers would be hired at any given wage. Decreases in $MRP_L$ would similarly shift the labor demand to the left.

## 9.2   CHANGES IN FACTOR DEMAND AND FACTOR SUPPLY

Remember that the law of demand says that as the price of a good increases, the quantity demanded decreases, all other things being held equal. In this chapter, you will study how and why the law of demand holds true. You will also study how and why demand changes. It is important to distinguish between a **change in the quantity demanded** and a **change in demand**. A movement of the equilibrium *along* a stationary demand curve represents a change in the quantity demanded.

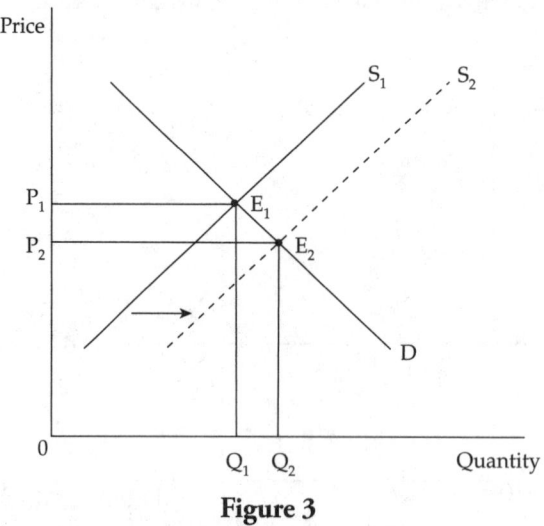

**Figure 3**

For example, when the supply increases from $S_1$ to $S_2$ in Figure 3, the equilibrium moves from $E_1$ to $E_2$, and the equilibrium price moves from $P_1$ to $P_2$. This results in a change in the quantity demanded from $Q_1$ to $Q_2$. Because the demand curve shows the relationship between quantity demanded and price, changes in price simply bring us to different points on the same demand curve, thereby causing changes in the quantity demanded. In contrast, a *shift* in the demand curve represents a change in demand. Keep in mind that the demand curve maps out the value of each additional unit of a good to consumers. A shift in demand would result from any change that affects the value of that good to consumers or the number of consumers in the market. Anything other than a lower price that induces increased consumption of a good causes a shift to the right of the demand curve as in Figure 4.

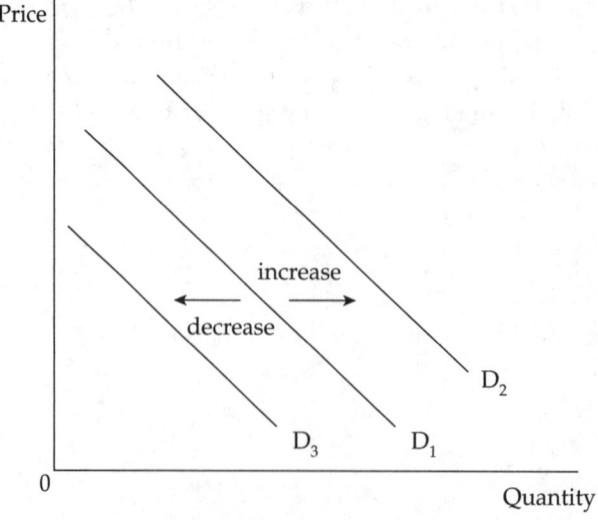

**Figure 4: Shifts in Demand**

Specifically, an increase (shift to the right) in demand can result from the following:

- **A positive change in tastes or preferences**. Such a change could result from a successful advertising campaign or a research report finding the good to have positive effects on health.

- **An increase in the price of substitute goods**. For example, if the price of Pepsi goes up, the demand for Coke will increase.

- **A decrease in the price of complements**. For example, if the price of gasoline goes down, the demand for large cars will increase.

- **An increase in income for normal goods**. By definition, a **normal good** is one that the consumer buys more of when income increases. For example, a higher income might lead to a higher demand for steak.

- **A decrease in income for inferior goods**. By definition, an **inferior good** is one that the consumer buys more of when income decreases. For example, a lower income might lead to a higher demand for hot dogs if people start substituting them for steak.

- **An increase in the number of buyers**. With more buyers, more individual demand curves are added to find the market demand curve.

- **Expectations of higher future income**. If you pass your board exam and realize you're going to make big money, you will probably start spending more now. This is called **consumption smoothing**.

- **Expectations of higher future prices**. This is a good reason to buy more now rather than later.

- **Expectations of future shortages**. For example, when a severe storm is predicted, people often stock up on canned goods and bottled water beforehand.

- **Lower taxes or higher subsidies**. Either of these changes will make more money available for consumption.

- **Regulations that promote use**. For example, the adoption of regulations that require fire alarms in every room of the house would increase the demand for fire alarms.

Of course, the opposite of each of the above changes will cause the demand curve to decrease (shift to the left). Remember, *changes in the price of a good do not change the demand for that good. They change only the quantity demanded*. This is because changes in the price of a good do not change the value of that good to us. They change only the quantity of the good that we can buy before the value of the good falls below the price.

You can remember the primary reasons for a shift in demand with the acronym TRIBE.

    **T**  –  **T**astes and preferences of consumers

    **R**  –  the prices of **R**elated goods (substitutes and complements)

    **I**  –  the **I**ncome of buyers

    **B**  –  the number of **B**uyers

    **E**  –  **E**xpectations for the future

## Concurrent Shifts in Demand and Supply

Let's explore how shifts in both supply and demand affect each other. It can be confusing to sort out in one's head but easy to determine by simply drawing the graph.

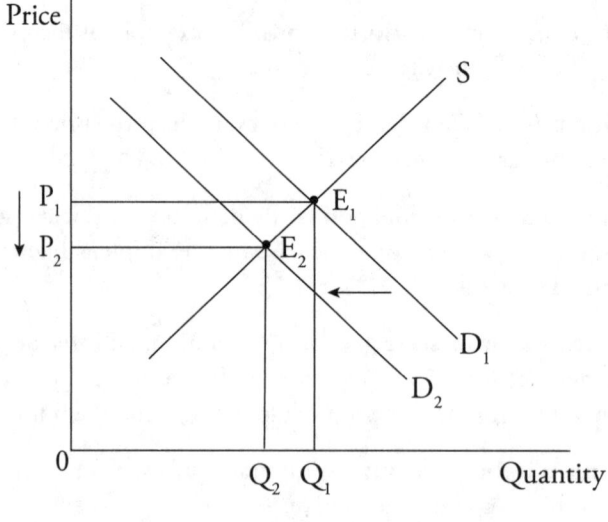

**Figure 5**

If demand decreases (for example, as the result of a decrease in income), a comparison of the old and new equilibrium prices and quantities in a quick sketch like Figure 5 will immediately indicate that both price and quantity decrease.

> It is a common mistake on AP Exams to shift both supply and demand when only one of the two should be shifted. Think carefully about whether the influence described in an exam question will affect production costs and therefore the supply curve, or consumers' willingness and ability to pay and therefore the demand curve.

It is always possible that two influences will occur at once. Suppose there is a massive beetle infestation in the farm belt and at the same time a study finds that carrots prevent heart disease. The beetles will increase the cost of producing carrots and thus decrease their supply. The study will increase consumers' willingness to pay for carrots and thus increase the demand. Figure 6 illustrates the new equilibrium.

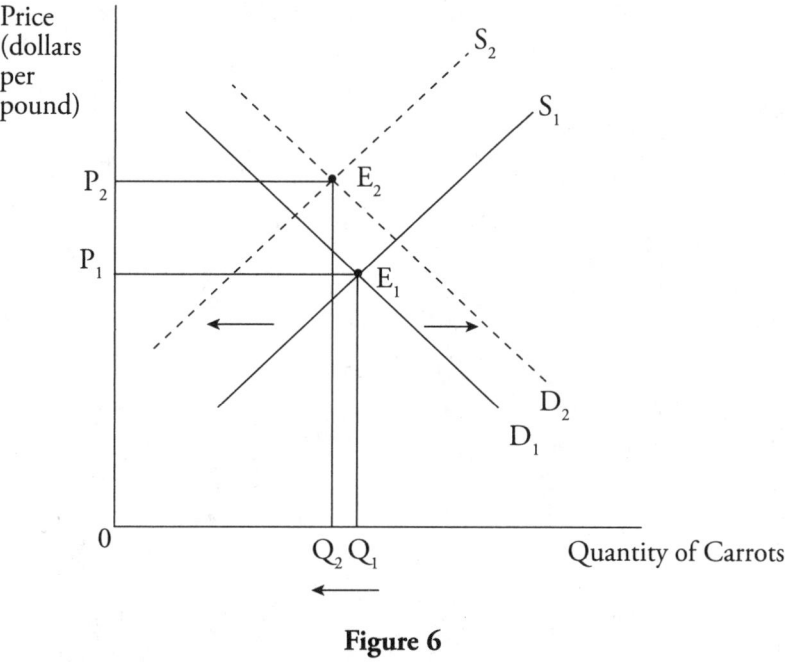

**Figure 6**

Whenever both supply and demand shift at the same time, the effect on equilibrium price OR quantity will be certain, and the effect on the other will depend on the relative size of the shifts in supply and demand. In Figure 6, it is clear that the equilibrium price increases, because both a decrease in supply and an increase in demand result in a higher price. However, because a decrease in supply decreases the equilibrium quantity and an increase in demand increases the equilibrium quantity, the net effect on quantity depends on the relative sizes of the shifts. As it is drawn here, the supply shift dominates the demand shift and there is a net decrease in quantity. Don't let supply- and demand-shifting questions intimidate you; simply draw the graph and describe the evident outcomes. It may help to clearly label the original equilibrium and the new equilibrium so that you don't get confused about the four points of intersection while you are interpreting the graph. When both supply and demand shift and you do not know the relative size of the shifts, it is appropriate to state that the change in the variable (price or quantity) that is pulled in both directions is "indeterminate" (cannot be determined).

A tip on shifting curves: It can be confusing that a decrease in supply shifts the supply curve up, while a decrease in demand shifts the demand curve down. To clear things up, remember that for both curves, **L**eft is **L**ess and **R**ight is **R**ising!

## Measuring Consumer Preference

Remember that utility is a measure of individuals' satisfaction. **Marginal utility** (MU) is the additional utility gained from consuming one more unit of a good and is often quantified in terms of the amount of money an individual would be willing to spend on that good. The principle of diminishing marginal utility suggests that as one consumes more and more of a good, the additional satisfaction gained from subsequent units (MU) decreases.

Suppose the dollar value of Austin's marginal utility from cheese slices is as indicated in Figure 7 and Table 1.

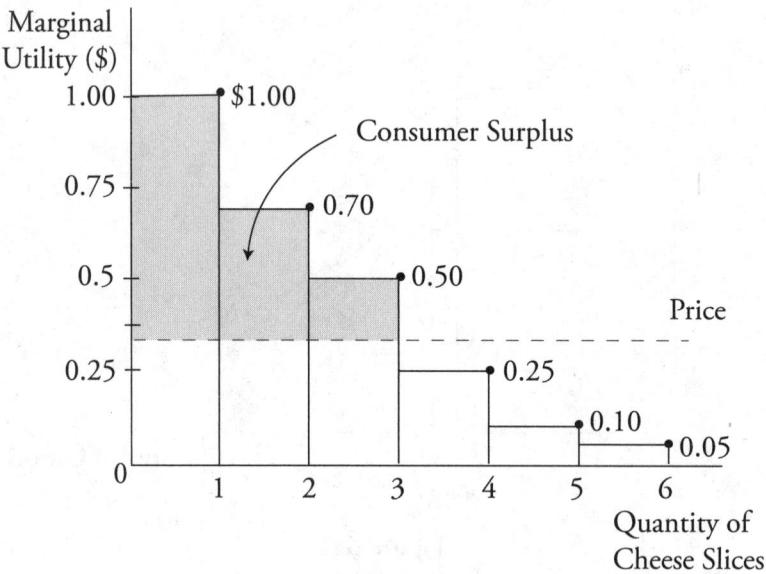

**Figure 7**

| Quantity of Cheese Slices | Marginal Utility (in dollars) | Total Utility (in dollars) |
|:---:|:---:|:---:|
| 1 | 1.00 | 1.00 |
| 2 | 0.70 | 1.70 |
| 3 | 0.50 | 2.20 |
| 4 | 0.25 | 2.45 |
| 5 | 0.10 | 2.55 |
| 6 | 0.05 | 2.60 |

**Table 1**

The first slice is worth $1.00 to him, the second is worth $0.70, and so forth. He will choose to consume until one more slice would be worth less to him than the price. If the price were $0.35, he would consume the first three, which are worth $1.00, $0.70, and $0.50 to him. He would not pay $0.35 for the fourth slice, which is worth only $0.25 to him. The points drawn on this graph outline Austin's demand curve, and tell us everything we need to know to calculate his total utility and consumer surplus (explained below).

**Total utility** is found by adding the marginal utility values gained from each of the units consumed. Because Austin consumes three slices of cheese, his total utility is $1.00 + $0.70 + $0.50 = $2.20. More generally, the relationship between marginal utility and total utility is as illustrated in Figure 8. As more and more of a typical good is consumed, the total utility received from that good increases at a decreasing rate, reaches a peak, and then decreases at an increasing rate. This is because marginal utility—the contribution to total utility from the last unit consumed—diminishes as more of the good is consumed. Total utility reaches a maximum at the quantity for which marginal utility is zero, after which point each additional unit provides a negative marginal utility and therefore detracts from total utility.

Take note of the graphical relationship between the curves representing total and marginal utility: the marginal utility at any particular quantity is the slope of the total utility curve at that quantity. Thus, when marginal utility is positive, total utility is rising with a positive slope. When marginal utility is zero, total utility is at a peak with a zero slope. When marginal utility is negative, total utility is declining with a negative slope.

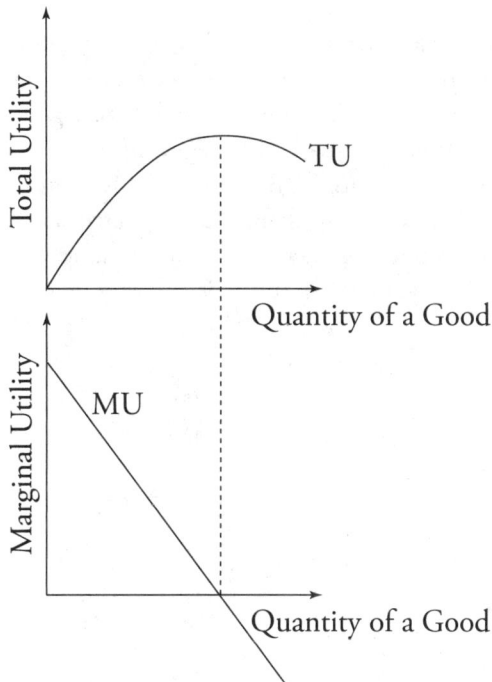

**Figure 8: Total Utility and Marginal Utility**

**Consumer surplus** is the value a buyer receives from the purchase of a good *in excess of what is paid for it*. With a price of $0.35 for the first, second, and third slices, Austin receives consumer surpluses of $1.00 − $0.35 = $0.65, $0.70 − $0.35 = $0.35, and $0.50 − $0.35 = $0.15, respectively. To be more general, consumer surplus is the area below the demand curve and above the price line up to the quantity that is consumed. **Producer surplus** is the difference between the price a seller receives for a good and the minimum price for which she would be willing to supply a quantity of the good. Producer surplus is thus the area below the price line and above the supply curve. Figure 9 illustrates consumer surplus and producer surplus in a general case.

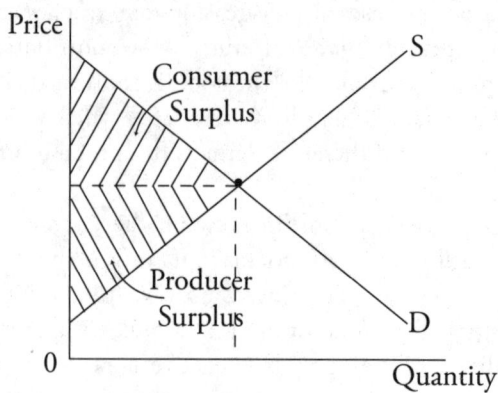

Note: The AP Exam may refer to economic surplus, generally. In this context, economic surplus equals consumer surplus plus producer surplus.

**Figure 9: Consumer and Producer Surplus**

The distinction between total and marginal utility helps to sort out a paradox that dates back to Plato. It may seem strange that we pay very little money for some goods, such as water, which are essential to life, while we pay much more money for some goods that are inessential, such as diamonds. Although the value of water is very high, this value is reflected in the total utility gained from it, not in the marginal utility. Because water is plentiful, we consume it until the marginal utility is very small. In contrast, diamonds are scarce, so although the initial units are worth less to us than the life-sustaining first units of water, supply restricts our consumption of diamonds to a point at which the marginal utility is still very high.

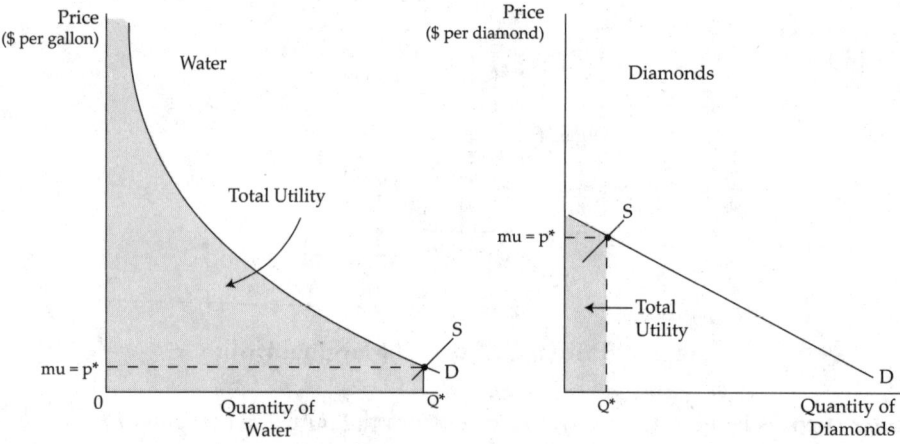

**Figure 10: The Water–Diamond Paradox**

In Figure 10, notice that the total utility from water is much larger than that for diamonds, but the marginal utility is much smaller for water than for diamonds. Thankfully, price corresponds with the marginal utility rather than the total utility.

## 9.3 PROFIT-MAXIMIZING BEHAVIOR IN PERFECTLY COMPETITIVE FACTOR MARKETS

In contrast to the allocative, distributive, and production efficiencies that are achieved when a perfectly competitive market is in long-run equilibrium, firms with market power can challenge the efficiency of the market if left unchecked. Consider a monopoly as in Figure 11.

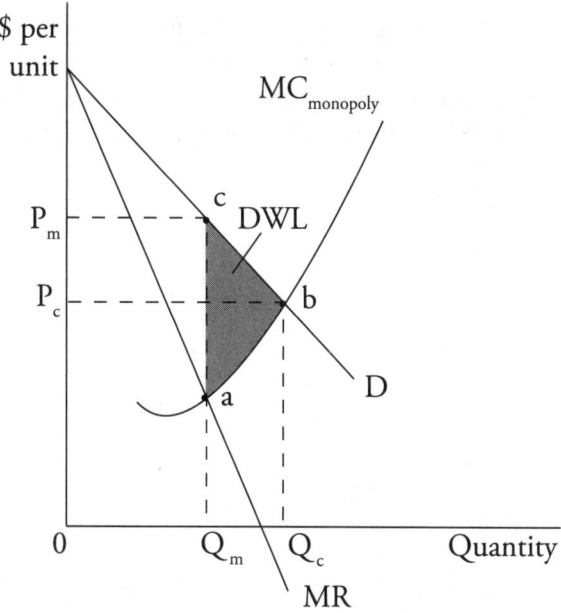

**Figure 11**

The monopoly price will be $P_m$, and the monopoly will produce $Q_m$. To simplify the comparison of monopoly and competitive outcomes, let's assume constant returns to scale, meaning that many smaller firms could produce a fraction (say, one one-thousandth) of the market's output for that same fraction of the cost. The competitive market's supply curve would be the monopoly's MC curve, and the competitive market's equilibrium would be at the intersection of MC and the demand curve. Note that at this intersection, $P_c = MC$ is the condition for allocative efficiency. The competitive price $P_c$ is below the monopoly price $P_m$, and the competitive quantity $Q_c$ is more than the monopoly quantity $Q_m$.

Along with the potential for higher prices and lower quantities in a monopoly market comes a welfare loss. In the absence of externalities (to be discussed later in this chapter), the demand curve reflects the benefits to consumers of additional units of the good, and the marginal cost curve reflects the additional cost of resources needed to provide those benefits. Thus, the area *abc* between the demand curve and the MC curve from $Q_m$ to $Q_c$ represents the deadweight loss (DWL), sometimes called "efficiency loss" (in essence, DWL is lost consumer and producer surplus), due to a monopoly market structure. The potential for monopolies to decrease quality is an added detriment of monopoly power.

Monopolies also have some positive attributes. The potential for sustainable monopoly profits can induce individuals and firms to invent new products. Some argue that the quest for monopoly profits motivates research and development expenditures that result in important drugs and technology. In other situations, competition is not an option. Industries such as power generation and rail service have such high fixed costs that it would be impossible for a particular service area to support more than one firm. Firms in these industries are called **natural monopolies**.

As illustrated in Figure 12, the high fixed costs in natural monopolies cause the average total cost curve to fall throughout the relevant range of production, and the demand curve intersects average total cost while the average total cost curve is still falling. In this case, the allocatively efficient price ($P_{SO}$), at which marginal cost equals demand, would not allow profits because $P_{SO}$ is less than average total cost at the corresponding quantity of $Q_{SO}$. However, the monopoly price of $P_M$ is also undesirable because it is considerably higher than the socially optimal price and the associated quantity of $Q_M$ is below the socially optimal quantity.

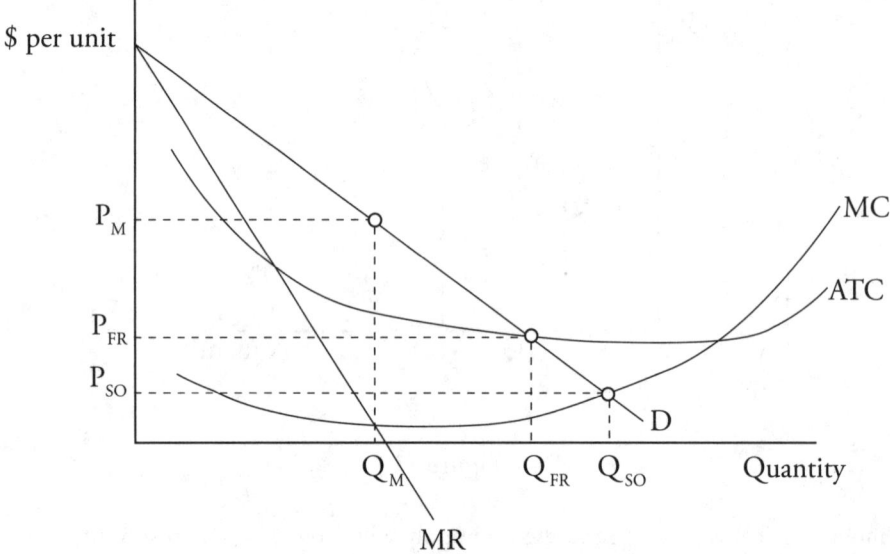

**Figure 12: Natural Monopoly**

Because competition can't temper prices in this situation, it is common for natural monopolies to be regulated. The challenge, then, is to decide on a regulated price. If a price ceiling is set at $P_{SO}$, production will satisfy the MB = MC condition for social optimality (assuming there are no externalities), but the monopoly will require financial assistance in order to survive because it will experience a loss of the difference between price and average total cost for every unit sold.

An available compromise is to set a **"fair return" price ceiling** at $P_{FR}$. This price is equal to average total cost at the corresponding quantity of $Q_{FR}$. Thus, the firm will break even. The fair return price falls between the monopoly price and the socially optimal price, providing what many regulators see as a desirable middle ground between the resource misallocation caused by higher prices and the losses caused by lower prices.

The threats of excessive prices, limited quantities, and inferior quality have led the government to foster competition in industries in which it is considered beneficial. The primary tool used to restrict market power is antitrust legislation. Congress created the Interstate Commerce Commission (ICC) in 1887 to oversee and correct abuses of market power in the railroad industry; in 1914, Congress created the Federal Trade Commission (FTC) to investigate the structure and conduct of firms engaging in interstate commerce.

A summary of landmark antitrust legislation follows:

- The **Sherman Act (1890)** declared attempts to monopolize commerce or restrain trade among the states illegal.

- The **Clayton Act (1914)** strengthened the Sherman Act by specifying that monopolistic behavior such as price discrimination, tying contracts, and unlimited mergers is illegal.

- The **Robinson-Patman Act (1936)** prohibits price discrimination except when it is based on differences in cost, difference in marketability of product, or a good faith effort to meet competition.

- The **Celler-Kefauver Act (1950)** authorized the government to ban **vertical mergers** (mergers of firms at various steps in the production process from raw materials to finished products) and **conglomerate mergers** (combinations of firms from unrelated industries) in addition to **horizontal mergers** (mergers of direct competitors).

There are several formal measures of market power. The **Herfindahl-Hirschman Index** (HHI) takes the market share of each firm in an industry as a percentage, squares each percentage, and adds them all up. $\text{HHI} = \sum_{i=1}^{m} S_i^2$. For example, if one firm holds a 100-percent market share, the HHI $= 100^2 = 10,000$. If two firms hold 30-percent market shares and one holds a 40-percent market share, the HHI $= 30^2 + 30^2 + 40^2 = 3,400$. The HHI increases as the number of firms in the industry decreases or as the firms become less uniform in size. The $n$-firm **concentration ratio** is the sum of the market shares of the largest $n$ firms in an industry, where $n$ can represent any number. For example, if the four largest firms in the cola industry hold 21-, 18-, 11-, and 6-percent market shares, the four-firm concentration ratio is the sum of these numbers, 56.

# 9.4   MONOPSONISTIC MARKETS

As in the previous section, labor will be used here as an example in the explanation of factor markets. The determination of other factor prices is analogous.

In a perfectly competitive labor market, each firm is a **wage taker**, just as firms are price takers in a perfectly competitive output market. The market demand for labor is the sum of the firm demand curves. Market demand will thus increase or decrease in response to changes in the number of firms or the $\text{MRP}_L$ in the individual firms. The market supply of labor is the sum of all of the individual labor supply curves, and thus depends on the number of workers in the market and each worker's willingness to provide labor services at various wage rates. Figure 13 illustrates labor market supply and demand curves on the right, and the horizontal labor supply confronting a competitive firm on the left.

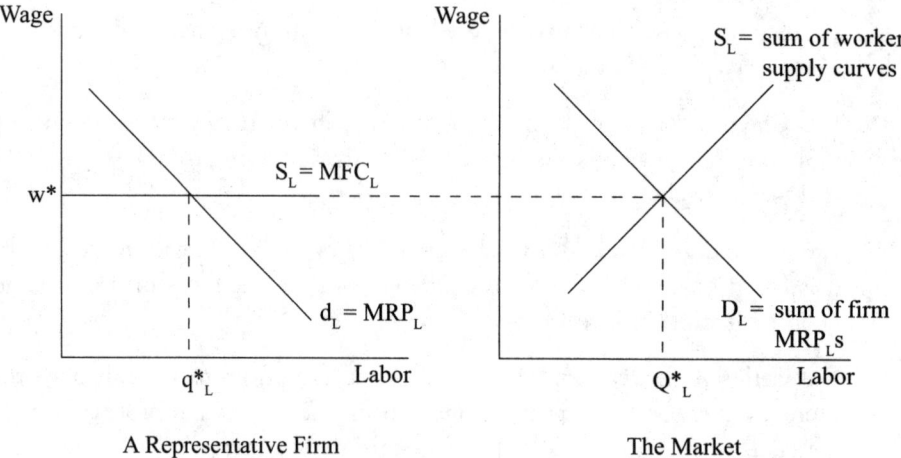

**Figure 13: A Perfectly Competitive Labor Market**

The intersection of the labor market demand and supply curves establishes the equilibrium wage. At this wage, everyone who would like to work has the opportunity to do so, meaning that there is no unemployment in this market. As described above, legislation that sets a minimum wage above the market equilibrium can act as a price floor for labor and cause unemployment. We will discuss unemployment further in the review of macroeconomic concepts.

According to Figure 14, the monopsony desires to hire $L_m$ workers and pay them $W_m$. The union will seek a wage of $W_u$, which is the marginal revenue product of the last worker hired (the MRP is what the last worker is worth to the employer, and the employer will most likely not pay workers more than what they are worth).

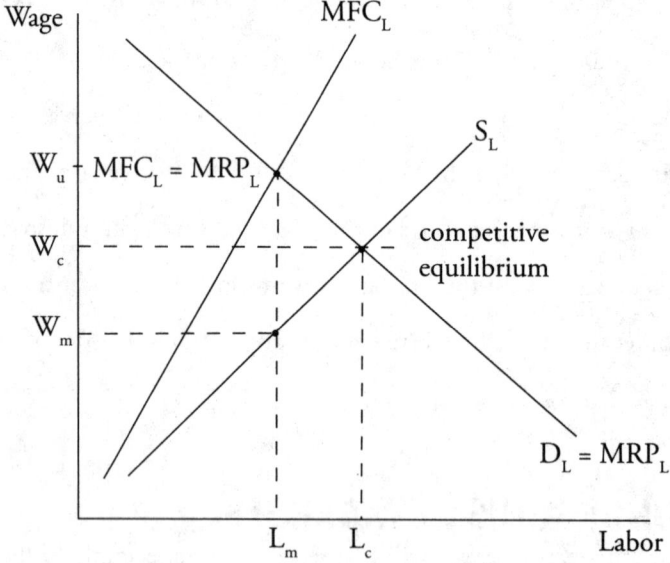

**Figure 14: Monopsony**

When one firm is the sole purchaser of labor services in a market, as a mining company might be in a small mining town, this firm is called a **monopsony**. Recall that marginal revenue is below price for a monopoly because it faces a downward-sloping market demand curve and must lower its price on *all* units sold in order to sell more. Similarly, a monopsony faces the entire upward-sloping labor supply curve as in Figure 14 and must raise wages to hire more workers. This results in a **marginal factor cost** or **MFC** (the additional cost of hiring one more worker) that is above the wage. For example, suppose a firm employing three workers for $10 per hour must pay $12 per hour to attract a fourth worker. The marginal factor cost of the fourth worker per hour is $12 *plus* the additional $2 per hour it must pay each of the first three workers to bring their wages from $10 to $12. The MFC is thus $12 + $2 + $2 + $2 = $18. Firms in a competitive labor market are wage takers, and their marginal factor cost equals the wage because they can hire all the workers they want at the same market wage.

A monopsony chooses the employment level at which $MRP_L = MFC_L$, indicated by $L_m$ in Figure 14. The lowest wage the firm can pay to attract $L_m$ workers, $W_m$, is determined by the labor supply curve directly above $L_m$. Notice that relative to the competitive labor market wage ($W_c$) and quantity of workers ($L_c$), the monopsony hires fewer workers and pays them less.

# 9.5 SOCIALLY EFFICIENT AND INEFFICIENT MARKET OUTCOMES

Fair and optimized allocation of economic resources in a society is called social efficiency. Social efficiency is subject to the following relationship:

Marginal Social Benefit (MSB) = Marginal Social Cost (MSC)

## Market Failure

**Market failure** occurs when resources are not allocated optimally. That is, allocative efficiency is not achieved. This can result from the following:

- imperfect information
- imperfect competition
- externalities
- public goods

**Imperfect information** means that buyers and/or sellers do not have full knowledge about available markets, prices, products, customers, suppliers, and so forth. For example, imperfect information occurs when buyers pay too much for a product because they do not know about a lower-priced alternative. Another example of this occurs when producers make too much of a specific product, and not enough of another because they don't understand the demand of their customers. Solutions to imperfect information include truth-in-advertising regulations, consumer information services, and market surveys by firms. As another example of available solutions, some countries require restaurants and hotels to post price lists so that potential customers can easily compare prices.

## 9.6 EXTERNALITIES

**Externalities** are costs or benefits felt beyond or "external to" those causing the effects. Inefficiencies arise as the result of externalities because those making decisions do not consider all of the repercussions of their behavior. When your neighbor decides how many dogs to own, she is likely to weigh the price of the dogs, their food, their health care, etc., against the joy she receives from owning them. On the other hand, she might not consider the costs imposed on you due to the dogs' barking and biting, and the droppings left in your yard. This is an example of a **negative externality** because the external effects of your neighbor's dog ownership are hurtful to you. The result of her failure to consider the costs she is imposing on you is that she will buy too many dogs. Negative externalities lead to overconsumption.

On the other hand, when your neighbor decides how many flowers to plant in her yard, she might plant fewer than the optimal amount for society if she does not consider the enjoyment you and others in the neighborhood get out of seeing and smelling them. When you decided whether or not to get a flu shot last winter, did you consider the benefits to others of not getting the flu from you if you were immunized? Flowers and flu shots are sources of **positive externalities,** which lead to underconsumption. It is important to note that externalities are also known as spillover effects: negative externalities are called **spillover costs** and positive externalities are called **spillover benefits.**

Figure 15 illustrates the dog ownership decision for your neighbor, whom we'll call Mary.

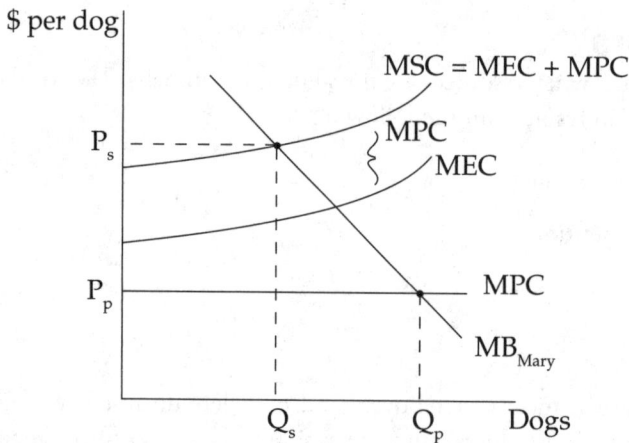

**Figure 15: Negative Externalities**

Mary's marginal benefit per dog decreases as she acquires more and more dogs, in accordance with the law of diminishing marginal utility. The **marginal private cost** (MPC) per dog (the additional cost Mary pays for each additional dog) is assumed to be constant, although the analysis is the same if it is increasing. The **marginal external cost** (MEC) per dog (the additional cost imposed on the neighbors) might increase because each additional dog not only barks, bites, and makes droppings but also helps provoke the existing dogs to cause even more ruckus. Looking only at her MB and MPC, Mary will own $Q_p$ dogs. To find the optimal quantity for society, add the MEC and the MPC to find the **marginal social cost** (MSC). The MSC intersects the MB at the socially optimal quantity of $Q_s$ dogs. This is the number of dogs Mary would own if she paid the full marginal social cost of $P_s$ for that particular quantity. As shown with Mary's dogs, when there are negative externalities associated with a good, an **over allocation of resources** will occur, meaning more goods will be produced than the market demands.

Figure 16 illustrates the flower-purchasing decision for Mary.

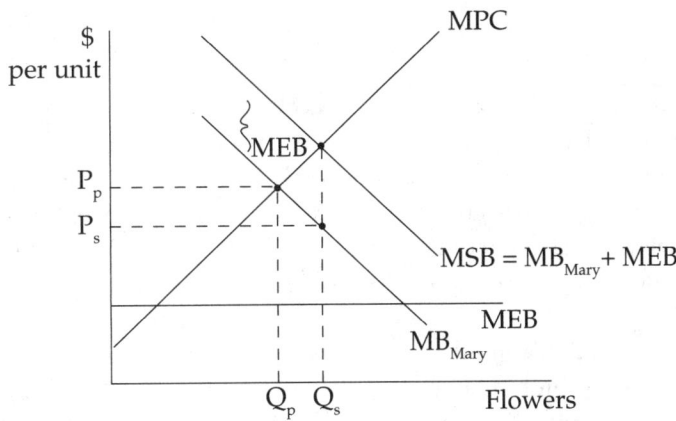

**Figure 16: Positive Externalities**

While Mary's marginal benefit decreases, her marginal private cost increases as she purchases more flowers because she must forego increasingly valuable alternative activities to plant more and more. The marginal external benefit (MEB) is assumed to be constant for simplicity. Mary will purchase $Q_p$ flowers, short of the socially optimal $Q_s$, which equates the marginal social benefit (MSB = MB + MEB) and the marginal cost. Mary would purchase $Q_s$ if the price were $P_s$ rather than $P_p$. As shown with Mary's flowers, when there is a positive externality associated with a good, an **under allocation of resources** will occur, meaning fewer flowers will be produced than the market demands.

There are several solutions to problems with externalities. Those causing negative externalities can be taxed by the amount of the MEC, causing them to feel or "internalize" the full costs of their behavior. Likewise, those causing positive externalities can be subsidized by the amount of the MEB so that their private benefit equals the marginal social benefit. This is one reason why it is a good idea to subsidize immunizations and education and tax liquor and gasoline. Ronald Coase suggested that those who are helped or hurt by positive or negative externalities might be able to pay the decision makers to produce more or less of their product. The viability of such payoffs is contingent on the clarity of each side's rights (for example, the right for a firm to pollute), and the ability of the affected parties to organize and collect the necessary funds. Alternative solutions for negative externalities include restricting the output to the socially optimal quantity ($Q_s$) or imposing a price floor at the socially optimal price ($P_s$).

Note that an individual's marginal benefit curve is synonymous with their demand curve, and the marginal cost curve (above average variable cost) is equivalent to the supply curve for a competitive firm. Don't be confused if you see presentations of the externality story that replace MB and MPC with D and S. Also note that for the purpose of finding the social optimum, it makes no difference whether the MEC is added to the MPC curve or subtracted from the MB curve. Either way, the MEC creates the same sized wedge between MB and MPC, and the resulting socially optimal quantity and price are the same. Likewise, the MEB could be subtracted from the MPC rather than being added to the private MB to yield identical results.

## 9.7   PUBLIC AND PRIVATE GOODS

**Public goods** are those that many individuals benefit from at the same time. They are characterized as being *nonrival in consumption and nonexcludable*. A **nonrival good** is one for which the consumption of that good does not affect its consumption by others. For example, Donna's use of a radio signal does not detract in any way from Dina's use of the same radio signal. **Rival goods** like food and parking spaces cannot be consumed by multiple users simultaneously.

Once available, **nonexcludable goods** cannot be held back from those who desire access. For example, once a country is protected by a military system, it is impossible to prevent particular individuals within the country from benefiting from that defense. Other examples of public goods include police protection, disease control, clean air, and the preservation of animal species.

Because multiple users benefit from a public good at the same time, the demand curve for society that reflects the marginal benefit from each additional unit of the good is found by adding each individual's demand curve vertically. Figure 17 illustrates a market for police protection that consists of only two individuals, Vernon and Linda.

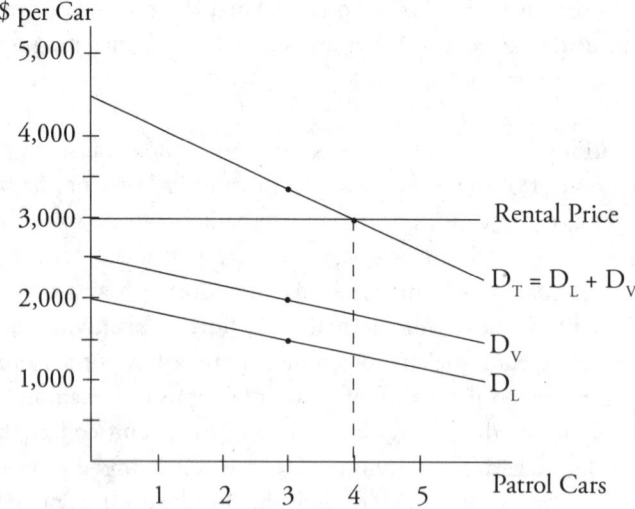

**Figure 17: A Public Good**

Vernon's annual benefits from the protection of various numbers of police cars are represented by his demand curve, $D_V$, and Linda's benefits from the same police cars are represented by $D_L$. The total annual benefit from the third patrol car, for example, is Vernon's $2,000 benefit plus Linda's $1,500 benefit, or $3,500. Their town should purchase police cars until the total social demand, $D_T$, equals the annual price of renting a police car—$3,000—which occurs with the rental of four police cars.

The problem that arises with public goods is that consumers know that they can benefit from the provision of these goods whether or not they pay for them. Even if each household gains $1,000 per year worth of benefits from military protection, a door-to-door collection to pay for the military would come up short due to the temptation for households to be free riders. A **free rider** is one who attempts to benefit from a public good without paying for it. Given the nonrival and nonexcludable nature of national defense, individuals have little incentive to reveal their true preferences. Instead, they might say they would rather risk invasion than pay for national defense, and then benefit from the protection paid for by others. Another classic example of the free rider problem is the difficulty of getting neighbors to pay for a streetlight in a cul-de-sac. The solution to the free rider problem in most cases is to have some form of government (federal government for national defense, a neighborhood association for streetlights) provide the public goods. Governmental units can collect money in the form of taxes, fees, or dues from everyone who benefits from the public goods and then fund their provision.

## 9.8  INCOME AND WEALTH INEQUALITY

You've heard it before—the rich are getting richer and the poor are getting poorer. In relative terms, this is correct. The *gap* between rich and poor continues to widen. This is generally true on the basis of the share of income held by the richest and poorest 20 percent of the U.S. population over the past few decades. Some argue that income inequality is greater than these statistics suggest, because the rich also receive nonmonetary perks like fancy meals, housing, travel, and so on that do not show up in income reports. Others argue that the inequality trends are influenced by changing demographics such as the average age, the number of wage earners in a family, and the divorce rate. Comparisons over time of households with similar demographics yield smaller changes in income inequality.

Income equality is often measured using the **Lorenz curve,** as illustrated in Figure 18, and the associated **Gini coefficient**.

You're nearing the end of the Microeconomics review! If you're going to dive into Macro, be sure to give yourself some downtime to let your brain absorb the information you've been studying.

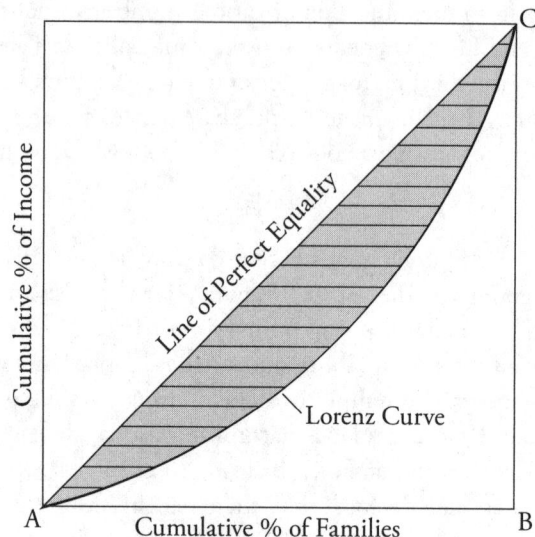

**Figure 18: The Lorenz Curve**

The vertical axis measures the cumulative percentage of income. The horizontal axis measures the cumulative percentage of families, starting with the poorest and ending with the richest. The straight line from corner to corner represents perfect income equality because the proportion of families equals the proportion of income—the "poorest" 10 percent hold fully 10 percent of the income and so forth. The line below it is the Lorenz curve, which depicts the actual relationship between families and income in the United States. The poorest 20 percent hold only 4 percent of income, the poorest 40 percent hold 14 percent of income, and so on.

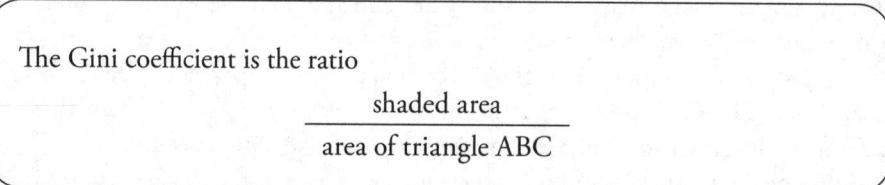

The Gini coefficient is the ratio

$$\frac{\text{shaded area}}{\text{area of triangle ABC}}$$

If income were divided equally, both the shaded area and the Gini coefficient would be 0. If the richest family made all of the income, the Gini coefficient would be 1. The Gini coefficient in the United States is about 0.48.

The **poverty line** is the official benchmark of poverty. It is set at three times the minimum food budget as established by the Department of Agriculture. The poverty line for a family of four is about $30,000. Nearly 12.8 percent of Americans live below the poverty line. The list below includes some of the programs that seek to redistribute income and assist the disadvantaged.

- With a **progressive tax,** the government receives a larger percentage of revenue from families with larger incomes. In contrast to a progressive tax, which helps redistribute income to the poor, a **regressive tax** collects a larger percentage of revenue from families with smaller incomes. A **proportional tax** collects the same percentage of income from all families.

- The **Social Security** program provides cash benefits and health insurance (Medicare) to retired and disabled workers and their families.

- **Public assistance** or **welfare** typically provides temporary assistance to the very low-income families.

- **Supplemental Security Income (SSI)** assists very poor elderly individuals who have virtually no assets and little or no Social Security entitlement.

- **Unemployment compensation** provides temporary assistance to unemployed workers.

- **Medicaid** provides health insurance and hospitalization benefits to the low-income families.

- The **Supplemental Nutrition Assistance Program (SNAP)**, also known as **Food Stamps**, and **Public Housing programs** provide food and shelter for the low-income families.

## Unions

Workers in many industries increase their collective bargaining and lobbying strengths by forming **labor unions**. Unions use three general methods to increase the wages for their members. They attempt to:

- increase the demand for labor

- decrease the supply of labor

- negotiate higher wages

Because the demand for labor is derived from the demand for the products labor produces, one way to increase labor demand is to increase product demand. This is accomplished with calls for consumers to "look for the union label," to lobby for favorable regulations and government expenditures, and to support protective tariffs and quotas that impede foreign competition.

**Featherbedding agreements** require employers to hire union members for particular tasks whether they are needed or not. Although the Taft-Hartley Act attempted to outlaw featherbedding and similar "make-work" agreements, the Supreme Court has permitted payments for nonproductive work. Examples include unnecessarily large minimum crew sizes on trains, and agreements that theaters will pay union musicians for performances even when orchestras from out of town are brought in to play.

Using an approach called exclusive unionism, some craft unions such as plumbers and electricians attempt to increase wages by restricting the supply of workers with their skills. When employers agree to hire only union workers, restricting the labor supply is as simple as restricting union membership. In other situations, unions can reduce the labor supply by lobbying for child labor laws, immigration restrictions, compulsory retirement, and occupational licensing.

For unskilled and semiskilled workers, it makes less sense to form an exclusive union because there are many available workers who could provide the same services. Instead, these groups tend to form inclusive or industrial unions that encourage as many workers as possible to join. Industrial unions try to use their size to their advantage when negotiating wage floors and compensation packages. On average, union members earn about 18 percent more than nonunionized workers in similar positions.

# CHAPTER 9 KEY TERMS

## 9.1
marginal revenue product of labor

## 9.2
change in quantity demanded
change in demand
normal good
inferior good
determinants of demand (TRIBE)
marginal utility
total utility
consumer surplus
producer surplus

## 9.3
natural monopoly
"fair return" price ceiling
Sherman Act
Clayton Act
Robinson-Patman Act
Celler-Kefauver Act
vertical mergers
conglomerate mergers
horizontal mergers
Herfindahl-Hirschman Index
concentration ratio

## 9.4
wage taker
monopsony
marginal factor cost (MFC)

## 9.5
market failure
imperfect information

## 9.6
externalities
negative externality
positive externality
spillover costs
spillover benefits
marginal private cost
marginal external cost
marginal social cost
over allocation of resources
under allocation of resources

## 9.7
public goods
nonrival goods
rival goods
nonexcludable goods
free rider

## 9.8
Lorenz curve
Gini coefficient
poverty line
progressive tax
regressive tax
proportional tax
Social Security
public assistance (welfare)
Supplemental Security Income (SSI)
unemployment compensation
Medicaid
Supplemental Nutrition Assistance Program
    (SNAP) (Food Stamps)
Public Housing program
labor unions
featherbedding agreements

# CHAPTER 9 DRILL QUESTIONS

See Chapter 10 for answers and explanations.

**1** ☐ Mark for Review

Which of the following could have caused an increase in the demand for ice cream cones?

- (A) A decrease in the price of ice cream cones
- (B) A decrease in the price of ice cream, a complimentary good to ice cream cones
- (C) An increase in the price of ice cream, a complimentary good to ice cream cones
- (D) A decrease in the price of lollipops, a close substitute for ice cream
- (E) An increase in the supply of ice cream cones

**2** ☐ Mark for Review

A student eats 3 slices of pizza while studying for his Economics exam. The marginal utility of the first slice of pizza is 10 utils, that of the second slice is 7 utils, and that of the third slice is 3 utils. Which of the statements below holds true with the above data?

- (A) The student would not eat any more pizza.
- (B) The marginal utility of the fourth slice of pizza will be 0.
- (C) The student should have stopped eating pizza after 2 slices.
- (D) The total utility this student received from eating pizza is 20 utils.
- (E) The total utility decreases after the first slice of pizza because of diminishing marginal utility.

**3** ☐ Mark for Review

The total utility from sardines is maximized when they are purchased until

- (A) marginal utility is zero
- (B) marginal benefit equals marginal cost
- (C) consumer surplus is zero
- (D) distributive efficiency is achieved
- (E) deadweight loss is zero

**4** ☐ Mark for Review

Relative to a competitive input market, a monopsony

- (A) pays less and hires more workers
- (B) pays less and hires the same number of workers
- (C) pays more and hires more workers
- (D) pays more and hires fewer workers
- (E) pays less and hires fewer workers

**5** ☐ Mark for Review

Which of the following is NOT among the methods unions use to increase wages?

(A) Negotiations to obtain a wage floor

(B) Restrictive membership policies

(C) Efforts to decrease the prices of substitute resources

(D) Featherbedding or make-work rules

(E) Efforts to increase the demand for the product they produce

**6** ☐ Mark for Review

If the government regulates a monopoly to produce at the allocative efficient quantity, which of the following would be true?

(A) The monopoly would break even.

(B) The monopoly would incur an economic loss.

(C) The monopoly would make an economic profit.

(D) The deadweight loss in this market would increase.

(E) The deadweight loss in this market would decrease.

**7** ☐ Mark for Review

If the government subsidizes producers in a perfectly competitive market, then

(A) the demand for the product will increase

(B) the demand for the product will decrease

(C) the consumer surplus will increase

(D) the consumer surplus will decrease

(E) the supply will decrease

**8** ☐ Mark for Review

If corn is produced in a perfectly competitive market and the government placed a price ceiling above equilibrium, which of the following would be true?

(A) There would be no change in the amount of corn demanded or supplied.

(B) A shortage of corn would be created.

(C) A surplus of corn would be created.

(D) The producers of corn would lose revenue due to the decreased price.

(E) Illegal markets for corn might develop.

**9** ☐ Mark for Review

Which of the following relationships represents fair and efficient allocation of resources?

(A) Monopolies

(B) Oligopolies

(C) Marginal Social Benefit (MSB) = Marginal Social Cost (MSC)

(D) Marginal Social Benefit (MSB) > Marginal Social Cost (MSC)

(E) Marginal Social Benefit (MSB) < Marginal Social Cost (MSC)

**10** ☐ Mark for Review

Because people with relatively low incomes spend a larger percentage of their income on food than people with relatively high incomes, a sales tax on food would fall into which category of taxes?

(A) Progressive

(B) Proportional

(C) Regressive

(D) Neutral

(E) Flat

# Chapter 9 Summary

## 9.1 Factor Markets

o The **marginal revenue product of labor** is the amount of revenue generated by one additional unit of labor; calculate using this formula:

$$MRP_L = MP_L \times P_{output}$$

o The above equation can be used for any of the factors of demand.

## 9.2 Changes in Factor Demand and Factor Supply

o The demand curve shifts with
  - **T**astes and preferences of consumers
  - the prices of **R**elated goods
  - the **I**ncome of buyers
  - the number of **B**uyers
  - **E**xpectations for the future

o **Marginal utility** is the additional utility gained from consuming one more unit of a good.

o **Total utility** is the sum of all marginal utility values gained from each unit consumed.

o **Consumer surplus** is the value a buyer receives from the purchase of a good *in excess* of what the consumer pays for it; **producer surplus** is the difference between the price a seller receives for a good and the minimum price for which she would be willing to supply a quantity of the good.

## 9.3 Profit-Maximizing Behavior in Perfectly Competitive Factor Markets

o **Natural monopolies** occur when fixed costs are so high as to prohibit a second firm from entering the market.

o The **Sherman Act**, the **Clayton Act**, the **Robinson-Patman Act**, and the **Celler-Kefauver Act** are important pieces of antitrust legislation.

o A **vertical merger** is a merger of firms at various steps in the production process.

o A **conglomerate merger** is a combination of firms from unrelated industries.

o A **horizontal merger** is a merger of direct competitors.

## 9.4 Monopsonistic Markets

o A **monopsony** occurs when one firm is the sole purchaser of labor services.

o The **marginal factor cost (MFC)** is the additional cost of one more unit of labor.

o A monopsony will choose an employment level at which $MRP_L = MFC_L$.

## 9.5 Socially Efficient and Inefficient Market Outcomes

o Fair and optimized allocation of economic resources in a society is called social efficiency. Otherwise, the economic process will result in inefficient market outcomes.

o A **market failure** occurs whenever resources aren't allocated optimally. This can result from
  • imperfect competition
  • **externalities:** costs or benefits felt beyond those causing the effects
  • **public goods:** goods that many individuals benefit from at the same time
  • **imperfect information:** buyers and/or sellers do not have full knowledge about available markets, prices, products, customers, suppliers

## 9.6 Externalities

○ **Negative externalities** lead to overconsumption; **positive externalities** lead to underconsumption.

○ The **marginal private cost** (MPC) of a good is the cost paid by the consumer for an additional unit of a good; the **marginal external cost** is the cost paid by people other than the buyer for an additional unit of a good.

## 9.7 Public and Private Goods

○ A **nonrival good** is one for which the consumption of that good does not affect its consumption by others.

○ **Nonexcludable** goods cannot be held back from those who desire access.

○ A **free rider** is one who attempts to benefit from a public good without paying for it.

## 9.8 Income and Wealth Inequality

○ The **Gini coefficient** uses the **Lorenz curve** to calculate income inequality.

○ The **poverty line** is the official benchmark for poverty; it is set at three times the minimum food budget as established by the Department of Agriculture.

○ Workers increase their collective bargaining and lobbying strengths by forming **labor unions.** They attempt to:
- increase the demand for labor
- decrease the supply of labor
- negotiate higher wages

# Chapter 10
# Microeconomics Drill Questions: Answers and Explanations

# CHAPTER 5 DRILL QUESTIONS: ANSWERS AND EXPLANATIONS

1. **B**  Producing some combination of goods can be considered *impossible* if the combination lies outside the production-possibilities frontier. Points $P$ and $S$ lie within the production-possibilities frontier, so eliminate (A) and (D). Points $R$ and $T$ lie directly on the production-possibilities frontier and are thus still possible, so eliminate (C) and (E). Point $Q$ lies outside the production-possibilities frontier, so the correct answer is (B).

2. **A**  Goods are considered capital goods when they are used to produce other goods. A screwdriver could be used to produce goods that require screws (for example, a computer), so eliminate (B). Factory machinery would be used in factories that produce various other goods, so eliminate (C). A milk-transporting truck may not be a tool in the production of milk, but is a type of capital in that it helps milk become a consumer good (e.g., driving it to a grocery store where consumers may purchase it), so eliminate (D). A large baking oven would be used to produce baked goods, so eliminate (E). An expensive necktie is a consumer good that is not used as a tool or ingredient in producing other goods, so the correct answer is (A).

3. **D**  Because maximizing Lauren's utility relies on knowing the price of each good, eliminate (A), (B), and (C) because they disregard the price of each good. If the price of a burger is $3 and the price of a milkshake is $3, then the marginal utility per dollar of a burger is $6, and the marginal utility per dollar of a milkshake is $4. Because these values are not equal, this combination of goods and prices would not maximize Lauren's utility. So, eliminate (E). If the price of a burger is $6 and the price of a milkshake is $4, then the marginal utility per dollar of both goods is $3, and Lauren's utility is maximized. Therefore, (D) is the correct answer.

4. **E**  You are asked for the combination that maximizes Diego's utility. Recall that maximizing utility requires you to find the marginal utility divided by the price of each good and find the values for which these equations are equal for either good ($\frac{MU_x}{P_x} = \frac{MU_y}{P_y}$ for goods $X$ and $Y$). The marginal utilities per dollar for each poster and for each figurine are as given:

| Quantity of Posters | Marginal Utility of Posters (in dollars) | Marginal Utility per dollar spent on posters | Quantity of Figurines | Marginal Utility of Figurines (in dollars) | Marginal Utility per dollar spent on figurines |
|---|---|---|---|---|---|
| 1 | 30 | 10 | 1 | 72 | 12 |
| 2 | 27 | 9 | 2 | 60 | 10 |
| 3 | 24 | 8 | 3 | 48 | 8 |
| 4 | 21 | 7 | 4 | 36 | 6 |
| 5 | 18 | 6 | 5 | 24 | 4 |
| 6 | 15 | 5 | 6 | 12 | 2 |

Maximize Diego's marginal utility by adding up the combination of goods each of which have the highest marginal utility per dollar while staying within Diego's budget. Choices (B) and (D) propose combinations that cost $33. However, Diego could buy one more poster to spend the total of his budget and increase his utility slightly more. So, eliminate (B) and (D). Choices (A), (C), and (E) cost exactly $36, so pick which of these yields the greatest marginal utility with each poster or figurine purchased. In (E), Diego purchases 6 posters and 3 figurines. Diego would have to give up two posters (11 marginal utility in total) in order to purchase a fourth figurine that adds 6 to his total utility. Because the marginal utility of the two posters is higher than that of the extra fourth figurine, this combination maximizes Diego's utility. In (A) and (C), Diego would have the option to increase his total utility at the margin by purchasing two more posters instead of one of his figurines, so neither (A) nor (C) maximizes Diego's utility. Eliminate (A) and (C). The correct answer is (E).

5.  **C**  According to the graph, Country A can produce 40 TVs or 30 cell phones (or some combination in the middle). Therefore, 1 cell phone costs 1.3 TVs in Country A. Similarly, in Country B, 1 cell phone costs 2.0 TVs. Trade would benefit both countries—eliminate (A)—and the opportunity (relative) costs of cell phones to TVs in (D) and (E) don't match the calculations above—eliminate (D) and (E). As cell phones cost less in Country A compared to Country B, Country A has a comparative advantage in cell phones. Therefore, the answer is (C).

6.  **D**  Choices (A), (B), (C), and (E) all refer to factors of production. The cost of the car designer's studio can be considered either land or capital. The car designer's time is labor, and the car designer's creativity can be considered either labor or entrepreneurship. Steel is capital, and rubber is a natural resource. Choice (D) refers to opportunity cost, which is not a factor of production. Therefore, the correct answer is (D).

7.  **E**  In an economic activity, the comparison of expected costs and anticipated benefits is called a cost-benefit analysis. Variable and opportunity costs are parts of the total costs, not all of them. Choices (A) and (B) are not related to the question. Effectiveness of an economic decision does not guarantee a certain reward for an economic event; (D) is not an admissible answer. Production of a commodity is not associated with analyzing the rewards of an economic decision, eliminating (C). Therefore, (E) is the correct answer for this question.

# CHAPTER 6 DRILL QUESTIONS: ANSWERS AND EXPLANATIONS

1.  **A**  The question asks about demand, so eliminate any answer choices that focus on supply—eliminate (B), (D), and (E). The Fisher effect relates to monetary supply, so eliminate (C). The demand curve is downward-sloping because each additional unit a consumer consumes gives that consumer less utility than the previous one; therefore, the consumer is willing to pay less for additional units, creating a downward-sloping demand curve. The answer is (A).

2. **B** The question asks about supply, so eliminate (C) because it focuses on demand. Scale (including decreasing marginal costs) and scope refer to a particular firm, whereas the question asks about the aggregate supply of lawn-mowing services. Eliminate (A), (D), and (E). The supply curve is upward-sloping because as the price of lawn-mowing services increases, more suppliers are willing to enter the market as their opportunity cost for supplying these services increases compared to their other economic opportunities. In other words, a physician will take the job of a dishwasher if the pay for washing dishes is higher than the pay for being a physician. The answer is (B).

3. **B** If the supply increases, then at any price point, the quantity of that good increases, and the supply curve shifts to the right. If the demand increases, then at every price point, the quantity demanded increases, and the demand curve shifts to the right (see the figure below). The combination of an increase in both supply and demand will result in an increase in quantity—eliminate (A) and (C). The change in equilibrium price depends on the relative size of the increase in demand and supply, as well as the relative elasticity of supply and demand. The answer is (B).

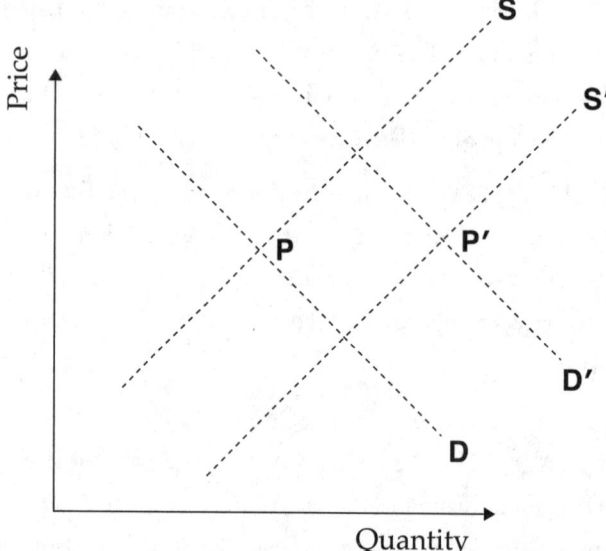

4.  **A**  When your choices include "None of the above," it is important to eliminate all other choices before settling on your answer. In this case, the change is from point M to point M′ in the figure below. This change necessarily results in a lower equilibrium price, but undetermined equilibrium quantity. Therefore, the answer is (A).

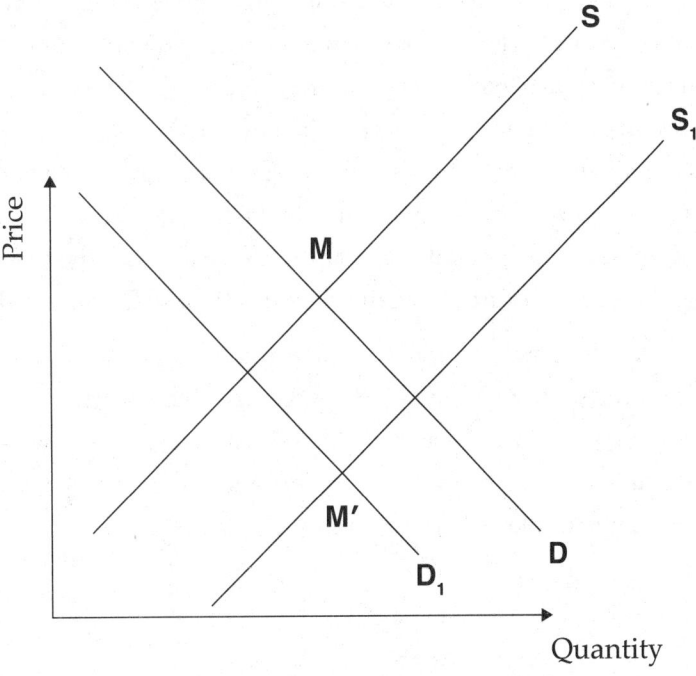

5.  **E**  For the same quantity, the supply price has increased. This means that the price of producing that good has increased. The answer that states an increase in production price is (E), so the correct answer is (E).

6.  **D**  The question gives data on the supply curve, so answer choices that refer to demand can be eliminated—eliminate (B) and (C). Elasticity $= \dfrac{\text{Percent Change in Quantity}}{\text{Percent Change in Price}} = \dfrac{5}{3} = 1.6 > 1$. As the elasticity of supply is greater than 1, the supply is elastic. Therefore, the answer is (D).

7.  **E**  Normal goods are defined with respect to consumer income levels; therefore, answers that do not reference income—(A), (B), and (C)—can be eliminated. As income increases, the demand for a normal good increases. Therefore, the answer is (E).

8.  **C**  Cross-price elasticity refers to the demand for a good when the equilibrium price of another good changes. Choices (A), (B), and (E) can be eliminated as they are not functions of cross-price elasticity. A negative cross-price elasticity means that the demand for a good has decreased when the equilibrium price of another good increases. This means that the two goods are complements. For example, the quantity for rental skis decreases when ticket prices for ski resorts increase. The answer is (C).

9. **D** If the elasticity quotient of demand is less than 1, the demand is inelastic. Choices (A), (B), and (E) can be eliminated as they incorrectly describe the demand price elasticity given in the question, 0.78, as elastic or unit elastic. Because of the direct relationship between price and total revenue for inelastic goods, the firm should increase its price, as it will increase its revenue. The answer is (D).

10. **D** Choice (D) is the correct answer because imposing a price ceiling, which is usually done by governments, directly affects the relations between supply and market price and results in a sudden equilibrium shockwave. Economic externalities are the result of the impact of the production or consumption of a specific good or service indirectly on the third economic variable or entity. Choice (A) is not a correct choice and should be eliminated. Bankruptcy of firms or banks does not directly disturb the economic equilibrium conditions. Therefore, (B) and (C) are not correct choices. Changing both supply and demand at the same rate when the economic conditions are at equilibrium level does not disturb the equilibrium conditions. This makes (E) incorrect, as well.

11. **A** The best approach is to draw the supply and demand for labor (see the following figure). As the minimum wage increases from W to W', the wages rise, but the quantity of labor needed drops. Therefore, increasing the minimum wage would be beneficial for some workers (for those who are employed at the higher wage), but detrimental for others (those who were employed at the lower wage, but are no longer employed). The answer is (A).

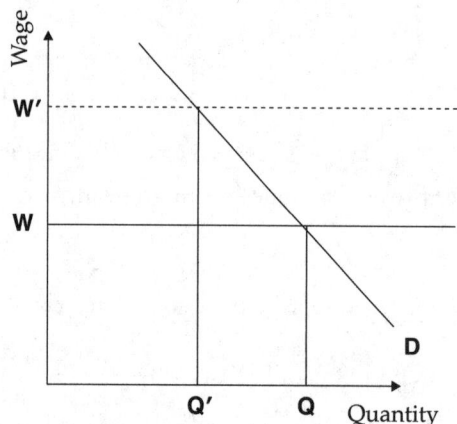

12. **E** The side with the more relative inelasticity would bear the greater tax burden. If consumers are to bear the majority of the tax burden, then the demand curve should be inelastic and the supply curve should be elastic. Look carefully at the answer choices. Whereas (C) would result in the correct conditions, the question asks which will result in consumers paying for the largest burden of the tax. Therefore, (E) is the best choice.

13. **B** Contractionary monetary policy occurs when the government's actions reduce the overall money supply in the economy. Purchasing bonds, increasing taxes (and spending the additional tax revenue), increasing government spending, and decreasing the discount rate all increase the supply of money, so eliminate (A), (C), (D) and (E). Selling bonds reduces the overall money supply in the economy; therefore, the answer is (B).

14. **E** Contractionary fiscal policy starts with the government decreasing its spending (or increasing taxes). As the government demand for loanable funds has decreased, the interest rate drops, leading to a decrease in demand of the domestic currency. Eliminate (A) and (C) because they give the incorrect effect on the interest rate due to contractionary fiscal policy. Eliminate (B) and (D) because they give the incorrect effect on the value of the dollar due to a decrease in interest rates. Therefore, the answer is (E).

# CHAPTER 7 DRILL QUESTIONS: ANSWERS AND EXPLANATIONS

1. **E** The long-run average cost curve is always below the short-run average cost curve except at the cost-minimizing point for that short-run average cost curve. To the left of that point, the firm is using too much capital and fixed costs are too high. To the right of this point, the firm is using too little capital and diminishing returns to scale are causing costs to increase. See Figure 3 on page 117. Choices (A), (B), and (C) can be eliminated because the SRAC and LRAC curves will intersect at the quantity for which the amount of capital in question is the cost minimizing amount. Choice (D) can be eliminated because the LRAC is below the SRAC due to lack of fixed costs in the long term. Therefore, the answer is (E).

2. **D** The marginal cost curve always intersects the average variable cost curve at the lowest point of the latter (see Figure 2 on page 115). Choice (A) can be eliminated because MC intersects MR to find the profit-maximizing quantity. Choices (B) and (E) can be eliminated because the AVC, by definition, represents an average of marginal costs and will not intersect at marginal cost's minimum or maximum point. Choice (C) can be eliminated because AVC is a U-shaped curve that opens upward and doesn't have a single maximum point. Therefore, the answer is (D).

3. **C** As the firm is a price taker in the labor market, wages will not be affected, so eliminate (B) and (D). As marginal product of labor has increased (workers have become more productive), the marginal revenue product (amount earned by each worker) has also increased. This will cause the firm to hire more workers until the marginal cost of labor equals the marginal product of labor, so (A) can be eliminated. Therefore, the answer is (C).

4. **D** A competitive firm's demand for labor is determined by the quantity at which the marginal productivity of labor is equal to the marginal cost of labor (i.e., when the last worker produces just enough to cover their wages). Eliminate (B) because the question is framed in regard to the firm's demand for work, not the employee's willingness to work. Eliminate (C) and (E) because demand for labor is not restricted by physical products produced or the marginal utility and cost. Eliminate (A) because profits alone do not determine demand for labor. Therefore, the answer is (D).

5. **B** If the third worker's MP = 10, then that worker generated income of 10 × $3 = $30. As the worker is paid $15, the firm is making economic profit. Therefore, it should hire more workers until the productivity of the last worker just equals the revenue generated by that worker. Eliminate (C), (D) and (E). As more workers are hired (and no other investment in the business is made), each subsequent worker will generate lower and lower marginal revenue and $MRP_L$ will decrease. Therefore, the answer is (B).

6.  **A**  When a firm produces at a point at which MR = MC, then it is maximizing its profits, which is to say that it is producing at the point at which its revenues most exceed its costs. Therefore, the answer is (A).

7.  **B**  The gross profit is the difference between the revenue from the sales of a product or a service and total costs associated with the product or the service. Cost of production, cost of labor, and fixed costs are parts of the total costs. Therefore, (A), (C), and (E) are not admissible answers. Choice (D) includes only one variable of the gross product, so you can eliminate that answer. This leaves you with (B), the correct answer.

8.  **D**  Before trade, the price and quantity of cotton would be P and Q, respectively (as shown in the figure below). As the world price is below the domestic equilibrium price, the domestic price would fall to P′ and the equilibrium quantity would rise to Q′. As domestic producers would not be able to produce the higher quantities at the lower price, the United States would become a net importer of cotton. The answer is (D).

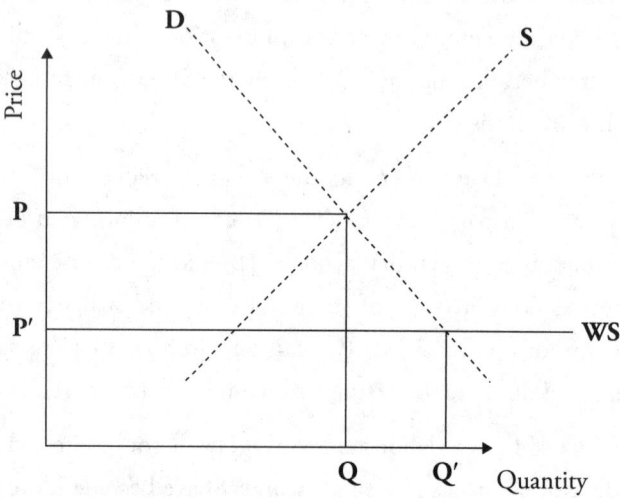

# CHAPTER 8 DRILL QUESTIONS: ANSWERS AND EXPLANATIONS

1.  **D**  With a question like this one, it is easier to work out the possible outcomes and compare them to the given choices. First look at Company's A strategies. If Company B expands, then Company A does not expand. If Company B does not expand, then Company A does not expand. Therefore, no matter what Company B does, Company A's strategy would be to not expand. And therefore Company A has a dominant strategy, so eliminate (B), (C), and (E).

Turning to Company B, if Company A were to expand, Company B would not want to expand. If Company A does not expand, Company B does not expand. Therefore, no matter what Company A does, Company B has a dominant strategy of not expanding, so eliminate (A). As both companies have a dominant strategy, the answer is (D). (Note that as both companies benefit from not expanding, a Nash equilibrium also exists.)

2. **B**  If a monopoly faces a straight, downward-sloping demand curve, then the marginal revenue for a monopoly is halfway between the demand curve and the vertical axis. See Figure 1 on page 131. Therefore, the answer is (B).

3. **B**  The best approach to this question is to use Process of Elimination. Consider that in oligopolistic markets, there are a few (possibly large) firms that dominate the market, so eliminate (D). As perfect competition is reduced, these firms do make economic profit, so eliminate (A). As there are only a few firms that would most probably be subjected to antitrust legislation, and some of the antitrust legislation may have been developed in response to the actions of these oligopolies, eliminate (C). Typically in oligopolistic markets there are several buyers and few sellers. Therefore, the sellers have market power, so eliminate (E). While interdependence is not a prerequisite for oligopolistic markets, it is a common feature of such markets. Therefore, the answer is (B).

4. **A**  Consider that monopolistic markets are characterized by one supplier and several buyers. The seller thus has the ability to control prices by either fixing prices or limiting quantity. As the firm is limiting quantity to maximize its revenue, it is causing more deadweight loss than a firm ordinarily would in a perfectly competitive market. A monopoly is unlikely to lower prices; in fact, it is likely to raise prices, so eliminate (B). A monopoly reduces supply by limiting production, so eliminate (C). A monopoly has only one firm, so eliminate (D). Quality of goods is not discussed, as economics assumes that the goods are identical and meet the minimum quality standards, so eliminate (E). Therefore, the answer is (A).

5. **E**  To determine Company A's strategy, suppose Company B opts for a small budget. Company A would opt for a large budget. If Company B opts for a large budget, Company A would opt for a small budget. As Company A opts for either a small or large budget based on Company's B position, Company A does not have a dominant strategy, so eliminate (A), (B), (C), and (D). Look at Company B's strategy instead. If Company A opts for a small budget, Company B would opt for a small budget. If Company A were to opt for a large budget, Company B would choose the large budget as well. Therefore, there isn't a dominant strategy for either company. The answer is (E).

6. **B**  A monopoly produces less and sells for more than firms in perfect competition, so eliminate (A). As no short-run-versus-long-run data is given, eliminate (C) and (D). Cost data is not given so eliminate (E). Therefore, the answer is (B).

7. **C**  Price discrimination occurs when a company can charge different prices to different customers for essentially the same product with the goal of maximizing revenue. Therefore, any company that can engage in price discrimination will earn higher revenues than those companies that do not. Therefore, the answer is (C).

8. **E**  The quantity a monopoly supplies is determined by that quantity for which MR = MC (point D). Therefore, the quantity supplied would be G (see the following figure). The total revenue a monopoly receives is area $P_2$EGO. The cost is area PDGO, and the profit is $P_2$EDP. Therefore, the answer is (E).

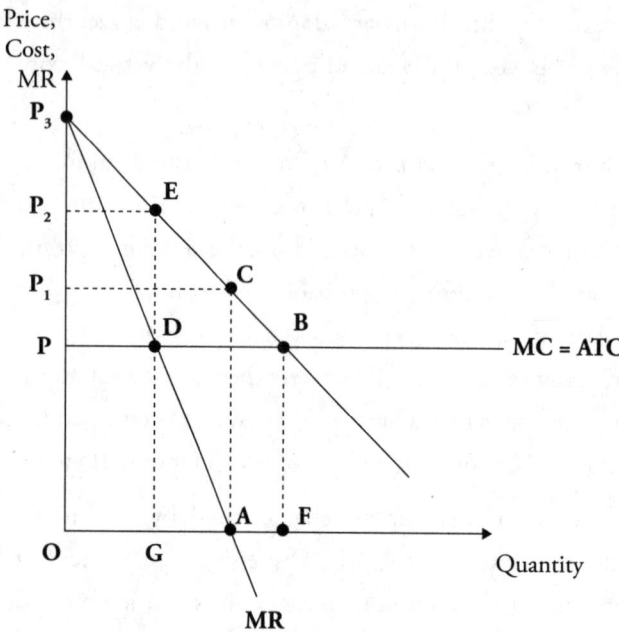

9.   **A**   A bilateral monopoly exists when a monopsony buys from a monopoly—i.e., there is only one seller and one buyer of a good or service. See page 134. Remember that "mono" in "monopoly" means "one," so (B) can be eliminated because it references more than one buyer. Eliminate (D) and (E) because what is sold is irrelevant in determining a bilateral monopoly. Eliminate (C) because the term "monopsony" is specific to buyers. Therefore, the answer is (A).

# CHAPTER 9 DRILL QUESTIONS: ANSWERS AND EXPLANATIONS

1.   **B**   Increase in demand refers to a shift in the demand curve. An increase in the demand for a good could be caused by an increase in real income (assuming that it is a normal good), a drop in price of a complimentary good, or a rise in price of a substitute. Eliminate (A) because a change in price would change the quantity demanded, not cause an overall shift in the curve. Eliminate (C) and (D) because they incorrectly apply the effects of changes in compliments and substitutes. Eliminate (E) because a shift in the supply curve does not necessarily affect the demand curve. In this case, the best answer is (B).

2.   **D**   As the question makes no prediction of the utility derived from eating more than three slices of pizza, any answer that mentions consequences after the third slice or makes a non-economic judgment on pizza eating—(A), (B), and (C)—can be eliminated. Total utility increases with the consumption of each subsequent slice, as the marginal utility for the three slices is positive, so eliminate (E). The total utility is the sum of the utility received from consuming each slice. In this case it is 10 + 7 + 3 = 20. Therefore, the total utility from consuming three slices of pizza is 20 utils. The answer is (D).

3. **A**  The question asks about total utility, which refers to consuming sardines. This question focuses on the demand for sardines, so answer choices that refer to supply (D) can be eliminated. As the question does not refer to supply, any answer choices that need the supply and demand curves—(C) and (E)—can be eliminated. Similarly, utility is independent of cost, so (B) can be eliminated. To maximize the total utility of sardines, they need to be consumed until the marginal utility is equal to zero (regardless of the price). Therefore, the answer is (A).

4. **E**  A monopsony occurs when there is only one buyer for a specific good (for example, a large company in a small town is virtually the only buyer of labor). As the buyer is interested in maximizing its own revenue, the net result is that wages are depressed, and fewer workers are hired. Eliminate (C) and (D) because they claim that a monopsony pays more rather than less. Eliminate (A) and (B) because they claim that a monopsony hires more or the same number of workers, rather than fewer. Therefore, the answer is (E).

5. **C**  Unions are interested in increasing their members' wages. They do this through collective bargaining, wage floors, featherbedding, increasing the demand for their goods (the "Buy American" campaign, for example), and other such tactics. One way to approach this question is through Process of Elimination (which is probably the most efficient way as the tactics listed are all union tactics). Another is to realize that decreasing the price of substitute resources makes those resources more attractive and therefore would hurt union wages. Therefore, the answer is (C).

6. **E**  As the question does not give any information on the profits the monopoly is making, one cannot comment on them, so eliminate (A), (B), and (C). Regulating a monopoly to allocative efficiency is a measure designed to reduce deadweight loss. Therefore, the answer is (E).

7. **C**  As the demand curve does not change, answers focusing on demand—(A) and (B)—can be eliminated. A subsidy increases supply, so eliminate (E). Consumer surplus is the area under the demand curve between the equilibrium price and the vertical axis (see the following figure). The consumer surplus before the subsidy is shown by region A, and after the subsidy, consumer surplus increases to include regions B and C. Therefore, the answer is (C).

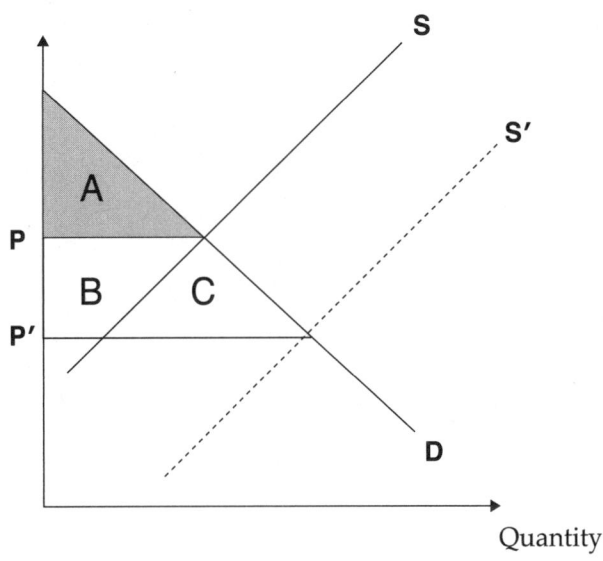

8.  **A**  The best way to approach this question is to draw the supply and demand curves (see the following figure). Remember that a price ceiling sets a maximum price a producer may charge. Since the price ceiling (PC) is above the equilibrium price, the equilibrium price and quantity do not change as a result of the price ceiling. Therefore, the answer is (A).

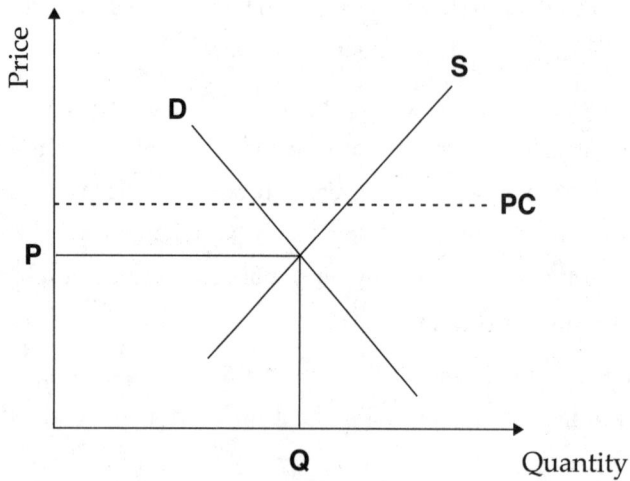

9.  **C**  Both monopolies and oligopolies generate an inefficient quantity. This condition, in turn, generates inefficiency of allocation of resources. This means (A) and (B) are incorrect. Only when the marginal social benefit is the same as the marginal social cost is the allocation of resources fair and efficient. Hence, (C) is the correct answer. Since (D) and (E) contradict this condition, they are incorrect.

10.  **C**  Extracting proportionally more tax income from the poor is by definition a regressive tax (see page 164). Therefore, the answer is (C).

# Review of
# Macroeconomics
# Concepts

# Chapter 11
# Macro Units 1 and 2: Basic Economics Concepts, Economic Indicators, and the Business Cycle

**Economics** is the study of how to allocate scarce resources among competing ends. **Macroeconomics** is the branch of economics that deals with the whole economy and issues that affect most of society. These issues include inflation, unemployment, Gross Domestic Product, national income, interest rates, exchange rates, and so on. **Microeconomics** is the branch of economics that looks at decision-making at the firm, household, and individual levels, and studies behavior in markets for particular goods and services. For example, it models a firm's decision of how much to produce and what price to charge for its goods or services.

The concepts of scarcity, opportunity costs, production possibilities, specialization and comparative advantage, functions of an economic system, demand, supply, and price determination are important to both microeconomic and macroeconomic analysis. Because there is overlap, these concepts are covered only once, in the microeconomics chapters.

## 11.1   THE CIRCULAR FLOW AND GDP

A country's annual **Gross Domestic Product** (GDP) is the total value of all final goods and services produced in a year within that country. The expression "*final* goods and services" is worded the way it is to avoid double counting: GDP does not include the value of intermediate goods like lumber and steel that go into the production of other goods like homes and cars, or the repurchase of used goods, which were included in GDP in the year in which they were first produced. Also excluded from the calculation of GDP are financial transactions such as the buying and selling of stocks and bonds, since there is no productive activity associated with them to measure. Public and private transfer payments also are not considered in GDP, nor are underground economic activities (both legal and illegal) and home production. The media is prone to using changes in GDP as indicators of societal well-being. Although an increase in this measure might reflect an increase in the standard of living, GDP also increases with expenditures on natural disasters, deadly epidemics, war, crime, and other detriments to society. Unless "bads" such as these are subtracted, be cautious in interpreting changes in GDP.

> **Be Careful!**
>
> Some textbooks ignore the intermediate step of personal income and just mention national income and disposable income. If the intermediate step is not used, then you would have to deduct taxes and add back in government transfers to go from national income to disposable income.

**National income** (NI) is the sum of income earned by the factors of production owned by a country's citizens. It includes wages, salaries, and fringe benefits paid for labor services, rent paid for the use of land and buildings, interest paid for the use of money, and profits received for the use of capital resources. **Personal income** (PI) is the money income received by households before personal income taxes are subtracted, and **disposable income** (DI) is personal income minus personal income taxes.

There are two primary methods for calculating GDP—the expenditure approach and the income approach. The **expenditure approach** adds up spending by households, firms, the government, and the rest of the world using the following formula:

$$GDP = C + I + G + (X - M)$$

Here **C** represents personal consumption expenditures by households, such as purchases of durable and nondurable goods and services. **I** represents investment in new physical capital, new construction (both commercial and residential), and additions to business inventories. **G** represents government purchases, **X** represents exports, and **M** represents imports.

The **income approach** makes use of the fact that expenditures on GDP ultimately become income. National income can thus be modified slightly to arrive at GDP. To begin with, depreciation must be added to national income. **Depreciation** is the decline in the value of capital over time due to wear or obsolescence. Depreciation expenses are subtracted from corporate profits before the NI calculation, so they must be re-added to capture the value of output needed to replace or repair worn-out buildings and machinery. **Subsidy payments** made by the government to farmers (for example) are part of the farmers' income but are not made in exchange for goods or services, so they are not part of GDP. Thus, they must be subtracted from NI to find GDP.

Finally, we must add the income of foreign workers in the country whose GDP is being calculated, and we also must subtract the income of citizens working abroad. This addition of the **net income of foreign workers** accounts for the fact that NI includes the income of all citizens everywhere, whereas GDP includes the value of goods produced domestically by anyone. If George Lucas makes a film in France, his income will be part of the U.S. national income because he is a U.S. citizen, but his foreign-made film is part of France's GDP. We must subtract his income from NI when calculating the U.S. GDP. The opposite is true for citizens of France, for example, who produce in the United States. In summary:

GDP = NI + Depreciation – Subsidies + Net income of foreigners

**Net domestic product** is GDP minus depreciation. This indicates how much output is left over for consumption and additions to the capital stock after replacing the capital used up in the production process.

# Circular Flow

It is useful to visualize the flow of resources through the economy with a diagram such as Figure 1.

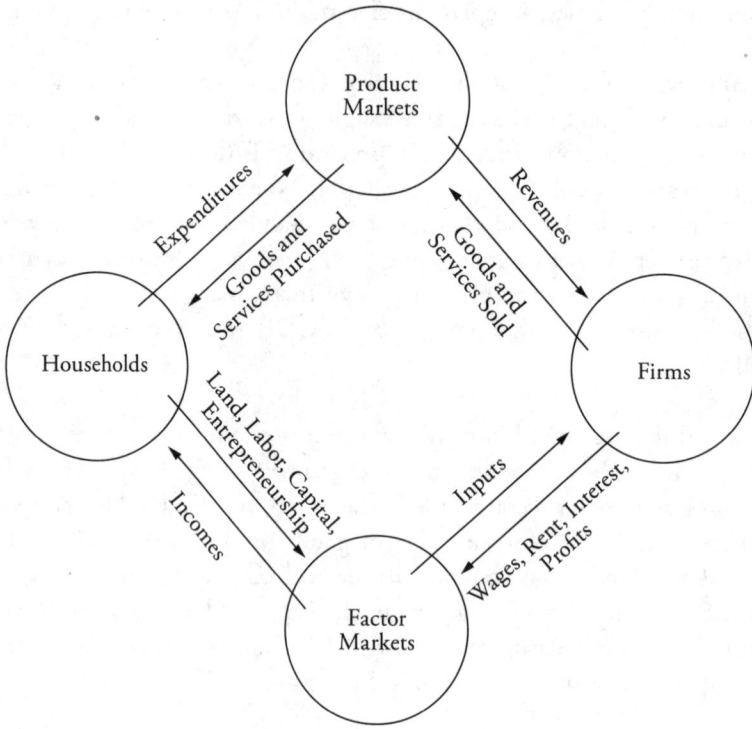

**Figure 1**

> Questions regarding figures such as Figure 1 have shown up on past AP Exams, so be sure to take the time to study and draw the circular flow diagram yourself.

Goods flow from firms to households through the product markets, and inputs flow from households to firms through the factor markets. This simplified model highlights the interdependence between firms and households and the equality of aggregate income and expenditure. If the payments from firms to households for inputs differ from the payments from households to firms for goods and services, the owners of the firms experience profits or losses. Because the firm owners themselves represent households, the full value of expenditures, including any profits or losses, ends up as household income. As for GDP, whether production is valued at what is paid for it or what is paid to produce it doesn't matter because of the equality of **aggregate income** and **aggregate expenditure**.

$$\text{Aggregate income} = \text{Aggregate expenditure} = \text{GDP}$$

These equalities hold even when the government and international transactions are included in the model, as discussed on the following page.

Before we move on, let's get even broader and look at a larger circular-flow diagram (Model 1) to see how money flows throughout the economy at large:

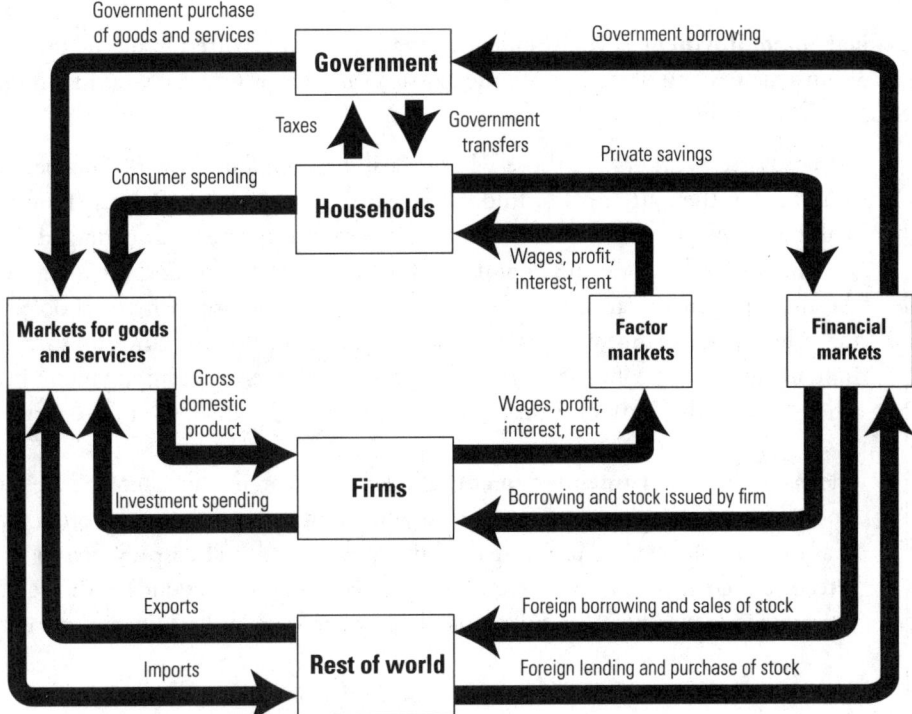

**Model 1: Expanded Circular-Flow Diagram**

## 11.2 UNEMPLOYMENT

The **labor force** includes employed and unemployed adults. To be considered **unemployed**, a labor force participant must be willing and able to work, and must have made an effort to seek work in the past four weeks. The **labor force participation rate** is the number of people in the labor force divided by the working-age population. The **unemployment rate** is the number of unemployed workers divided by the number in the labor force and then multiplied by 100 to get the percent. The various categories of unemployment are defined below.

- **Frictional unemployment** occurs as unemployed workers and firms search for the best available worker-job matches. Included in this category are new labor force entrants looking for their first jobs and workers who are temporarily unemployed because they are moving to a new location or occupation in which they will be more productive.

- **Structural unemployment** is the result of a skills mismatch. As voice recognition software is perfected, skilled typists may find themselves out of work. The same was true for blacksmiths skilled at making horseshoes after the advent of the automobile made horse-drawn buggies obsolete. Poorly educated people may find themselves structurally unemployed because they lack marketable skills.

- **Cyclical unemployment** results from downturns in the business cycle. During recessions and depressions, firms are likely to hire fewer workers or let existing workers go. When the economy recovers, many of these cyclically unemployed workers will again find work.

- **Seasonal unemployment** is the result of changes in hiring patterns due to the time of year. Ski instructors and lifeguards are the classic examples of workers who lose their jobs because of the season.

**Employ This Tip to Remember Unemployment**

You can remember the categories of unemployment using the following irreverent acrostic mnemonic:

**F**ire—Frictional

**S**ome—Structural

**C**ut—Cyclical

**S**ome—Seasonal

**Discouraged workers** are those who are willing and able to work, but become so frustrated in their attempts to find work that they stop trying. Because they are not making an effort to find a job at least once every four weeks, discouraged workers are not counted among the unemployed in official statistics, and are a reason why the unemployment rates might understate the true unemployment problem. On the other hand, **dishonest workers** bias the unemployment figures upward. These individuals claim to be unemployed in order to receive unemployment benefits when, in fact, they do not want a job or are working for cash in an unreported job.

The **natural rate of unemployment**, about 5 percent in the United States, is the typical rate of unemployment in a normally functioning economy and is often thought of as the sum of frictional and structural unemployment. **Full employment** is *not* 100 percent employment, but the level of employment that corresponds with the natural rate of unemployment. With full employment there is no cyclical unemployment.

Some unemployment can be a good thing. Frictional unemployment often allows workers to move into new jobs that are more satisfying for both the worker and the employer than a previous matching. But high rates of unemployment can be devastating, leading to personal loss of self-confidence, crime, the breakup of families, and depression. There are also losses to output and income. Economists, including the late Arthur Okun, have estimated that for every one percentage point increase in the unemployment rate above the natural rate, output falls by 2 to 3 percentage points. This is called **Okun's Law.**

## 11.3   PRICE INDICES AND INFLATION

**Inflation** is a sustained increase in the overall price level. An increase in the price of one good is not necessarily inflation, although it might be part of a broader increase in the general price level that would constitute inflation. The opposite of inflation—a sustained decrease in the general price level—is called **deflation**. If all prices, wages, salaries, rents, and so forth increase by the same percentage, the real effects of inflation might be minimal. For example, suppose Ted's salary is $10 per day and he uses it to buy a pizza for $6 and two mochas for $2 each. With inflation at the rate of 100 percent per day, all prices and salaries are doubled by the next day. Ted earns $20, pizzas cost $12, and mochas cost $4. In economic terms, Ted's **nominal salary** (the actual number of dollars) has increased, but his **real salary** (the purchasing power of the dollars) has remained the same. There should be no real effect because Ted can still purchase exactly what he did before with his salary—one pizza and two mochas. If Ted notes the increase in his salary but does not notice the similar increase in all prices, he might think he is better off. This is called **money illusion,** and can lead to excessive spending.

Other detrimental effects of inflation include the following:

- Stores must change price listings on signs, shelves, computers, and wherever else they are recorded to keep up with inflation. The costs of such changes are called **menu costs,** a name that originated with the classic example of restaurants having to print new menus after price changes.

- Fixed incomes and incomes that increase at a rate less than the inflation rate decrease in value, imposing a burden on the recipients.

- The value of interest payments does not increase in step with inflation decreases, which hurts lenders and savers.

- Social tensions tend to increase with inflation, in part due to the uncertainty and redistribution of income that it entails.

- Increased shoe leather costs are the cost of time and effort that people spend trying to counteract the effects of inflation. Examples of this include holding less cash on hand and having to make frequent trips to the ATM.

- The unit of account (the standard monetary unit of measurement of value/costs of goods, services, and assets) is unstable because of inflation.

- Inflation is a monetary-related economic problem. A high rate of inflation for a sustained period of time in any economy results in significant growth in the money supply (for more on the money supply, see Chapter 13).

## 11.4   REAL VS. NOMINAL GDP

There are also benefits from inflation. Those who borrowed money at fixed interest rates pay back amounts that are worth less in real terms due to inflation. Suppose the interest rate on Stephanie's $100 loan is fixed at five percent, meaning that she makes a nominal interest payment of $5 per year. If the price of apples is $1 this year, the real purchasing power of her interest payment is five apples. If inflation takes the price of apples up to $1.25, the real value of her interest payment decreases to the equivalent of four apples. Price indices are used to measure inflation and adjust nominal values for inflation to find real values. The **Consumer Price Index** (CPI) is the government's gauge of inflation. It is used, for example, to adjust tax brackets and social security payments for inflation. To find it, the Bureau of Labor Statistics checks the prices of items in a fixed representative "market basket" of thousands of goods and services used by typical consumers in a base year.

The CPI is calculated as

$$\text{CPI} = \frac{\text{Cost of base year market basket at current prices}}{\text{Cost of base year market basket at base year prices}} \times 100$$

The inflation between years Y and Z (Z being the more recent year) can be calculated using the following formula:

$$\text{Inflation between years Y and Z} = \left[ \frac{\text{CPI in Year Z}}{\text{CPI in Year Y}} - 1 \right] \times 100$$

And any year's nominal GDP (or any other nominal figure) can be converted into real base year dollars using the following formula:

$$\text{Real GDP} = \frac{\text{Nominal GDP}}{\text{CPI for the same year as the nominal figure}} \times 100$$

The CPI may overestimate the inflation rate, primarily due to its inflexible dependency on the base year market basket. If the price of concert tickets goes up considerably, you might substitute movies for concerts. Because the CPI relies on a fixed market basket, such substitutions for less expensive goods and services are not accounted for in its measure of inflation. Quality improvements and price changes in new products that were not in the base year basket are also excluded from CPI inflation estimates.

The **Producer Price Index** (PPI) is similar in calculation to the CPI, but it applies to the prices of wholesale goods such as lumber and steel. The PPI is sometimes a good predictor of future inflation because producers often pass their cost increases on to consumers.

The **Gross Domestic Product Deflator** is an alternative general price index that reflects the importance of products in current market baskets, rather than in base year market baskets, which become less relevant over time. Its formula is

$$\text{GDP Deflator} = \frac{\text{Cost of current year market basket at current prices}}{\text{Cost of current year market basket at base year prices}} \times 100$$

This formula differs from the CPI calculation in that current year quantities are used. The value of the GDP Deflator can be substituted for CPI values in the formulas for inflation and real GDP above. Because the GDP Deflator reflects both price changes and substitutions away from goods that have become relatively expensive, it generally registers a lower inflation rate than the CPI.

The primary causes of inflation are discussed in the section on aggregate demand.

## 11.5   BUSINESS CYCLES

As real GDP is a measure of aggregate output, it can be used to track the overall growth of the economy. Generally speaking, economies fluctuate between periods of expansion and contraction in the short run. Despite these short-run fluctuations, economic growth can still occur in the long-run.

**Business cycles** are fluctuations in aggregate output and employment. These fluctuations are caused by changes in aggregate supply and aggregate demand. (See the following chapter for a detailed explanation of what causes shifts in the aggregate supply and demand curves.) The phases of the business cycle are known as **recession** and **expansion**. The turning points between these phases are known as **peaks** and **troughs**.

These concepts are illustrated on the Business Cycle Graph:

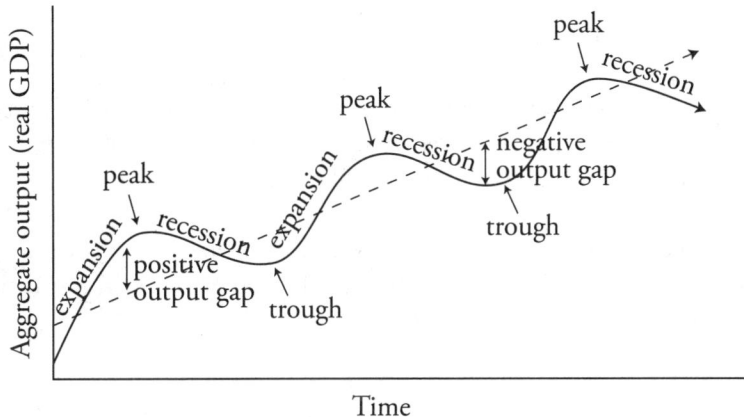

On the Business Cycle Graph, real GDP appears on the *y*-axis and time appears on the *x*-axis. The portions of the real GDP curve with a negative slope are recessions, and the portions of the curve with a positive slope are expansions. A peak occurs when the slope transitions from positive to negative, and a trough occurs when the slope transitions from negative to positive. Note that in the long run, growth occurs despite recessions in the short run.

When an economy's unemployment rate equals its natural rate of unemployment, it's considered by economists to be reaching its **potential output**. Potential output is also known as **full-employment output**. As output is measured by real GDP, the potential output curve can be illustrated alongside the business cycles curve.

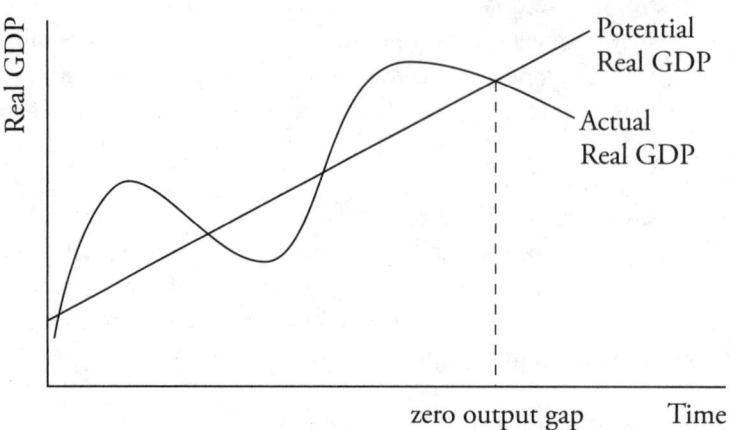

The **output gap** is the difference between potential output and actual output. Where the two curves above intersect, the output gap is zero.

Another way to measure economic growth is to consider the growth rate in real GDP per capita over time. For instance, output per employed worker is a measure of average labor productivity. Productivity is a function of technology and capital per worker.

As a result, employment and aggregate output are directly related. This is because firms must employ more workers to produce more output, if all other factors are held constant. This is represented by the Aggregate Production Function.

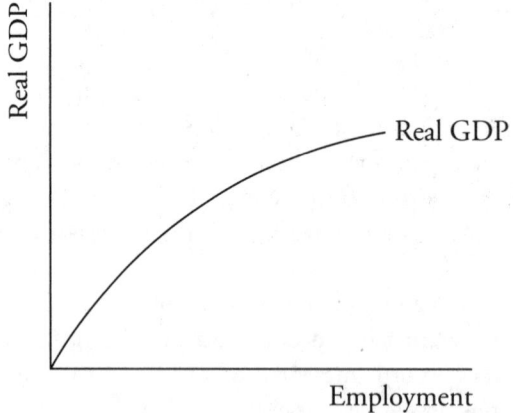

Though real GDP increases along with employment, it does so at a decreasing rate. This is another example of diminishing marginal returns. Keep in mind that the Aggregate Production Function is also beneficial in considering potential real GDP. When an economy's employment equals its natural rate of unemployment, real GDP reflects potential output.

## Classical Analysis

**Classical economists** theorize that wages, prices, and interest rates fluctuate quickly, clearing (bringing to equilibrium) labor and capital markets, and allowing input and output prices to stay in line with each other. Classical economists also believe in **Say's Law**—the idea that supply creates its own demand. In other words, when supplying goods, workers earn money to spend or save, and savings end up being borrowed and spent on business investments. There should be no problem finding demand for the goods and services produced, because the income from making them will be spent purchasing them. This supports the classical contention that the government does not need to concern itself with policies that maintain demand at a desirable level.

Critics of Say's Law argue that savings might not equal investment, because the interest rate does not fluctuate freely enough to clear the capital market (see Figure 2).

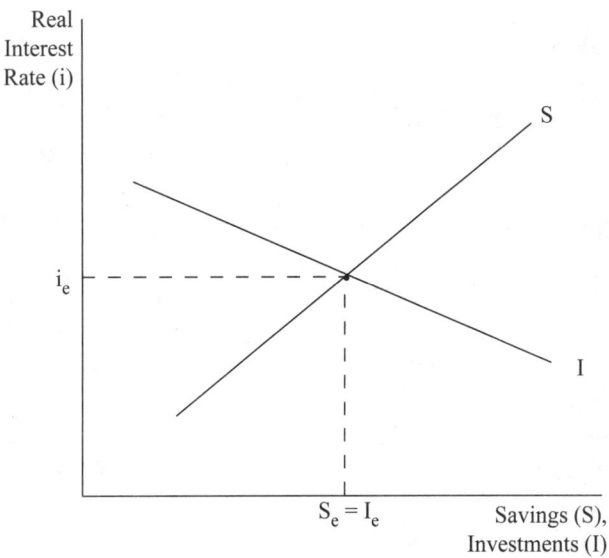

**Figure 2: The Capital Market**

John Maynard Keynes (see next page) argued that investment demand depends more on expectations about the prosperity of the economy than on interest rates. If savings exceed investment, some of the nation's real GDP will not be purchased and firm inventories will expand, resulting in layoffs and subsequent production below full employment output. Likewise, if savings are less than investment, expenditures will exceed real GDP and firm inventories will deplete, resulting in inflation and production beyond full employment output.

The general description of the long-run aggregate supply curve explains that real GDP rests at $Y_f$ in the long run after wage adjustments have had a chance to catch up with price adjustments. If wages can adjust quickly, as classical theory suggests, they will remain in line with prices, and changes in the price level will not result in changes in real GDP even in the short run. The assumption of flexible wages thus corresponds with a vertical aggregate supply curve as in the left side of Figure 3. One result of a vertical AS is that increases in aggregate demand (due to expansionary policy or otherwise) will increase the price level while having no effect on real GDP.

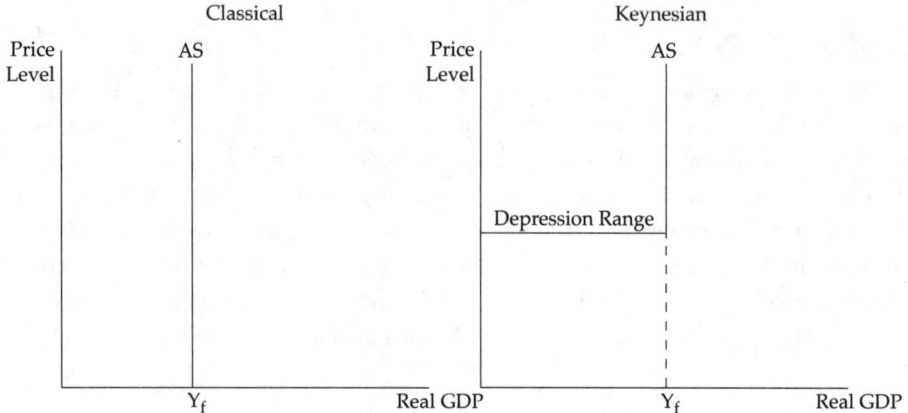

**Figure 3: Classical and Keynesian Aggregate Supply Curves**

## Keynesian Analysis

British economist John Maynard Keynes had a somewhat different view of the aggregate supply curve. As illustrated on the right side of Figure 3, the Keynesian AS curve is horizontal until the full-employment level of output, when it becomes vertical, as classical theory predicts. Keynes focused on the horizontal "depression range" of AS when excess capacity and unemployment allow increases in output and income without forcing the price level to increase.

Keynes blamed the existence of unemployment and the inability of the economy to self-adjust to full-employment output largely on "sticky" wages, particularly in the downward direction. Keynesians argue that wage contracts are typically adjusted no more than once a year, and such influences as unions, tradition, and a reluctance to threaten company morale effectively prohibit decreases in wages. If wages cannot adjust to match changes in price levels, deviations from full employment output might persist until the government steps in with monetary or fiscal policy (explained in Chapter 13) to bolster or tame the economy. This is in contrast with the classical economists' preference for laissez-faire (hands-off) governmental policy.

# CHAPTER 11 KEY TERMS

## 11.1

economics
macroeconomics
microeconomics
Gross Domestic Product
national income
personal income
disposable income
expenditure approach
income approach
depreciation
subsidy payments
net foreign income
net domestic product
aggregate income
aggregate expenditure

## 11.2

labor force
unemployed
labor force participation rate
unemployment rate
frictional unemployment
structural unemployment
cyclical unemployment
seasonal unemployment
discouraged worker
dishonest worker
natural rate of unemployment
full employment
Okun's Law

## 11.3

inflation
deflation
nominal salary
real salary
money illusion
menu cost

## 11.4

Consumer Price Index
Producer Price Index
Gross Domestic Product Deflator

## 11.5

business cycle
recession
expansion
peak
trough
potential output
full-unemployment output
output gap
classical economists
Say's Law
Keynesian analysis

# CHAPTER 11 DRILL QUESTIONS

See Chapter 16 for answers and explanations.

**1** ☐ Mark for Review

Gross Domestic Product is a close approximation of

(A) national income

(B) societal welfare

(C) the Consumer Price Index

(D) the GDP deflator

(E) the current account balance

**2** ☐ Mark for Review

The government measures inflation using the

(A) GNP

(B) URL

(C) CPI

(D) FED

(E) GDP

**3** ☐ Mark for Review

If global warming raises temperatures so high that snow can never again exist anywhere, snow ski instructors will experience which type of unemployment?

(A) Structural

(B) Frictional

(C) Seasonal

(D) Institutional

(E) Cyclical

**4** ☐ Mark for Review

| Goods | Quantity | Year 1 price per unit | Year 2 price per unit |
|-------|----------|-----------------------|-----------------------|
| Pizza | 5 | $12.00 | $11.00 |
| Soda | 10 | $2.00 | $1.25 |
| Napkins | 100 | $0.05 | $0.15 |

The diagram above shows data about the change in prices for a variety of goods. What happened to the CPI for this consumer from year 1 to year 2?

(A) It rose by 3%.

(B) It fell by 3%.

(C) It fell by one-third.

(D) It rose by one-third.

(E) It remained unchanged.

**5** ☐ Mark for Review

Which of the following would be classified under C when calculating GDP?

(A) A homeowner mowing her own lawn

(B) $50.00 spent eating out at a restaurant

(C) The purchase of new computer software by an accounting firm

(D) Flour purchased by a baker to make donuts

(E) Old clothing donated to charitable causes

**6** ☐ Mark for Review

Which transactions will NOT be counted in GDP?

(A) Pirated goods entering the country illegally

(B) The services of a physician

(C) A retiree's social security benefits

(D) A and C

(E) B and C

**7** ☐ Mark for Review

Which of the following unemployment conditions in an economy can be the result of one of the business cycles?

(A) Frictional unemployment

(B) Structural unemployment

(C) Cyclical unemployment

(D) Seasonal unemployment

(E) Discouraged employers

# Chapter 11 Summary

## 11.1 The Circular Flow and GDP

o A country's annual **Gross Domestic Product** (GDP) is the total value of all final goods and services produced in a year within that country. GDP is calculated using either the **expenditure approach** or the **income approach**.

o **National income** (NI) is the sum of income earned by the factors of production owned by a country's citizens.

o **Personal income** (PI) is the money income received by households before personal income taxes are subtracted, and **disposable income** (DI) is personal income minus personal income taxes.

o **Depreciation** is the decline in the value of capital over time due to wear or obsolescence.

o Aggregate income = Aggregate expenditure = GDP

## 11.2 Unemployment

o The **labor force** includes employed and unemployed adults. To be **unemployed**, a labor force participant must be willing and able to work, and must have made an effort to seek work in the past four weeks.

o The **labor force participation rate** is the number of people in the labor force divided by the working-age population.

o **Discouraged workers** are those who are willing and able to work, but become so frustrated in their attempts to find work that they stop trying; **dishonest workers** claim to be unemployed to receive benefits, but don't want to work or are working for cash in an unreported job.

o **Full employment** is the level of unemployment that corresponds with the natural rate of unemployment (about 5% in the United States).

o **Okun's Law** states that for every one percentage point increase in the unemployment rate above the natural rate, output falls by 2 to 3 percentage points.

## 11.3    Price Indices and Inflation

o    **Inflation** is a sustained increase in the overall price level. **Deflation** is a sustained decrease in the overall price level.

o    One's **nominal** salary is the actual number of dollars that a person earns; one's **real salary** is the purchasing power of those dollars.

## 11.4    Real vs. Nominal GDP

o    The **Consumer Price Index** (CPI) is the government's gauge of inflation.

o    Calculate CPI using the following formula:
$$\text{Inflation between years Y and Z} = \left[ \frac{\text{CPI in Year Z}}{\text{CPI in Year Y}} - 1 \right] \times 100$$

o    The **Producer Price Index** (PPI) measures changes in the prices of wholesale goods such as lumber and steel.

o    The **Gross Domestic Product Deflator** is an alternative general price index that reflects the importance of products in current market baskets, rather than in base year market baskets, which become less relevant over time.

## 11.5    Business Cycles

o    **Business cycles** are fluctuations in aggregate output and employment. The phases of the business cycle are known as **recession** and **expansion**. The turning points between these phases are known as **peaks** and **troughs**.

o    When an economy's unemployment rate equals its natural rate of unemployment, it's reaching its **potential output**. Potential output is also known as **full-employment output**.

o    The **output gap** is the difference between potential output and actual output.

o    **Say's Law** is the idea that supply creates its own demand.

o    British economist John Maynard Keynes theorized a flat AS curve in the depression range and argued that wages cannot adjust to match changes in prices levels. Further, he argued that deviations from full employment output might persist until the government steps in with monetary or fiscal policy.

# Chapter 12
# Macro Unit 3:
# National Income
# and Price
# Determination

## 12.1   AGGREGATE DEMAND

**Aggregate demand** is the total demand for goods and services in the economy. Economists are interested in aggregate demand (AD) because, in the same way the market demand curve illustrates microeconomic patterns, the AD curve illustrates macroeconomic patterns such as inflation, unemployment, or the relative value of national currencies. The curve as depicted in Figure 1 is the relationship between real GDP and the price level.

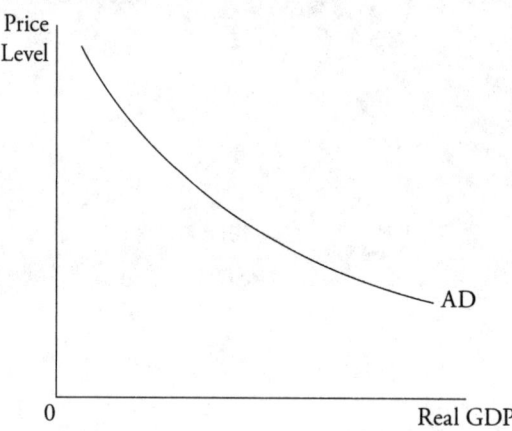

**Figure 1: Aggregate Demand**

It is not a simple aggregation of individual demand curves for particular goods, and it is not a market demand curve. The difference is that the AD curve reflects changes in demand when the price level for all goods increases or decreases, not when the price of one good changes relative to the price of another. When only the price of tea goes up, it is clear that the demand for tea will go down because we can substitute coffee or another product. The aggregate demand curve shows what happens when the prices of tea and coffee and most other goods and services all go up or down at the same time. When the general price level increases, we do not substitute one good for another; rather, we as a nation buy fewer goods and services. The substitutes in this case are money and financial assets, future goods and services, and imports.

Price and GDP have an indirect relationship, so the AD curve has a negative slope. When price decreases, GDP increases; when price increases, GDP decreases. Economists identify three primary effects that cause this relationship.

- **The Foreign Trade Effect:** When the price level in one country increases, the prices of imports from other countries become relatively less expensive. At the same time, exports from the country whose price level rose become relatively more expensive. Thus, more imported goods and services are purchased and fewer exports are sold. Domestic firms will also find it relatively more profitable to invest abroad. The decrease in exports and the increase in imports resulting from a higher price level lead to a decrease in real GDP (and vice versa).

- **The Interest Rate Effect:** When the price level increases, the real quantity of money (its purchasing power) decreases. People need more money even to continue their current consumption levels. This increases the demand for money in the form of loans, and decreases the supply of loanable funds. To reach equilibrium in the money market, the interest rate (which is effectively the price of money) must increase. The higher interest rate leads to a decrease in real GDP as households and firms put off major purchases and investment until future periods when the interest rate might be lower. Likewise, a decrease in the price level decreases interest rates and increases real GDP.

**A Memorable Relationship**

You can remember the effects that cause the indirect relationship between price and GDP using the following uplifting acrostic mnemonic:

**F**riends—Foreign Trade Effect

**I**nspire—Interest Rate Effect

**R**elationships—Real Wealth Effect

- **The Real Wealth Effect (or Real Balances Effect):** When the price level increases, the value of assets such as cash and checking-account balances falls. Given amounts of each of these assets will purchase fewer goods when prices are higher. The real value (or purchasing power) of the assets thus declines, and people buy less. Likewise, when the price level falls, the purchasing power of people's assets increases, and they buy more.

Because aggregate demand is the demand for all goods and services in the economy, it is measured in terms of real GDP. The components of aggregate demand are consumption (C), investment (I), government purchases (G), and exports minus imports (X – M).

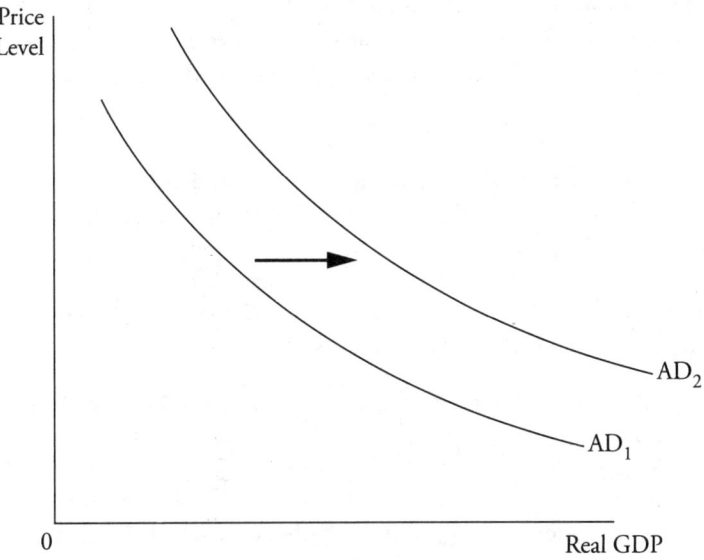

**Figure 2: Shifting Aggregate Demand**

The AD curve will shift to the right, as in Figure 2, when the following changes occur for reasons other than a change in the price level:

- Consumption increases due to:
    - expectations of inflation or shortages in the future
    - increased incomes or wealth
    - optimism about jobs and income

- Investment increases due to:
    - interest rates dropping
    - investors gaining optimism

- Government carries out expansionary policy such as a(n):
    - increase in spending
    - increase in the money supply
    - decrease in taxes

- Net exports increase because:
    - the exchange rate decreases (imports decrease)
    - foreign income increases (exports increase)

Of course, the opposite of each of these effects would shift the AD curve to the left.

## 12.2   SHORT-RUN AND LONG-RUN AGGREGATE SUPPLY

The **aggregate supply** (AS) curve indicates the total value of output that producers are willing and able to supply at alternative price levels in a given time period, holding other influences constant. Aggregate supply lives on the same graph as **aggregate demand** (AD), which is total demand for goods and services in the economy. Do not confuse the aggregate supply curve and the firm supply curve. The vertical axis of the aggregate supply curve measures the price level, not the price, of any particular good. Think of the **price level** as the average level of all prices—essentially what a price index like the CPI or the GDP Deflator measures. The horizontal axis measures the real value of all goods and services produced domestically in a given period—real GDP. Remember that expenditures on output (GDP) ultimately become income (NI), so the horizontal axis can be considered a measure of national output and income. Because it is the *real* value of GDP, it changes only when the quantity of goods and services produced changes, and not when only the price level changes.

It is important to remember that while aggregate supply and demand curves appear and behave in similar ways to individual market supply and demand curves, they illustrate fundamentally different relationships in the economy.

- When graphing individual markets, the *y*-axis represents the price of an individual good or service in the market. The *x*-axis represents the quantity of a specific good or service.

- When graphing aggregate markets, the *y*-axis represents the price level, a quantity that considers the collective value of goods and services produced by one nation, usually in an international marketplace. The *x*-axis represents the real GDP.

Figure 3 illustrates a typical **short-run aggregate supply curve** (labeled AS). It has a flat depression range (sometimes called the "Keynesian stage"), a positively sloped intermediate range, and a vertical physical limit (sometimes called the "Classical stage").

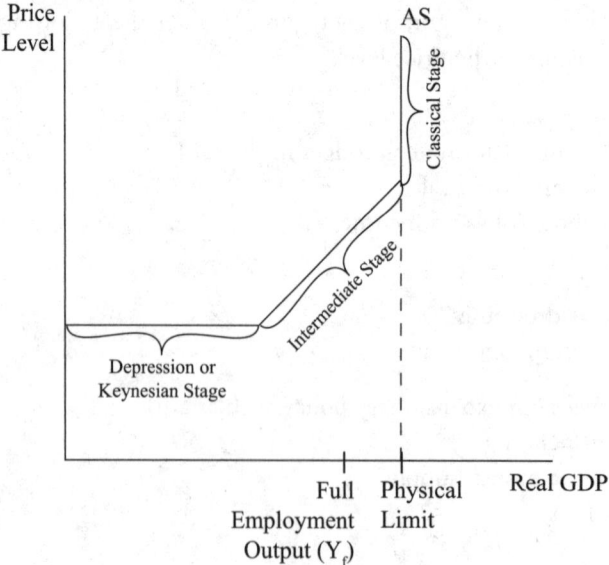

**Figure 3: Aggregate Supply**

During a depression, firms have large inventories and excess capacity and would be glad to sell more output at the existing price level. Likewise, workers and other factors of production are plentiful, and the economy can increase its output without placing upward pressure on prices or wages. This results in the horizontal segment of the aggregate supply curve. In other words, during a depression, changes in aggregate demand affect real GDP but not the price level.

The economy normally operates in the intermediate range of the AS curve, which is why many diagrams illustrate only this positively sloped segment of the curve. At these intermediate levels of output, there are no excessive inventories, and firms are closer to their productive capacities. Expansions in output require firms to hire additional inputs and work their plants and equipment at a faster pace, actions that require a profit incentive. While firms demand higher prices for increased output, wages and other input prices are relatively slow to adjust due to long-term contracts. If output prices increase faster than input prices, real factor prices (the buying power of payments to factors of production) decrease and the profit per unit of output increases. This gives firms the incentive they need to increase employment and produce more goods and services. Of course, the opposite of the above analysis is true for decreases in the price level and output. So changes in aggregate demand affect both price level and GDP in the intermediate range of the AS curve.

A change in the price level can also cause firms to produce more or less as the result of short-run misperceptions. If a firm sees the price of its product going up and does not realize that all prices are increasing at the same time, the firm might think that the relative value of its good has increased and be fooled into producing more.

As the economy reaches full employment, it becomes more difficult for firms to find new workers at the existing wage rate, and firms must increase wages (among other factor prices) in order to hire more inputs and increase output. The price level required to induce additional output then escalates until the economy reaches its physical limit for output. When factories cannot run any faster and workers cannot work any more overtime, the short-run AS cannot increase any more, and increases in aggregate demand simply increase the price level.

The AS curve shifts in response to changes in input prices and availability, technology, public policy, and other macro disturbances.

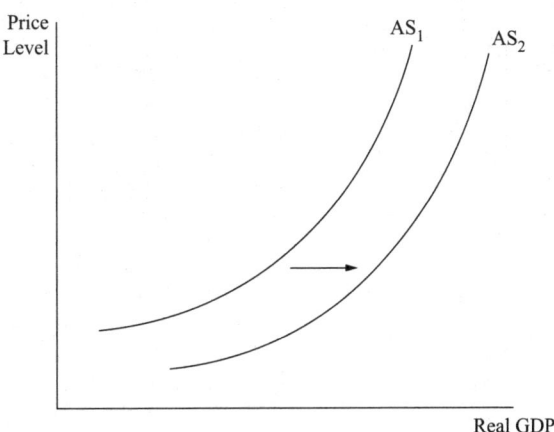

**Figure 4: Shifting Aggregate Supply**

More specifically, the AS will shift to the right, as in Figure 4, when

- Inputs become cheaper, more productive, or more plentiful, as with:
  - new discoveries of raw materials
  - increases in the labor supply
  - decreases in wages or other input prices
  - improvements in education or training
  - decreased inflationary expectations
  - increased investment (more capital)
  - technological advances
  - predictable or beneficial weather conditions

- Government policies reduce production costs, as with:
  - tax cuts
  - deregulation
  - reform in welfare or unemployment insurance programs

- Macro disturbances, such as wars and natural disasters, cease

The *opposite* of each of the above influences would cause the short-run AS curve to shift to the *left*.

## Long-Run Aggregate Supply

In the long run, wages and other input prices will adjust in accordance with output prices, and vice versa. This eliminates the incentive to produce more or less output at higher or lower price levels, because the purchasing power of per-unit profits has not changed. For example, suppose a firm sells phones for $100 each, has production costs of $60 per phone, and uses its $40 in profits per phone to buy two $20 CDs. If all prices and production costs increase by 10 percent, this firm will sell its phones for $110, spend $66 per phone on production, and make $44 in profits with which it can buy two $22 CDs. There is no reason to produce more just because all values increase by the same percentage. Thus, the **long-run aggregate supply curve** (LAS) is vertical, and stands at the level of output that corresponds with full employment, $Y_f$, as illustrated in Figure 5.

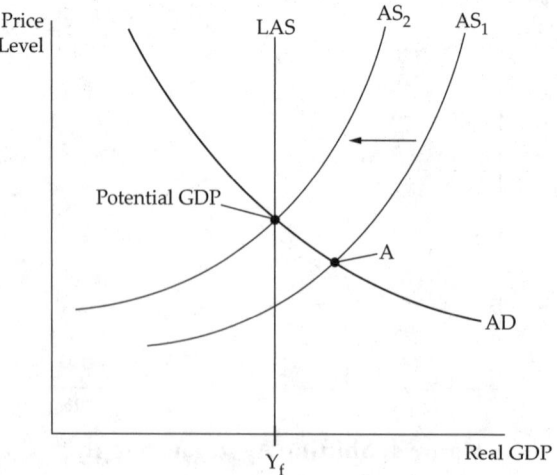

**Figure 5: Long-Run Aggregate Supply**

The LAS curve is located at $Y_f$ because at real GDP levels greater than $Y_f$, there is no cyclical unemployment and increases in output place upward pressure on wages and other input prices. In Figure 5, consider an economy operating at point A, the short-run equilibrium of aggregate supply ($AS_1$) and aggregate demand. Because real GDP exceeds $Y_f$, upward pressure on input prices will shift the short-run AS curve to the left until it resembles $AS_2$ and equilibrium real GDP equals $Y_f$. Likewise, at output levels less than $Y_f$, excess capacity and unemployment lead to decreases in wages and other input prices that shift the short-run AS curve to the right until real GDP again equals $Y_f$.

The LAS curve and $Y_f$ will shift to the right as the result of improved skill levels due to education and training, increased capital levels thanks to investment in previous periods, improved technology resulting from research and development, or increased resource availability due to new discoveries or population increases.

## One Last Thing

The transition from short-run equilibrium to long-run equilibrium as the economy "self" corrects is summarized in this handy series of figures:

Initially, the economy is at equilibrium at $E_1$, where $AD_1$ and $SRAS_1$ intersect and the price level is at $P_1$, as shown in Figure 6.

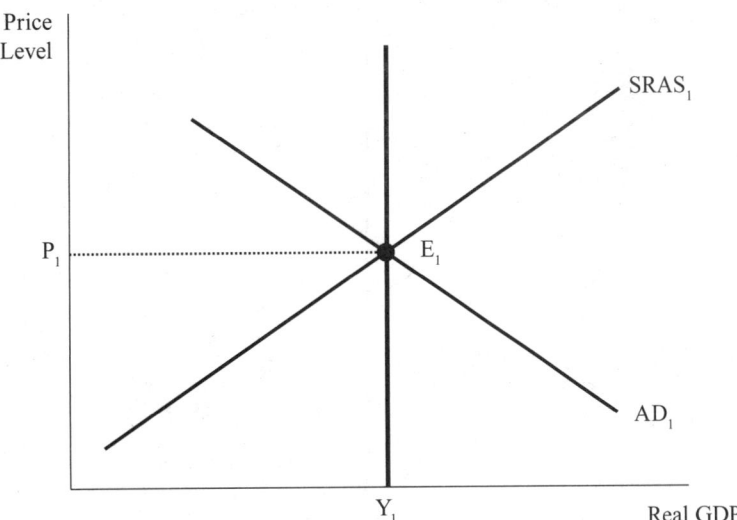

**Figure 6**

An initial negative demand shock decreases the aggregate demand to the left to $AD_2$, as shown in Figure 7.

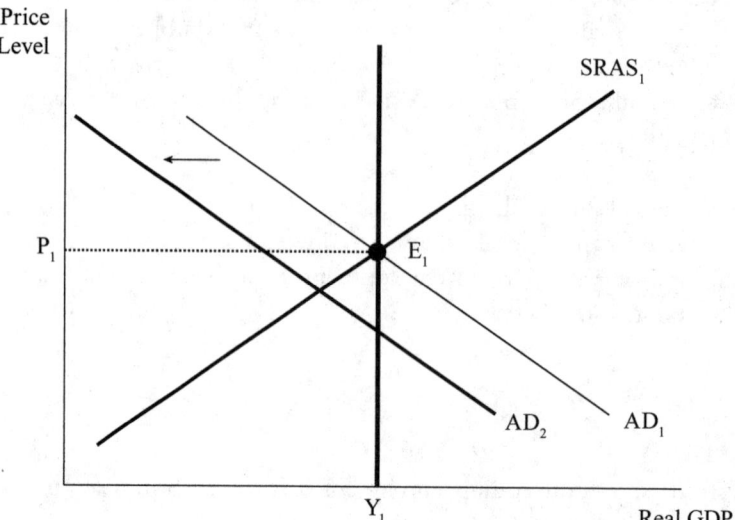

**Figure 7**

This reduces the price level to $P_2$ and aggregate output to $Y_2$, leading to higher unemployment in the short run and shifting equilibrium to $E_2$, as shown in Figure 8.

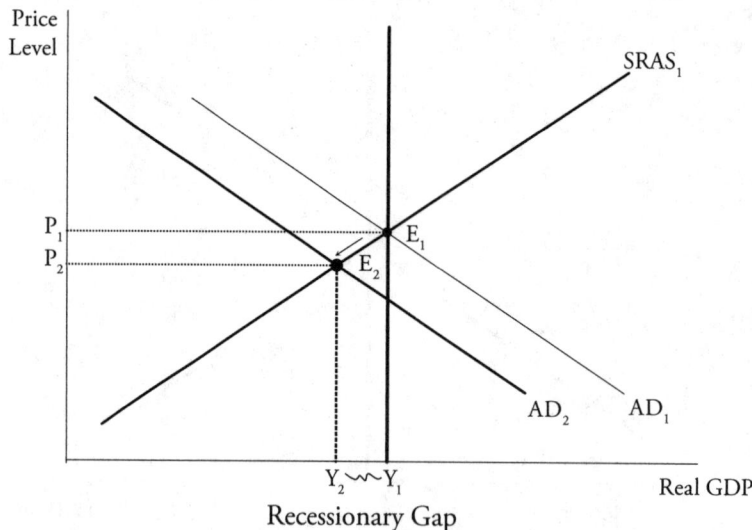

**Figure 8**

The reduction in price level leads to a decrease in nominal wages in the long run, which increases short-run aggregate supply to $SRAS_2$, bringing the economy into equilibrium at $E_3$, at which point, aggregate output is back to potential output at $Y_1$, as shown in Figure 9.

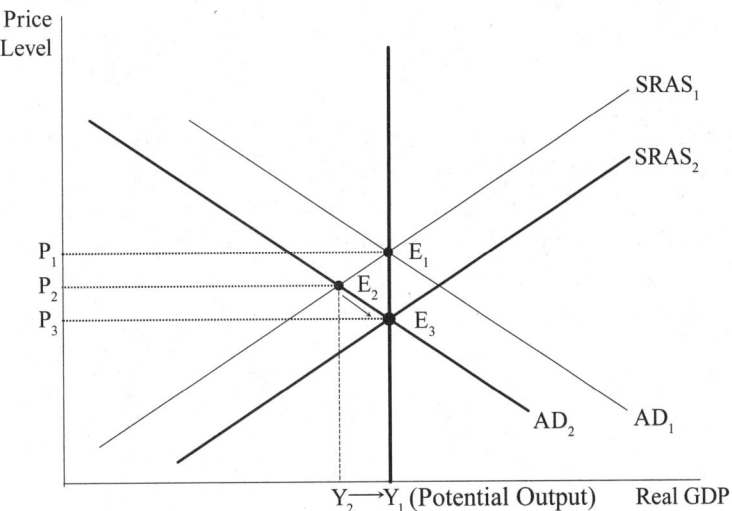

**Figure 9**

## 12.3 EQUILIBRIUM AND CHANGES IN THE AGGREGATE DEMAND-AGGREGATE SUPPLY MODEL

As with the market supply and demand curves, AS and AD intersect at an equilibrium point that designates an equilibrium level of real GDP as in Figure 10.

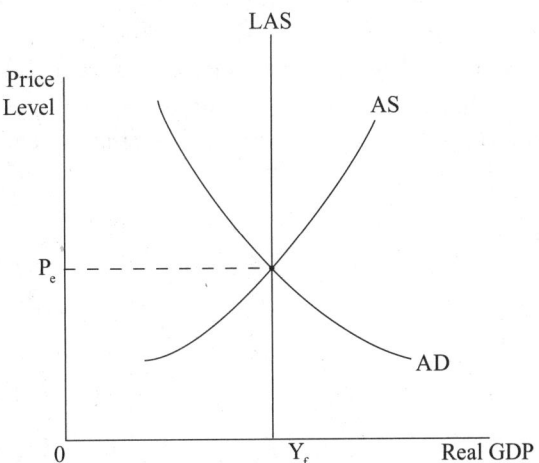

**Figure 10: Long-Run Equilibrium**

When the price level is above equilibrium, surpluses lead to a decrease in the price level. When the price level is below equilibrium, shortages bring increases in the price level. Because aggregate supply is vertical at full-employment output in the long run (or sooner, according to classical theory), the long-run equilibrium will occur at full-employment output regardless of the position of AD. Note that when AD intersects AS but not on the LRAS, you have only short-term equilibrium.

The behavior of AS and AD determines both real GDP and the price level, and studying AS and AD can give economists more information about inflation. Inflation can result from decreases in AS or increases in AD. When prices rise due to an increase in the costs of the factors of production, this is called **cost-push** or **supply-side inflation**. Graphically, this is illustrated by shifting the AS curve to the left, as shown in Figure 11.

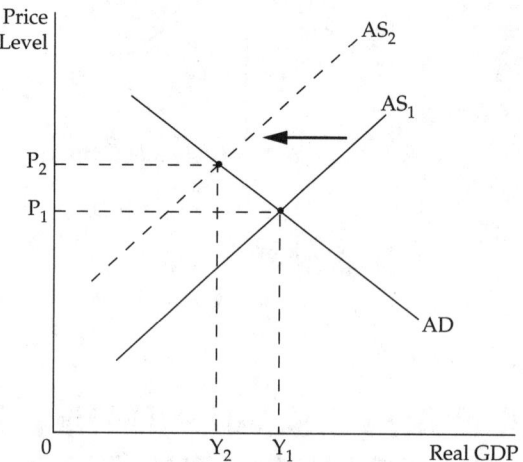

**Figure 11: Cost-Push Inflation**

Notice that this inflation is accompanied by a decrease in real GDP. **Stagflation** occurs when inflation is concurrent with relatively high unemployment and a reduction in GDP. **Demand pull inflation** is the result of the AD curve shifting out to the right relative to the AS curve for any of the reasons explained earlier in this section. Inflation that remains steady for a long period at a low rate is sometimes called **creeping inflation**. Unsteady inflation that exceeds 10 percent per year and grows month after month is sometimes called **galloping inflation**. Very rapid price increases in excess of 50 percent per year are sometimes called **hyperinflation**.

# The Multiplier

Common economic problems can occur when equilibrium between AS and AD occurs above or below LAS.

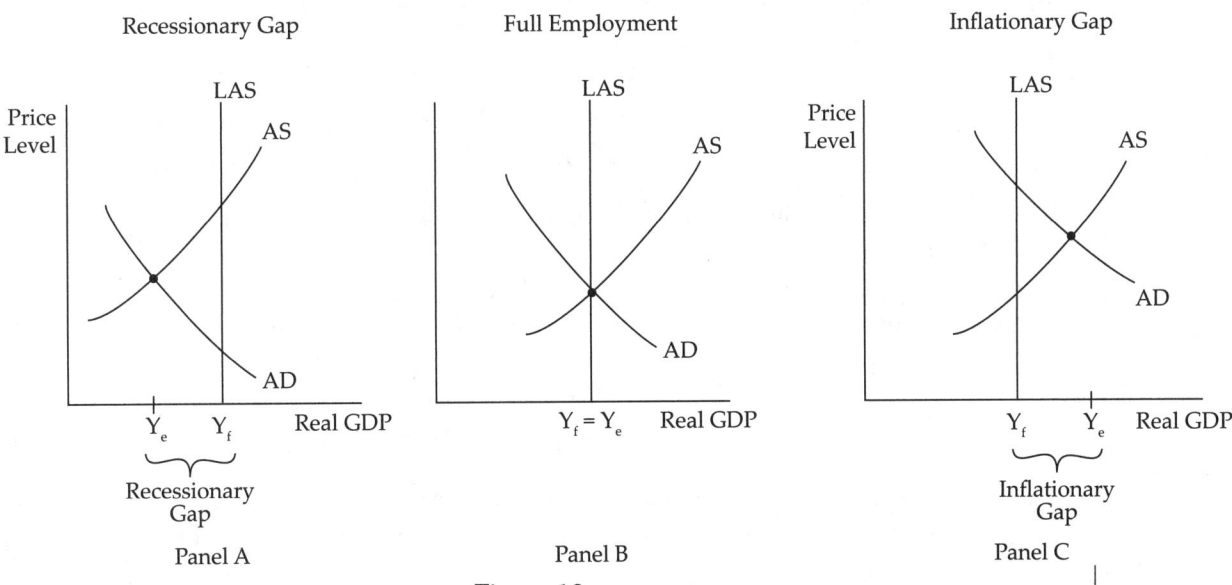

**Figure 12**

In Panel A of Figure 12, the equilibrium real GDP level, $Y_e$, is below the full employment output level, $Y_f$. When $Y_e < Y_f$, a **recessionary gap** exists as the amount by which equilibrium real GDP would have to increase to reach $Y_f$. In Panel B, equilibrium occurs at $Y_f$. This is a long-run equilibrium that can persist without recession or inflation, because there is no cyclical unemployment and no need to raise wages and overextend the labor force as would be necessary to produce beyond $Y_f$. In Panel C, equilibrium occurs at a real GDP level above $Y_f$. When $Y_e > Y_f$, an **inflationary gap** exists as the amount by which equilibrium real GDP would have to decrease to reach $Y_f$.

Classical theory suggests that when a recessionary gap exists, the surplus of workers and other inputs will cause wages and other input prices to fall, thus shifting AS to the right, lowering the price level, and increasing real GDP until equilibrium is at $Y_f$. Likewise, according to classical theory, an inflationary gap will quickly be cured as production beyond $Y_f$ necessitates high wages that lead AS to shift left, the price level to increase, and real GDP to fall until $Y_e = Y_f$. Keynesian theory counters that wages are not flexible enough to respond quickly to inflationary and recessionary pressures, and government intervention may be called for.

If the government wants to resolve inflationary and recessionary gaps with changes in expenditures, it becomes increasingly important to understand the effect on real GDP of each additional dollar of government purchases (or other types of spending). This is where the spending multiplier comes in. An additional dollar of spending adds more than a dollar to real GDP. This is because the initial dollar ends up in someone's pocket as income, and that person will turn around and spend some of it, creating more income and more spending and so on. The **spending multiplier**, or **expenditure multiplier**, is the number by which the initial amount of new spending should be multiplied to find the total resulting increase in real GDP.

At the introductory level, the spending multiplier is discussed in the context of a simplified economy in which all income is either spent on consumption or saved. The opportunity to spend income on imports is ignored for the sake of simplicity. The government can be included in this model by referring to disposable income—income net of taxes, or Y – T.

The **marginal propensity to consume** (MPC) is the amount by which consumption increases for every additional dollar of real income.

$$MPC = \frac{\text{change in consumption}}{\text{change in real income}}$$

If another dollar of real income would bring you to spend another 76 cents on consumption, your MPC is 0.76.

The **marginal propensity to save** (MPS) is the fraction of each additional dollar of income that is saved.

$$MPS = \frac{\text{change in saving}}{\text{change in real income}}$$

When the government and foreign trade are omitted, or when income means disposable income, the marginal propensity to save is the complement to the marginal propensity to consume.

$$MPC + MPS = 1$$
$$\text{or}$$
$$MPS = 1 - MPC$$

The formula for the spending multiplier or expenditure multiplier is

$$\text{Multiplier} = \frac{1}{1 - MPC} = \frac{1}{MPS}$$

The derivation of the multiplier formula is beyond the scope of the AP Exam, but an example might convince you of its strength. Suppose spending (C, I, or G) increases by $100. This $100 will end up in people's pockets as income. If the marginal propensity to consume is 0.75, 75 percent of the initial spending increase—or $75—will be spent and becomes new income. Of that $75, 75 percent—or $56.25—will again be spent, and so on until 75 percent of the final amount of additional income won't buy a piece of penny candy. This process is carried out through nine rounds of spending in Table 1.

| Spending Round | Increase in Spending | Cumulative Increases in Real GDP |
|:---:|:---:|:---:|
| 1 | $100.00 | $100.00 |
| 2 | $75.00 | $175.00 |
| 3 | $56.25 | $231.25 |
| 4 | $42.19 | $273.44 |
| 5 | $31.64 | $305.08 |
| 6 | $23.73 | $328.81 |
| 7 | $17.80 | $346.61 |
| 8 | $13.35 | $359.95 |
| 9 | $10.01 | $369.97 |
| ⋮ | ⋮ | ⋮ |
| All others | $30.03 | $400.00 |

**Table 1**

In the end, real GDP increases by a total of $400. With an initial expenditure of $100 and a multiplier of $\frac{1}{(1-0.75)} = \frac{1}{0.25} = 4$, this is exactly what the multiplier would predict: $4 \times \$100 = \$400$. Likewise, when expenditures decrease, the resulting total decrease in real GDP is found by multiplying the amount of the initial decrease by the spending multiplier.

## 12.4   FISCAL POLICY

The government exercises **fiscal policy** when it tries to counter fluctuations in aggregate expenditure with changes in purchases, transfer payments (e.g., unemployment insurance, social security, or welfare), or taxes. **Expansionary fiscal policy** involves increasing government purchases, increasing transfers, or decreasing taxes in order to shift aggregate demand to the right and boost real GDP. **Contractionary fiscal policy** involves decreasing purchases, decreasing transfers, or increasing taxes, thus shifting aggregate demand to the left, which will lower the price level and decrease real GDP.

Because government purchases are a component of autonomous expenditures, the **government spending multiplier** is the same as the autonomous spending multiplier.

$$\text{Government spending multiplier} = \frac{1}{1-\text{MPC}} = \frac{1}{\text{MPS}}$$

### Automatic Stabilizers

When fiscal policy makes headlines, it's usually because the government is responding to a specific situation or crisis. The government relies on **automatic stabilizers** to protect individuals and businesses from routine fluctuations in the economy. Automatic stabilizers include ongoing government policies such as unemployment insurance, welfare, and social security. Automatic stabilizers also include tax policies that are closely related to economic activity, such as personal income tax, payroll tax, and corporate income tax.

If the MPC is 0.5 and equilibrium real GDP exceeds full employment real GDP by $1 trillion, the government can use the multiplier formula to determine the amount by which its purchases should decrease to bring $Y_e$ down to $Y_f$.

The multiplier in this case is $\dfrac{1}{(1-0.5)} = \dfrac{1}{0.5} = 2$, meaning that for every dollar that G decreases, $Y_e$ will decrease by two dollars. Thus, a decrease in G by $500 billion will decrease $Y_e$ by the desired $1 trillion.

When the government changes taxes or transfer payments, the multiplier is a bit smaller, because for each $1 decrease in taxes or increase in transfers, a fraction (the MPS) is saved, and only the MPC is initially spent. This is in contrast to a $1 increase in government spending, all of which falls into the hands of the initial sellers of goods and services. The tax multiplier is negative because tax increases lead to expenditure decreases, and vice versa. The **tax multiplier**, which indicates the total change in real GDP resulting from each $1 change in taxes, is thus:

$$\text{Tax multiplier} = -\frac{\text{MPC}}{\text{MPS}}$$

The multiplier for transfer payments is the same except that the MPC is positive.

The above multipliers apply when only government spending, transfers, or taxes are changed. If an increase in government spending is accompanied by an equivalent increase in taxes, or likewise both G and T decrease in order to balance the budget, the government spending multiplier and the tax multiplier are combined to form the **balanced budget multiplier**.

$$\text{Balanced budget multiplier} = \frac{1}{1-\text{MPC}} + \left(\frac{-\text{MPC}}{1-\text{MPC}}\right) = \frac{1-\text{MPC}}{1-\text{MPC}} = 1$$

Thus, the change in real GDP resulting from an equivalent change in G and T is no different from the initial change in G and T.

There are both direct and indirect effects of fiscal policy. Consider the repercussions of an increase in government purchases. The expenditure increase will increase real GDP as can be illustrated with the AE diagram in Figure 13. In macroeconomics, we often use a 45° line as a guide. In Figure 13, the 45° line signifies the point at which AE = real GDP. The economy achieves equilibrium when AE intersects the 45° line.

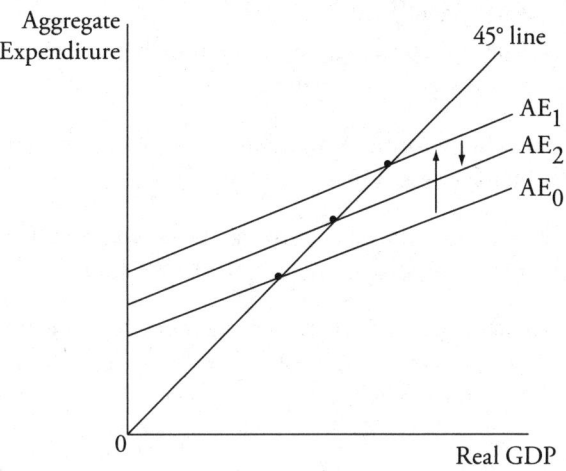

**Figure 13**

With an increase in real GDP, more money will be demanded for the purpose of making the additional expenditures. Figure 14 illustrates the demand and supply of money.

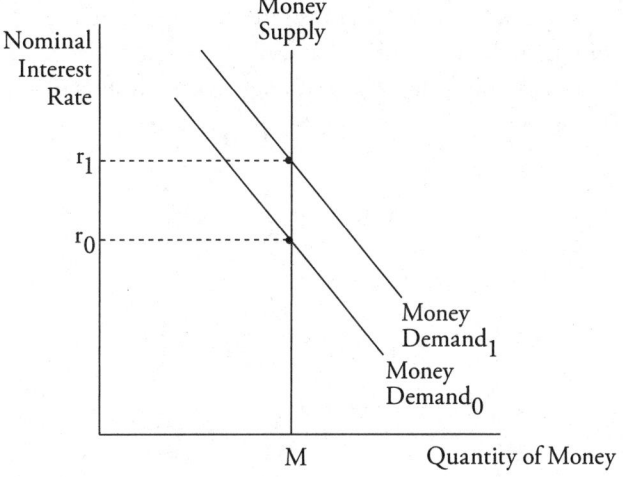

**Figure 14: The Money Market**

We assume that the supply of money is vertical. The increase in the demand for money drives up the equilibrium interest rate. Investment decreases as interest rates rise, thus bringing AE back down to $AE_2$ in Figure 13.

# Supply-Side Fiscal Policy

**Supply-side economists** believe that changes in tax rates will affect aggregate supply as well as aggregate demand. These are their primary arguments.

- With lower taxes, households will save more, and businesses will invest more. The investment will increase capital levels and make workers more productive.

- Lower income-tax rates increase the take-home pay of workers and thus increase the incentive for individuals to enter the workforce or increase their work hours.

- Entrepreneurship involves many risks. Lower tax rates increase the after-tax rewards to successful entrepreneurs and may encourage them to take risks with new products and technologies.

If a tax cut prompted both an increase in aggregate demand and an increase in aggregate supply, the supply-side effect would bolster the increase in real GDP caused by the increase in aggregate demand. Inspired by the work of Arthur Laffer, supply-side economists also argue that tax cuts might actually lead to increases in tax revenue. The idea is that although the tax rate is lower, increases in production (for the reasons given above) might increase the tax base by more than enough to compensate for the lower tax rate.

Critics of supply-side economics contend that tax rates in the United States are already low relative to those in many industrialized nations, that any supply-side effects are likely to be smaller and longer in coming than supply-siders suggest, and that the results of supply-side tax cuts in the 1980s were unconvincing.

# CHAPTER 12 KEY TERMS

## 12.1

aggregate demand
foreign trade effect
interest rate effect
Real Wealth Effect (real balances effect)

## 12.2

aggregate supply
aggregate demand
price level
short-run aggregate supply curve
long-run aggregate supply curve

## 12.3

cost push (supply-side) inflation
stagflation
demand pull inflation
creeping inflation
galloping inflation
hyperinflation
recessionary gap
inflationary gap
spending multiplier (expenditure multiplier)
marginal propensity to consume
marginal propensity to save

## 12.4

fiscal policy
expansionary fiscal policy
contractionary fiscal policy
government spending multiplier
tax multiplier
balanced budget multiplier
supply-side economist
automatic stabilizers

# CHAPTER 12 DRILL QUESTIONS

See Chapter 16 for answers and explanations.

**1** ☐ Mark for Review

Operating in the intermediate range of the aggregate supply curve, an increase in aggregate demand results in an increase in

(A) price level only

(B) real GDP only

(C) neither price level nor real GDP

(D) nominal GDP only

(E) price level and real GDP

**2** ☐ Mark for Review

If the marginal propensity to consume is 0.8, what is the largest total increase in GDP that can result from $500 of new spending?

(A) $400

(B) $500

(C) $625

(D) $2,500

(E) $5,000

**3** ☐ Mark for Review

Stagflation occurs when

(A) the price level rises for two consecutive quarters

(B) the price level rises and output falls

(C) the price level stays the same and output increases

(D) the price level stays the same and output decreases

(E) the price level and output both fall

**4** ☐ Mark for Review

A recessionary gap exists when the short-run equilibrium level of real GDP

(A) decreases over time

(B) equals the full-employment level of real GDP

(C) is above the full-employment level of real GDP

(D) is below the full-employment level of real GDP

(E) increases over time

**5** ☐ Mark for Review

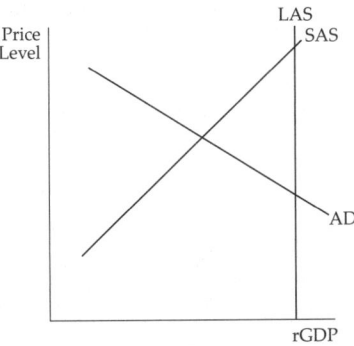

On the graph of the aggregate supply and demand model above, a recessionary gap exists, and the economy is in

Ⓐ neither short-run nor long-run equilibrium

Ⓑ long-run, but not short-run, equilibrium

Ⓒ short-run equilibrium

Ⓓ both long- and short-run equilibrium

Ⓔ neutral equilibrium

**6** ☐ Mark for Review

Long-run aggregate supply is most likely to increase as the result of

Ⓐ an increase in the real interest rate

Ⓑ increased investment in capital

Ⓒ an increase in aggregate demand

Ⓓ an increase in the unemployment rate

Ⓔ an increase in the exchange rate

**7** ☐ Mark for Review

Which of the following statements would "supply-side" economists disagree with?

Ⓐ Tax changes cause shifts in aggregate supply that work against shifts in aggregate demand, thus reducing the effect of the tax change on real GDP.

Ⓑ A tax cut is likely to increase aggregate supply by boosting saving, investment, and thus capital accumulation.

Ⓒ A tax increase is likely to decrease aggregate supply by decreasing after-tax wages and thus providing disincentives to work.

Ⓓ A tax cut is likely to increase aggregate supply by providing greater rewards for risk taking.

Ⓔ A decrease in tax rates does not necessarily result in a decrease in tax revenues.

**8** ☐ Mark for Review

The Fed decides to sell bonds on the open market. How is this likely to affect interest rates and the value of the dollar?

Ⓐ The interest rate decreases, and the value of the dollar decreases.

Ⓑ The interest rate decreases, and the value of the dollar increases.

Ⓒ The interest rate increases, and the value of the dollar increases.

Ⓓ The interest rate increases, and the value of the dollar decreases.

Ⓔ The interest rate increases, and the value of the dollar remains the same.

**9**  ☐ Mark for Review

How will an increase in investment from businesses and consumers affect aggregate demand?

Ⓐ Investment from businesses and consumers doesn't affect aggregate demand.

Ⓑ Aggregate demand will increase.

Ⓒ Aggregate demand will decrease.

Ⓓ Aggregate demand will spike before equalizing.

Ⓔ Aggregate demand will remain the same.

# Chapter 12 Summary

## 12.1  Aggregate Demand

o   **Aggregate demand** is the total demand for goods and services in the economy.

o   Three effects cause the inverse relationship between price and GDP.
   - **The Real Wealth Effect**
   - **The Foreign Trade Effect**
   - **The Interest Rate Effect**

## 12.2 Short-Run and Long-Run Aggregate Supply

o   The **aggregate supply** (AS) curve indicates the total value of output that producers are willing and able to supply at alternative price levels in a given time period, holding other influences constant.

o   **Aggregate demand** (AD) is the total demand for goods and services in the economy.

o   The **price level** is the average level of all prices.

o   The **long-run aggregate supply curve** (LAS) is vertical and stands at the level of output that corresponds with full employment.

## 12.3  Equilibrium and Changes in the Aggregate Demand-Aggregate Supply Model

o   **Cost-push** or **supply-side inflation** occurs when inflation results from an increase in resource costs that shifts the AS curve to the left.

o   **Stagflation** is defined by the combination of rising prices and falling output.

o **Demand pull inflation** is the result of the AD curve shifting out to the right relative to the AS curve.

o Inflation that remains steady for a long period at a low rate is called **creeping inflation**.

o Unsteady inflation that exceeds 10 percent per year and grows month after month is **galloping inflation**.

o **Hyperinflation** is very rapid price increases in excess of 50 percent per year.

o A **recessionary gap** exists as the amount by which equilibrium real GDP would have to increase to reach LAS.

o An **inflationary gap** exists as the amount by which equilibrium real GDP would have to decrease to reach LAS.

o The **spending multiplier** is the number by which the initial amount of new spending should be multiplied to find the total resulting increase in real GDP.

o The **marginal propensity to consume** (MPC) is the amount by which consumption increases for every additional dollar of real income.

$$MPC = \frac{\text{change in consumption}}{\text{change in real income}}$$

o The **marginal propensity to save** (MPS) is the fraction of each additional dollar of income that is saved.

$$MPS = \frac{\text{change in saving}}{\text{change in real income}}$$

o The formula for the **spending multiplier,** or **expenditure multiplier,** is

$$\text{Multiplier} = \frac{1}{1 - MPC} = \frac{1}{MPS}$$

## 12.4 Fiscal Policy

o The government exercises **fiscal policy** when it tries to counter fluctuations in aggregate expenditure with changes in purchases, transfer payments, or taxes.

o Because government purchases are a component of autonomous expenditures, the **government spending multiplier** is the same as the autonomous spending multiplier.

$$\text{Government spending multiplier} = \frac{1}{1 - \text{MPC}} = \frac{1}{\text{MPS}}$$

o The **tax multiplier** is the total change in real GDP resulting from each $1 change in taxes.

$$\text{Tax multiplier} = -\frac{\text{MPC}}{\text{MPS}}$$

# Chapter 13
# Macro Unit 4:
# Financial Sector

## 13.1   FINANCIAL ASSETS

**Financial assets** are a subcategory of economic assets. These are entities over which institutional units or individuals assert ownership rights. The owners can derive economic benefits through their possession or use over a period of time. Most financial assets are financial claims arising from contractual relationships in which one institutional unit provides funds to another. The contracts thus established are the basis of the creditor/debtor relationship by which the owners of assets obtain an unconditional claim on the economic resources of other institutional units.

## 13.2   DEFINITION, MEASUREMENT, AND FUNCTIONS OF MONEY

**Money** is any commonly recognized item used to exchange goods and services within an economy. Though the word *money* is commonly used to refer to anything of value that is exchanged between individuals, the formal definition is more rigorous. For an item to formally be considered money, it must have the following characteristics:

- Portability: money must be easily transferred between individuals

- Durability: money must endure and hold value through time

- Divisibility: money must be broken down into smaller units to make change

- Fungibility: money must carry interchangeable value across place and time (in other words, a buyer and seller must agree on the value of the item being used as money, and future buyers and sellers must agree, too)

Many items have been used as money throughout history with varying degrees of success. Economists generally agree that precious metals have been some of the most effective monies humans have used, pointing to the gold and silver exchanged in ancient Egypt that is still used as money today. Other items have been less successful. For example, because packs of cigarettes are portable and easily divided, they have been used as money in prisons. However, cigarettes do not function well as money in the larger economy. Cigarettes aren't fungible; individuals who don't smoke don't think they have value. Nor are cigarettes durable: if set on fire or dropped in a puddle, a cigarette is obsolete.

Money has three primary functions.

1. **Medium of exchange**. Without money, we would have to barter for everything. This is hard enough when there is a **double coincidence of wants**, meaning that the person who owns the goods or services you want (for example, flour) has a desire for what you have to barter with (for example, chickens). But if you have chickens, you want flour, and the flour owner wants a shovel, you will have to try to trade your chickens for a shovel that you can trade for flour. If the shovel maker doesn't want chickens, the complexity grows. A common medium of exchange greatly simplifies such transactions.

2. **Store of value.** If the goods or services you produce are perishable, you will benefit from a nonperishable item that will hold the value of past production into the future. The output of a tomato farmer or a ski instructor will have little value six months after production. By

exchanging this output for something that carries value across place and time, the benefits of production can be transferred into the future. (Note: storing value is the key characteristic that distinguishes money from currency.)

3. **Unit of account.** Money provides a standard unit for price listings and comparisons. If there were no common unit of account, price listings would be in terms of arbitrary units (three chickens per shovel, two sacks of flour per telephone) and price comparisons would involve a complex set of conversions. The recent adoption of the euro as a standard unit of account in the European Union was largely an attempt to eliminate the burden of reconciling the many different measures of value there.

Money is commonly confused with two other concepts: wealth and currency. **Currency** is an item that is used as money but does NOT act as a store of value or carry intrinsic value. Consider, for example, the difference between a silver coin and paper cash that are both worth one U.S. dollar. If the United States ceases to exist, the silver coin would still have value; people in other countries would want to use it as money or perhaps melt it down into jewelry. The silver coin carries intrinsic value beyond that of the U.S. dollar. The paper cash, however, would be worthless and have no value beyond that of scratch paper. As a result, silver coins are money and paper cash is currency. (Another way to conceptualize this relationship: all money is currency, but not all currency is money.)

Because confusion between money and currency is so common, economists sometimes use the terms commodity money and fiat money to describe the same relationship. **Commodity money** refers to any raw material with intrinsic value that is used in exchange for other goods in an economy (such as a silver coin), while **fiat money** refers to currency without intrinsic value (such as paper cash).

**Wealth** is the value of the total assets owned by an individual or entity. While there are a variety of ways to measure and think about wealth, it is most commonly the sum of one's assets, minus any debts.

## 13.3 BANKING AND THE EXPANSION OF THE MONEY SUPPLY

Most nations and territories utilize a central bank to maintain macroeconomic stability. Central banks influence the value and supply of money by setting a **policy rate**. The policy rate is the interest rate at which depository institutions lend reserve balances to each other overnight.

Because banks can invest and borrow from each other instantaneously to maximize returns (a strategy known as arbitrage), changes in the policy rate directly impact interest rates throughout the economy. Consumers are more likely to borrow and spend when interest rates are low, so decreasing the policy rate increases the money supply. Conversely, when the policy rate is high, money is expensive, so lending and spending decrease.

In the United States, the central bank is called the Federal Reserve Bank (the Fed). Established by Congress in 1913, the Fed has a "dual mandate," or two primary goals: 1) to maximize the employment rate and 2) to maintain price stability. Essentially, maintaining price stability equates to limiting inflation, or maintaining the value and buying power of the US dollar. In the United States, the policy rate is known as the **federal funds rate (FFR).**

Here's how it works:

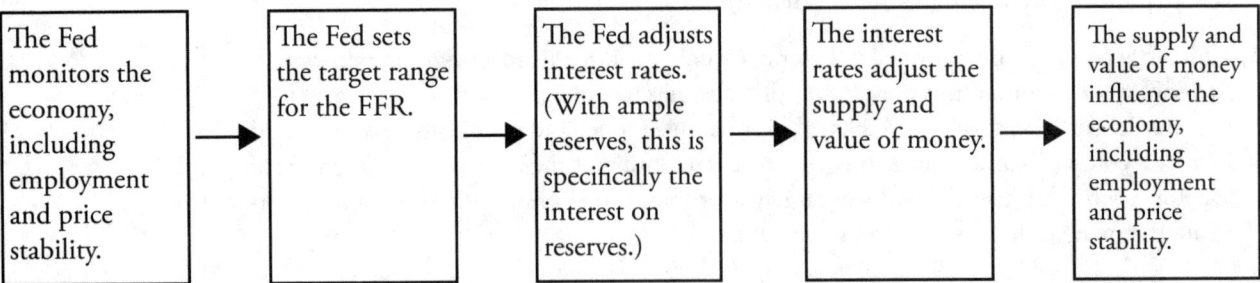

Monitoring the money supply is a key operation for any central bank. Confusingly, the term **money supply** does not refer to the supply of money within the United States; the money supply refers to the supply of currency and other liquid assets held within the United States. The term **liquidity** refers to how easily an asset can be transferred into currency; in other words, liquidity refers to how easily an asset can be sold for its cash value. The Fed tracks money supply totals in categories ranked in decreasing order of liquidity:

- **M1** is the sum of coin and paper money plus checking deposits and savings deposits.

- **M2** is M1 plus small-time deposits (deposits less than $100,000 with a fixed term of maturity such as CDs), money market mutual funds, and Eurodollar deposits (overnight, dollar-denominated deposits in European banks).

This section will explore the various tools the Fed uses to manipulate the money supply and ensure the FFR falls within its target range. The following section will explore models illustrating exactly how changes in FFR impact the economy.

Due to the financial crisis of 2008, the Fed made a series of large-scale asset purchases that dramatically increased the amount of money it holds in its own reserves. Prior to 2008, excess reserves held by the Fed hadn't exceeded $2 billion. By December 2008, the Fed held $767 billion in reserves. In August of 2014, reserves held by the Fed reached an all-time high of $2.7 trillion. As a result, the Fed has changed its practices to reflect the shift from **limited reserves** to **ample reserves**.

To be clear, the Fed plans to move forward using tools appropriate to holding ample reserves. For success on the AP Exam, be prepared to compare the tools used in limited and ample reserves. Let's look more closely.

# Tools of Central Bank Policy with Limited Reserves

With limited reserves, the Fed utilized three tools to control the money supply.

- Adjustments in the required reserve ratio, the fraction of its own assets a commercial bank is required to hold in liquid reserves

- Adjustments in the discount rate paid by banks to borrow from the Fed

- Open market operations (buying and selling of government securities)

As detailed below, the **required reserve ratio** was a key factor in the process of money creation. If the required reserve ratio was high, banks were required to hold a large portion of their deposits as reserves and lend out less. If the Fed wanted to increase the money supply, it could decrease the required reserve ratio and thereby require banks to hold less money in reserves. Note: In the current state of ample reserves, the Fed no longer requires banks to hold reserves, and the reserve ratio is obsolete.

The **discount rate** is the interest rate banks pay to borrow money from the Fed. When the rate is low, banks are more likely to borrow from the Fed when the banks' excess reserves do not satisfy their demand for loans. The Fed can thus increase the money supply by decreasing the discount rate or vice versa.

**Open market operations** involve the Fed's purchase and sale of government securities. When the government runs a deficit (G > T), the Treasury (not the Fed) borrows money by selling government securities—bonds, bills, and notes—on the open market. Congress has authorized the Fed to buy and sell these government securities just like individuals and other institutions, which enables it to inject money into the economy or remove it from circulation. When the Fed sells a bond for $1,000, it is effectively giving a piece of paper to the buyer that says "bond" on it and taking in the buyer's money. This removes money from circulation. It may also have a multiplied effect if the $1,000 to buy the bond is withdrawn from a bank account, bringing the bank's reserves below the required level, and causing the bank to call in loans from others who will subsequently remove deposits from other banks and cause further contraction. To expand the money supply, the Fed can buy securities. If the Fed buys a bond, it gives money to someone in exchange for a piece of paper. This new money in the economy is likely to be deposited into someone's bank account, where most of it will be lent out again, and the whole multiplier process works its magic once more.

Economies with limited reserves utilize a **fractional reserve banking system** in which only a fraction of total deposits is held on reserve and the rest is lent out. The ratio of a bank's reserves to its total deposits is called the **reserve ratio**.

$$\text{Reserve ratio} = \frac{\text{bank reserves}}{\text{total deposits}}$$

With limited reserves, the Fed set a minimum reserve ratio for all banks. Banks earn profits by lending the amount of their deposits beyond the required reserves out to borrowers who paid an interest rate higher than the interest rate the banks pay to their depositors.

Central to the accounting practices of a bank was a **balance sheet** called a **T account,** as shown in Figure 1.

Panel A

| Assets | | Liabilities | |
|---|---|---|---|
| Required Reserves | 10 | Deposits | 100 |
| Excess Reserves | 10 | | |
| Loans | 80 | | |
| | 100 | | 100 |

Panel B

| Assets | | Liabilities | |
|---|---|---|---|
| Required Reserves | 6 | Deposits | 60 |
| Excess Reserves | 0 | | |
| Loans | 54 | | |
| | 60 | | 60 |

Panel C

| Assets | | Liabilities | |
|---|---|---|---|
| Required Reserves | 6 | Deposits | 60 |
| Excess Reserves | 0 | Borrowed Reserves | 26 |
| Loans | 80 | | |
| | 86 | | 86 |

**Figure 1**

The **assets** side includes required reserves, excess reserves that can be loaned out, and loans. The **liabilities** side includes deposits and reserves that can be borrowed from the Fed. The two sides of the T account must always balance, so when something changes the total on one side of the T account, there must also be a change on the other side. Consider a bank with assets and liabilities as in Panel A (in millions of dollars). This bank has $100 million in deposits, and with a reserve ratio of 10 percent, its required reserves are $10 million. Loans could increase from $80 million to $90 million by reducing excess reserves from $10 million to zero. Now suppose a major depositor reduced her deposits by $40 million. The required reserves are now 10 percent of the remaining $60 million in deposits, or $6 million. There are several options for how the bank can come back into balance. It could call in $26 million in loans, bringing assets and liabilities to $60 million, as shown in Panel B. It could also borrow $26 million in reserves from the Fed as in Panel C, balancing each side of the T account with $86 million.

The fractional reserve banking system enables what economists call **money creation**. Money creation is the generation of assets caused when an initial deposit to a bank is held partially in reserve and partially redistributed as a loan over and over again. Suppose $100 million of new deposits enters a banking system which, for simplicity, we will assume has no initial holdings and loans out all of its excess reserves. We will also assume there are no cash holdings, meaning that all loans are either deposited in a bank or paid to people who deposit them in a bank. When the $100 million deposit enters the first bank, 10 percent must be held as reserves, and $90 million is loaned out. That $90 million is deposited in another bank and 90 percent of that, or $81 million, is loaned out. The $81 million is deposited and enables a $72.9 million loan, which is deposited and enables a $65.61 million loan and so on. In the end, as illustrated in Figure 2, the entire $100 million initial deposit is held as reserves; there are $900 million in loans stemming from this deposit; and total deposits are $1,000 million, or $1 billion.

| | | | | | |
|---|---|---|---|---|---|
| Bank 1 | Reserves | 10 | | Deposits | 100 |
| | Loans | 90 | | | |
| Bank 2 | Reserves | 9 | | Deposits | 90 |
| | Loans | 81 | | | |
| Bank 3 | Reserves | 8.1 | | Deposits | 81 |
| | Loans | 72.9 | | | |
| Bank 4 | Reserves | 7.29 | | Deposits | 72.9 |
| | Loans | 65.61 | | | |
| • | | | • | | |
| • | | | • | | |
| • | | | • | | |
| Total | Reserves | 100 | | Deposits | 1,000 |
| | Loans | 900 | | | |

**Figure 2**

The total amount of deposits resulting from an initial deposit that is ultimately held as reserves is conveniently found using the **money multiplier**.

$$\text{Money multiplier} = \frac{1}{\text{required reserve ratio}}$$

In the above example, the required reserve ratio was 0.10, so the money multiplier was $\frac{1}{0.10} = 10$, and the $100 million new deposit created a total of $10 \times \$100$ million = $1 billion in deposits.

Remember that the money multiplier was used when the United States had limited reserves. The Fed currently has ample reserves and no longer mandates a reserve ratio. As a result, the money multiplier is obsolete. (But is still fair game on the AP Exam!)

## Tools of Central Bank Policy with Ample Reserves

As discussed, the 2008 crisis prompted the Fed to take dramatic action. The Fed reduced the FFR to nearly 0 to encourage borrowing and spending and to support economic recovery. To achieve this FFR, the Fed relied on open-market operations, purchasing long-term securities issued by the government. Interest rates dropped, and there was a dramatic increase to the reserves held in the United States.

In response, the Fed adjusted the mechanisms through which it influences the FFR and manages the economy.

- **Interest on reserves.** With ample reserves, small changes to the reserve ratio no longer have an effective impact on the FFR. Instead, *the Fed allows banks to earn interest on whatever they choose to hold in reserve.* This interest rate impacts the interest rates at which banks are willing to lend money.

- **Adjustments to the discount rate.** As in economies with limited reserves, the interest rate at which the Fed lends to other banks influences the interest rates at which banks are willing to lend to consumers, and thus interest rates throughout the economy.

- **Open market operations**. The Fed still engages in open market operations. However, it does so with the intention of maintaining its own reserves, not to manage the FFR.

The key differences between limited and ample reserves merit repeating. Economies with limited reserves rely upon direct changes in the money supply, via the reserve ratio, to manage the economy. In economies with ample reserves, the Fed influences the economy via **administered interest rates**, specifically interest held on reserves and adjustments to the discount rate.

## 13.4   MONETARY POLICY

**Monetary policy** describes the way in the which the Fed uses its tools to influence interest rates, inflation, exchange rates, unemployment, and real GDP. In other words, when economists talk about changes in monetary policy, they are talking about whether the Fed is trying to make the economy expand or contract. Here we will examine how changes in monetary policy impact the economy.

# Monetary Policy with Limited Reserves

Figure 3 illustrates the direct effects of expansionary monetary policy with limited reserves.

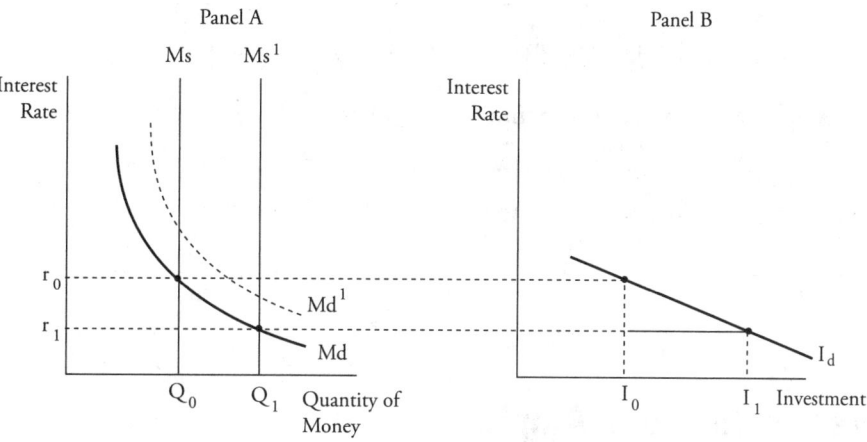

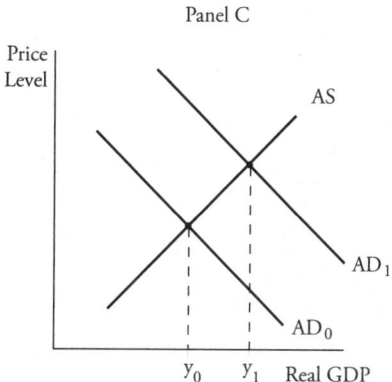

**Figure 3**

In Panel A, the money supply increases, resulting in a lower interest rate. In Panel B, the lower interest rate is seen to induce an increase in the quantity of investment demanded. Panel C illustrates the result of the increase in I on AD, and the resulting increase in real GDP, including multiplier effects, as explained above. Note that the key mechanism for impacting interest levels, and therefore prices, is the money supply, or the reserve ratio.

As is the case for fiscal policy, an increase in real GDP due to expansionary monetary policy spurs a second round of effects. With more output being purchased and more income being earned, the demand for money increases from Md to $Md^1$ in Panel A of Figure 3. This will increase the interest rate and decrease investment. However, the magnitude of these second-round effects is likely to be smaller than that of the direct effects, so the end result of expansionary monetary policy will be a decrease in the interest rate and an increase in real GDP.

In summary, the effects of **expansionary monetary policy** are

$$Ms \uparrow \Rightarrow \ r \downarrow \Rightarrow \ I \uparrow \Rightarrow \ AD \uparrow \Rightarrow \ Y \uparrow \Rightarrow \ Md \uparrow \Rightarrow \ r \uparrow$$

(but not enough to counteract the previous effects)

The effects of **contractionary monetary policy** are summarized as

$$Ms \downarrow \Rightarrow \ r \uparrow \Rightarrow \ I \downarrow \Rightarrow \ AD \downarrow \Rightarrow \ Y \downarrow \Rightarrow \ Md \downarrow \Rightarrow \ r \downarrow$$

(but not enough to counteract the previous effects)

## Monetary Policy with Ample Reserves

The following model (Figure 4) reflects the differences in monetary policy with limited and ample reserves.

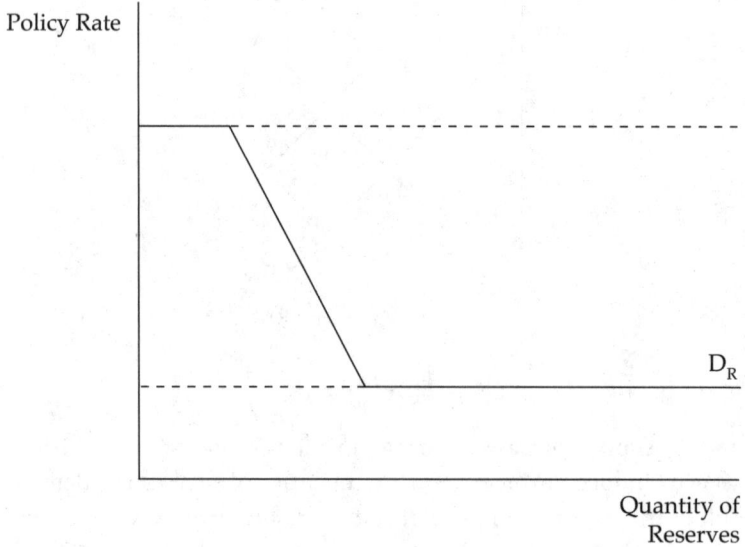

**Figure 4: Demand for Reserves**

The initial horizontal portion of the demand curve represents the discount rate, the interest rate banks pay the Fed in order to borrow money. In effect, this creates a ceiling for the value of the dollar as banks generally want to pay the lowest interest rates on the market. The downward-sloping portion of the curve represents economies with limited reserves, wherein changes in the quantity of reserves impact the policy rate. The final horizontal segment represents economies with ample reserves, for which changes in the quantity of reserves have no impact on the policy rate.

Modeling the supply of reserves illustrates the impact of changing the reserve ratio with limited reserves. Remember that the supply of reserves is vertical because it is controlled directly by central banks.

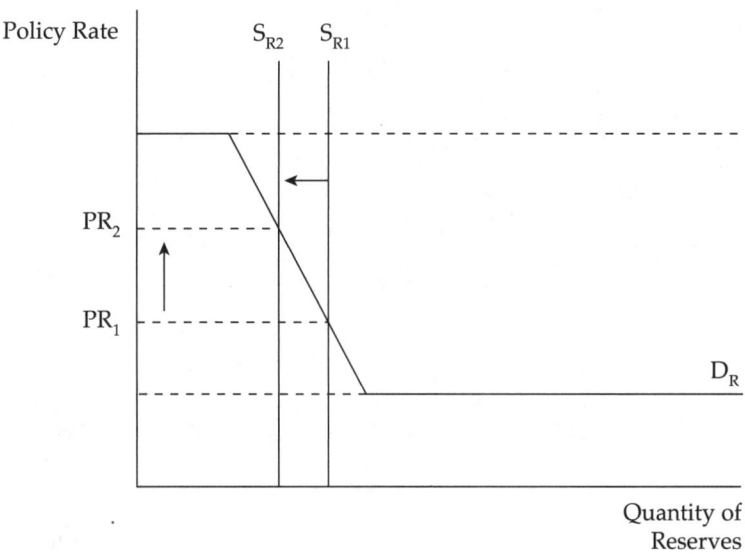

**Figure 5: Decrease in the Supply of Reserves in an Economy with Limited Reserves**

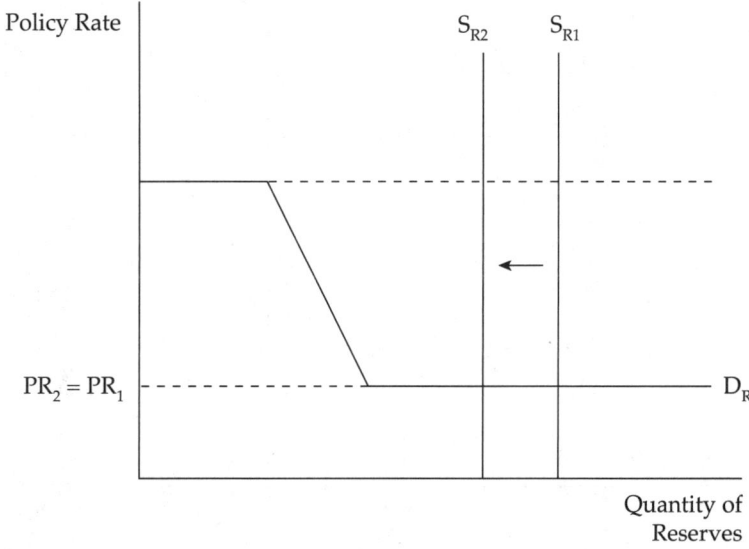

**Figure 6: Decrease in the Supply of Reserves in an Economy with Ample Reserves**

As illustrated in Figure 5, a decrease in the supply of reserves in economies with limited reserves results in an increase in the policy rate. The converse is also true: increases in the supply of reserves decrease the policy rate. In economies with ample reserves, adjusting the supply of reserves via the reserve ratio has no impact on the policy rate or the overall economy. Figure 6 illustrates economies with ample reserves. A shift in the supply of reserves, or the reserve ratio, has no impact on the policy rate.

By contrast, economies with ample reserves use administered interest rates—the discount rate and interest earned on reserves—to influence demand for reserves and the policy rate. Look at Figures 7 and 8.

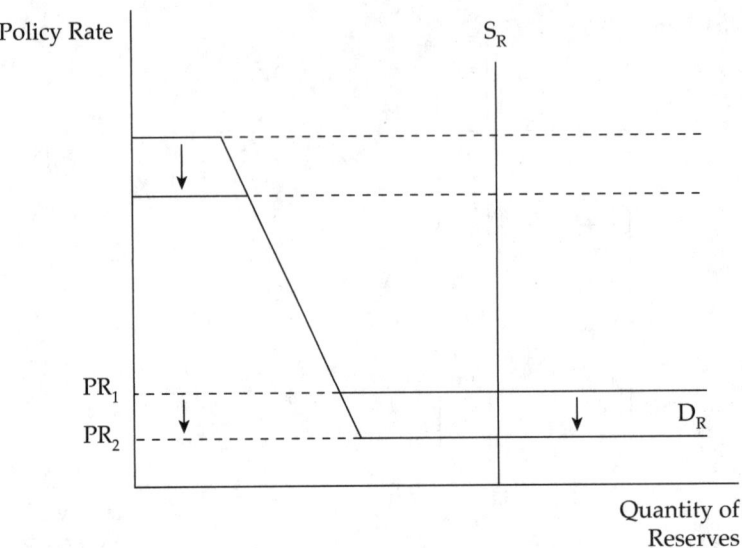

**Figure 7: Decrease in Administered Interest Rates**

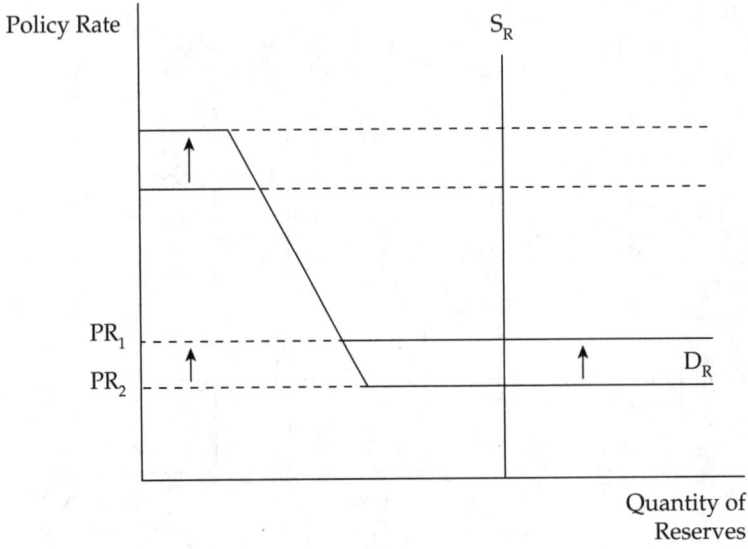

**Figure 8: Increase in Administered Interest Rates**

When understanding these graphs, remember that the interest rate on reserves directly influences demand for reserves. When central banks increase and decrease administered interest rates, they are increasing and decreasing demand for reserves. While the supply of reserves held by the Fed is mandated and therefore vertical, commercial banks will hold more in reserves (an increase in demand for reserves) when they can earn higher interest rates and will hold less in reserves (a decrease in demand for reserves) when they earn lower interest rates. As a result, administered interest rates influence the policy rate in economies with ample reserves.

## Interaction of Fiscal and Monetary Policies

Fiscal and monetary policy need not operate in isolation. By combining the two types of policy into an orchestrated policy mix, a preferable macro outcome may result. For example, expansionary fiscal policy may boost output at the expense of higher interest rates that crowd out investment. To expand the problem, when investment in capital resources goes down in the current period, future output is sacrificed because there is less capital for use in production. (Reread this sentence twice—this point is often missed on AP Exam!) In order to limit or eliminate the crowding out of investment that may result from expansionary fiscal policy, it can be combined with expansionary monetary policy that will increase the money supply and decrease the interest rate.

# CHAPTER 13 KEY TERMS

## 13.1

financial assets

## 13.2

money
medium of exchange
double coincidence of wants
store of value
unit of account
currency
commodity money
fiat money
wealth

## 13.3

policy rate
federal funds rate (FFR)
money supply
liquidity
M1
M2
limited reserves
ample reserves
required reserve ratio
discount rate
open market operation
fractional reserve banking system
reserve ratio
balance sheet
T account
assets
liabilities
money creation
money multiplier
interest on reserves
adjustments to the discount rate
open market operations
administered interest rates

## 13.4

monetary policy
expansionary monetary policy
contractionary monetary policy

# CHAPTER 13 DRILL QUESTIONS

See Chapter 16 for answers and explanations.

**1** ☐ Mark for Review

The term *liquidity* refers to

- (A) the value of the total assets owned by an individual or entity
- (B) the ability of money to retain its value over time
- (C) how easily an asset can be transferred into cash
- (D) how easily an asset can be transferred between two individuals or entities
- (E) the ability of money to be broken down into smaller units

**2** ☐ Mark for Review

Which of the following could the Federal Reserve do to increase the money supply?

- (A) Buy government securities on the open market
- (B) Increase the discount rate
- (C) Increase the Federal Funds Rate
- (D) Increase the required reserve ratio
- (E) Reduce their purchases of large-scale assets

**3** ☐ Mark for Review

Which of the following is NOT an effect of contractionary monetary policy?

- (A) The real interest rate increases.
- (B) Aggregate demand decreases.
- (C) Capital investment decreases.
- (D) The demand for money decreases.
- (E) Real output increases.

**4** ☐ Mark for Review

Which of the following is NOT a true statement about the money supply?

- (A) Paper money is included in both the M1 and the M2 money supply.
- (B) Money market mutual funds are not included in the M1 money supply.
- (C) Checking deposits are included in the M2 money supply.
- (D) Fiat money is included in the M1 money supply.
- (E) Small-time deposits like CDs are included in the M1 money supply.

**5** ☐ Mark for Review

If a total $10 million in deposits results from an initial deposit of $2 million, what is the required reserve ratio?

Ⓐ 5%

Ⓑ 10%

Ⓒ 15%

Ⓓ 20%

Ⓔ 25%

**6** ☐ Mark for Review

Which of the following policies might a central bank with limited reserves adopt to counter a recession?

Ⓐ A decrease in taxes

Ⓑ An increase in government spending

Ⓒ An increase in the discount rate

Ⓓ An increase in the required reserve ratio

Ⓔ The purchase of bonds

**7** ☐ Mark for Review

Which of the following elements CANNOT be considered as a financial asset?

Ⓐ Bank deposits

Ⓑ Stocks

Ⓒ Bonds

Ⓓ Loans

Ⓔ Net worth

# Chapter 13 Summary

## 13.1 & 13.2   Financial Assets and Definition, Measurement, and Functions of Money

- o   **Financial assets** are a subcategory of economic assets. These are entities over which institutional units or individuals assert ownership rights.

- o   **Money** is anything that is commonly accepted as a means of payment for goods and services.

- o   Money has three functions:
  - •   medium of exchange
  - •   store of value
  - •   unit of account

- o   **Currency** is any item that is used as money that does NOT act as a store of value or carry intrinsic value.

- o   **Commodity money** is any raw material with intrinsic value (such as a silver coin) that is used in exchange for other goods in an economy.

- o   **Fiat money** is a currency without intrinsic value (such as paper cash). Fiat money is also known as currency.

- o   **Wealth** is the value of the total assets owned by an individual or entity.

## 13.3   Banking and the Expansion of the Money Supply

- o   Economies rely on central banks to manage their macroeconomic indicators. Central banks influence economies via the **policy rate**. In the United States, the central bank is the Federal Reserve Bank, and the policy rate is known as the **federal funds rate**.

- o   **Money supply** is the amount of currency and other liquid assets available on the market; **liquidity** refers to how easily that money can be accessed.
  - •   **M1** is the sum of coin and paper money plus checking deposits and savings deposits.
  - •   **M2** is M1 plus investments.

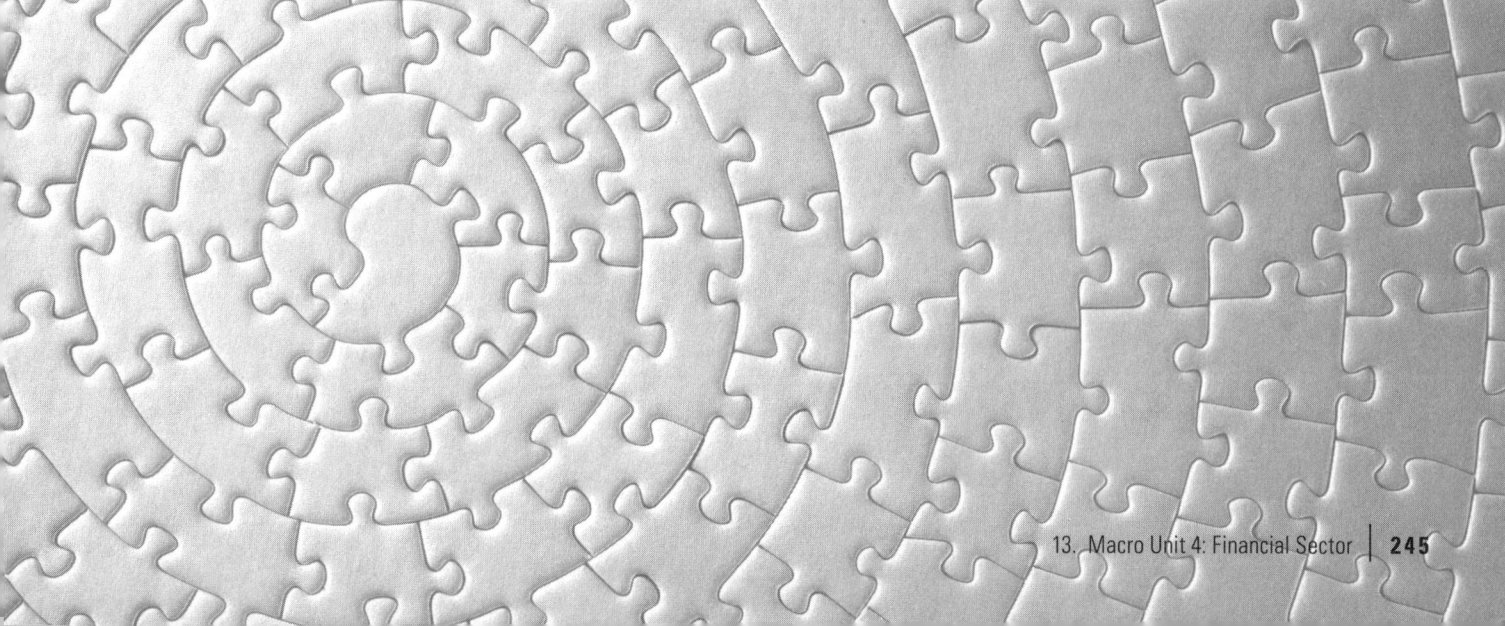

o   Economies with **limited reserves** use a **fractional reserve banking system** in which only a fraction of total deposits is held on reserve and the rest is lent out.

$$\text{Reserve ratio} = \frac{\text{bank reserves}}{\text{total deposits}}$$

o   **Money creation** is the generation of assets caused by an initial deposit to a bank being held partially in reserve and partially redistributed as a loan over and over again.

o   The **money multiplier** is the total amount of deposits resulting from an initial deposit that is ultimately held as reserves.

$$\text{Money multiplier} = \frac{1}{\text{required reserve ratio}}$$

o   The **discount rate** is the interest rate banks pay to borrow money from the Fed.

o   **Open market operations** involve the Fed's purchase and sale of government securities.

o   Economies with **ample reserves** rely on administered interest rates, the discount rate and **interest on reserves**, to influence the economy.

# 13.4   Monetary Policy

o   **Monetary policy** is the use of money and credit controls to influence interest rates, inflation, exchange rates, unemployment, and real GDP.

o   The effects of expansionary monetary policy are

$$Ms \uparrow \Rightarrow \ r \downarrow \Rightarrow \ I \uparrow \Rightarrow \ AD \uparrow \Rightarrow \ Y \uparrow \Rightarrow \ Md \uparrow \Rightarrow \ r \uparrow$$

o   The effects of contractionary monetary policy are

$$Ms \downarrow \Rightarrow \ r \uparrow \Rightarrow \ I \downarrow \Rightarrow \ AD \downarrow \Rightarrow \ Y \downarrow \Rightarrow \ Md \downarrow \Rightarrow \ r \downarrow$$

# Chapter 14
# Macro Unit 5: Long-Run Consequences of Stabilization Polices

# 14.1   THE PHILLIPS CURVE

Currency exchange provides another lens through which to view inflation: inflation occurs when the value of one nation's currency drops relative to that of other nations' currency.

When there is an oversupply of one nation's currency, that nation will experience **monetary inflation**, increased prices due to the decreased purchasing power of currency. Though slow rates of monetary inflation are accepted by most nations, if one nation experiences inflation at a higher rate, its currency will purchase fewer goods in the international market than other nations, and citizens of that nation will face higher prices.

Economists use aggregate supply and demand curves to illustrate the relationship between inflation and unemployment. Changes in output and associated unemployment fluctuations resulting from shifts in the AD curve suggest an inverse relationship between inflation and unemployment. As the AD curve shifts to the right in Figure 1, the price level increases and unemployment decreases.

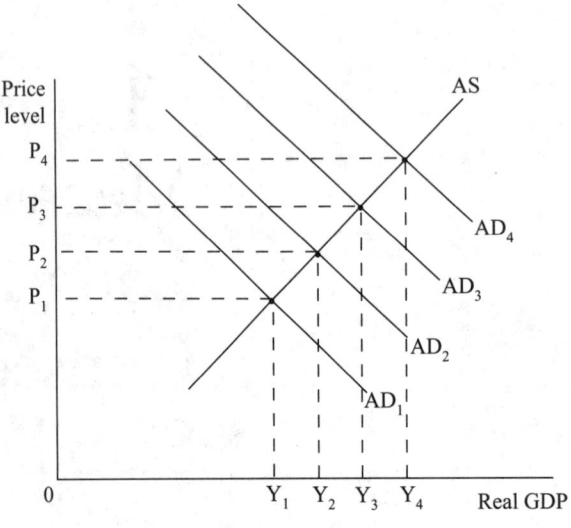

**Figure 1**

Shifts to the left in AD result in lower price levels but higher unemployment. This inverse relationship between inflation and unemployment is portrayed in Figure 2 (on the next page) in what is called a short-run **Phillips curve**, named after English economist A.W. Phillips.

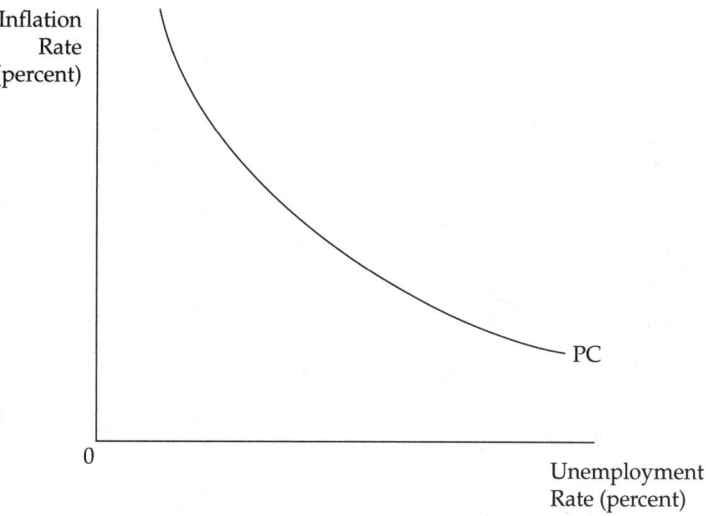

**Figure 2: Short-Run Phillips Curve**

A fixed output level in the long run at full employment output corresponds with unemployment at the natural rate of unemployment. As explained in Chapter 11, the natural rate of unemployment is the sum of frictional and structural unemployment. This implies a vertical long-run Phillips curve, as illustrated in Figure 3.

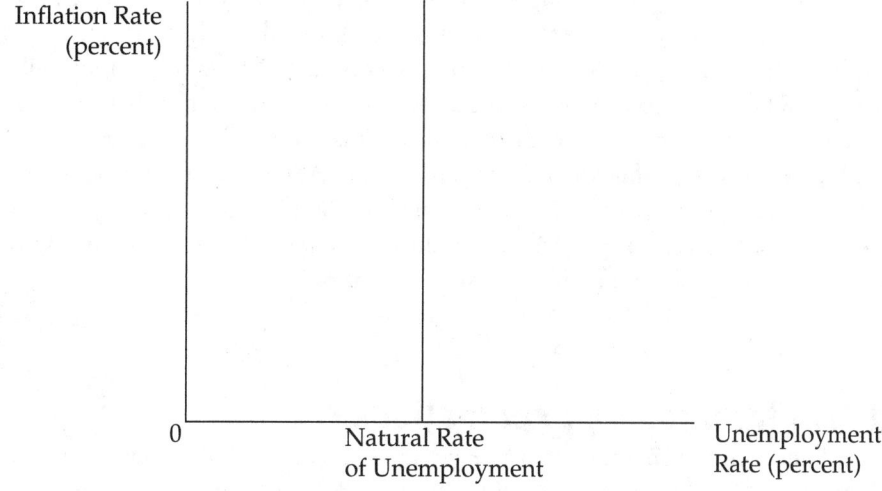

**Figure 3: Long-Run Phillips Curve**

# Supply Shocks

This trade-off between inflation and unemployment that Phillips suggested is supported by real-world data from the 1960s, but data from the 1970s exhibits stagflation—an increase in both the price level and unemployment. Stagflation is caused by shocks to supply that shift AS leftward and result in a rightward shift in the Phillips curve, as illustrated in Figure 4.

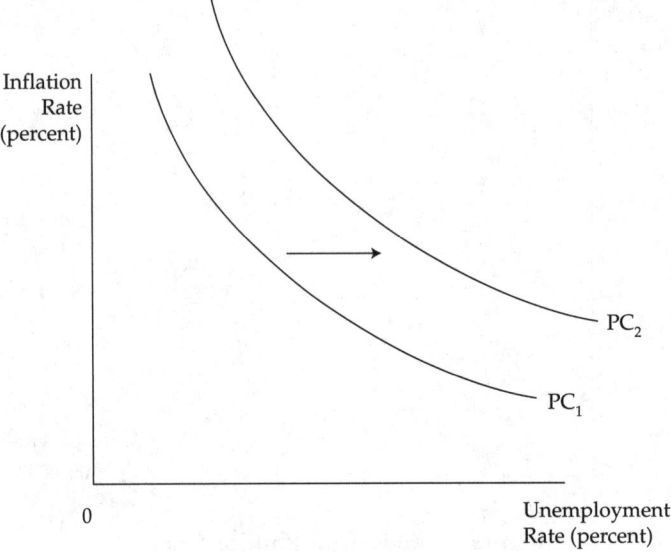

**Figure 4**

Supply shocks can be caused by natural disasters such as droughts, technical snafus such as computer viruses, or restrictions on the use of resources, as occurred with oil in the 1970s.

Modern Keynesian theory notes that wages and prices are particularly "sticky" in the downward direction (firms are reluctant to lower wages and prices) and that the structure or composition of AD changes over time. When some components of AD become more popular, their prices increase. When other components of AD fall out of favor, rather than lowering their prices and decreasing the payments to their inputs, firms respond with cutbacks and layoffs. The result of these **structural shocks** to the composition of AD is unemployment and inflation. Expansionary policies can increase AD and thereby cure the unemployment but fan the inflation. Alternatively, contractionary policies can reduce price levels but increase unemployment. There lies the trade-off between unemployment and inflation.

## The Role of Inflationary Expectations

Shifts in the Phillips curve can result from changes in expectations about inflation. **Inflationary expectations** are a self-fulfilling prophecy. If inflation is expected, workers and firms build these expectations into their wage and price contracts, and these higher wages and prices result in inflation. Expectations of inflation thus increase the inflation rate for any given level of unemployment, causing a shift to the right in the Phillips curve. If prices are expected to rise more slowly in the future, inflation will decrease for any given unemployment rate and the Phillips curve will shift to the left.

## 14.2  MONEY, GROWTH, AND INFLATION

The theory of **rational expectations** suggests that people learn to anticipate government policies designed to influence the economy, thereby making the policies ineffectual. With an understanding of the true sources of inflation (for more on inflation, see Chapter 11), and using all available information, workers and consumers respond quickly to policies unless they are somehow caught off guard or fooled. For example, if the government predictably attempts to boost real GDP by increasing the money supply or government spending (and thus aggregate demand) as in Figure 5, people will anticipate the resulting inflation and build it into their wage and price demands.

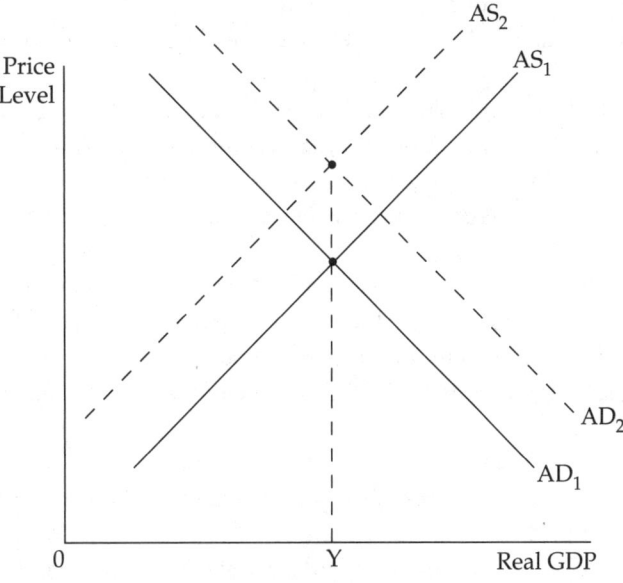

**Figure 5**

The increased wages will shift AS back from $AS_1$ to $AS_2$ and the government policy will have no real effect on output or income. In concert with the classical theory, the rational expectations theory assumes that wages, prices, and interest rates adjust quickly to keep real GDP at the full-employment level. Unemployment is seen as a temporary result of random shocks, because on average, wages and prices are set at the levels that equate supply and demand in both the goods and labor markets. The bottom line of the rational expectations theory is that government intervention is not necessary or useful for stabilizing the economy.

## 14.3  GOVERNMENT DEFICITS AND NATIONAL DEBT

The **budget deficit** is the difference between federal government spending and tax collections (G – T) in one year. The **national debt** is the accumulation of past deficits—the total amount that the federal government owes at a given time. The Keynesian emphasis on fiscal policy to spur and cool the economy has an associated requirement for deficit spending during recessions, which can be balanced with budget surpluses during booms. The government finances deficits by selling Treasury bonds, bills, and notes on the open market. Although the United States has had a multi-trillion-dollar debt since the early 1980s, there is little agreement over how much debt is too much. Some adhere to the **Ricardian Equivalence Theory** that deficit financing is no different from tax financing because if the former is chosen, people will simultaneously increase their savings by the amount they would have been taxed in preparation for the inevitable repayment of the debt at a later time. Others worry that government spending crowds out private economic activity and feel that debt or deficit ceilings should be in place to limit the burden of repayment.

When governments use expansionary fiscal policy, they increase spending, decrease taxes, or a combination of both. These expansionary policies will move an economy toward deficit, as now the government will be spending more and/or receiving less. On the other hand, when a government imposes a contractionary fiscal policy, the decreased spending/increased taxes will move an economy toward surplus, as now the revenue will be greater and total spending less.

Deficits can be financed by either borrowing or creating money. When the government borrows, it competes with private borrowers and bids up the interest rate. This can crowd out private investment and interest-sensitive consumption. By creating money, the government can spend money without raising interest rates, but this is likely to cause inflation.

As of December 2024, the U.S. national debt was $36.13 trillion. Defenders of high debt levels argue that it is wise to borrow now for educational programs, national defense, infrastructure, and research if the benefits to present and future generations exceed the eventual costs to those same parties. They also note that much of the debt is held domestically, meaning that we simply owe money to ourselves.

Those who wish to pay off the debt sooner argue that most of the benefits will be received by present generations and paid for by future generations. They note that most individuals are not able to make debt repayments as the Ricardian Equivalence Theory would predict. And they state that by crowding out private investment in capital, research, and development, the government reduces labor productivity, incomes, and living standards for the same future generations that will be saddled with repaying the debt.

## 14.4   CROWDING OUT

The decrease in real investment stemming from higher interest rates (r) due to government purchases is called **crowding out**. The effect of crowded-out investment on real GDP is most likely smaller than the initial increase in real GDP due to the purchases, in which case we call it **partial crowding out**. If the decrease in investment eliminates the entire boost in real GDP from the increased purchases, this is called **complete crowding out**. To summarize the effects of expansionary fiscal policy

$$G \uparrow \text{ or } T \downarrow \Rightarrow \ AD \uparrow \Rightarrow \ Y \uparrow \Rightarrow \ Md \uparrow \Rightarrow \ r \uparrow \Rightarrow \ I \downarrow \Rightarrow \ Y \downarrow$$

(typically falling by less than the initial increase in Y)

The effects of contractionary fiscal policy are summarized as

$$G \downarrow \text{ or } T \uparrow \Rightarrow \ AD \downarrow \Rightarrow \ Y \downarrow \Rightarrow \ Md \downarrow \Rightarrow \ r \downarrow \Rightarrow \ I \uparrow \Rightarrow \ Y \uparrow$$

(typically increasing by less than the initial decrease in Y)

# 14.5 ECONOMIC GROWTH

**Economic growth** is measured in terms of annual increases in real GDP or real GDP per capita (per person). Growth can be modeled as a rightward shift in the long-run aggregate supply curve or as an outward shift in the production possibility frontier, as illustrated in Figure 6.

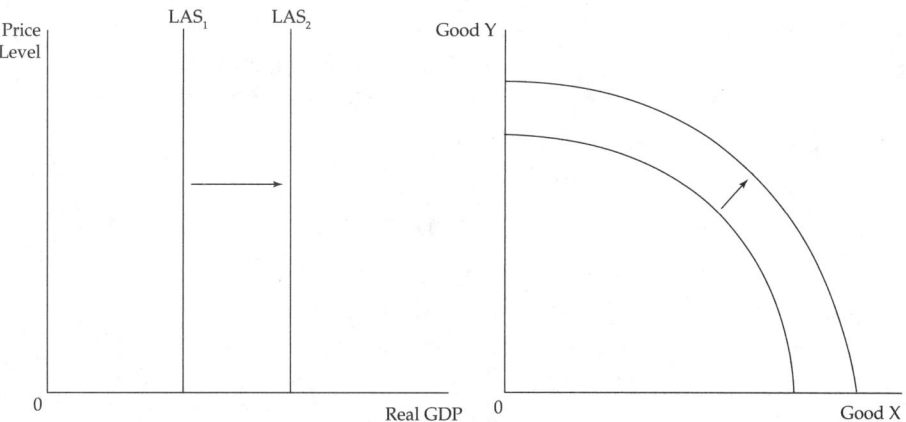

**Figure 6: Models of Economic Growth**

Government policies to promote economic growth include support for education systems, vocational training, research grants, and development programs, which can increase the output levels achievable with a given set of resources. As explained in the section on monetary policy, the central bank can promote growth with actions that lower interest rates and thereby increase investments in capital.

Economic growth permits expanded consumption levels and lessens the burden of scarcity. The Reverend Thomas Malthus put forth perhaps the most famous concern about economic growth. He suggested that output, and food in particular, would grow at an **arithmetic rate**—adding a constant amount each period—while population would grow at a **geometric rate**—increasing by a constant proportion each period. The eventual result would be a population that far exceeded its supplies of food. Fortunately, technological improvements in food and other types of production have provided geometric output growth that meets or exceeds population growth.

Beyond fears of starvation, there are additional constraints on population and output growth that may be more binding. Resources that exist in fixed supply are unlikely to disappear completely because prices will become prohibitively high before the resources vanish. However, as the availability of fossil fuels, clean air and water, life-sustaining forests, and similar limited resources diminishes, we will have to make do with alternatives, some of which may be inferior. This is what makes economics—the allocation of scarce resources among competing ends—so important for you to study.

Sources of growth include

- **Increased investments in human capital,** which come from education, training, practice, and experience. For example, as more people receive training in solar panel installation, more solar panels can be purchased and installed.

- **Increased investments in physical capital.** For example, with more tractors, farmers can harvest more grain from a given area of land.

- **Improvements in technology,** as can result from research and development efforts. For example, the use of robots in automobile manufacturing plants permits assembly lines to move more rapidly.

- **Enhanced resource utilization** results from better management and distribution of productive resources. For example, if there is underutilized capital or labor in an economy, better use of those resources will allow production levels to increase. This type of growth can be illustrated on the production-possibilities frontier graph by a movement from a point lying below the production-possibilities frontier toward a point on the frontier.

# CHAPTER 14 KEY TERMS

## 14.1

monetary inflation
Phillips curve
structural shocks
inflationary expectations

## 14.2

rational expectations

## 14.3

budget deficit
national debt
Ricardian Equivalence Theory

## 14.4

crowding out
partial crowding out
complete crowding out

## 14.5

economic growth
arithmetic rate
geometric rate

**More Great Books**

Check out The Princeton
Review's test prep titles
*ACT Prep* and *SAT Prep*,
and many more!

# CHAPTER 14 DRILL QUESTIONS

See Chapter 16 for answers and explanations.

**1** ☐ Mark for Review

A leftward shift in the short-run aggregate supply curve would also cause

- (A) a leftward shift in full-employment output
- (B) a rightward shift in the short-run Phillips Curve
- (C) an increase in resource prices
- (D) a rightward shift in the long-run Phillips Curve
- (E) a leftward shift in aggregate demand

**2** ☐ Mark for Review

Which of the following scenarios is LEAST likely to promote economic growth?

- (A) The government writes a new grant to fund healthcare research.
- (B) A company invests in a training program for its employees to boost productivity.
- (C) A hotel chain opens a new location and hires workers.
- (D) The Federal Reserve lowers the reserve requirement.
- (E) The Federal Reserve sells bonds on the open market.

**3** ☐ Mark for Review

Which of the following scenarios provides an example of the theory of rational expectations?

- (A) Commercial banks hold more in reserves when the central bank administers higher interest rates.
- (B) A farmer offers flour to a cobbler in exchange for shoes, and the cobbler accepts because he wants the flour more than he wants the shoes.
- (C) A self-interested lender offers a fixed-rate interest loan to a borrower anticipating that the government will lower the interest rate in the future.
- (D) The government increases unemployment insurance in response to an inflation crisis.
- (E) Real investment decreases because government expenditures cause increases in real interest rates.

**4** ☐ Mark for Review

The short-run Phillips curve indicates a

- (A) direct relation between unemployment and inflation
- (B) direct relation between price and quantity demanded
- (C) inverse relation between price and quantity demanded
- (D) inverse relation between unemployment and inflation
- (E) vertical relation between unemployment and inflation

**5** ☐ Mark for Review

Which of the following statements is correct in regard to the federal budget deficit and the federal debt?

Ⓐ When the debt is negative, the deficit decreases.

Ⓑ When the debt is positive, the deficit decreases.

Ⓒ The deficit is the accumulation of past debts.

Ⓓ When the deficit is negative, the debt decreases.

Ⓔ When the deficit is negative, the debt increases.

**6** ☐ Mark for Review

There is relatively more crowding out as the result of expansionary fiscal policy when

Ⓐ expansionary monetary policy accompanies the fiscal policy

Ⓑ the investment demand curve is inelastic

Ⓒ government spending improves profit expectations among businesses

Ⓓ aggregate supply is vertical

Ⓔ the investment demand curve is elastic

**7** ☐ Mark for Review

Which of the following variables can cause inflation?

Ⓐ Growth in bank capitals

Ⓑ Higher rate of employment

Ⓒ Higher rate of unemployment

Ⓓ Increase in demand

Ⓔ Money growth

# Chapter 14 Summary

## 14.1 The Phillips Curve

o **Monetary inflation** occurs when prices increase due to an oversupply of currency.

o A **Phillips curve** illustrates the inverse relationship between the inflation rate and unemployment.

## 14.2 Money, Growth, and Inflation

o The theory of **rational expectations** suggests that people learn to anticipate government policies designed to influence the economy, thereby making the policies ineffectual.

o Inflation is a sustained increase in the overall price level. The opposite of inflation—a sustained decrease in the general price level—is called deflation. Very high inflation for a sustained period of time results in money growth.

## 14.3 Government Deficits and National Debt

o The **budget deficit** is the difference between federal government spending and tax collections in one year.

o The **national debt** is the accumulation of past deficits—the total amount that the federal government owes at a given time.

o The **Ricardian Equivalence Theory** states that deficit financing is no different from tax financing because if the former is chosen, people will simultaneously increase their savings by the amount they would have been taxed in preparation for the inevitable repayment of the debt at a later time.

## 14.4   Crowding Out

○   **Crowding out** is the decrease in real investment stemming from higher interest rates due to government purchases.

## 14.5   Economic Growth

○   Sources of growth include:
   - increased investments in human capital
   - increased investments in physical capital
   - improvements in technology
   - enhanced resource utilization

# Chapter 15
# Macro Unit 6:
# Open Economy,
# International Trade,
# and Finance

## 15.1 BALANCE OF PAYMENTS ACCOUNTS

As markets become increasingly global, international transactions have a large bearing on virtually every economy. The **balance of payments** is a statement of all international flows of money over a given period. Below, you'll find a graph that illustrates the difference between imports and exports in the United States from 2019 through 2024.

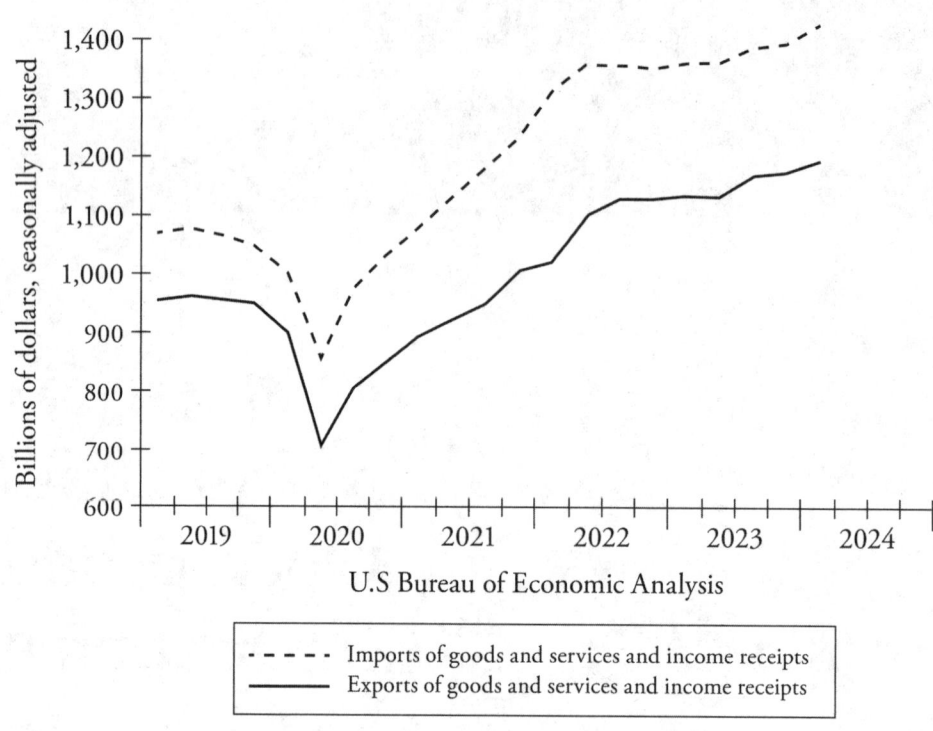

Quarterly U.S. Current-Account Balances

U.S Bureau of Economic Analysis

- - - - - Imports of goods and services and income receipts
———— Exports of goods and services and income receipts

Source: U.S. Bureau of Economic Analysis, www.BEA.gov

**Figure 1**

There are three balances within the balance of payments statement. The **merchandise trade balance** is

Merchandise trade balance = merchandise exports – merchandise imports

A merchandise **trade deficit** exists when imports exceed exports, which is typically the case in the United States. The opposite of a trade deficit is a **trade surplus.** Merchandise trade deficits or surpluses must be offset elsewhere in the **current-account** or **financial account balances**.

The current-account balance includes the merchandise trade balance plus the trade of services and transfers between countries.

Current-account balance = trade balance + services balance + transfers

The financial account balance considers other types of assets that change ownership across international borders, including securities, currency, capital (such as machinery), and land. In the equation below, "home" refers to the home country for which the financial account balance is made.

Financial account balance =
foreign purchases of home assets – home purchases of foreign assets

## 15.2 EXCHANGE RATES AND THE FOREIGN EXCHANGE MARKET

International **currency markets** exist so nations with different currencies can trade with each other. To purchase merchandise, services, capitals, or financial assets from other nations, buyers must first purchase that nation's currency. An international market for U.S. dollars exists when:

- international citizens want to purchase U.S. goods or services
- international citizens want to invest in U.S. firms
- international citizens want to give monetary gifts to individuals in the United States

Though the market for foreign currency exchange has unique characteristics, the market behavior can be illustrated using supply and demand curves like any other commodity. Figure 2 illustrates the market for U.S. dollars in Japan:

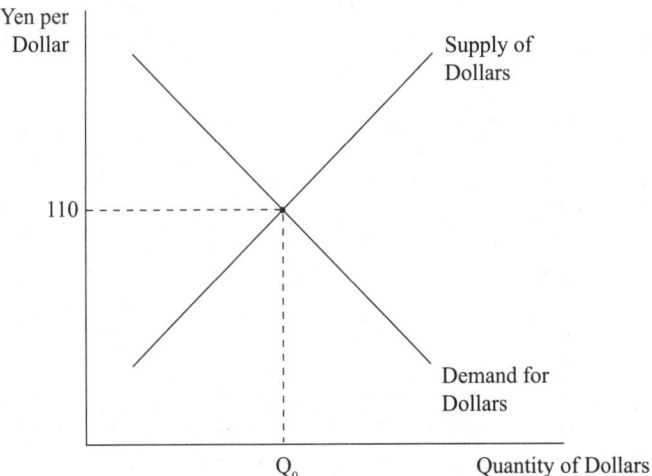

**Figure 2: The Currency Market**

As the value of yen per dollar increases, the quantity of dollars demanded goes down and the quantity of dollars supplied goes up. The reasoning behind this is the same as for the dollar-zucchini market—at a higher price, consumers desire fewer zucchinis and farmers are willing to produce more. Likewise, when dollars increase in value relative to the yen, fewer dollars are demanded for purchase of U.S. imports, travel, securities, and so forth in Japan. More people are willing to exchange dollars for yen when they receive more yen per dollar.

The equilibrium in the dollar-yen market determines the **exchange rate**—the rate at which dollars are exchanged for yen, or more generally, the value for which one nation's currency can be exchanged for another. In Figure 2 on the previous page, the exchange rate is 110 yen per dollar.

Pay particular attention to the price of dollars on the *y* axis: Japanese yen per U.S. dollar. In the foreign exchange market, one national currency is purchased with another, creating a reciprocal relationship between the two currencies. When someone in Japan demands (or purchases) U.S. dollars, they inherently create a supply of Japanese yen in the international currency market. Consider Japanese travelers newly arrived in the Unites States: they supply their yen to the teller in the airport and ask for dollars. Because the transaction inherently involves both currencies, when the value of the dollar changes, the relative value of the yen changes in an equal and opposite amount.

Though the interconnectedness of currencies makes calculating the absolute value of any given currency highly complex, relative relationships therein can be illustrated with the supply and demand curve(s) like any other commodity. Compare Figure 3 on the left with Figure 4 on the right; in Figure 4, the demand curve for U.S. dollars has shifted to the right, reflecting an increase in demand:

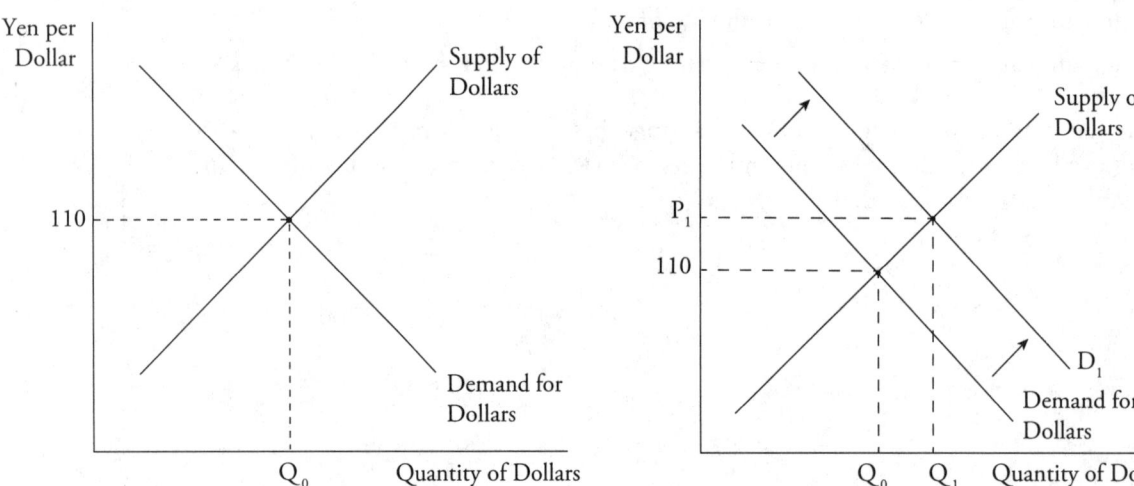

**Figure 3: The Currency Market**　　　　**Figure 4: Increased Demand for Dollars**

While there isn't enough information to calculate the value of $P_1$, the graph illustrates that the price of yen per U.S. dollar will increase with demand like any other commodity. In other words, the U.S. dollar has increased in value relative to the yen and therefore costs more yen to purchase. It is critical to remember that the basic laws of supply and demand apply to the relative values of currency when analyzing international currency exchange.

The following factors will cause the demand for the U.S. dollar (or any currency) to shift in the market for international currency exchange:

- **Change in relative income levels between countries.** Because imports are often normal goods, an increase in another nation's income will increase the demand for U.S. goods and the dollars with which to buy them.

- **Change in relative inflation rates.** If inflation occurs at a lower rate in the United States, then U.S. exports are slower than others to increase in price in the international market. This means U.S. products are less expensive than international competitors, and therefore in higher demand.

- **Change in consumer preferences for U.S. goods.** If U.S. goods are more popular than those of international competitors, they will be in higher demand.

- **Increase in national confidence.** Investors are more likely to invest in nations with strong, stable economies and minimal conflict.

Consider the following scenarios and try to predict the effect on the value of the U.S. dollar relative to the Japanese yen:

- Japan has a bumper crop of food, importing less and demanding fewer dollars. (The dollar loses value.)

- Interest rates increase in the United States relative to Japan, and depositors increase the demand for dollars in order to put their funds into U.S. banks. (The dollar increases in value.)

- Prices rise relatively fast in the United States, and the demand for dollars decreases. The supply of dollars increases as consumers purchase more goods elsewhere. (The dollar loses value.)

- Incomes in Japan increase relative to those in the United States, and Japanese consumers tend to spend more, increasing the demand for U.S. exports and currency. (The dollar increases in value.)

## Related Terms

A currency that **depreciates** or becomes weaker is one that falls in value relative to other currencies. It takes relatively more units of a depreciated currency to buy a unit of another country's currency. For example, if it cost 110 yen to buy a dollar yesterday and it costs 120 yen to buy a dollar today, the yen has depreciated. Depreciation decreases imports because they become more expensive for domestic consumers, and increases exports because they become relatively less expensive for foreigners to purchase. A weaker currency thus helps exporting industries and domestic tourism while hurting importing industries and citizens traveling abroad. As a result, currency depreciation makes a trade deficit smaller (or a trade surplus larger).

**Appreciation**, which is the opposite of depreciation, results in a stronger currency. When a currency appreciates or becomes stronger, it takes fewer units of that currency to buy a unit of another currency. For example, if it cost 110 yen to buy a dollar yesterday and it costs 100 yen to buy a dollar today, the yen has appreciated. Appreciation increases imports because they become less expensive, and decreases exports because they become more expensive. A stronger currency thus helps importing industries and citizens traveling abroad, while hurting exporting industries and domestic tourism. As a result, currency appreciation leads to a larger trade deficit (or a smaller trade surplus).

**Arbitrage** is the practice of buying at a low price and selling at a high price for a certain profit. Arbitrage will prevent exchange rates from being different in one place than in another for any significant period. If Shigeyuki can purchase dollars in Osaka for 90 yen and sell them in Kyoto for 110 yen, he will do so, thus increasing the supply of dollars in Kyoto and increasing the demand for dollars in Osaka until the exchange rate is equalized between the two locations.

## 15.3 EFFECTS OF CHANGES IN POLICIES AND ECONOMIC CONDITIONS ON THE FOREIGN EXCHANGE MARKET

### Exchange Rate Policy

There are several options for the management of exchange rates, as illustrated in Figure 5.

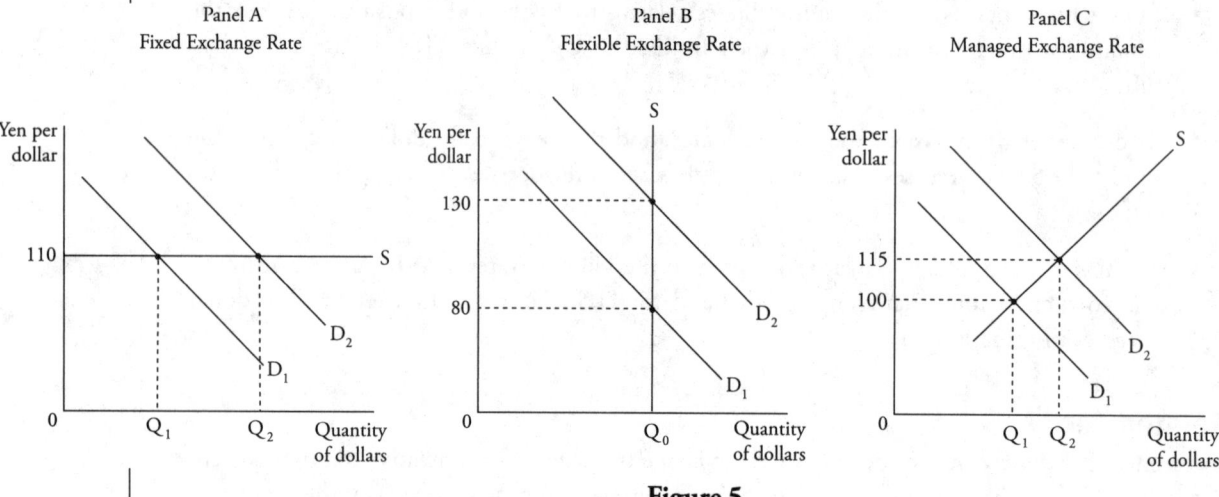

**Figure 5**

Most central banks hold reserves in each of the major currencies that can be increased or decreased to influence the exchange rate. The central bank can set a **fixed exchange rate** as in Panel A, in which case changes in demand affect only the quantity of dollars purchased, or the central bank can fix the quantity of assets denominated in the home currency and permit a **flexible exchange rate** that changes with demand as in Panel B. Or the central bank can have a **managed exchange rate** as in Panel C. In this case, changes in demand result in changes in the exchange rate, but the exchange rate fluctuations are dampened by a positively sloped supply curve.

## 15.4 CHANGES IN THE FOREIGN EXCHANGE MARKET AND NET EXPORTS

The United States has an **open economy**, meaning it trades with other nations to acquire goods that cannot be supplied within its borders and sells goods in international markets. By contrast, if a country did not engage in foreign trade it would be considered to have a **closed economy.** In open economies, the effects of fiscal policy on interest rates can have additional implications on international trade. For example, **expansionary fiscal policy** can cause the following chain of events, leading to a decline in net exports:

Government (G) spending increases or Taxes (T) decrease $\Rightarrow$

Higher interest rates (the crowding-out effect) $\Rightarrow$

Increased demand for the domestic currency for investment purposes (e.g., Treasury bonds) $\Rightarrow$

Appreciation of the domestic currency relative to foreign currencies $\Rightarrow$

Exports (X) decrease and Imports (M) increase

- Net Exports (X – M) decrease, partially offsetting the effects of the expansionary policy

Likewise, **contractionary fiscal policy** can cause the following events, leading to an increase in net exports:

Government (G) spending decreases or Taxes (T) increase $\Rightarrow$

Lower interest rates (due to the government demanding fewer loanable funds) $\Rightarrow$

Decreased demand for the domestic currency for investment purposes (e.g., Treasury bonds) $\Rightarrow$

Depreciation of the domestic currency relative to foreign currencies $\Rightarrow$

Exports (X) increase and Imports (M) decrease $\Rightarrow$

- Net Exports (X – M) increase, partially offsetting the effects of the contractionary policy

## 15.5   REAL INTEREST RATES AND INTERNATIONAL CAPITAL FLOWS

## The Loanable Funds Market and the Money Market

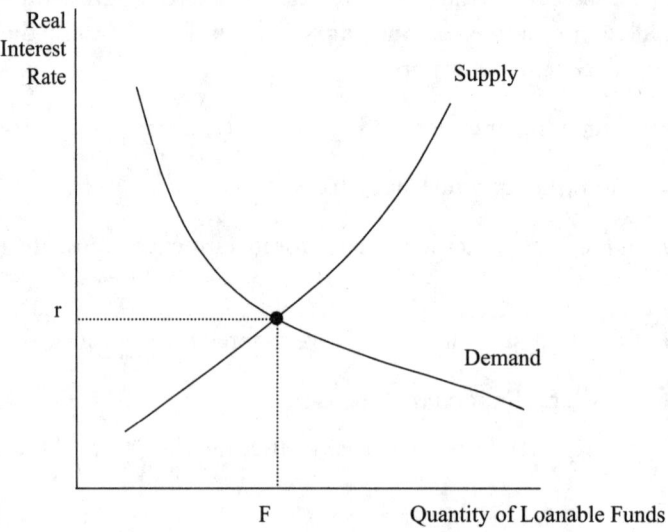

**Figure 6: The Loanable Funds Market**

An exam question might ask you to illustrate the **loanable funds market** (Figure 6) rather than the **money market**. The workings of these markets are similar, although the loanable funds market has a positively sloped supply curve. This is because higher interest rates don't increase the total money supply, but they do increase the supply of loanable funds. As interest rates increase, households become more willing to forgo current consumption and make their money available to banks and borrowers. Considering the two graphs side by side can offer further comparison:

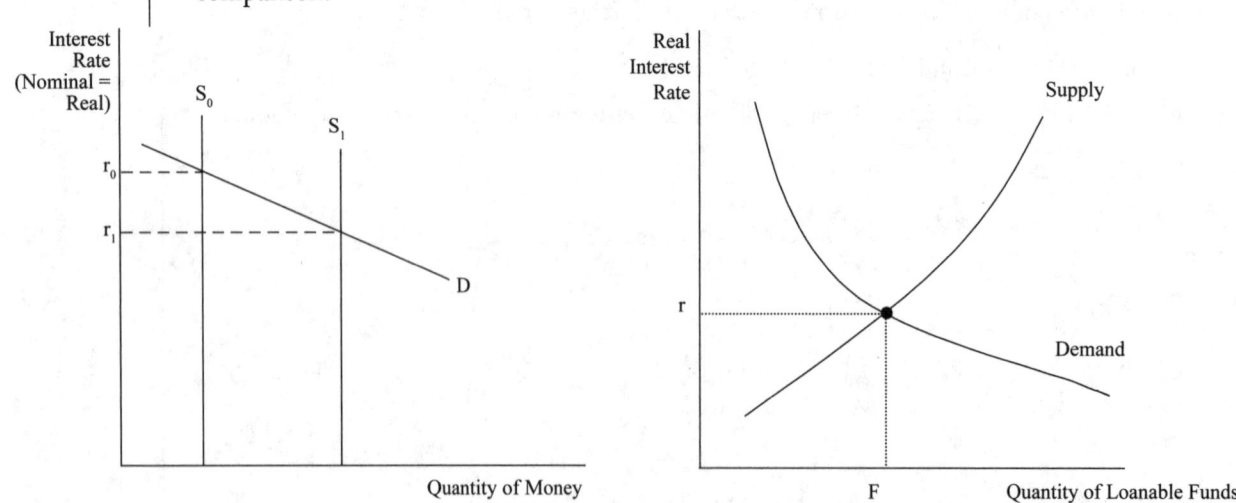

**Figure 7: The Money Market**

Both of these graphs serve a similar function: to find the equilibrium point between the quantity of money demanded and the quantity of money supplied to determine the interest rate, which is used as a measure of the value of money. However, each illustrates fundamentally different relationships. The money market graph illustrates how actions by a central bank affect the interest rate in the short run. For example, Figure 7 illustrates how increasing the supply of money through open market operations decreases the interest rate. On the other hand, the loanable funds market illustrates only the market specific to loans from financial institutions over the long run. In the short run, the money market can be used to assess the interest rate as normal and real interest rates are held equal; in the long run, only the real interest rate applies, thus the need to utilize the loanable funds market instead. Generally speaking, the money market graph is used to determine the value of money in the short run, and the loanable funds market is used to determine the value of money in the long run.

It can be helpful to simply remember that the money supply is held constant in the short run. When you're taking the AP Exam, read the exam questions carefully. If a question refers to the money market, draw a vertical money supply curve. If the question refers to the loanable funds market, draw the loanable funds supply curve with a positive slope to reflect the sensitivity of loanable funds to the interest rate.

## Monetarist-Keynesian Controversy

Part of learning macroeconomics is understanding the variety of ideas put forth about the behavior of the economy and the different policy prescriptions that result. Here we will contrast some of the most extreme views of Keynesian and monetarist theory. Of course, the truth and most economists' views are somewhere in the middle.

As illustrated in the top section of Figure 8 (shown on the next page), Keynesians believe that changes in the money supply will have little effect on interest rates because the demand curve for money is relatively flat. If it is perfectly flat, a **liquidity trap** exists, meaning that changes in the money supply will have no effect on interest rates. Notice that as the money supply increases from $M_s$ to $M_s^1$ in the top left graph, there is no change in the equilibrium interest rate and therefore no change in real investment. Even if interest rates were to change, Keynesians believe that the investment demand curve is relatively inelastic (steep), making it largely unresponsive to changes in the interest rate. As a result, Keynesians see little place for monetary policy in spurring the economy, and favor fiscal policy measures instead.

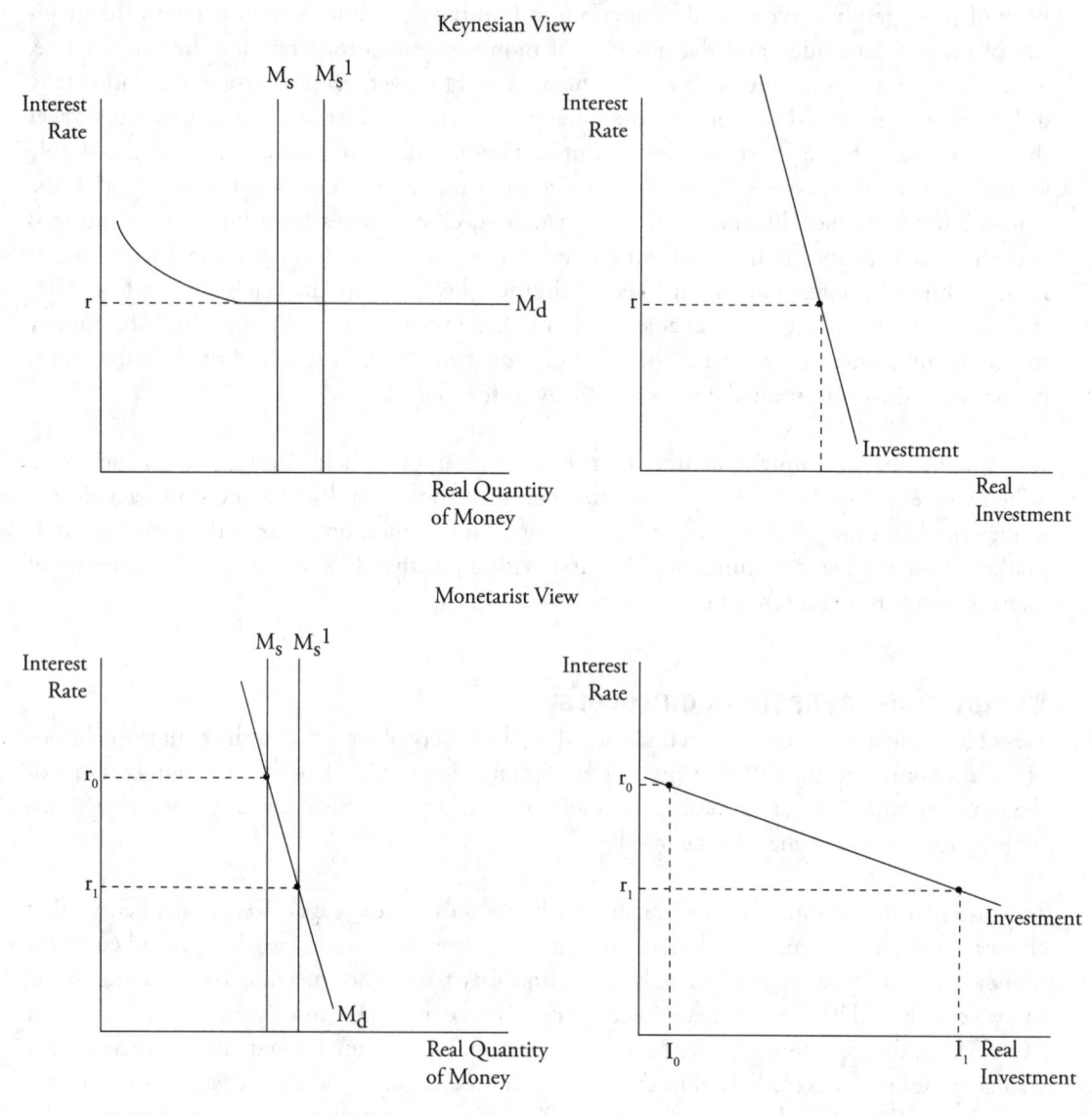

**Figure 8**

In contrast, monetarists believe that the demand for money is very sensitive to the interest rate. As shown in the lower half of Figure 8, the result of a steep demand curve for money is that an increase in the money supply lowers interest rates substantially. Monetarists further believe that investment demand is relatively elastic, making it very responsive to decreases in the interest rate. Given this, the money supply is a useful tool for keeping the economy on an even keel. Monetarists believe that the economy is inherently stable and recommend a steady increase in the money supply proportional to the increase in real GDP. At the same time, this theory does not favor fiscal policy, both because it can be ill-timed, and due to the problem of crowding out when investment is sensitive to the interest rate. If either the demand curve for money is vertical (totally unresponsive to the interest rate) or the investment demand curve is horizontal, complete crowding out occurs. In this case, fiscal policy has no effect because any increase in government spending increases the demand for money and induces an increase in interest rates that eliminates an equivalent amount of investment.

Monetarists also explain the power of monetary policy using the **equation of exchange**. According to the following equation, the money supply (M) times the velocity of money (V) equals the average price (P) times the quantity of goods and services sold in a period (Q):

$$MV = PQ$$

The **velocity of money** is the number of times per period (typically a year) that the average dollar is spent on final goods and services. The same dollar will bounce around the economy several times each year. Mauricio will spend $20 to purchase groceries from David, and then David will spend the same $20 to purchase CDs from Keyshia the banker, and then Keyshia will loan the same $20 out to Stephanie for home improvements, and so forth. Simply put, the equation of exchange states that the number of dollars multiplied by the number of times they are used per year must equal the total number of dollars spent in a year.

If one item in the equation of exchange changes, another item must change to maintain the balance. Thus, if M changes, either V, P, or Q must also change. Monetarists claim that velocity is stable, so increases in M must increase P and/or Q and thus increase total spending (P × Q). Classical economists and some monetarists also subscribe to the **quantity theory of money**, which states that in addition to V being stable, Q is stable. This implies that increases in M will have no effect other than to increase the price level. All of these direct linkages between the money supply and expenditures are in contrast with the Keynesian view, which is that the money supply has a small and indirect influence on expenditures by affecting interest rates that affect investment, which affects aggregate expenditures.

Keynesians and monetarists also differ in their approach to inflation and interest rates. Real interest rates are adjusted for anticipated inflation.

> **Real interest rate** = nominal interest rate – anticipated inflation,
>
> and likewise,
>
> **Nominal interest rate** = real interest rate + anticipated inflation

Keynesians advocate fighting inflation by decreasing the money supply to drive up both real and nominal interest rates and to reduce consumption and investment. Monetarists believe that there is a fairly stable **natural rate of real interest**, in which case fluctuations in the nominal interest rate simply reflect changes in anticipated inflation. From their perspective, the real interest rate must change in order to influence investment. If market participants can predict that the Fed will counter inflation by reducing money supply growth, anticipated inflation and nominal interest rates will begin to fall, not rise, when the Fed tightens the money supply. This is called the **Fisher effect**.

A summary of classical, Keynesian, and monetarist views appears in Table 1 below.

| | |
|---|---|
| **Monetarists** | Monetarists see the money supply as the primary tool to bring economic stability. For stability, they suggest following a strict "monetary rule," such as increasing the money supply at a rate equal to the average growth in real output. They believe that fiscal and monetary policy, intended for fine-tuning, threaten to destabilize the economy. They also feel that changes in government spending will crowd out private spending and have little or no effect on aggregate spending, prices, real output, or real interest rates. Unemployment and output are expected to tend toward their natural rates without active intervention. |
| **Classical Economists** | Classical economists agree with monetarists that the economy is fairly stable and will naturally adjust to full employment. They feel that attempts to fine-tune the economy are ineffective because individuals come to anticipate the government's actions and act to offset them. Classical economists emphasize that the velocity of money is constant, meaning that an increase in the money supply has a direct effect on total spending. |
| **Keynesians** | Keynesians view the economy as inherently unstable and blame inadequate demand for periods of stagnation. They recommend active government policy to respond to inflationary and recessionary gaps. They feel that changes in government spending can affect aggregate spending, real interest rates, and real output. Keynesians also believe that changes in the money supply have a relatively small and indirect effect on output. Changes in the money supply affect interest rates, which affect investment, which affects aggregate expenditures, which affect income and output. |

**Table 1**

# CHAPTER 15 KEY TERMS

## 15.1

balance of payments
merchandise trade balance
trade deficit
trade surplus
current account balance
financial account balance

## 15.2

currency market
exchange rate
depreciation
appreciation
arbitrage

## 15.3

fixed exchange rate
flexible exchange rate
managed exchange rate

## 15.4

open economy
closed economy
expansionary fiscal policy
contractionary fiscal policy

## 15.5

loanable funds market
money market
liquidity trap
equation of exchange
velocity of money
quantity theory of money
real interest rate
nominal interest rate
natural rate of interest
Fisher effect

# CHAPTER 15 DRILL QUESTIONS
See Chapter 16 for answers and explanations.

**1** ☐ Mark for Review

When a nation's currency appreciates

(A) members of this nation demand more goods from markets in other countries

(B) the nation's income increases

(C) a greater quantity of the nation's currency is supplied in the foreign exchange market

(D) the nation achieves a trade surplus

(E) interest rates increase as a result

**2** ☐ Mark for Review

Expansionary fiscal policy is associated with all of the following EXCEPT

(A) depreciation of the domestic currency

(B) the crowding-out effect

(C) a decrease in taxes

(D) an increase in aggregate demand

(E) an increase in net exports

**3** ☐ Mark for Review

The quantity theory of money supports the idea that

(A) fluctuations in the nominal interest rate reflect changes in inflation

(B) deficit financing and tax financing encourage the same behaviors in consumers

(C) unemployment varies inversely with inflation

(D) increases in the money supply cause inflation

(E) the money supply has a relatively small effect on aggregate expenditures

**4** ☐ Mark for Review

A crisis in the United States causes investors to prioritize opportunities in Europe and Japan. How does this affect the demand for the U.S. dollar?

(A) Demand for the dollar increases, and the value depreciates.

(B) Demand for the dollar increases, and the value appreciates.

(C) Demand for the dollar decreases, and the value depreciates.

(D) Demand for the dollar decreases, and the value appreciates.

(E) Demand for the dollar increases, and the value will remain the same.

**5** ☐ Mark for Review

Depreciation of the dollar is most likely to

Ⓐ increase imports

Ⓑ increase travel abroad

Ⓒ increase exports

Ⓓ decrease a trade surplus

Ⓔ increase a trade deficit

**6** ☐ Mark for Review

Japan decides to reduce taxes, causing growth. How does this affect the U.S. dollar?

Ⓐ Reducing taxes in Japan has no effect on the U.S. dollar.

Ⓑ Reducing taxes in Japan increases the demand of the U.S. dollar.

Ⓒ Reducing taxes in Japan decreases the demand for the U.S. dollar.

Ⓓ Reducing taxes in Japan causes the Fed to reduce taxes in the United States.

Ⓔ Reducing taxes in Japan causes the Fed to keep taxes in the United States the same.

**7** ☐ Mark for Review

Income in Japan grows at a faster rate than income in the United States. How does this affect the demand for the U.S. dollar and the value of the U.S. dollar?

Ⓐ Demand for the dollar will increase, and the dollar will depreciate.

Ⓑ Demand for the dollar will increase, and the dollar will appreciate.

Ⓒ The supply of the dollar increases, and the dollar will appreciate.

Ⓓ Demand for the dollar decreases, and the dollar will appreciate.

Ⓔ The supply of the dollar decreases, and the dollar will remain the same.

# Chapter 15 Summary

## 15.1 Balance of Payments Accounts

o The **balance of payments** is a statement of all international flows of money over a given period.

o A **trade deficit exists** when imports exceed exports; the opposite is a **trade surplus**.

## 15.2 Exchange Rates and the Foreign Exchange Market

o A currency that **depreciates** or becomes weaker is one that falls in value relative to other currencies; **appreciation** occurs when a currency gains value relative to others.

o **Arbitrage** is the practice of buying at a low price and selling at a high price for a certain profit.

## 15.3 Effects of Changes in Policies and Economic Conditions of the Foreign Exchange Market

o When a central bank sets a **fixed exchange rate**, changes in demand affect only the quantity of dollars purchased; with a **flexible exchange rate**, a central bank can fix the quantity of assets denominated in the home currency.

## 15.4 & 15.5 Changes in the Foreign Exchange Market and Net Exports and Real Interest Rates and International Capital Flows

o A **liquidity trap** exists when the demand for money is perfectly flat, meaning that changes in the money supply will have no effect on interest rates.

o  The **equation of exchange** states that the number of dollars multiplied by the number of times they are used per year must equal the total number of dollars spent in a year.

$$MV = PQ$$

o  The **velocity of money** (V) is the number of times per period that the average dollar is spent on final goods and services.

o  The **quantity theory of money** states that Q is stable in addition to V.

o  Monetarists believe that there is a fairly stable **natural rate of real interest**, in which case fluctuations in the nominal interest rate simply reflect changes in anticipated inflation.

o  The **Fisher effect** occurs when market participants can predict that the Fed will counter inflation by reducing money supply growth, causing anticipated inflation and nominal interest rates to fall when the Fed tightens the money supply.

# Chapter 16
# Macroeconomics
# Drill Questions:
# Answers and
# Explanations

# CHAPTER 11 DRILL QUESTIONS: ANSWERS AND EXPLANATIONS

1. **A** GDP measures the worth of a country's goods and services. Eliminate (C) and (D) because they are indicators of inflation. Eliminate (E) because it is vague, and the question doesn't reference a specific account. Eliminate (B) because societal welfare is broader in scope than just GDP. Therefore, the answer is (A).

2. **C** Eliminate (B) and (D) because they are irrelevant and misleading. Eliminate (A) and (E) because they exist independently from inflation. Inflation is measured by the Consumer Price Index (CPI); therefore, the answer is (C).

3. **A** Structural unemployment occurs when workers have to either move to new industries or learn new skills (types of unemployment are summarized on pages 191–192). Eliminate (C) because the question indicates that snow loss is permanent, not seasonal. Therefore, the answer is (A).

4. **B** The cost of goods for Year 1: 5 × $12.00 + 10 × $2.00 + 100 × $0.05 = $60 + $20 + $5 = $85.00. The cost of goods for Year 2: 5 × $11.00 + 10 × $1.25 + 100 × $0.15 = $55 + $12.5 + $15 = $82.50. As the cost of goods decreased, CPI must have dropped, so eliminate (A), (D), and (E). The change in CPI is $\frac{85-82.5}{85} \times 100 = \frac{2.5}{85} \times 100 \approx 3\%$. Therefore, the answer is (B).

5. **B** C is the consumption that gets captured in the GDP calculation. Nonmonetary transactions are not captured by the GDP, so eliminate (A) and (E). Goods purchased by a company for producing goods and services are not counted as consumed goods, so eliminate (C) and (D). Therefore, the answer is (B).

6. **D** Transactions that do not include an exchange of goods or services (such as transfer payments) and transactions not reported to the government (such as off-the-book payments or illegal activities) are not counted in GDP. Therefore, the answer is (D). Side note: Some countries are trying to estimate and include parallel market transactions in their GDP calculations!

7. **C** Cyclical unemployment results from downturns in the business cycle (types of unemployment are summarized on page 191–192). Choice (A) is incorrect because frictional unemployment occurs as unemployed workers and firms search for the best available worker-job matches. Structural unemployment is the result of a skills mismatch. Choice (B) is not a right answer for this question. Choice (D) is incorrect because seasonal unemployment is the result of changes in hiring patterns due to the time of year. Choice (E) is not acceptable because discouraged workers are those who are willing and able to work, but become so frustrated in their attempts to find work that they stop trying; "discouraged employers" is a made-up term meant to distract. The correct answer is (C).

# CHAPTER 12 DRILL QUESTIONS: ANSWERS AND EXPLANATIONS

1. **E** The best strategy for this question is to sketch the intermediate range of the AS and AD curves with price on the vertical axis and GDP on the horizontal axis. (See Figure 3 on page 208.) Shift the AD curve to the right as indicated in the question. Visually, you can see that this will cause both price and GDP to increase. Therefore, the answer is (E).

2. **D** The largest increase in GDP = multiplier × $500. Multiplier = $\frac{1}{MPS} = \frac{1}{1 - MPC} = \frac{1}{1 - 0.8} = \frac{1}{0.2} = 5$. Therefore, the maximum increase in GDP is 5 × $500 = $2,500. The answer is (D).

3. **B** Stagflation occurs when an increase in prices is concurrent with a decrease in output and, usually, employment. By definition, the correct answer is (B). Stagflation is often caused by cost-push inflation. This increase in cost of resources causes the aggregate supply curve to shift to the left ($AS_1$ in the figure below), causing prices to increase and GDP to fall. Therefore, a correctly drawn graph also reveals that the answer is (B).

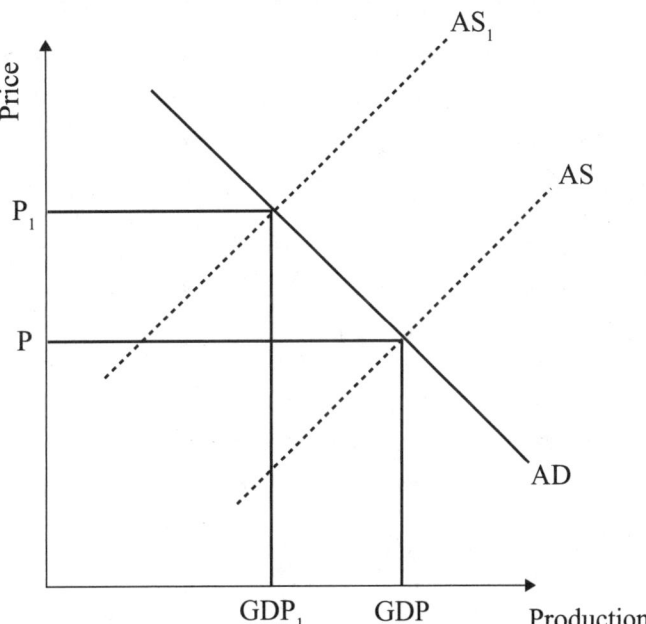

4. **D** Eliminate (A) and (E) because the recessionary gap refers to the relationship between short-run equilibrium and LAS, a function of the full-employment level of real GDP. A recessionary gap occurs when the equilibrium GDP is below full employment level. Therefore, the answer is (D).

5. **C** The equilibrium GDP is where the short-term aggregate supply (SAS) curve and the aggregate demand (AD) curve intersect. The GDP at this level is lower than the GDP of where AD and LAS intersect. The economy is, therefore, not at long-run equilibrium or neutral equilibrium, so eliminate answers (B), (D), and (E). As the economy is in short-run equilibrium, the answer is (C).

6. **B** Long-run aggregate supply increases when industry can produce more. This can happen if the country invests in equipment (i.e., capital). Therefore, the answer is (B).

7.  **A**  Supply-side economists believe that tax rates impact both aggregate demand and aggregate supply (in the same direction). More specifically, a decrease in taxes would lead to an increase in aggregate demand and an increase in aggregate supply. The question is asking what these economists would disagree with; therefore, the answer is (A).

8.  **C**  The interest rate and the value of money have a direct relationship, so (B) and (D) can be eliminated. Selling bonds decreases the money supply, shifting the supply curve to the left. As a result, the interest rate and the value of money both increase. Choice (C) is correct.

9.  **B**  An increase in investment from businesses and consumers causes aggregate demand to increase. Choices (A) and (C) are incorrect. There is not enough information to determine the rate at which aggregate demand will change, so (D) is incorrect. Choice (B) is correct.

# CHAPTER 13 DRILL QUESTIONS: ANSWERS AND EXPLANATIONS

1.  **C**  The term *liquidity* refers to how easily an asset can be transferred into cash or currency. Choice (A) is defining the term *wealth*, (B) is defining the function of money as a *store of value*, (D) is defining the term *portability*, and (E) is defining the term *divisibility*. So, eliminate (A), (B), (D), and (E). The correct answer is (C).

2.  **A**  The Federal Reserve can increase the money supply by buying government securities—for example, bonds—on the open market. Eliminate (B), (C), (D), and (E) because these actions decrease the money supply. The correct answer is (A).

3.  **E**  Real output decreases when contractionary monetary policy is implemented. Choices (A), (B), (C), and (D) are all correct effects of contractionary monetary policy. Choice (E), an increase in real output, is the effect of an *expansionary* monetary policy. So, eliminate (A), (B), (C), and (D). The correct answer is (E).

4.  **E**  Choices (A), (B), (C), and (D) are all true statements about the money supply, so eliminate these answer choices. Small-time deposits, including CDs, are included in the M2 money supply, but not in the M1 money supply. Therefore, (E) is not a true statement, and so the correct answer is (E).

5.  **D**  Because the question deals with $10 million in total deposits resulting from a $2 million initial deposit, this question pertains to the money multiplier (which depends on the required reserve ratio). The money multiplier can be expressed as $\dfrac{1}{required\ reserve\ ratio}$, and because the ratio of $10 million to $2 million is 5, perform the following operations. Set 5 equal to the money multiplier equation, divide by 5 on both sides and multiply the *reserve ratio* on both sides to get a *reserve ratio* equal to 0.2. So, eliminate (A), (B), (C), and (E). The right answer is (D).

6.  **E**  To counter a recession, a central bank with limited reserves needs to decrease the interest rates or increase the money supply. Increasing the discount rate increases the interest rate, and increasing the required reserve ratio lowers the money supply. Eliminate (C) and (D). Changes in taxes or government spending may not affect the money supply or the interest rate, so eliminate (A) and (B). Purchasing bonds increases the money supply, and therefore the answer is (E).

7.  **E**  The first four answer choices, (A), (B), (C), and (D), are the main types of financial assets. Net worth is calculated based on various financial assets, so it is not a financial asset per se. The answer is (E).

# CHAPTER 14 DRILL QUESTIONS: ANSWERS AND EXPLANATIONS

1.  **B**  Full-employment output and aggregate demand are not shifted by a shift in the aggregate supply, so eliminate (A) and (E). An increase in resource prices would cause a leftward shift in aggregate supply, but the shift would not cause the increased prices. Eliminate (C). A leftward shift in the short-run aggregate supply curve would cause a rightward shift in the short-run Phillips Curve, not the long-run Phillips Curve, so eliminate (D). Choice (B) is the correct answer.

2.  **E**  Choices (A), (B), (C), and (D) would all promote economic growth, so eliminate these answer choices. If the Federal Reserve sells bonds on the open market, then the money supply would decrease, real interest rates would increase, investment would decrease, aggregate demand would decrease, and output would decrease. Because investment and output are decreasing, economic growth is not promoted but instead impeded. Therefore, (E) would promote economic growth the *least*, and (E) is thus the correct answer.

3.  **C**  The theory of rational expectations claims that when people are fully informed about the state of the economy and they can anticipate the government taking certain actions, then they will adjust their behaviors in a way that dampens or contradicts the intentions of the policy.

4.  **D**  The short-run Phillips curve illustrates the inverse relationship between unemployment and inflation rate (illustrated in Figure 2 on page 249). Therefore, the answer is (D).

5.  **D**  The deficit is the difference between government spending and tax revenue (G − T) for a given year. The debt is the accumulation of past deficits (an accounting of total difference between government spending and tax revenues). The sign of debt gives no information on deficit, as it is changes in debt that the deficit measures, so eliminate (A) and (B). Choice (C) is reversed in that debt is the accumulation of past deficits, so eliminate (C). When the deficit is negative, then tax revenues exceed government spending. This leads to a decrease in debt. Therefore, the answer is (D).

6.  **E**  Crowding out is a decrease in real investment as a result of government purchases. Government purchases are part of the fiscal policy, so eliminate (A). Impact of government purchases is felt on the demand side, so eliminate (D). When the investment demand curve is elastic, a small increase in government purchases will cause a larger reduction in demand for money. Therefore, the answer is (E).

7.  **E**  When there is more supply of money associated with the same number of products and services in the market, it is normal that the producers and service providers take advantage of the extra money and increase their prices. Therefore, (E) is correct. Choice (A) is incorrect because an increase in bank capitals does not affect the rate of inflation. Fluctuating rates of employment are not a vital factor of inflation, though they may cause some other economic crises. Therefore, (B) and (C) are incorrect. Increase in demand can be resolved by increasing the supply, so (D) is not an effective factor of inflation.

# CHAPTER 15 DRILL QUESTIONS: ANSWERS AND EXPLANATIONS

1.  **C**  A nation's currency appreciates when other nations demand more of it in order to purchase the nation's goods or invest in this nation's assets, (C). Choice (A) says that this nation is demanding more goods from other nations, which is the opposite of what causes a nation's currency to appreciate. Choice (B) says that this nation's income necessarily increases, but the nation's income does not necessarily *have* to increase in this case. Choice (D) says that the nation achieves a trade surplus, and when a nation's currency appreciates, the nation's imports tend to increase while their exports decrease. An increase in imports and a decrease in exports moves the nation toward a trade deficit and away from a trade surplus, depending on the situation. The appreciation of a nation's currency does not cause interest rates to increase, so eliminate (E).

2.  **A**  Expansionary fiscal policy is actually associated with an increase in the nation's currency, not a decrease.

3.  **D**  The quantity theory of money supports the idea that increases in the money supply cause inflation. Choice (A) describes the monetarist view on the natural rate of real interest, which is a different theory of inflation. Choice (B) describes the Ricardian Equivalence Theory. Choice (C) describes a phenomenon modeled by the Phillips Curve. Choice (E) describes a key Keynesian economic view, which contrasts with the quantity theory of money. So, eliminate (A), (B), (C), and (E). Choice (D) is the correct answer.

4.  **C**  When investors pull their money from the United States, the demand for the dollar decreases and the value depreciates. Eliminate (A), (B), and (E) because they state that demand for the dollar increases; eliminate (D) because it states that the value of it appreciates. Therefore, the answer is (C).

5.  **C**  Depreciation of the dollar will make American goods cheaper to export, and will make imports more expensive for Americans. A direct consequence is that American companies will export more, and demand for foreign goods in America will decrease. Eliminate (D) and (E) because depreciation alone won't necessarily affect the amount of national debt. Eliminate (A) and (B) because they describe effects of appreciation of the dollar. Therefore, the answer is (C).

6.  **B**    Reducing taxes in Japan will increase the supply of yen in the market, increasing demand for imports from the United States, and therefore increasing the demand for the U.S. dollar. The correct answer is (B).

7.  **B**    When incomes abroad increase faster than those in the United States, the demand for the dollar will increase and the dollar will appreciate. Most imports are normal goods, so when incomes increase so does the demand for imports. Choice (A) is incorrect because increased demand for dollars causes dollars to appreciate, not depreciate. Choice (C) incorrectly addresses supply instead of demand. Choice (D) confuses the relationship between demand and appreciation; therefore, the answer is (B).

# Part V
# Practice Tests

17  Microeconomics Practice Test 1
18  Microeconomics Practice Test 1: Answers and
    Explanations
    How to Score Practice Test 1
19  Macroeconomics Practice Test 1
20  Macroeconomics Practice Test 1: Answers and
    Explanations
    How to Score Practice Test 1

# Chapter 17
# Microeconomics
# Practice Test 1

# AP® Microeconomics Exam

**SECTION I: Multiple-Choice Questions**

## DO NOT OPEN THIS BOOKLET UNTIL YOU ARE TOLD TO DO SO.

### At a Glance

**Total Time**
1 hour, 10 minutes
**Number of Questions**
60
**Percent of Total Grade**
66.7%

**DISCLAIMER: The official multiple-choice section of the AP Microeconomics Exam will be administered digitally. Instructions for the digital exam may differ from those for this practice test.**

### Instructions

Section I of this examination contains 60 multiple-choice questions. Fill in all of the ovals for numbers 1 through 60 on your answer sheet.

Indicate all of your answers to the multiple-choice questions on the answer sheet. Give only one answer to each question.

Use your time effectively, working as quickly as you can without losing accuracy. Do not spend too much time on any one question. Go on to other questions and come back to the ones you have not answered if you have time.

**SECTION II: Free-Response Questions**

### Instructions

You are advised to spend the first 10 minutes reading all of the questions and planning your answers. You will then have 50 minutes to answer all three of the following questions. It is suggested that you spend 25 minutes on question 1 and roughly 12 minutes each on questions 2 and 3. You may use scratch paper to plan your work, but you must write your answers in the free-response booklet.

### At a Glance

**Total Time**
60 minutes
**Number of Questions**
3
**Percent of Total Grade**
33.3%
**Writing Instrument**
Pencil or pen (with dark blue or black ink)

Include correctly labeled diagrams, if useful or required, in explaining your answers. A correctly labeled diagram must have all axes and curves clearly labeled and must show directional changes.

If the question prompts you to "Calculate," you must show how you arrived at your final answer. A calculator is allowed in this section.

**GO ON TO THE NEXT PAGE.**

This page intentionally left blank.

**GO ON TO THE NEXT PAGE.**

## AP MICROECONOMICS
### SECTION I
#### Time—70 Minutes
#### 60 Questions

**Directions**: Each of the questions or incomplete statements below is followed by five suggested answers or completions. Select the one that is best in each case and then fill in the corresponding oval on the answer sheet.

**1** ☐ Mark for Review

Resource allocation involves answering all EXCEPT which of the following basic questions?

(A) What goods and services should be produced?

(B) At what price should goods and services be sold?

(C) Who consumes goods and services?

(D) How should goods and services be produced?

(E) What opportunity costs are associated with producing a good?

**2** ☐ Mark for Review

How is economic growth reflected in a production possibilities curve (PPC)?

(A) An outward shift

(B) An inward shift

(C) An increase in slope

(D) A decrease in slope

(E) Economic growth doesn't impact the PPC.

**3** ☐ Mark for Review

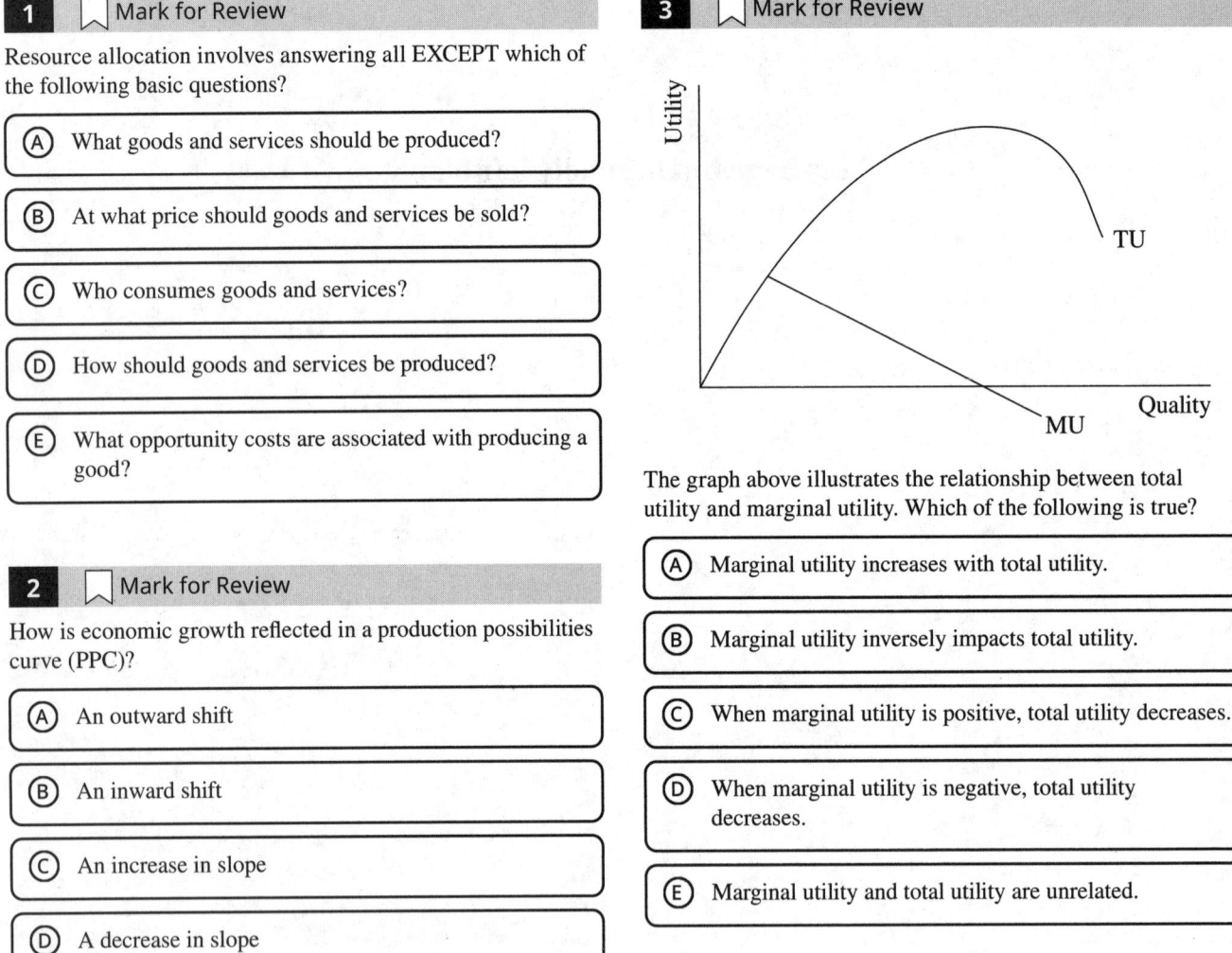

The graph above illustrates the relationship between total utility and marginal utility. Which of the following is true?

(A) Marginal utility increases with total utility.

(B) Marginal utility inversely impacts total utility.

(C) When marginal utility is positive, total utility decreases.

(D) When marginal utility is negative, total utility decreases.

(E) Marginal utility and total utility are unrelated.

**GO ON TO THE NEXT PAGE.**

**4** ☐ Mark for Review

Country A can produce more widgets at a lower opportunity cost than Country B. This is best described as

(A) opportunity cost advantage

(B) absolute advantage

(C) comparative advantage

(D) production possibilities advantage

(E) utility advantage

**5** ☐ Mark for Review

Which of the following results if the price of shoes falls below the equilibrium price?

(A) The quantity demanded of shoes is greater than the quantity supplied.

(B) The quantity purchased of shoes is greater than the quantity sold.

(C) The quantity supplied of shoes is greater than the quantity sold.

(D) The quantity supplied of shoes is greater than the quantity demanded.

(E) There is a surplus of shoes.

**6** ☐ Mark for Review

Assume that a seven percent increase in the price of jackets causes a 14 percent increase in the quantity demanded of sweaters. What is the cross-price elasticity of demand between these goods, and how are these goods related?

(A) Cross-price elasticity of demand equals –0.5, and these goods are complements.

(B) Cross-price elasticity of demand equals –0.5, and these goods are substitutes.

(C) Cross-price elasticity of demand equals +2.0, and these goods are complements.

(D) Cross-price elasticity of demand equals +2.0, and these goods are substitutes.

(E) Cross-price elasticity of demand equals –2.0, and these goods are complements.

**7** ☐ Mark for Review

When the equilibrium price for a regulated good falls above the price ceiling, which of the following scenarios likely results?

(A) A surplus of the regulated good

(B) A shortage of the regulated good

(C) An outward shift of the demand curve for the regulated good

(D) An inward shift of the demand curve for the regulated good

(E) A reduction of queuing costs

**GO ON TO THE NEXT PAGE.**

**8** ☐ Mark for Review

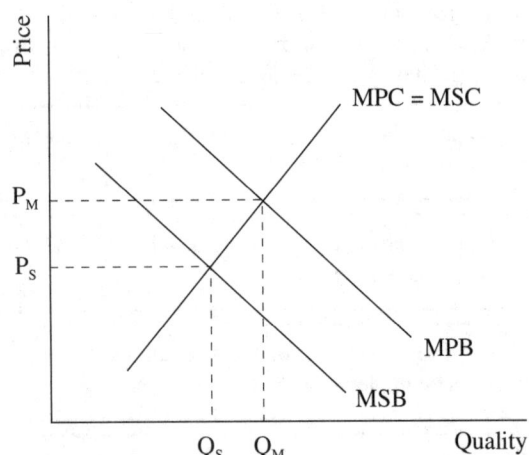

The above graph illustrates the externalities associated with a given good. Which of the following best describes the externality associated with this good?

(A) Negative production externality

(B) Positive production externality

(C) Positive consumption externality

(D) Negative consumption externality

(E) There are no externalities associated with this good.

**9** ☐ Mark for Review

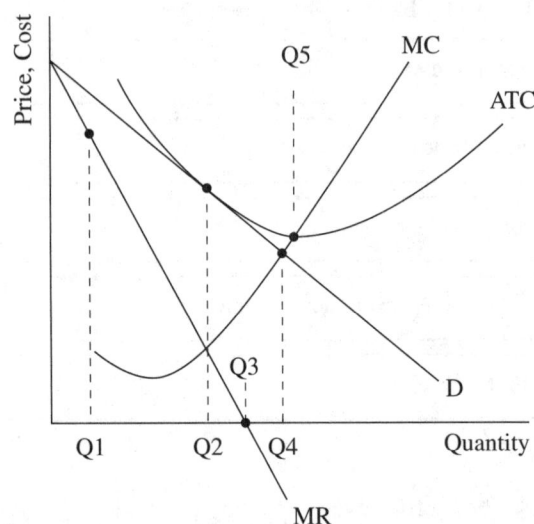

The above graph illustrates monopolistically competitive firms in the long run. Which quantity represents the equilibrium point for firms in this market?

(A) Q1

(B) Q2

(C) Q3

(D) Q4

(E) Q5

**10** ☐ Mark for Review

In the long run, which operating costs are variable?

(A) Natural resources

(B) Labor

(C) Capital

(D) Entrepreneurship

(E) All operating costs

**GO ON TO THE NEXT PAGE.**

**11** ☐ Mark for Review

Which of the following is true in a perfectly competitive market?

Ⓐ Firms produce at a level for which marginal cost equals marginal revenue.

Ⓑ Firms face barriers to entry and exit.

Ⓒ Firms independently set the prices of their goods.

Ⓓ Firms maintain market power.

Ⓔ The market is inefficient and requires intervention to prevent market failure.

**12** ☐ Mark for Review

Which of the following is true about monopolies?

Ⓐ Monopolies must raise prices to sell additional units.

Ⓑ Monopolies occur when there are no barriers to enter the market.

Ⓒ Monopolies will set prices lower than their marginal costs.

Ⓓ Monopolies will supply a quantity at which marginal revenue equals marginal cost.

Ⓔ Monopolies will supply a quantity at which average total revenue equals marginal cost.

**13** ☐ Mark for Review

Which of the following will NOT cause a shift in the supply curve?

Ⓐ Changes in input costs

Ⓑ Changes in quantity produced

Ⓒ Changes in the price of substitutes of production

Ⓓ Changes in the price of complements of production

Ⓔ Changes in relevant regulations

**14** ☐ Mark for Review

In a decreasing cost industry, productive efficiency occurs when

Ⓐ firms produce when marginal cost equals average costs

Ⓑ firms' average production costs decrease because multiple products are being produced

Ⓒ firms do not experience increased production costs as a result of output growth

Ⓓ firms experience zero net growth

Ⓔ firms face decreasing returns to scale

**15** ☐ Mark for Review

Economies of scale exist when

Ⓐ an unlimited number of sellers can enter the market

Ⓑ firms are continuously earning profits

Ⓒ long-run average costs remain constant

Ⓓ the short-run average cost curve slopes downward

Ⓔ the long-run average cost curve slopes downward

**16** ☐ Mark for Review

Which economic condition can be generated by imposing a price ceiling on a certain commodity?

Ⓐ Increasing the supply of the commodity

Ⓑ Shifting the price above the equilibrium level

Ⓒ Increasing consumer purchase power

Ⓓ Decreasing production of the commodity

Ⓔ Increasing production of the commodity

**GO ON TO THE NEXT PAGE.**

**17** ☐ Mark for Review

Which of the following statuses results when a competitive firm is making zero economic profits?

(A) The firm goes bankrupt.

(B) The firm becomes a monopoly.

(C) Other firms are motivated to enter the market.

(D) Other firms go out of business.

(E) The firm becomes stable in both long and short term.

**18** ☐ Mark for Review

How can profit maximization occur for a monopolistic firm?

(A) When price covers average variable costs

(B) When price covers total variable cost

(C) When price covers only its fixed costs

(D) When average cost of production is lowest

(E) When marginal cost equates to marginal revenue

**19** ☐ Mark for Review

Which statement comparing a perfectly competitive firm and a monopoly firm is valid?

(A) Both have horizontal demand curves.

(B) Both have downward-sloping demand curves.

(C) A perfectly competitive firm has a horizontal demand curve, while a monopoly firm has a downward-sloping demand curve.

(D) A perfectly competitive firm has a downward-sloping demand curve, while a monopoly firm has an upward-sloping demand curve.

(E) A perfectly competitive firm has an upward-sloping demand curve, while a monopoly firm has a downward-sloping demand curve.

**20** ☐ Mark for Review

Which of the following groups of factors results in market failure?

(A) Imperfect competition, imperfect information, externalities, and public goods with no intervention

(B) Perfect competition, imperfect information, positive externalities, and public goods with intervention

(C) Perfect competition, imperfect information, negative externalities, and public goods with intervention

(D) Only imperfect information, positive externalities, and public goods with no intervention

(E) Only imperfect information, negative externalities, and public goods with no intervention

**21** ☐ Mark for Review

A food company makes a product that is entirely produced from seaweed. As the product becomes more popular in the market, the need to gather seaweed from the oceans increases. On the basis of the relationship between demand for the product in the market and increasing demand for seaweed, which of the following types of industries best characterizes this food company?

(A) Competitive industry

(B) Decreasing-cost industry

(C) Monopolistic industry

(D) Wide-bargaining industry

(E) Profit-making industry

**GO ON TO THE NEXT PAGE.**

**22**  ☐ Mark for Review

Medicare provides benefits beyond just supporting the health of certain groups of people. Which of the following can be used to characterize Medicare?

(A) Negative externalities, which should be privatized

(B) Positive externalities, which should be subsidized

(C) An example of a positional externality

(D) An example of an inframarginal externality

(E) An example of a technological externality

**23**  ☐ Mark for Review

Which of the following factors is determined by the equilibrium wage?

(A) The market labor demand curve

(B) The market labor supply curve

(C) The marginal demand curve

(D) The marginal supply curve

(E) The quantity of labor demanded

**24**  ☐ Mark for Review

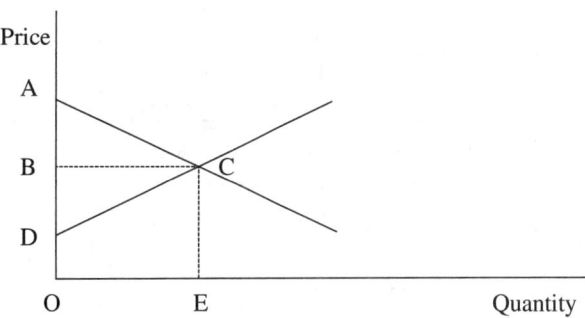

Which region in the figure above represents producer surplus?

(A) ABC

(B) ACD

(C) BCD

(D) BCEO

(E) OACE

**25**  ☐ Mark for Review

Which of the following events would shift the supply curve of donuts to the right?

(A) All government institutions forbid donuts from being eaten on the premises.

(B) A donut plant is damaged by an unexpected event.

(C) The cost of sugar increases.

(D) The sales tax rate on snack food products is reduced worldwide.

(E) Health research indicates donuts are less healthy as compared to other snacks.

**GO ON TO THE NEXT PAGE.**

**26** 🔖 Mark for Review

Which of the following is true about a profit-maximizing firm?

Ⓐ They will produce a good at the quantity where marginal revenue equals fixed average cost.

Ⓑ They will produce a good at the quantity where demand equals average variable cost.

Ⓒ They will produce a good at a quantity where marginal revenue equals marginal cost.

Ⓓ They will produce a good at a quantity on the elastic portion of the demand curve.

Ⓔ They will produce a good at a quantity where marginal revenue exceeds demand.

**27** 🔖 Mark for Review

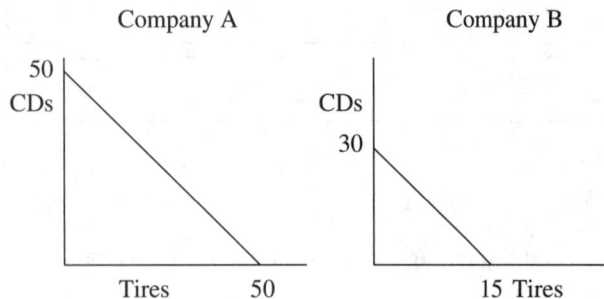

PPFs of Company A and Company B are shown above. Both companies have the same resources to work with. Which of the following conclusions can be drawn from the given data?

Ⓐ Company A has a comparative advantage in both goods.

Ⓑ Company B has an absolute advantage in CDs.

Ⓒ Company B has a comparative advantage in both goods.

Ⓓ Company A has a comparative advantage in tires, and Company B has a comparative advantage in CDs.

Ⓔ Company A has a comparative advantage in CDs, and Company B has a comparative advantage in tires.

**28** 🔖 Mark for Review

Which of the following would NOT be considered a factor of production for a paper company?

Ⓐ The water used to mill the trees

Ⓑ The equipment in the mill

Ⓒ The salespeople's time

Ⓓ The mill owner's time

Ⓔ The mill owner's preference for designing motorcycles

**29** 🔖 Mark for Review

A profit maximizing firm will produce at a quantity determined by the intersection of which two curves?

Ⓐ Total cost of labor and marginal product of capital

Ⓑ Total fixed costs and total variable costs

Ⓒ Average revenue and average cost

Ⓓ Marginal revenue and average cost

Ⓔ Marginal revenue and marginal cost

**GO ON TO THE NEXT PAGE.**

**30** ☐ Mark for Review

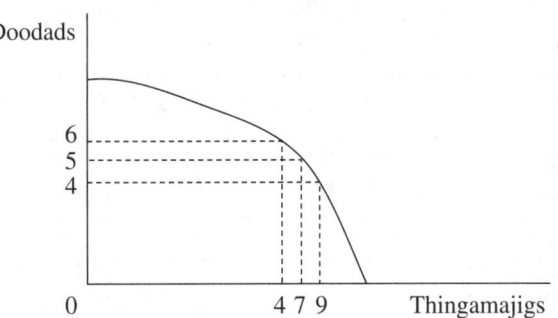

The graph above shows the PPF of producing doodads and thingamajigs. What is the opportunity cost of producing the fifth doodad?

Ⓐ 1 thingamajig

Ⓑ 2 thingamajigs

Ⓒ 3 thingamajigs

Ⓓ 4 thingamajigs

Ⓔ The slope of the PPF

**31** ☐ Mark for Review

Which of the following conditions characterizes the substitute nature of two related goods?

Ⓐ When goods are normal

Ⓑ When goods are inferior

Ⓒ When goods are luxurious

Ⓓ A negative cross-price elasticity

Ⓔ A positive cross-price elasticity

**Questions 32 through 33 refer to the following.**

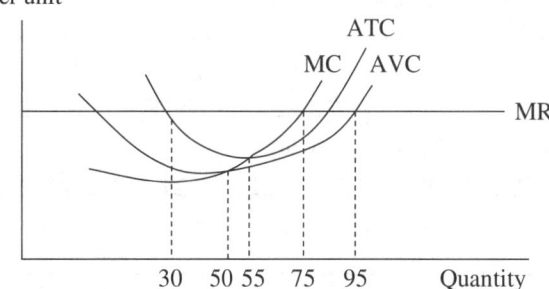

**32** ☐ Mark for Review

The graph above represents the cost and revenue curves of a product. Why does producing 75 units of the good maximize the profit?

Ⓐ Because producing 75 units results in MR < ATC

Ⓑ Because producing 75 units results in MR > ATC

Ⓒ Because producing 75 units results in MR = AVC

Ⓓ Because producing 75 units results in MR = ATC

Ⓔ Because producing 75 units results in MR = MC

**33** ☐ Mark for Review

Which is the best choice for the firm, if the price is determined to be below AVC?

Ⓐ The firm should raise its prices.

Ⓑ The firm should shut down.

Ⓒ The firm should try to lower labor costs.

Ⓓ The firm should borrow money.

Ⓔ No further action is required. The firm has achieved unexpected levels of profit.

**GO ON TO THE NEXT PAGE.**

**34**  ☐ Mark for Review

Which firm has equal price and marginal revenue at all levels of its demand curve?

Ⓐ Oligopolistic firm

Ⓑ Perfectly competitive firm

Ⓒ Monopoly firm

Ⓓ Firm with maximized profit

Ⓔ Firm with minimized cost

**35**  ☐ Mark for Review

Given their concentration ratios, which of the following firms is a monopoly?

Ⓐ TelTech Firm: Concentration ratio = 0

Ⓑ A&P Firm: Concentration ratio = 10

Ⓒ Publicom Firm: Concentration ratio = 100

Ⓓ DSL Connect Firm: Concentration ratio = 1,000

Ⓔ EduVille Firm: Concentration ratio = 10,000

**36**  ☐ Mark for Review

Which of the following conditions characterizes constant returns to scale?

Ⓐ Keeping the other input fixed, one input varies.

Ⓑ As output increases, the long-run average cost decreases.

Ⓒ As input increases, the marginal returns to scale decrease.

Ⓓ As input increases, the output increases proportionally to input.

Ⓔ Productivity increases at a rate proportional to work force incentives.

**37**  ☐ Mark for Review

Robin's income decreased by 20% and her consumption of cupcakes decreased by 50%. Which of the following conclusions is the most likely to be valid?

Ⓐ Robin's income elasticity of demand is 2.5.

Ⓑ Robin's income elasticity of demand is 0.4.

Ⓒ Robin's income elasticity of demand is 0.25.

Ⓓ Robin's income elasticity of demand is 12.5.

Ⓔ Robin's income elasticity of demand is 6.25.

**38**  ☐ Mark for Review

The unemployment rate is zero when

Ⓐ a competitive market is not in equilibrium

Ⓑ the unemployment rate is below one percent

Ⓒ a perfectly competitive market is in equilibrium

Ⓓ the unemployment rate is below five percent

Ⓔ demand curves of individual firms are downward sloping

**GO ON TO THE NEXT PAGE.**

**39** ☐ Mark for Review

| Printer | TC |
|---------|-------|
| 1 | 1,001 |
| 2 | 1,003 |
| 3 | 1,008 |
| 4 | 1,045 |

The table above lists the total costs (TC) for the production of different numbers of printers. Based on the pattern of the data in the table, if the total fixed costs are 1,000, which of the following conclusions is valid about the printer production?

(A) The marginal cost curve rises continuously.

(B) The marginal cost curve falls continuously.

(C) The marginal cost curve remains constant.

(D) The marginal cost of the fourth printer is 45.

(E) The average cost to produce four printers is 8.

**40** ☐ Mark for Review

When is an industry called a duopoly?

(A) If two firms engage in price gauging

(B) If two firms own all, or nearly all, of the market for a good or service

(C) When it is monopolistically competitive

(D) If it is an oligopoly firm with nonstandard product

(E) If two firms collude to divide the market

**41** ☐ Mark for Review

Adding demand curves vertically to find the demand curve for the entire society and having no competitive rival characterize what type of goods?

(A) Private goods

(B) Public goods

(C) Complementary goods

(D) Manufactured goods

(E) Capital goods

**42** ☐ Mark for Review

In a fictional world, if half the dogs die suddenly, how will the demand and supply curves of dog toys change?

(A) Only the supply curve shifts right.

(B) Only the supply curve shifts left.

(C) Only the demand curve shifts left.

(D) Only the demand curve shifts right.

(E) The demand curve shifts left and the supply curve shifts right.

**GO ON TO THE NEXT PAGE.**

**43** ☐ Mark for Review

Which of the following is accounted for in the calculation of a country's gross domestic product?

Ⓐ The repurchase of used goods.

Ⓑ Intermediate goods in the supply chain.

Ⓒ Trading of stocks and bonds.

Ⓓ Investment in new capital.

Ⓔ Public and private transfer payments.

**44** ☐ Mark for Review

Which of the following objectives are the basics of an economic system?

Ⓐ Analyzing monetary systems and circulations of financial sources

Ⓑ Analyzing demanded goods and services, consumers, and methods of production

Ⓒ Analyzing the production time, consumers, and methods of production

Ⓓ Analyzing demanded goods and services, and allocating resources of production

Ⓔ Analyzing monetary systems and allocating labor forces for production

**45** ☐ Mark for Review

Which of the following sources are factors of production?

Ⓐ Labor, human and physical capitals, natural resources

Ⓑ Outputs, human and physical capitals, natural resources

Ⓒ Human and physical capitals, outputs

Ⓓ Labor, outputs, inferior goods

Ⓔ Public goods, human and physical capitals, outputs

**46** ☐ Mark for Review

Which of the following statements best characterizes a monopolistically competitive firm?

Ⓐ A downward-sloping demand curve in the short-run and zero economic profits in the long run

Ⓑ A downward-sloping supply curve in both the short run and long run

Ⓒ Zero economic profits in both the short run and long run

Ⓓ A supply curve that shifts to the right as new competing firms enter the market

Ⓔ A supply curve that shifts to the left as the firm transforms into a true monopoly

**47** ☐ Mark for Review

How does dominant strategy equilibrium occur in game theory?

Ⓐ When one player wins and the other loses

Ⓑ When both players have a dominant strategy

Ⓒ When neither player has a dominant strategy

Ⓓ When the players work together

Ⓔ When Nash equilibrium occurs

**GO ON TO THE NEXT PAGE.**

**48** ☐ Mark for Review

Which of the following conditions most likely results in a shift to the right in the demand curve for specialty coffee drinks?

(A) Bankruptcies of several major coffee chains

(B) New farming techniques that increase the yield of coffee beans

(C) Optimizing the existing technology to lower costs of production

(D) Expectations of higher future income among specialty coffee drinkers

(E) Expectations of lower future income among specialty coffee drinkers

**49** ☐ Mark for Review

A perfectly competitive firm deals with which of the following conditions?

(A) Marginal revenue, average revenue, and price are equal.

(B) The demand curve lies above the marginal revenue curve.

(C) Marginal revenue differs from average revenue.

(D) Average revenue differs from price.

(E) The demand curve is vertical.

**50** ☐ Mark for Review

In which of the following market conditions does the government impose strong antitrust laws?

(A) Imperfect competition

(B) Imperfect information

(C) Perfect competition

(D) Perfectly elastic demand

(E) Elastic demand

**51** ☐ Mark for Review

Which of the following factors are barriers to entry?

(A) Control of resources, economies of scale, patents, and accounting profits

(B) Control of resources, economies of scale, patents, and exclusive licenses

(C) Economies of scale, patents, total revenue, and exclusive licenses

(D) Economies of scale, patents, and requirements for short-run profits

(E) Patents, exclusive licenses, and signs of market failure

**GO ON TO THE NEXT PAGE.**

**52** ☐ Mark for Review

Which of the following conditions in game theory occurs when neither party has a motivation to alter their strategy?

(A) A zero-sum game

(B) A dominant strategy

(C) A payoff

(D) A Nash equilibrium

(E) A prisoner's dilemma

**53** ☐ Mark for Review

A company has market power such that it can prevent resale of its products. The company can also offer different prices to different buyers. What are such advantages called?

(A) Profit maximization

(B) Profit minimization

(C) Efficiency in production

(D) Price discrimination

(E) Price determination

**54** ☐ Mark for Review

If the price of keyboards falls below the equilibrium price, which of the following will occur?

(A) The quantity demanded of pianos is greater than the quantity supplied.

(B) There is a keyboard surplus.

(C) The quantity supplied of keyboards is greater than the quantity demanded.

(D) The quantity purchased of keyboards is greater than the quantity sold.

(E) The quantity supplied of keyboards is greater than the quantity sold.

**55** ☐ Mark for Review

Why is a monopoly's marginal revenue curve below the demand curve?

(A) New products do not have much demand in a monopolistic market.

(B) Monopolies must lower their prices in order to sell more units of product.

(C) At all levels of output, labor costs are fixed for monopolies.

(D) The price of each unit produced is fixed in monopolies.

(E) Monopolies are not trying to earn a profit.

**GO ON TO THE NEXT PAGE.**

**56** ☐ Mark for Review

Decrease in price of output and in the marginal product of labor results in which of the following transformations?

Ⓐ The market supply curve for labor moves upward.

Ⓑ The market supply curve for labor moves downward.

Ⓒ The market demand curve for labor stretches.

Ⓓ The market demand curve for labor shifts to the left.

Ⓔ The market demand curve for labor shifts to the right.

**57** ☐ Mark for Review

Which curve does NOT typically have a negatively sloping section at any time?

Ⓐ Marginal product curve

Ⓑ Average product curve

Ⓒ Total product curve

Ⓓ Marginal cost curve

Ⓔ Total cost curve

**58** ☐ Mark for Review

Which of the following is the most likely to decrease wages for bookbinders?

Ⓐ An increase in the cost of bookbinding

Ⓑ An increase in the price of books

Ⓒ A new cost-effective automated process

Ⓓ The opening of a new book store

Ⓔ Half the existing bookbinders taking paid leave to participate in training programs

**59** ☐ Mark for Review

Which of the following conditions best describes a monopsony?

Ⓐ The marginal factor cost curve is below the labor supply curve.

Ⓑ The marginal revenue curve is below the demand curve.

Ⓒ The marginal revenue curve is above the demand curve.

Ⓓ The unit price always reflects a zero profit rate in the long term.

Ⓔ The marginal factor cost curve is above the labor supply curve.

**60** ☐ Mark for Review

Imagine a city has a population of 700,000, and the labor force has 650,000 people. If 505,000 people are employed, what is the unemployment rate?

Ⓐ 15%

Ⓑ 30%

Ⓒ 42%

Ⓓ 50%

Ⓔ 65%

**END OF SECTION I**

## AP MICROECONOMICS
## SECTION II

**Total Time—1 hour**
**Reading Period—10 minutes**
**Writing Period—50 minutes**
**3 Questions**

**Directions:** You are advised to spend the first 10 minutes reading all of the questions and planning your answers. You will then have 50 minutes to answer all three of the following questions. You may begin writing your responses before the reading period is over. It is suggested that you spend approximately half your time on the first question and divide the remaining time equally between the next two questions. Include correctly labeled diagrams, if useful or required, in explaining your answers. A correctly labeled diagram must have all axes and curves clearly labeled and must show directional changes. If the question prompts you to "Calculate," you must show how you arrived at your final answer. Use a pen with black or dark blue ink. Make sure to write all your answers in the free-response booklet.

---

**1** ☐ Mark for Review

In a certain country, Compumart is the only provider of Internet service. It is currently operating at a loss.

A. Using a correctly labeled graph, show each of the following.
  (i) Compumart's current operational status, including the loss-minimizing price and quantity.
  (ii) The area of dead weight loss
  (iii) The allocatively efficient quantity

B. If Compumart raised the price above the loss-minimizing price, would the total revenue increase, decrease, or not change? Explain.

C. Assume that a lump-sum subsidy is provided to Compumart by the county government. In the short run, what would happen to the following?
  (i) Will the deadweight loss increase, decrease, or not change? Explain.
  (ii) Will Compumart's economic losses increase, decrease, or not change? Explain.

D. Assume that a per-unit subsidy is provided to Compumart by the county.
  (i) Will the deadweight loss increase, decrease, or not change? Explain.
  (ii) Will Compumart's economic losses increase, decrease, or not change? Explain.

E. Suppose a new Internet service provider enters the market. What will happen to the equilibrium price and quantity of Internet service in the county? Explain.

**GO ON TO THE NEXT PAGE.**

**2** ☐ Mark for Review

Suppose there is a cheap synthetic substitute for natural gas found at the same time new natural gas deposits start being mined.

    A.  Draw a correctly labeled supply and demand diagram to represent this scenario.

    B.  Explain how the shift in part (A) will affect the equilibrium price and quantity of natural gas.

**3** ☐ Mark for Review

Lollipops (*y*-axis) vs. Chocolate Toffees (*x*-axis)

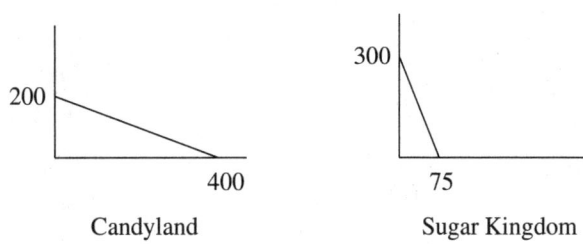

Candyland                   Sugar Kingdom

Refer to the PPFs above to answer the following.

    A.  Does either country have an absolute advantage in the production of either lollipops or chocolate toffees? Explain.

    B.  Does either country have a comparative advantage in the production of either lollipops or chocolate toffees? Explain.

**STOP**

**END OF EXAM**

_____

# Chapter 18
# Microeconomics
# Practice Test 1:
# Answers and
# Explanations

# MICROECONOMICS PRACTICE TEST 1 ANSWER KEY

## Section I

| | | | | | |
|---|---|---|---|---|---|
| 1. | B | 21. | B | 41. | D |
| 2. | A | 22. | B | 42. | C |
| 3. | D | 23. | E | 43. | D |
| 4. | C | 24. | C | 44. | B |
| 5. | A | 25. | D | 45. | A |
| 6. | D | 26. | C | 46. | A |
| 7. | B | 27. | D | 47. | B |
| 8. | D | 28. | E | 48. | D |
| 9. | B | 29. | E | 49. | A |
| 10. | E | 30. | B | 50. | A |
| 11. | A | 31. | E | 51. | B |
| 12. | D | 32. | E | 52. | D |
| 13. | B | 33. | B | 53. | D |
| 14. | A | 34. | B | 54. | A |
| 15. | D | 35. | C | 55. | B |
| 16. | C | 36. | D | 56. | D |
| 17. | E | 37. | A | 57. | E |
| 18. | E | 38. | C | 58. | C |
| 19. | C | 39. | A | 59. | E |
| 20. | A | 40. | B | 60. | B |

# MICROECONOMICS PRACTICE TEST 1: ANSWERS AND EXPLANATIONS

## Section I: Multiple-Choice

1. **B** The price of a good is determined by supply and demand, particularly the quantity supplied and the quantity demanded. Price is not a basic factor in resource allocation. Resource allocation concerns itself with what goods and services to produce, who will consume them, how they will be produced, and the opportunities that are lost when one good or service is selected for production. Choice (B) is the correct answer.

2. **A** In a production possibilities curve, the slope reflects the relative opportunity cost between producing two different goods, so (C) and (D) can be eliminated. Economic growth suggests that there is an increase in resources available to produce goods. When more goods can be produced, the PPC shifts outward. Choice (A) is the correct answer.

3. **D** Marginal utility and total utility are directly related, meaning that while marginal utility is positive, total utility will continue to increase. As a result, (B), (C), and (E) can be eliminated. Generally speaking, as more units of a good are consumed, the marginal utility gained from each consumed good decreases, so (A) can be eliminated. Choice (D) is the correct answer, as illustrated by the change in slope of TU when MU crosses the x-axis.

4. **C** By definition, comparative advantage occurs when an individual, business, or country can produce a good or service at a lower opportunity cost than another producer. Choice (C) is the correct answer.

5. **A** This is an example of a question for which sketching a quick supply and demand graph can be enormously helpful. If shoe price falls below the equilibrium price, there is no surplus, and the quantity supplied is clearly less than the quantity demanded. Choices (D) and (E) can be eliminated. When price falls below equilibrium, there is a shortage, so supply won't exceed quantity sold, so (C) can be eliminated. Choice (B) can be eliminated because "purchased" and "sold" are synonyms, so the quantities in (B) are equal. Choice (A) is the correct answer.

6. **D** Cross-price elasticity of demand is calculated by dividing the percentage change of good B, in this case sweaters, by the percentage change of good A, in this case jackets. The result is +2.0. When the result of this equation is positive, the goods are substitutes. Choice (D) is the correct answer.

7. **B** A price ceiling occurs when there is a maximum allowed price for a regulated good. There is no direct impact on demand, so (C) and (D) can be eliminated. The result is a shortage, and a potential increase in queuing costs, so (A) and (E) can be eliminated, and (B) is the correct answer.

8. **D** In the graph provided, marginal personal cost equals marginal social cost. Therefore, this is a consumption externality and not a production externality. The marginal social benefit is less than the marginal personal benefit, making this a negative consumption externality. Choice (D) is the correct answer.

9.  **B**   In the long run in a monopolistically competitive market, producers will produce when the average total cost (ATC) equals demand. Therefore, (B) is the correct answer.

10. **E**   Choices (A), (B), (C), and (D) are all factors of supply. In the long run, firms can adjust all their inputs. Therefore, all costs become variable. Choice (E) is the correct answer.

11. **A**   This question requires a thorough understanding of the qualities of competitive markets. In competitive markets, firms face no barriers to entry and exit, but have no market power. Further, prices are set by the market, and firms are price takers. Competitive markets are efficient and do not require intervention to prevent market failure. Choice (A) is the correct answer.

12. **D**   Monopolies occur when there are substantial barriers to entering a market, so eliminate (B). Monopolies are more likely to use advertising to increase their profits than they are to reduce prices. It's unlikely that a monopoly would set prices lower than their marginal costs as this would reduce profits, so eliminate (C). Monopolies determine their quantity supplied by maximizing their profits, when marginal revenue equals marginal cost. Eliminate (E); (D) is the correct answer.

13. **B**   Changes in the cost of inputs, complements, substitutes, and relevant regulations will all cause the supply curve to shift, whereas a change in the quantity supplied will cause the equilibrium point to shift along the supply curve itself. Eliminate (A), (C), (D), and (E); (B) is the correct answer.

14. **A**   Choice (B) describes economies of scope, not necessarily productive efficiency. Choice (C) describes a constant cost industry. Choice (E) describes an increasing cost industry. Net growth isn't necessarily related to decreasing costs, so eliminate (D). Therefore, (A) is the correct answer.

15. **D**   By definition, economies of scale exist over the range of output for which the long-run average cost curve slopes downward, meaning that the cost per unit is falling. The correct answer is (D).

16. **C**   In the case of shortage or economic crises, a price ceiling sets the maximum amount a seller can charge in order to empower consumer purchasing power. An effective price ceiling must be below the equilibrium price. Price ceilings stop sellers from selling at the price equilibrium. Increases in the quantity of the good supplied and surpluses in the supply of the good would result from a lowest possible price, not a highest possible price. Price ceilings do not cause the demand or supply curves to shift. The quantity of the good supplied would decrease rather than increase.

17. **E**   The long-term goal of all competitive firms is to make zero economic profit. Economic profit is calculated by subtracting all costs from revenues, including human capital and opportunity costs. Zero economic profit means that the firm is making what it should as a healthy competitor, not that it is losing money. With zero economic profit, a company can become immune against those factors that may cause bankruptcy or monopoly. Eliminate (A) and (B). When a firm earns positive or negative economic profits, other firms are motivated to enter or exit the market accordingly, so (C) and (D) can be eliminated. Choice (E) is the best answer.

18. **E**   Every firm in any of the market structures would prefer to maximize profits, when marginal cost equals marginal revenue, though there may be outside strictures such as price ceilings or subsidies.

19. **C**  Either a monopoly or a perfectly competitive firm can legally charge any price it wants, but in both cases prices that are too high can result in losses instead of profits. A perfectly competitive firm has horizontal marginal revenue and demand curves, with zero economic profit, ideally. A monopoly has a downward-sloping demand curve due to demand decreasing as price increases.

20. **A**  Prices are too high as a result of imperfect competition. Quantities may be too high when negative externalities exist, but are too low when there are positive externalities and public goods. All of these factors are sources of market failure, which occurs when resources are not allocated efficiently.

21. **B**  This question is challenging because it's not actually testing your knowledge of how seaweed, a factor of supply, defines the market. Instead, it's testing your knowledge of the five types of industry available in the answers. Use Process of Elimination. There is not enough information to make conclusions about profits. There is also insufficient information to determine whether the situation is a monopoly, a bargaining, or a competitive industry. This new industry uses so much seaweed that the overall seaweed demand is increased, making this a decreasing-cost industry.

22. **B**  When externalities are positive, subsidies are required to bring the marginal benefit to the creator(s) of the externalities up to the marginal social benefit. Otherwise, these goods and services will be too expensive for many people to consume, lowering the overall benefit of their consumption to society. Medicare should be encouraged up to the level of marginal social benefit. Therefore, it should be subsidized in order to lower costs to consumers.

23. **E**  Labor demand is a function of the marginal product of labor and the price of the output. The market labor demand curve is derived from the sum of individual demand curves. Supply is not determined by equilibrium price, but the quantity of labor is.

24. **C**  Producer surplus is generated by market prices in excess of the lowest price producers would otherwise be willing to accept for their goods. Graphically, this is the difference between the price line and the supply curve. In this figure, this is the area BCD. ABC is the consumer surplus, and OACE is the total utility.

25. **D**  This question is asking you to identify what would cause an increase in supply, which is represented by a shift of the supply curve to the right. When factors of supply such as sugar become more expensive, supply decreases, so eliminate (C). Unfavorable research might decrease demand, but it wouldn't impact supply, so eliminate (E). A loss of capital would most likely reduce production or make it more expensive, so eliminate (B). Increased regulations would also decrease supply, so eliminate (A). Choice (D) is the correct answer.

26. **C**  Theory holds that profit maximizing firms will produce a good at a quantity where marginal revenue equals marginal cost. If the marginal cost to produce a good exceeds the price the firm will earn for the good, the firm will no longer be maximizing profits. Marginal revenue is a downward sloping curve with half the slope of the demand curve, so eliminate (E). The elasticity of the demand curve alone doesn't necessarily impact profit, so eliminate (D). Any consideration of profit would need to consider total costs, not distinguish between fixed and variable costs, so eliminate (A) and (B). Choice (C) is the answer.

27. **D** Company A gives up one tire per CD, and Company B gives up $\frac{1}{2}$ of a tire per CD, giving Company B the comparative advantage in CDs, because it is giving up fewer tires to produce one more CD. Company A gives up one CD per tire and Company B gives up 2 CDs per tire, giving Company A the comparative advantage in tires because it is giving up fewer CDs to produce one more tire. Company A has an absolute advantage in both goods because it can produce more with the same resources.

28. **E** Choices (A), (B), (C), and (D) are factors of production. Choice (E) is an opportunity cost, but is not a factor of production.

29. **E** A profit maximizing firm will produce at a quantity for which marginal revenue equals marginal cost. Choice (E) is the best answer.

30. **B** When the fifth doodad is produced, production of thingamajigs goes from 9 to 7. Therefore, the opportunity cost is 2 thingamajigs. The slope of the PPF is the negative inverse of the opportunity cost of the doodad.

31. **E** Cross-price elasticity is the only type of elasticity that considers two particular goods. The cross-price elasticity is the percentage change in the quantity demanded of one good divided by the percentage change in the price of another good. If an increase in the price of one good causes an increase in the quantity demanded of another good, the cross-price elasticity is positive, and the goods are substitutes. When consumers decide they do not wish to pay the increased price of the first good, they feel comfortable substituting it with the second good. If an increase in the price of one good causes a decrease in the quantity demanded of another good, the cross-price elasticity is negative, and the goods are complements. A horizontal demand curve refers only to one good and has nothing to do with substitution.

32. **E** Firms maximize profit by producing when MR = MC. In the diagram, MR = MC at 75.

33. **B** The firm is not earning enough to pay for any of its fixed costs when the price is determined to be below AVC (average variable costs). Only by shutting down immediately can the firm minimize its losses by eliminating its variable costs and paying only its fixed costs.

34. **B** A perfectly competitive firm's demand curve is horizontal at the prices determined by the market equilibrium. Thus, each firm can sell as many units as it wants at the market price, and marginal revenue equals the price.

35. **C** The $n$-firm concentration ratio is the sum of the market shares of the largest $n$ firms in an industry. A monopoly holds 100 percent of the market share regardless of the value of $n$. Therefore, Publicom Firm is a monopoly.

36. **D** Marginal returns are gained when one input is varied and the other is fixed. Decreasing marginal returns and production incentives are separate from constant returns to scale. The long-run average cost is related to economies of scale. Specifically, when the long-run average costs decrease as output increases, there are increasing returns to scale. Constant returns to scale occur when output increases proportionally to input as input increases. For example, output doubles as input doubles.

37. **A** The income elasticity of demand is the percentage change in the quantity demanded divided by percentage change in income, or 50 ÷ 20 = 2.5.

38. **C** Of the options available, (C) is the best answer. When a perfectly competitive labor market is in equilibrium, individual firms face a horizontal labor demand curve and are considered price takers. Everyone who wants to work at the market wage rate can do so, resulting in an unemployment rate of zero.

39. **A** Marginal cost is the additional cost of producing one additional printer. With a total fixed cost of 1,000, the marginal costs for producing a first, second, third, and fourth printer are 1, 2, 5, and 37, respectively. Clearly, marginal cost to produce each extra printer is going up.

40. **B** The key is the number of firms in the system. A duopoly refers to a scenario in which two firms dominate the market for a specific good or service. The term "duopoly" doesn't describe the specific behaviors of those firms, such as whether or not they are colluding or engaging in price gauging. Choice (B) is the best answer.

41. **D** An absolute advantage occurs when any given good can be produced using fewer resources per unit than a competitor. A comparative advantage occurs when one good can be produced at a lower opportunity cost than another. In Company A you can buy one CD for one tire; In Company B a CD only costs half a tire! So Company B has the comparative advantage in tires. The reverse is also true for tires. In Company B, one tire costs two CDs, whereas in Company A, one tire costs one CD. Company A has the comparative advantage in tires. Choice (D) is correct.

42. **C** The sudden loss of half the dogs in the world decreases demand for specialty dog toys drastically. While the supply of dog toys is not affected, the demand curve shifts to the left.

43. **D** The expenditure approach uses the following data points to calculate the GDP: personal consumption expenditures by household, investment in new capital, government purchases, exports, and imports. Choice (D) is the correct answer.

44. **B** The fundamental questions that every economic system must answer include the following: What goods and services are produced? How will they be produced? For whom will they be produced? Choice (C) asks how long production will take, and (D) considers the specifics of where resources are produced, so they can be eliminated. Monetary systems and circulations of financial resources are examples of economics in action, as opposed to a basic tenets of economics. Choice (B) is the correct answer.

45. **A** Factors of production are inputs that are necessary for the production of supply. Human capital, labor, natural resources, and physical capital are all factors necessary in the production of the supply of a product. They are not public goods, because they can be excluded and there are rivals for them. They are not inferior, which would mean that demand for them would decrease as the price increased. They are inputs, necessary for the production of goods, rather than outputs, the end result of the production of goods.

46. **A** In the short run, a monopolistically competitive firm will face a downward-sloping demand curve because its products are differentiated. However, in the long run, the lack of barriers to entry will allow similar firms to compete until economic profits are zero. Supply curves will not necessarily shift under certain circumstances for monopolistically competitive firms.

47. **B** A dominant strategy equilibrium exists in game theory when both players have a dominant strategy. This means that both players have a strategy that is better for them regardless of the actions of the other player.

48. **D** Bankruptcies of coffee chains and new farming or production techniques affect the supply curve, not the demand curve. Expectations of lower future income among specialty coffee drinkers might cause them to start consuming fewer drinks right away, shifting the demand curve to the left. Expectations of higher future income among the same consumers might cause them to start consuming more drinks right away, shifting the demand curve to the right.

49. **A** The definition of a perfectly competitive firm is that P = MR = AR.

50. **A** Imperfect competition conditions occur when individual producers or consumers are allowed to exercise unfair control over the price of a good. Antitrust legislation prevents larger groups of producers and/or consumers from banding together to manipulate price levels.

51. **B** The factors outlined in (B) all provide obstacles to new firms trying to enter an industry. None of them are required for a firm to earn short-run profits. In fact, they can have the opposite effect for firms trying to enter the market. These items can create market power and allow firms to maintain economic profits.

52. **D** Nash equilibrium is a term from game theory that indicates that each party in a strategic game wants to stick with their strategy, based on the knowledge each has of the other's strategy. In other words, neither party has anything to gain from selling the other party out. A zero-sum game occurs when one player's gain is equal to another person's loss. A dominant strategy occurs when a player will make the same choice regardless of their opponent's choice, and a payoff is simply a term for what one player earns. The prisoner's dilemma is a specific of game theory example. Choice (D) is the correct answer.

53. **D** The definition of price discrimination involves the firm's having the power to set prices in the market, the ability to prevent the resale of its products, and buyers with differing, separable demand elasticities. Price discrimination involves charging customers or groups of customers different prices based on their willingness to pay.

54. **A** This question tests your knowledge of how the supply and demand curves illustrate market equilibrium. If a good is priced below the equilibrium point, there will be a shortage, and the demand for keyboards will be greater than the quantity supplied. The correct answer is (A).

55. **B** Monopolies by definition are trying to earn a profit. The demand curve is not affected by competition, which means that a monopoly must lower its prices to sell more units of its product. This means that the marginal revenue is not the price indicated on the demand curve. Labor costs are not fixed for monopolies at all levels of output. Levels of demand for new products are also not fixed for all monopolies.

56.  **D**  The market demand curve for labor is calculated by adding the individual firm labor demand curves. The labor demand curve is independent of the labor supply curve, so any market demand curve shift is independent of any changes in the labor supply curves. When the number of firms in the market increases or the price of output increases, the market demand curve for labor will shift to the right as consumer demand for the firm's products decreases. When the marginal product of labor decreases, the firm will be able to produce more of the product for the same price. When the price of output decreases, consumer demand for the product will increase. In both cases, the market demand curve for labor will shift to the left.

57.  **E**  A typical total cost curve is constantly increasing. While the slope of the total cost curve may change, it will remain positive at all times as the total costs will always increase over time. All of the other choices will have periods of decrease, or negative slope.

58.  **C**  A new automated process that will make bookbinding much cheaper will decrease the demand for labor by shifting the labor supply curve to the left, leading to a decrease in wages. An increase in the price of books or an increase in the cost of bookbinding increases the demand for labor by shifting the labor supply curve to the right, leading to an increase in wages. When bookbinders receive more specialized training, they leave their jobs, decreasing the number of bookbinders available and increasing wages. Opening a bookstore would increase demand for book production, likely increasing wages.

59.  **E**  A monopsony is a market condition in which there is only one buyer for a product. It is the mirror image of a monopoly, which has only one supplier for a product. The marginal revenue curve is below the demand curve for a monopoly because the monopoly can sell its products at a higher price due to the lack of competition in production. Similarly, the marginal factor cost curve is above the labor supply curve for a monopsony because it can force the suppliers to set a lower price up to a point.

60.  **B**  Use the following equation to calculate unemployment: $\left(\dfrac{\text{Number of people unemployed}}{\text{labor force}}\right) \times 100$.

To find the number of people unemployed, subtract the number of people employed from the population: $\dfrac{(700,000 - 505,000)}{650,000} \times 100 = 30\%$. Choice (B) is the correct answer.

# Section II: Free-Response

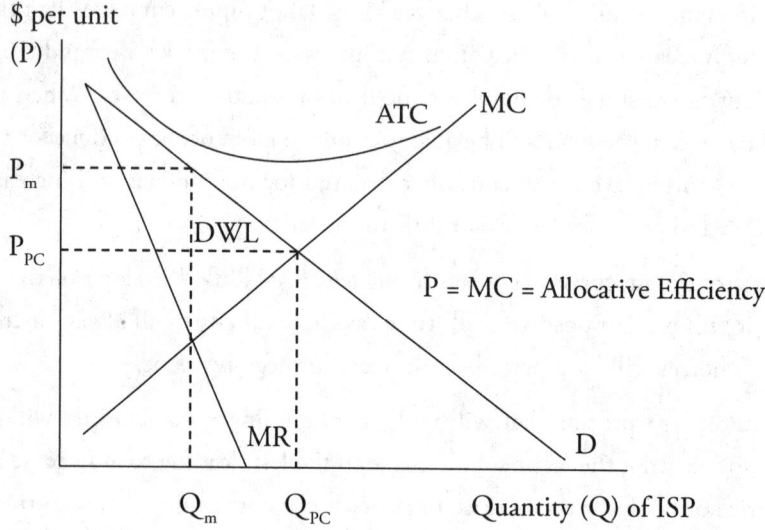

1.

A. The figure you drew should look similar to the figure above. A monopoly would charge $P_m$ and produce $Q_m$ in order to minimize its losses. The profit-maximizing equilibrium would occur when marginal revenue equals marginal cost (MR = MC). DWL is Dead Weight Loss to the economy as a whole.

B. If Compumart raised its prices above the loss-minimization price, revenue would increase because marginal revenue is greater than marginal cost.

C. A lump-sum subsidy affects only fixed costs. While the Average Total Cost will be lowered, the marginal cost will remain the same. While the overall economic losses will decrease, the Dead Weight Loss will remain the same.

D. In the short run, a per-unit subsidy would make the marginal cost curve shift downward as each unit would now cost less for the firm to produce. This would shift the loss-minimizing price down while increasing the loss-minimizing quantity produced. Compumart's economic losses will decrease and the deadweight loss will decrease.

E. The addition of one new firm turns the situation into a duopoly. The new firm would produce at a new loss-minimizing price and quantity. This would shift the marginal revenue curve for the existing firm down, making the quantity produced less and the price higher in the short run. However, depending on the equilibrium price for the new firm, the existing firm may need to lower prices in order to maintain its share of the market in the long run.

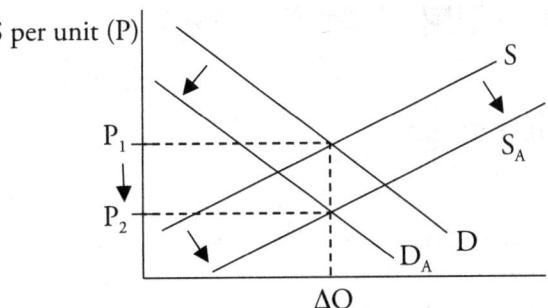

2.

A. The figure you drew should look similar to the figure above.

B. The cheap synthetic substitute will lower the demand, shifting the demand curve to the left and lowering the equilibrium price. Mining new natural gas deposits will increase the supply, shifting the supply curve to the right and also lowering the price. The new equilibrium price of natural gas will be much lower, while the change in quantity is minimal.

3.

A. Candyland can produce 400 chocolate toffees while Sugar Kingdom can produce only 75, giving Candyland the absolute advantage in the production of chocolate toffees. Sugar Kingdom, on the other hand, can produce 300 lollipops while Candyland can produce only 200, giving Sugar Kingdom the absolute advantage in the production of lollipops.

B. Candyland gives up 2 chocolate toffees for every lollipop it produces while Sugar Kingdom gives up $\frac{75}{300}$, or $\frac{1}{4}$, of a chocolate toffee for every lollipop it produces. Because the opportunity cost in Candyland is higher for chocolate toffees, Sugar Kingdom has a comparative advantage in the production of chocolate toffees. Candyland gives up $\frac{1}{2}$ of a lollipop for every chocolate toffee it produces while Sugar Kingdom gives up 4 lollipops for every chocolate toffee it produces. Because Sugar Kingdom gives up fewer chocolate toffees for each lollipop produced, Sugar Kingdom has the comparative advantage in producing lollipops.

# HOW TO SCORE YOUR PRACTICE TESTS

## Section I: Multiple-Choice

$$\underline{\hspace{3cm}} \times 1.66625 = \underline{\hspace{3cm}}$$

Number Correct                Weighted
(out of 60)                Section I Score
                (Do not round)

## Section II: Free-Response

Question 1   $\underline{\hspace{3cm}} \times 2.50125 = \underline{\hspace{3cm}}$

(out of 10)             (Do not round)

Question 2   $\underline{\hspace{3cm}} \times 2.50125 = \underline{\hspace{3cm}}$

(out of 5)             (Do not round)

Question 3   $\underline{\hspace{3cm}} \times 2.50125 = \underline{\hspace{3cm}}$

(out of 5)             (Do not round)

| AP Score Conversion Chart Microeconomics | |
| --- | --- |
| **Composite Score Range** | **AP Score** |
| 107–150 | 5 |
| 90–106 | 4 |
| 73–89 | 3 |
| 56–72 | 2 |
| 0–55 | 1 |

Sum = $\underline{\hspace{3cm}}$

Weighted
Section II Score
(Do not round)

## Composite Score

$$\underline{\hspace{3cm}} + \underline{\hspace{3cm}} = \underline{\hspace{3cm}}$$

Weighted        Weighted        Composite Score
Section I Score   Section II Score   (Round to nearest
                              whole number)

*Note: This score sheet is to help you estimate your approximate score for the official exam, not your actual score.*

# Chapter 19
# Macroeconomics
# Practice Test 1

# AP® Macroeconomics Exam

## DO NOT OPEN THIS BOOKLET UNTIL YOU ARE TOLD TO DO SO.

### At a Glance

**Total Time**
1 hour, 10 minutes
**Number of Questions**
60
**Percent of Total Grade**
66.7%

**DISCLAIMER:** The official multiple-choice section of the AP Macroeconomics Exam will be administered digitally. Instructions for the digital exam may differ from those for the practice test.

### Instructions

Section I of this examination contains 60 multiple-choice questions. Fill in all of the ovals for numbers 1 through 60 on your answer sheet.

Indicate all of your answers to the multiple-choice questions on the answer sheet. Give only one answer to each question.

Use your time effectively, working as quickly as you can without losing accuracy. Do not spend too much time on any one question. Go on to other questions and come back to the ones you have not answered if you have time.

### Instructions

You are advised to spend the first 10 minutes reading all of the questions and planning your answers. You will then have 50 minutes to answer all three of the following questions. It is suggested that you spend 25 minutes on question 1 and roughly 12 minutes each on questions 2 and 3. You may use scratch paper to plan your work, but you must write your answers in the free-response booklet.

### At a Glance

**Total Time**
60 minutes
**Number of Questions**
3
**Percent of Total Grade**
33.3%
**Writing Instrument**
Pencil or pen (with dark blue or black ink)

Include correctly labeled diagrams, if useful or required, in explaining your answers. A correctly labeled diagram must have all axes and curves clearly labeled and must show directional changes.

If the question prompts you to "Calculate," you must show how you arrived at your final answer. A calculator is allowed in this section.

GO ON TO THE NEXT PAGE.

This page intentionally left blank.

GO ON TO THE NEXT PAGE.

# AP MACROECONOMICS
## SECTION I
### Time—70 Minutes
### 60 Questions

**Directions:** Each of the questions or incomplete statements below is followed by five suggested answers or completions. Select the one that is best in each case and then fill in the corresponding oval on the answer sheet.

---

**1** ☐ Mark for Review

The population of Country X is 550,000, and the labor force is 500,000. If 475,000 people are unemployed, what is the unemployment rate?

(A) 2%

(B) 5%

(C) 7.5%

(D) 10%

(E) 50%

---

**2** ☐ Mark for Review

Which of the following is NOT accounted for in the calculation of a country's gross domestic product using the expenditure approach?

(A) Personal consumption by households

(B) Imports

(C) Government purchases

(D) Investment in new physical capital

(E) Income taxes

---

**3** ☐ Mark for Review

Which of the following would lead to a decrease in nominal interest rates?

(A) An expansionary monetary policy accompanied by an increase in the demand for money

(B) An expansionary monetary policy accompanied by a decrease in the demand for money

(C) A contractionary monetary policy accompanied by an increase in the demand for money

(D) A contractionary monetary policy conducted with no change in the demand for money

(E) A contractionary monetary policy accompanied by a decrease in the demand for money

---

**GO ON TO THE NEXT PAGE.**

**4** ☐ Mark for Review

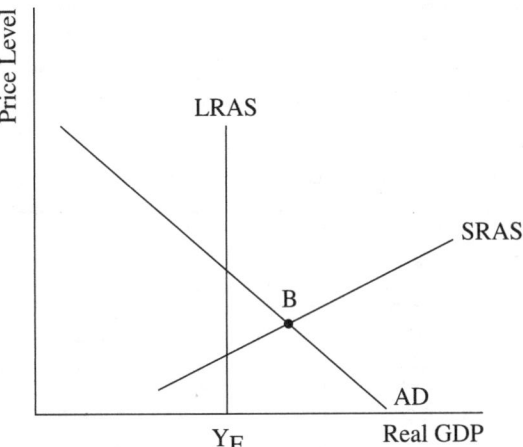

A country's economy is in equilibrium at point B. Which of the following policies would be most effective to increase the price level in the short run?

(A) Increasing income tax rates

(B) Increasing the required reserve ratio

(C) Decreasing government expenditures

(D) Decreasing interest on reserves

(E) Decreasing the minimum wage

**5** ☐ Mark for Review

A decrease in the demand for loanable funds could be best explained by which of the following?

(A) A decrease in political instability in the country

(B) A decrease in the firms' optimism about the future jobs and income

(C) A decrease in income or wealth

(D) An increase in government taxes

(E) An increase in investment spending

**6** ☐ Mark for Review

If expansionary monetary policy is carried out, what will most likely happen to interest rates and the money supply?

(A) Both interest rates and the money supply will increase.

(B) Both interest rates and the money supply will decrease.

(C) Interest rates will increase, and the money supply will decrease.

(D) Interest rates will decrease, and the money supply will increase.

(E) The money supply will increase, but the change in interest rates will be indeterminate.

**7** ☐ Mark for Review

If an economy is currently in an inflationary period, which of the following changes would result in a decrease in real GDP in the short run and an increase in the price level in the long run?

(A) There is a decrease in the productivity of the economy's resources.

(B) The government begins running a budget deficit.

(C) There is a decrease in the prices of the economy's productive resources.

(D) There is a decrease in real interest rates.

(E) The government decreases income taxes.

**GO ON TO THE NEXT PAGE.**

**8** ☐ Mark for Review

If the government increases taxes on businesses, what will be the most likely effect of this action?

Ⓐ An increase in government spending, an increase in aggregate demand, and an increase in real output

Ⓑ An increase in investment spending, an increase in the capital stock, and a decrease in real output

Ⓒ A decrease in consumption spending, an increase in aggregate demand, and an increase in real output

Ⓓ An increase in consumption spending, a decrease in aggregate demand, and a decrease in real output

Ⓔ A decrease in investment spending, a decrease in the capital stock, and a decrease in real output

**9** ☐ Mark for Review

If an economy experiences improvements in education, training, practice, and experience, what will happen to its production possibilities curve (PPC) and its long-run aggregate supply (LRAS) curve?

Ⓐ The PPC stays the same, and the LRAS curve shifts outward.

Ⓑ The PPC shifts outward, and the LRAS curve shifts inward.

Ⓒ The PPC shifts inward, and the LRAS curve stays the same.

Ⓓ Both curves shift outward.

Ⓔ Both curves shift inward.

**10** ☐ Mark for Review

If the United States budget deficit decreases, what will most likely happen to the United States dollar in the foreign exchange market?

Ⓐ It will appreciate because interest rates will increase.

Ⓑ It will depreciate because interest rates will increase.

Ⓒ It will depreciate because interest rates will decrease.

Ⓓ It will appreciate because interest rates will decrease.

Ⓔ It will not change because changes in the government budget have no effect on the exchange rate.

**11** ☐ Mark for Review

In economies with ample reserves, central banks are likely to use which of the following mechanisms to influence the economy?

Ⓐ The reserve ratio, discount rate, and open market operations

Ⓑ Administered interest rates, the reserve ratio, and the discount rate

Ⓒ The discount rate, open market operations, and the reserve ratio

Ⓓ Administered interest rates, the discount rate, and open market operations

Ⓔ The federal funds rate, the reserve ratio, and administered interest rates

**GO ON TO THE NEXT PAGE.**

**12** ☐ Mark for Review

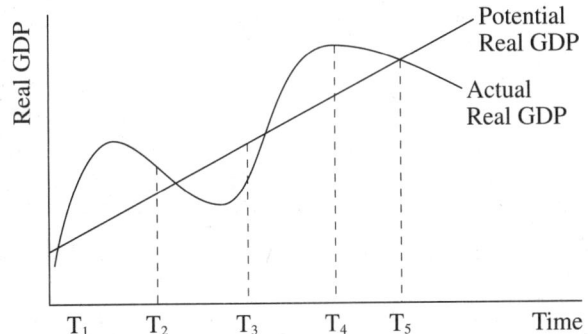

At which point in the above graph does the output gap equal zero?

Ⓐ  $T_1$

Ⓑ  $T_2$

Ⓒ  $T_3$

Ⓓ  $T_4$

Ⓔ  $T_5$

**13** ☐ Mark for Review

The price of money that is borrowed and saved is best measured by which of the following indicators?

Ⓐ  The money multiplier

Ⓑ  Interest rates

Ⓒ  Gross domestic product

Ⓓ  Exchange rates

Ⓔ  Reserve rate

**14** ☐ Mark for Review

A central bank would categorize which of the following as M1 while monitoring the money supply?

Ⓐ  Paper money, checking deposits, and savings deposits

Ⓑ  Paper money, small-time deposits, and mutual funds

Ⓒ  Checking deposits, savings deposits, and mutual funds

Ⓓ  Any money not currently held in a bank

Ⓔ  Small-time deposits, mutual funds, and Eurodollar deposits

**15** ☐ Mark for Review

In the loanable funds market, which of the following stakeholders determine the equilibrium real interest rate?

Ⓐ  Central banks and commercial banks

Ⓑ  Borrowers and commercial banks

Ⓒ  Central banks and savers

Ⓓ  Borrowers and savers

Ⓔ  Borrowers and central banks

**GO ON TO THE NEXT PAGE.**

**16** ☐ Mark for Review

Which of the following is most likely to occur when a nation's currency appreciates?

Ⓐ Exports, imports, and net exports will all decrease.

Ⓑ Exports, imports, and net exports will all increase.

Ⓒ Exports will decrease, imports will increase, and net exports will decrease.

Ⓓ Exports will increase, imports will decrease, and net imports will increase.

Ⓔ Exports will decrease, imports will decrease, and net imports will increase.

**17** ☐ Mark for Review

Which of the following will NOT cause a shift in the aggregate demand curve?

Ⓐ Consumption

Ⓑ Investment

Ⓒ Government spending

Ⓓ Net exports

Ⓔ Price level

**18** ☐ Mark for Review

When considering aggregate demand and aggregate supply, which of the following best describes the marginal propensity to consume (MPC)?

Ⓐ The MPC quantifies the size of the change in aggregate demand as a result of a change in any of the components of aggregate demand.

Ⓑ The MPC quantifies the size of the change in aggregate demand as a result of a change in taxes.

Ⓒ The MPC equals the expenditure multiplier divided by the tax multiplier.

Ⓓ The MPC is the change in consumer spending divided by the change in disposable income.

Ⓔ The MPC equals the tax multiplier divided by the expenditure multiplier.

**19** ☐ Mark for Review

Which of the following is best represented by the short-run aggregate supply (SRAS) curve?

Ⓐ The relationship between price level and the quantity of goods and services supplied in the economy

Ⓑ The overall flexibility of prices and wages

Ⓒ The trade-off between inflation and unemployment

Ⓓ The total output an economic system will produce in a set period of time if all resources are fully employed

Ⓔ Changes in the full-employment level of output and economic growth after a shock to aggregate demand

**GO ON TO THE NEXT PAGE.**

**20** ☐ Mark for Review

The Phillips curve model represents the relationship between which of the following?

(A) Real GDP and time

(B) Real GDP and employment

(C) Inflation and unemployment

(D) Nominal interest rates and quantity of money in an economy

(E) Capital goods and consumption goods

**21** ☐ Mark for Review

Country A has the ability to produce 200,000 cars or 500,000 motorcycles in a given year. Country B would like to import 300,000 cars. Why can't Country A produce all the cars that Country B wants to buy?

(A) Country A has limited resources.

(B) Country A has unlimited factors of production.

(C) Country A has limited motorcycle plants.

(D) Country B has limited resources.

(E) Country B has unlimited inputs.

**22** ☐ Mark for Review

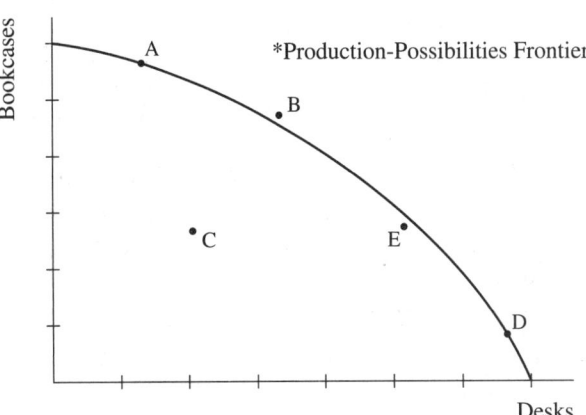

Based on the production-possibilities frontier for this simple economy that makes only desks and bookcases, which point illustrates the most inefficient use of the economy's resources?

(A) Point A

(B) Point B

(C) Point C

(D) Point D

(E) Point E

**GO ON TO THE NEXT PAGE.**

**23** ☐ Mark for Review

England and Spain can each produce T-shirts and backpacks. The two countries have different production-possibilities frontiers and different opportunity costs. In England, the opportunity cost of T-shirts in terms of backpacks is 1. In Spain, the opportunity cost of T-shirts in terms of backpacks is 0.5. Which statement accurately describes each country's comparative advantage?

Ⓐ England has a comparative advantage in backpacks, because 1 backpack costs only 1 T-shirt, while in Spain 1 backpack costs 2 T-shirts.

Ⓑ Spain has a comparative advantage in backpacks, because 1 backpack costs only 1 T-shirt, while in England 1 backpack costs 2 T-shirts.

Ⓒ England has a comparative advantage in T-shirts, because 1 T-shirt costs only 0.5 backpack, while in Spain 1 T-shirt costs 1 backpack.

Ⓓ Spain has a comparative advantage in T-shirts, because 1 T-shirt costs only 1 backpack, while in England 1 T-shirt costs 2 backpacks.

Ⓔ England has a comparative advantage in backpacks, because 1 backpack costs only 1 T-shirt, while in Spain 1 backpack costs 1.5 T-shirts.

**24** ☐ Mark for Review

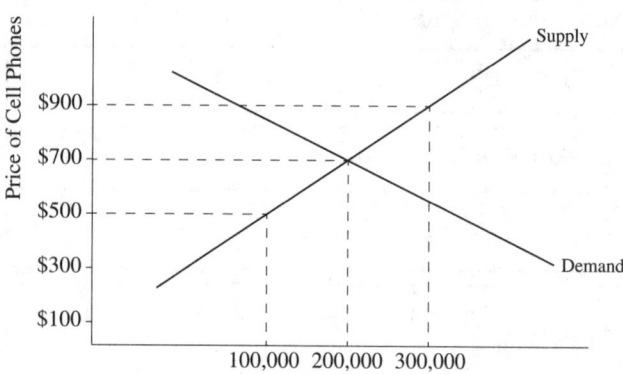

Based on the market for cellular phones as illustrated on this chart, if the current price of a phone is $500, how will phone producers change in order to achieve equilibrium?

Ⓐ Phone producers will lower supply until supply meets demand at the market clearing price of $700.

Ⓑ Phone producers will increase the price to $900 and triple production to 300,000.

Ⓒ Phone producers will increase supply to 200,000 units to achieve equilibrium and will not change the price.

Ⓓ Phone producers will increase production and raise the price to achieve equilibrium.

Ⓔ Phone producers will increase the price to $600.

**GO ON TO THE NEXT PAGE.**

**25** ☐ Mark for Review

Which of the following is a benefit of inflation?

(A) Net borrowers at fixed interest rates can make debt payments in inflated amounts that are worth less in real terms.

(B) Stores can print new menus with higher prices to cover inflation costs.

(C) People on fixed incomes get a boost in real purchasing power.

(D) The unit of account in an economy becomes more stable due to inflation.

(E) Lenders and savers holding long-term fixed-rate securities experience an increase in real returns.

**26** ☐ Mark for Review

Structural unemployment results from

(A) unemployed workers and firms searching for the best worker-job matches

(B) a mismatch between the skills of workers and changing demand in the market for those skills

(C) downturns in the economy

(D) hiring patterns during certain times of the year, such as holidays or summer

(E) workers becoming so frustrated in their attempts to find work that they stop trying to seek employment altogether

**27** ☐ Mark for Review

What are the different stages of business cycles?

(A) Expansion, peak, and growth

(B) Expansion, peak, recession, and trough

(C) Growth, recession, and trough

(D) Growth, peak, expansion, and trough

(E) Peak, recession, and trough

**28** ☐ Mark for Review

The aggregate demand curve is the relationship between the price level and the real GDP in an economy. Which of the following describes the slope of the AD curve?

(A) The slope of the AD curve is negative because as general price levels increase, there are fewer goods purchased.

(B) The slope of the AD curve is positive because as general price levels increase, there are more goods purchased.

(C) The slope of the AD curve is negative because as prices increase, consumers purchase substitute goods within the economy.

(D) The slope of the AD curve is positive because as prices decrease, consumers purchase substitute goods within the economy.

(E) The slope of the AD curve is negative because as demand increases, consumers negotiate lower prices for goods and services.

**GO ON TO THE NEXT PAGE.**

**29** Mark for Review

Which of the following describes one of the primary reasons for the indirect relationship between price and real GDP, as reflected on the AD curve?

(A) When prices rise in one economy, the prices of imports from other countries become relatively less expensive. This leads to a decrease in exports and an increase in imports, which reduces real GDP.

(B) When prices rise in one economy, the prices of imports from other countries become relatively more expensive. This leads to an increase in exports and a decrease in imports, which increases real GDP.

(C) When prices rise, a consumer's purchasing power increases. As a result, people need less money to continue the same level of consumption. This leads to a decrease in the demand for loanable funds, which leads to lower interest rates. Lower interest rates lead to an increase in real GDP as consumers complete major purchases.

(D) When prices rise, the value of assets such as cash increases because the same unit of cash purchases more goods. As a result, people buy more goods and services. This increases real GDP.

(E) When prices rise, the value of assets such as cash decreases because the same unit of cash purchases fewer goods. As a result, people buy more goods and services. This increases real GDP.

**30** Mark for Review

If the marginal propensity to consume is 0.65, what is the impact on GDP if spending increases by $300, due to the impact of the spending multiplier?

(A) $285.71

(B) $300.00

(C) $461.54

(D) $571.43

(E) $857.14

**31** Mark for Review

Which of the following statements describes the long-run aggregate supply curve (LAS)?

(A) The LAS is vertical and stands at the level of output that corresponds with full employment.

(B) The LAS is horizontal because changes in aggregate demand affect real GDP but not the price level.

(C) The LAS is upward sloping and reflects the fact that wages are relatively slow to adjust to price increases on goods from producers.

(D) The LAS is horizontal and lies at the level of output that corresponds with full employment.

(E) The LAS is vertical because changes in aggregate demand affect real GDP but not the price level.

**32** Mark for Review

Keynesian analysis supports government intervention in economies due to which of the following reasons?

(A) Prices of goods adjust rapidly in an economy, and consumers need protection from rapidly changing prices which only a government can provide.

(B) Consumers are not willing to lend out their savings, so only government can provide loans to businesses to encourage capital investments.

(C) Consumers are unwilling to invest in education or training without incentives from the government.

(D) Technological innovation will not occur without governmental incentives and intervention.

(E) Wages are "sticky" and CANNOT adjust to changing price levels quickly enough, particularly in the downward direction, so government must provide monetary or fiscal policy to alleviate unemployment.

**GO ON TO THE NEXT PAGE.**

**33** ☐ Mark for Review

Demand pull inflation occurs when

(A) prices rise due to an increase in the costs of the factors of production

(B) inflation occurs because the government increases the money supply

(C) inflation remains steady for a long period at a low rate

(D) inflation increases unsteadily and in excess of 10 percent per year

(E) inflation is concurrent with relatively high unemployment and a reduction in GDP

**34** ☐ Mark for Review

Expansionary fiscal policy consists of government policies that are intended to

(A) shift the AD curve to the right by increasing government purchases

(B) shift the AD curve to the right by increasing taxes

(C) shift the AD curve to the right decreasing transfer payments

(D) shift the AD curve to the left by increasing taxes

(E) shift the AD curve to the left by increasing government investments in capital projects such as highways

**35** ☐ Mark for Review

If the marginal propensity to consume is 0.7, and equilibrium real GDP is lower than full employment real GDP by $1 trillion, approximately how much should the government increase its purchases to bring the economy back to equilibrium, according to the government spending multiplier?

(A) $300 billion

(B) $588 billion

(C) $700 billion

(D) $800 billion

(E) $1,000 billion

**GO ON TO THE NEXT PAGE.**

**36** ☐ Mark for Review

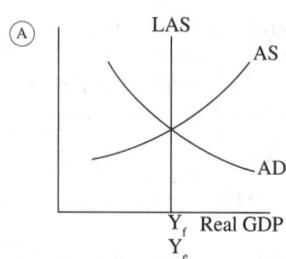

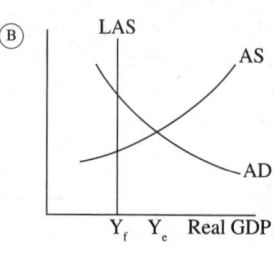

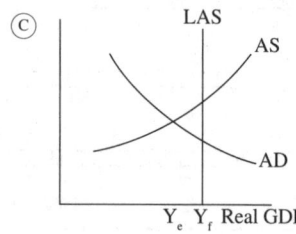

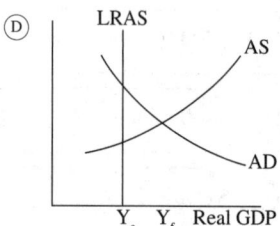

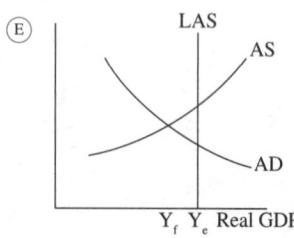

Which of the charts above illustrates a recessionary gap?

Ⓐ    Chart A

Ⓑ    Chart B

Ⓒ    Chart C

Ⓓ    Chart D

Ⓔ    Chart E

**37** ☐ Mark for Review

Which of the following describes an inflationary gap?

Ⓐ    The amount by which equilibrium real GDP would have to increase for the economy to reach full employment

Ⓑ    The amount by which the aggregate supply curve would have to shift to the right for the economy to reach full employment

Ⓒ    The amount by which equilibrium real GDP would have to decrease for the economy to reach full employment

Ⓓ    The amount by which the aggregate demand curve would have to shift to the right for the economy to reach full employment

Ⓔ    The amount by which the federal reserve would have to increase the money supply to lower inflation by 100 basis points

**GO ON TO THE NEXT PAGE.**

**38**  ☐ Mark for Review

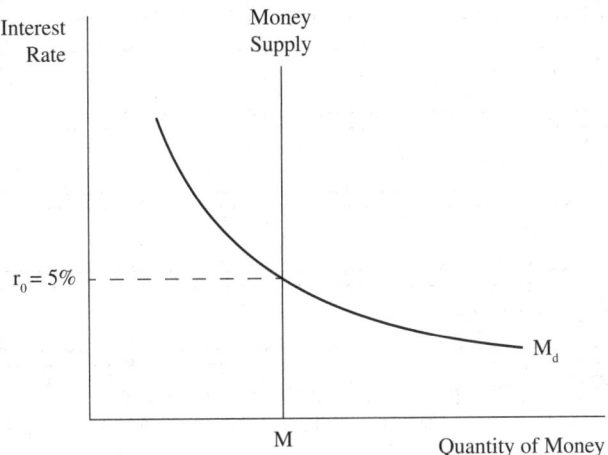

The graph above represents a current economy in which the money supply is stable and interest rates are $r_0 = 5\%$. Suppose a government with limited reserves wants to use expansionary monetary policy to increase real GDP. Which of the following describes the impact of expansionary monetary policy?

(A) The government would take actions to increase the money supply, the MS line would shift to the right, and interest rates would decrease to below 5%. This would spur investment, resulting in an increase in GDP.

(B) The government would take actions to increase the money supply, the MS line would shift to the right, and interest rates would increase above 5%. This would spur investment, resulting in an increase in GDP.

(C) The government would take actions to decrease the money supply, the MS line would shift to the left, and interest rates would decrease to below 5%. This would spur investment, resulting in an increase in GDP.

(D) The government would take actions to decrease the money supply, the MS line would shift to the right, and interest rates would increase above 5%. This would spur investment, resulting in an increase in GDP.

(E) The government would take actions to increase the money supply, the MS line would shift to the left, and interest rates would decrease to below 5%. This would spur investment, resulting in an increase in GDP.

**39**  ☐ Mark for Review

Which of the following best describes monetary policy?

(A) A government's use of changes in government purchases, transfer payments, or taxes to impact aggregate demand

(B) The policy that states that the money supply and the quantity of goods are stable, indicating that any changes in the money supply will only result in increased prices

(C) The ability of money to generate additional assets from an initial deposit to a bank as a result of a reserve banking system

(D) The policy describing a government's use of central banking tools to influence interest rates, inflation, exchange rates, unemployment, and real GDP

(E) A government's use of a required reserve ratio to govern the amount of loanable funds

**GO ON TO THE NEXT PAGE.**

**40** ☐ Mark for Review

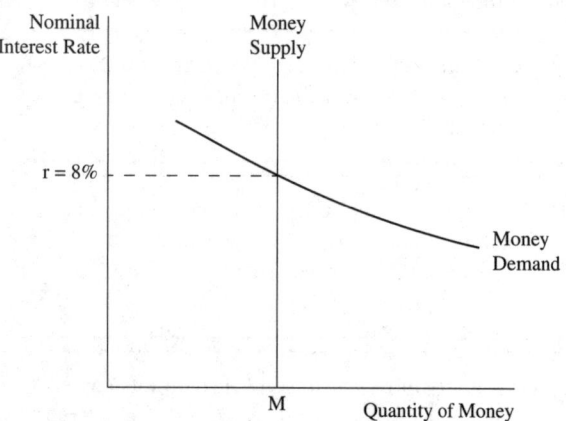

The chart above illustrates the money market in an economy in which current interest rates are 8%. If the central bank lowers the discount rate, which of the following describes how the chart will change?

(A) Banks will borrow less money from the central bank to satisfy demand for loans, which will result in the MS curve moving to the right and the interest rate decreasing to below 8%.

(B) Banks will borrow less money from the central bank to satisfy demand for loans, which will result in the MS curve moving to the left and the interest rate increasing to above 8%.

(C) Banks will borrow more money from the central bank to satisfy demand for loans, which will result in the MS curve moving to the right and the interest rate decreasing to below 8%.

(D) Banks will borrow more money from the central bank to satisfy demand for loans, which will result in the MS curve moving to the left and the interest rate increasing to above 8%.

(E) There will be no impact on the money market if the central bank lowers the discount rate.

**41** ☐ Mark for Review

The Phillips curve illustrates that the relationship between inflation and unemployment is which of the following?

(A) Stable and increasing

(B) Stable and inverse

(C) Stable and flat

(D) Stable and convex

(E) The Phillips curve proves there is no consistent relationship between inflation and unemployment.

**42** ☐ Mark for Review

What is the difference between the budget deficit and the national debt?

(A) The national debt is the difference between the federal government spending and tax collections (G – T) in one year, while the budget deficit is the accumulation of past years' national debt.

(B) The national debt is the difference between the tax collections and the federal government spending (T – G) in one year, while the budget deficit is the accumulation of past years' national debt.

(C) The budget deficit is the difference between the federal government spending and tax collections (G – T) in one year, while the national debt is the accumulation of past years' budget deficits.

(D) The budget deficit is the difference between the tax collections and the federal government spending (T – G) in one year, while the national debt is the accumulation of past years' budget deficits.

(E) The budget deficit is the difference between the federal government spending and the net exports (G – (X – M)), while the national debt is the accumulation of past years' budget deficits.

**GO ON TO THE NEXT PAGE.**

**43** ☐ Mark for Review

The principle of crowding out describes which of the following?

(A) When the government borrows money, it competes with private borrowers and bids up the interest rate. The higher interest rate causes some private investments and individual consumption to decrease.

(B) When the government creates money rather than raising interest rates, inflation decreases and private investments and individual consumption increase.

(C) When businesses compete for investment projects, the competition crowds out the weakest companies, resulting in business failures and unemployment.

(D) When the government repurchases bonds in the open market, the money supply decreases, which causes businesses to compete for loans, crowding out some investments.

(E) When businesses borrow money, they compete with the government and bid down interest rates. The lower interest rates cause some government investments to decrease.

**44** ☐ Mark for Review

Supply-side economists believe which of the following with respect to an expansionary policy of tax cuts?

(A) A tax cut will decrease aggregate supply because the higher take-home pay of workers will reduce the incentive to enter the workforce or take on extra hours, resulting in lower production.

(B) A tax cut will increase aggregate supply because consumers will save more and businesses will invest more, resulting in higher production.

(C) A tax cut will have no impact on aggregate supply because entrepreneurship involves risks that are not impacted by the tax structure.

(D) A tax cut will decrease both aggregate demand and aggregate supply, because consumers and businesses will decrease savings and investments.

(E) A tax cut will decrease aggregate demand but increase aggregate supply because consumers will save more, reducing demand but businesses will invest more, resulting in lower production.

**45** ☐ Mark for Review

Assume marginal propensity to consume is 0.80 and equilibrium real GDP ($Y_e$) falls short of full employment real GDP ($Y_f$) by $2 trillion. Using the government spending multiplier, what is the amount by which the government should increase its purchases to increase $Y_e$ to $Y_f$?

(A) $50 billion

(B) $400 billion

(C) $500 billion

(D) $1.6 trillion

(E) $8 trillion

**GO ON TO THE NEXT PAGE.**

**46** ▢ Mark for Review

Assume marginal propensity to consume is 0.80 and the government reduces taxes by $1 trillion. Using the tax multiplier, what is the amount by which GDP will change, as a result of this tax policy change?

Ⓐ GDP will increase by $250 billion.

Ⓑ GDP will decrease by $250 billion.

Ⓒ GDP will increase by $1 trillion.

Ⓓ GDP will increase by $4 trillion.

Ⓔ GDP will decrease by $4 trillion.

**47** ▢ Mark for Review

What is the impact on imports and exports as a result of expansionary fiscal policy such as an increase in government spending or a decrease in taxes?

Ⓐ Exports (X) increase and imports (M) decrease such that Net Exports (X – M) increase, partially offsetting the effects of expansionary policy.

Ⓑ Exports (X) decrease and imports (M) increase such that Net Exports (X – M) decrease, partially offsetting the effects of the expansionary policy.

Ⓒ Exports (X) increase and imports (M) remain unchanged, such that Net Exports (X – M) increase, partially offsetting the effects of expansionary policy.

Ⓓ Exports (X) remain unchanged and imports (M) increase, such that Net Exports (X – M) decrease, partially offsetting the effects of the expansionary policy.

Ⓔ Exports (X) and Imports (M) will remain unchanged.

**48** ▢ Mark for Review

Assume the per capita income level in Country A increases, while the per capital income level in Country B remains unchanged. Which of the following describes the impact on Country B's currency?

Ⓐ Country A's demand for Country B's products will increase, and Country A's demand for the currency of Country B will increase, causing the price of Country B's currency to increase in value.

Ⓑ Country A's demand for Country B's products will increase, and Country A's demand for the currency of Country B will increase, causing the price of Country B's currency to decrease in value.

Ⓒ Country A's demand for Country B's products will increase, and Country A's demand for the currency of Country B will increase, causing the price of Country A's currency to increase in value.

Ⓓ Country B's demand for Country A's products will increase, and Country B's demand for the currency of Country A will increase, causing the price of Country A's currency to increase in value.

Ⓔ Country B's demand for Country A's products will increase, and Country B's demand for the currency of Country A will decrease, causing the price of Country A's currency to increase in value.

**GO ON TO THE NEXT PAGE.**

**49** ☐ Mark for Review

Suppose inflation increases 10% in the United States and increases 4% in Japan. Which of the following describes the impact on the value of Japanese yen?

Ⓐ U.S. exports will be slower to increase in price than other similar products in Japan. So, U.S. products will be relatively less expensive than other similar products in Japan. The demand for U.S. products will go up, and the Japanese yen will decrease in value.

Ⓑ U.S. exports will be faster to increase in price than other similar products in Japan. So, U.S. products will be relatively more expensive than other similar products in Japan. The demand for U.S. products will go down, and the Japanese yen will decrease in value.

Ⓒ Japan's exports will be slower to increase in price than other similar products in the United States. So, Japanese products will be relatively less expensive than other similar U.S. products. The demand for Japanese products will go up, and the Japanese yen will increase in value.

Ⓓ Japan's exports will be faster to increase in price than other similar products in the United States. So, Japanese products will be relatively more expensive than other similar U.S. products. The demand for Japanese products will go down, and the Japanese yen will increase in value.

Ⓔ Japan's exports will be faster to increase in price than other similar products in the United States. So, Japanese products will be relatively less expensive than other similar U.S. products. The demand for Japanese products will go down, and the Japanese yen will increase in value.

**50** ☐ Mark for Review

A Canadian car company introduces a new car with new features that consumers overwhelmingly prefer and are not available on cars produced by U.S. car manufacturers. Which of the following describes the impact on the value of the Canadian dollar?

Ⓐ The Canadian cars will be in high demand, and consumers will demand Canadian dollars to purchase these cars. The value of the Canadian dollar will increase.

Ⓑ The Canadian cars will be in high demand, and consumers will demand Canadian dollars to purchase these cars. The value of the Canadian dollar will decrease.

Ⓒ Cars produced by U.S. manufacturers will be relatively less expensive, and consumers will increase demand for U.S. cars. Consumers will demand U.S. dollars to purchase these cars, and the value of the Canadian dollar will decrease.

Ⓓ The Canadian cars will be relatively more expensive than U.S. cars, and consumers will have low demand for these cars. The value of the Canadian dollar will not change.

Ⓔ The Canadian cars will be relatively less expensive than U.S. cars, and consumers will have low demand for these cars. The value of the Canadian dollar will increase.

**GO ON TO THE NEXT PAGE.**

## 51 ☐ Mark for Review

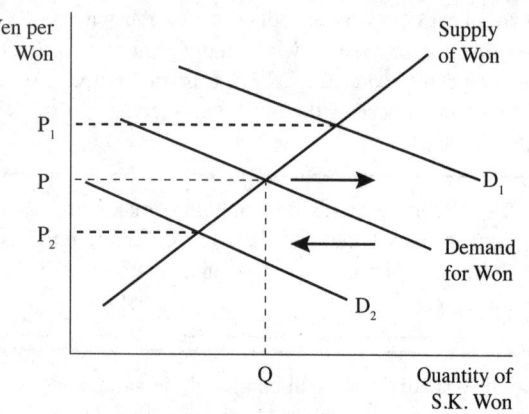

The chart above illustrates the relationship between the South Korean won and the Japanese yen. Interest rates in South Korea increase relative to Japan's interest rates. Which of the following describes the impact on the value of the South Korean won?

Ⓐ Depositors will demand more Japanese yen, pushing the demand line to $D_2$ (to the left). The price of yen per won will decrease to $P_2$ due to lower demand for won.

Ⓑ Depositors will demand more South Korean won, pushing the demand line to $D_2$ (to the left). The price of yen per won will decrease to $P_2$ due to lower demand for yen.

Ⓒ Depositors will demand more South Korean won, pushing the demand line to $D_1$ (to the right). The price of yen per won will increase to $P_1$ due to higher demand for won.

Ⓓ Depositors will demand more Japanese yen, pushing the demand line to $D_1$ (to the right). The price of yen per won will increase to $P_1$ due to lower demand for won.

Ⓔ Savers will demand more Japanese yen, pushing the demand line to $D_2$ (to the left). The price of yen per won will decrease to $P_2$ due to higher demand for yen.

## 52 ☐ Mark for Review

A weaker currency

Ⓐ decreases imports, increases exports, and makes a trade deficit larger (or a trade surplus smaller)

Ⓑ decreases imports, increases exports, and makes a trade deficit smaller (or a trade surplus larger)

Ⓒ increases imports, decreases exports, and makes a trade deficit larger (or a trade surplus smaller)

Ⓓ increases imports, decreases exports, and makes a trade deficit smaller (or a trade surplus larger)

Ⓔ increases imports, decreases exports, and has a net zero impact on the trade deficit or surplus

**GO ON TO THE NEXT PAGE.**

**53** ☐ Mark for Review

When a currency appreciates, it

(A) becomes stronger, and it takes fewer units of that currency to buy a unit of another currency

(B) becomes stronger, and it takes more units of that currency to buy a unit of another currency

(C) becomes stronger, and takes the same number of units of that currency to buy a unit of another currency

(D) becomes weaker, and it takes fewer units of that currency to buy a unit of another currency

(E) becomes weaker, and it takes more units of that currency to buy a unit of another currency

**54** ☐ Mark for Review

Which of the following describes a flexible exchange rate?

(A) The central bank can fix the quantity of assets denominated in the home currency so that the exchange rate changes with demand.

(B) The central bank holds the supply curve of the home currency fixed (horizontal) so that changes in demand of a currency affect only the quantity purchased.

(C) The demand curve of the home currency is positively sloped (rather than vertical) and changes in demand result in changes in the exchange rate.

(D) The central bank can fix the quantity of assets denominated in the home currency so that the exchange rate remains fixed.

(E) The demand curve of the home currency is negatively sloped so that the exchange rate remains fixed.

**GO ON TO THE NEXT PAGE.**

**Questions 55 through 58 refer to the following.**

Country A Balance of Payments, 2025

| | Item | Amount (Billions) |
|---|---|---|
| 1. | Merchandise exports | 1,658.4 |
| 2. | Merchandise imports | −2,877.2 |
| | Merchandise trade balance | −1,218.8 |
| 3. | Service exports | 852.5 |
| 4. | Service imports | −321.7 |
| 5. | Income from Country A overseas investments | 522.1 |
| 6. | Income outflow for foreign Country A investments | −288.1 |
| 7. | Net Country A government grants and transfers | −52.0 |
| 8. | Net private transfers | −167.8 |
| | Current-account balance | 1,397.5 |
| 9. | Country A capital inflow | 343.5 |
| 10. | Country A capital outflow | −541.1 |
| | Financial account balance | −197.6 |
| 11. | Statistical discrepancy | 178.3 |
| | Net Balance | 1,378.2 |

**55** ☐ Mark for Review

According to the chart above, what does the financial account balance of −197.6 indicate about Country A?

(A) Country A's domestic ownership of foreign assets exceeds the foreign ownership of Country A's assets.

(B) The foreign ownership of Country A's assets exceeds Country A's domestic ownership of foreign assets.

(C) Country A's government ownership of foreign assets exceeds foreign government ownership of Country A's assets.

(D) Foreign government ownership of Country A's assets exceeds Country A's government ownership of foreign assets.

(E) Country A's domestic ownership of foreign stocks exceeds the foreign ownership of Country A's stocks.

**56** ☐ Mark for Review

According to the chart, does Country A have a merchandise trade deficit?

(A) No, because current-account balance is positive

(B) No, because the financial account balance is negative

(C) No, because the service exports are greater than the service imports

(D) Yes, because the service exports are greater than the service imports

(E) Yes, because the merchandise trade balance is negative

**57** ☐ Mark for Review

What is included in lines 9. Country A capital inflow and 10. Country A capital outflow?

(A) Country A exchanges of securities, currency, capital, and land

(B) Country A purchases and sales of merchandise

(C) Country A purchases and sales of merchandise, services, investments, and transfers

(D) Country A exchanges of securities, currency, and merchandise

(E) Country A exchanges of securities, currency, merchandise, and services

**GO ON TO THE NEXT PAGE.**

**58** ⬚ Mark for Review

What is the Balance of Payments for Country A?

(A) −1,218.8 billion

(B) −541.1 billion

(C) −197.6 billion

(D) 1,378.2 billion

(E) 1,397.5 billion

**59** ⬚ Mark for Review

Which of the following is NOT a source of growth for an economy?

(A) Increased education and training of a country's workforce

(B) Increased purchases of capital equipment

(C) Developments in technology

(D) Improved management and distribution of productive resources

(E) Improvements in the exchange rate policy

**60** ⬚ Mark for Review

The Phillips curve describes the relationship between inflation and unemployment as

(A) an inverse relationship in the short run and vertical in the long run at the natural rate of unemployment

(B) a positively correlated relationship in the short run and vertical in the long run at the natural rate of unemployment

(C) an inverse relationship in the short run and positively correlated in the long run

(D) an inverse relationship in the short run and negatively correlated in the long run

(E) a positively correlated relationship in the short run and positively correlated in the long run

**END OF SECTION I**

## AP MACROECONOMICS
## SECTION II

**Total Time—1 hour**
**Reading Period—10 minutes**
**Writing Period—50 minutes**
**3 Questions**

**Directions:** You are advised to spend the first 10 minutes reading all of the questions and planning your answers. You will then have 50 minutes to answer all three of the following questions. You may begin writing your responses before the reading period is over. <u>It is suggested that you spend approximately half your time on the first question and divide the remaining time equally between the next two questions.</u> Include correctly labeled diagrams, if useful or required, in explaining your answers. A correctly labeled diagram must have all axes and curves clearly labeled and must show directional changes. If the question prompts you to "Calculate," you must show how you arrived at your final answer. Use a pencil or pen with black or dark blue ink. Make sure to write all your answers in the free-response booklet.

---

**1** ◻ Mark for Review

Assume that in Baselo, a nation with limited reserves, the economy is stalled. In Baselo, the marginal propensity to consume is 0.70. The Baselo government wants to enact expansionary fiscal policy.

A. Explain two actions that Baselo's government can take to enact the desired expansionary fiscal policy. Assume that Baselo cannot change its transfer payments.

B. Draw a correctly labeled graph that illustrates the impact of expansionary fiscal policy on aggregate expenditures and real GDP. Label the following:
   (i)     The original aggregate expenditure curve AE
   (ii)    The revised aggregate expenditure curve $AE_2$
   (iii)   The reference line RL that represents the points at which aggregate expenditures equal real GDP
   (iv)    The original GDP Y before the policy is enacted
   (v)     The revised GDP $Y_2$ after the expansionary fiscal policy is enacted

C. Draw a correctly labeled graph that illustrates the impact of expansionary fiscal policy on the money market. Label the following:
   (i)     The money supply curve MS
   (ii)    The money demand curve MD
   (iii)   The revised money demand curve $MD_2$ after the policy is enacted
   (iv)    The interest rates r (before the policy) and $r_2$ (after the policy)

D. Explain the concept of the government spending multiplier in relation to the autonomous spending multiplier.

E. Calculate the amount that the Baselo government must increase or decrease its purchases to increase real GDP by $5 trillion. Show your work.

F. Calculate the amount that Real GDP will increase or decrease if the Baselo government reduces taxes by $1 trillion. Show your work.

G. Use the balanced budget multiplier to explain the impact if Baselo increases government spending by $1 trillion and increases taxes by $1 trillion.

H. Explain the principle of crowding out as it applies to expansionary fiscal policy. Summarize the effects of expansionary fiscal policy using an equation with the following variables:
   (i)     G—government spending
   (ii)    T—taxes
   (iii)   AD—aggregate demand
   (iv)    Y—real GDP
   (v)     Md—money demand
   (vi)    r—interest rates
   (vii)   I—investments
   (viii)  $Y_2$—real GDP, revised

**GO ON TO THE NEXT PAGE.**

**2** ☐ Mark for Review

Country A, a nation with limited reserves, wants to enact contractionary monetary policy.

A. Explain one action that Country A's central bank can take to enact the desired contractionary monetary policy. Assume that Country A cannot change its reserve requirement.

B. Draw a correctly labeled graph of that illustrates the supply and demand curves of money with the impact of the contractionary monetary policy. Label the following:
   (i)    The original supply curve S
   (ii)   The revised supply curve $S_2$
   (iii)  The interest rates r (before the policy) and $r_2$ (after the policy)

C. Draw a correctly labeled graph that illustrates the impact of contractionary monetary policy on Investments. Label the following:
   (i)    The  original quantity of Investments I
   (ii)   The revised quantity of Investments $I_2$
   (iii)  The interest rates r (before the policy) and $r_2$ (after the policy)

D. Draw a correctly labeled graph that illustrates aggregate supply and demand, Real GDP, and price levels, with the impact of the contractionary monetary policy. Label the following:
   (i)    The original aggregate demand curve AD
   (ii)   The revised aggregate demand curve $AD_2$
   (iii)  Real GDP Y (before the policy) and $Y_2$ (after the policy)

**GO ON TO THE NEXT PAGE.**

**3**  ☐ Mark for Review

Explain the relationship between interest rates and the quantity of money and interest rates and the quantity of loanable funds. In your answer, include the following:

A.  Explain the different time frame represented by the money market and the loanable funds market.

B.  Explain why the supply curve in the money market has a different shape than the supply curve in the loanable funds market.

C.  Draw a correctly labeled graph of the money market that illustrates the impact of rising interest rates on the quantity of money. Label the following:
   (i)   The demand curve D
   (ii)  The original interest rate r and the higher interest rate $r_2$
   (iii) The original supply curve S and the revised supply curve $S_2$
   (iv)  The original quantity of money Q and the revised quantity of money $Q_2$

D.  Draw a correctly labeled graph of the loanable funds market that illustrates the relationship between interest rates and the quantity of loanable funds. Label the following:
   (i)   The supply curve S for loanable funds
   (ii)  The interest rate r
   (iii) The demand curve D

**STOP**
**END OF EXAM**
_____

# Chapter 20
# Macroeconomics Practice Test 1: Answers and Explanations

# MACROECONOMICS PRACTICE TEST 1 ANSWER KEY

## Section I

| | | | | | |
|---|---|---|---|---|---|
| 1. | B | 21. | A | 41. | B |
| 2. | E | 22. | C | 42. | C |
| 3. | B | 23. | A | 43. | A |
| 4. | D | 24. | D | 44. | B |
| 5. | B | 25. | A | 45. | B |
| 6. | D | 26. | B | 46. | D |
| 7. | A | 27. | B | 47. | B |
| 8. | E | 28. | A | 48. | A |
| 9. | D | 29. | A | 49. | C |
| 10. | C | 30. | E | 50. | A |
| 11. | D | 31. | A | 51. | C |
| 12. | E | 32. | E | 52. | B |
| 13. | B | 33. | B | 53. | A |
| 14. | A | 34. | A | 54. | A |
| 15. | D | 35. | A | 55. | A |
| 16. | C | 36. | C | 56. | E |
| 17. | E | 37. | C | 57. | A |
| 18. | D | 38. | A | 58. | D |
| 19. | A | 39. | D | 59. | E |
| 20. | C | 40. | C | 60. | A |

# MACROECONOMICS PRACTICE TEST 1: ANSWERS AND EXPLANATIONS

## Section I: Multiple-Choice

1. **B** The unemployment rate is equal to the number of unemployed people divided by the labor force multiplied by 100. The correct answer is (B).

2. **E** Using the expenditure approach, GDP is a function of personal consumption expenditures by households, investment in new physical capital, government purchases, exports, and imports. Therefore, (E) is the correct answer.

3. **B** To answer this question, it's helpful to draw a graph with nominal interest rates on the *y*-axis and quantity of money on the *x*-axis. The money supply curve is a vertical line, and the demand for money is a downward-sloping curve. A contractionary monetary policy causes the money supply curve to shift inward; an expansionary monetary supply causes the supply curve to shift outward. An increase in the demand for money causes the demand curve to shift outward; a decrease of the demand for money causes the demand curve to shift inward. Of the answers available, only (B) results in a reduction of the nominal interest rate.

4. **D** This question is testing your knowledge of what causes shifts in the aggregate demand curve. Increasing income taxes, increasing the required reserve ratio, decreasing government expenditures, and decreasing the minimum wage all cause the aggregate demand curve to shift inward, resulting in a decrease in price levels. Decreasing interest on reserves is the only change listed that would cause an increase in aggregate demand and an increase in price levels. Therefore, the correct answer is (D).

5. **B** A decrease in political instability, a decrease in income or wealth, an increase in government taxes, and an increase in investment spending would all cause an increase in demand in the loanable funds market. The correct answer is (B).

6. **D** The goal of expansionary monetary policy is to grow the economy, thereby expanding the money supply, so (B) and (C) can be eliminated. One of the primary means of doing that, particularly in economies with ample reserves, is by decreasing interest rates, so (D) is the correct answer.

7. **A** A budget deficit, a decrease in real interest rates, a decrease in income taxes, and a decrease in the prices of the economy's productive resources would all cause an increase in real GDP and a decrease in the price level in the long run. Therefore, the correct answer is (A).

8. **E** Increasing business taxes is an example of contractionary monetary policy. As a result, investment spending will decrease, capital stocks will decrease and real output will decrease. Choice (E) is the correct answer.

9. **D** Increased investment in human capital, such as education, training, practice, and experience are a primary source for economic growth. Under conditions of economic growth, both the PPC and the LRAS curve shift outward. The correct answer is (D).

10.  **C**  The size of the deficit has a direct relationship with administered interest rates. If the budget deficit decreases, it will cause a decrease in interest rates and the value of the U.S. dollar will depreciate. The correct answer is (C).

11.  **D**  The reserve ratio is used only in situations of limited reserves. With ample reserves, the reserve ratio is no longer relevant. Instead, central banks rely upon administered interest rates, the discount rate, and open market operations to influence the economy. Choice (D) is the correct answer.

12.  **E**  The output gap equals the difference between actual output and potential output. Graphically, this occurs when the potential real GDP curve intersects with the actual real GDP curve. Choice (E) is the correct answer.

13.  **B**  Gross domestic product is a measure of the final output of the economy. The money multiplier is used to calculate the amount of money held in reserves in economies with limited reserves. Exchange rates measure the value of one currency against another. The reserve rate is the percentage of assets that a central bank requires commercial banks to hold in reserve. Interest rates provide a measure of the price of money that is borrowed and saved. Choice (B) is the correct answer.

14.  **A**  By definition, M1 is the sum of coin and paper money, checking deposits, and savings deposits. M2 is M1 plus small-time deposits, money market mutual funds, and Eurodollar deposits. Choice (A) is the correct answer.

15.  **D**  The interaction of borrowers, who demand loanable funds, and savers, who supply loanable funds, determines the equilibrium real interest rate. Choice (D) is the correct answer.

16.  **C**  Factors that cause a currency to appreciate cause that country's exports to decrease and its imports to increase. As a result, net exports will decrease. Choice (C) is the correct answer.

17.  **E**  Any change in the components of aggregate demand (consumption, investment, government spending, or net exports) that is not due to changes in the price level leads to a shift in the aggregate demand curve. Choice (E) is the correct answer.

18.  **D**  Choice (A) describes the expenditure multiplier and (B) describes the tax multiplier. The expenditure multiplier and tax multiplier depend on the MPC, but dividing the two doesn't result in the MPC, so (C) and (E) can be eliminated. Choice (D) is the correct answer.

19.  **A**  The short-run aggregate supply curve describes the relationship between the price level and the quantity of goods and services supplied in an economy. Choices (B) through (E) all apply to the long-run supply curve. Choice (A) is the correct answer.

20.  **C**  The Phillips curve model is used to represent the relationship between inflation and unemployment and to illustrate how macroeconomic shocks affect inflation and unemployment. Choice (A) describes the business cycle graph. Choice (B) describes the aggregate production function. Choice (D) describes the money market. Choice (E) describes the production possibilities curve model. Choice (C) is the correct answer.

21. **A** Country A is experiencing scarcity due to limited resources, (A). If Country A had unlimited factors of production, (B), then Country A could easily produce enough cars. Country A does not need more motorcycle plants to build more cars, (C); Country A would need more car plants. Choices (D) and (E) are incorrect because Country B is not the producer.

22. **C** The production-possibilities frontier illustrates the choices an economy faces and the opportunity cost of making one good rather than another. Points A and D are on the PPF and represent an efficient use of the economy's resources. Point B is above the PPF and is unobtainable. Point C is significantly below the PPF and illustrates an inefficient use of the economy's resources. Point E is very close to the PPF and represents a mostly efficient allocation of resources.

23. **A** In England, 1 backpack costs 1 T-shirt. In Spain, 1 backpack costs 2 T-shirts. So, England has a comparative advantage in backpacks. Choice (B) is incorrect because the costs are reversed between the two countries. Choice (C) is incorrect because England has a comparative advantage in backpacks. Choice (D) in incorrect because the cost of 1 T-shirt in Spain is 0.5 backpack, and the cost in England of 1 T-shirt is 1 backpack. Choice (E) is incorrect because in Spain, 1 backpack costs 2 T-shirts.

24. **D** Phone producers will increase production and raise the price and will achieve equilibrium at $700 and 200,000 units. Choice (A) is incorrect because the amount of supply at $500 is already below demand and lowering supply will not increase the price. Choice (B) is incorrect because at this price and supply, there will be a surplus. Choice (C) is not correct because the price will also have to increase to achieve equilibrium. Choice (E) is incorrect because at a price of $600, there is still a shortage.

25. **A** In times of inflation, borrowers of money at fixed interest rates can repay the debts with lower amounts in real terms. Choice (B) is incorrect because these menu costs harm stores. Choice (C) is incorrect because people on fixed incomes experience reduced purchasing power in times of inflation. Choice (D) is incorrect because the unit of account becomes unstable in times of inflation. Choice (E) is incorrect because lenders and savers holding long-term fixed rate securities experience a decrease in real purchasing power during times of inflation.

26. **B** Choice (B) is correct because structural unemployment results from a skills mismatch in the marketplace for labor. Choice (A) is the definition of frictional unemployment. Choice (C) is the definition of cyclical unemployment. Choice (D) is the definition of seasonal unemployment. Choice (E) is the definition of discouraged workers.

27. **B** Choice (B) correctly lists the stages of business cycles. Choice (A) does not mention recession or trough. Choice (C) is incorrect because it does not include peak. Choice (D) is incorrect because it does not include recession/contraction. Choice (E) is incorrect because it does not include expansion.

28. **A** The AD curve reflects the changes in demand as the price level for all goods and services increases or decreases. The slope is negative because when the overall price level in an economy increases, the consumers in the economy purchase fewer goods and services. Choices (B) and (D) are incorrect because the slope of the AD curve is negative. Choice (C) is incorrect because the AD curve

reflects all goods and services, and does not illustrate substitution between different product markets within an economy. Choice (E) is incorrect because consumers cannot negotiate lower prices as demand increases.

29. **A** As prices rise, real GDP falls due to the foreign trade effect. Choice (B) is incorrect because when prices rise, the prices of imports from other countries become relatively less expensive. Choice (C) is incorrect because, according to the Interest Rate Effect, when prices rise, a consumer's purchase power decreases. Choice (D) is incorrect because according to the Real Wealth Effect, as prices rise, the value of assets such as cash decreases. Choice (E) is incorrect because as prices rise, the value of cash assets falls, and consumers purchase fewer goods and services.

30. **E** The multiplier equals $\dfrac{1}{(1-\text{MPC})}$. In this case, the multiplier equals $\dfrac{1}{0.35}$ or 2.8571. $300 × 2.8571 = $857.14. Choice (A) is incorrect because it is the multiplier multiplied by a $100 increase in spending. Choice (B) is incorrect because the multiplier would need to be 1 to get only a $300 increase in GDP per $300 increase in spending. Choice (C) is incorrect because it is $\dfrac{1}{0.65}$ × $300 rather than $\dfrac{1}{(1-0.65)}$. Choice (D) is incorrect because it is the multiplier multiplied by a $200 increase in spending.

31. **A** Choice (A) provides the definition of the LAS. Choice (B) is incorrect because the horizontal AS curve is a recessionary curve and not the long-run aggregate supply curve. Choice (C) is incorrect because the upward-sloping AS curve is the intermediate stage between recession and LAS. Choice (D) is incorrect because the horizontal AS curve reflects underemployment. Choice (E) is incorrect because on the LAS, changes in aggregate demand affect the price level but not real GDP.

32. **E** Keynesian analysis blames unemployment in an economy on "sticky" wages and suggests that government intervention is necessary to alleviate unemployment in an economy. Choice (A) is incorrect because Keynes did not assert that consumers need protection from changing prices. Choice (B) is incorrect because when consumers save in a financial institution, the funds are made available by that institution as loans for capital investment. Choice (C) is incorrect because consumers invest in education and training even without government incentive. Choice (D) is incorrect because technological innovation occurs in a market economy with or without government incentives or intervention.

33. **B** When the government increases the money supply, the AD curve shifts to the right. When the AD curve shifts to the right, this causes demand pull inflation. Choice (A) is incorrect because this is the definition of cost-push or supply-side inflation. Choice (C) is incorrect because this is the definition of creeping inflation. Choice (D) is incorrect because this describes galloping inflation. Choice (E) is incorrect because this is known as stagflation.

34. **A** An increase in government purchases will shift the AD curve to the right and increase GDP, which is an expansionary fiscal policy. Choice (B) is incorrect because increasing taxes will shift

the AD curve to the left and is contractionary. Choice (C) is incorrect because decreasing transfers will shift the AD curve to the left and is contractionary. Choice (D) is incorrect because increasing taxes is contractionary fiscal policy. Choice (E) is incorrect because the AD curve would shift to the right in the event of increased government investments.

35.  **A**  The multiplier equals $\dfrac{1}{(1-\text{MPC})}$. In this case, the multiplier equals $\dfrac{1}{0.3}$ or $3.\overline{3}$. $300 \times 3.\overline{3} =$ $1,000. Choice (B) is incorrect because $588 \times 1.7 \approx$ $1,000, but 1.7 is not the correct multiplier. Choice (C) is incorrect because it uses the multiplier $\dfrac{1}{0.7}$ = 1.43, which is incorrect. Choice (D) is incorrect because it uses the multiplier $\dfrac{1}{0.8}$ = 1.25, which is incorrect. Choice (E) is incorrect because this assumes the multiplier is 1.

36.  **C**  The chart in (C) correctly illustrates a recessionary gap. Choice (A) illustrates an economy at full employment. Choice (B) illustrates an inflationary gap. Choice (D) is an inflationary economy with $Y_e$ and $Y_f$ incorrect. Choice (E) is a recessionary economy with $Y_e$ and $Y_f$ incorrect.

37.  **C**  An inflationary gap occurs when the equilibrium between AS and AD is above the LAS. As a result, the inflationary gap is the amount by which equilibrium real GDP would have to decrease to move the economy to full employment. Choice (A) is incorrect because it describes a recessionary gap. Choice (B) is incorrect because if the AS curve shifts to the right, the economy would grow rather than decrease, and would not reach full employment. Choice (D) is incorrect because if the AD curve shifts to the right, the economy would grow rather than decrease. Choice (E) is incorrect because increasing the money supply would expand rather than contract the economy.

38.  **A**  Choice (B) is incorrect because if the MS line shifts to the right, interest rates would decrease to below 5%. Choices (C) and (D) are incorrect because the government has to increase the money supply to enact expansionary monetary policy. Choice (E) is incorrect because the MS line would shift to the right. Choice (A) is the correct answer.

39.  **D**  Choice (A) is incorrect because it describes fiscal policy. Choice (B) is incorrect because it describes the quantity theory of money. Choice (C) is incorrect because it describes the theory of money creation. Choice (E) is incorrect because it describes a fractional reserve banking system.

40.  **C**  Choices (A) and (B) are incorrect because banks will be willing to borrow more money from the central bank if the discount rate is lower. Choice (D) is incorrect because the MS curve will shift to the right. Choice (E) is incorrect because lowering the discount rate is one of the central bank's tools to control the money supply.

41.  **B**  The Phillips curve predicts that changes in unemployment will impact inflation, and lower unemployment leads to higher inflation. Choice (A) is incorrect because it is the opposite of what the Phillips curve depicts. Choices (C) and (D) are incorrect because a flat or convex curve is not consistent with lower unemployment and higher inflation. Choice (E) is incorrect because the Phillips curve does predict a consistent relationship between inflation and unemployment.

42. **C** Choices (A) and (B) are incorrect because they reverse the terms *budget deficit* and *national debt*. Eliminate (D) because T – G is a budget surplus, not a budget deficit. Lastly, (E) is incorrect because the budget deficit does not reflect net exports.

43. **A** If the government creates money, inflation increases. This means (B) doesn't work. Choice (C) is incorrect because crowding out happens when the government borrows money, not when businesses compete. Choice (D) is incorrect because if the government repurchases bonds in the open market, the money supply increases. Choice (E) is incorrect because if interest rates decrease, investments increase.

44. **B** Choices (A), (C), and (D) are incorrect because supply-side economists believe a tax cut will increase aggregate supply. Choice (E) is incorrect because higher investments would result in higher production. This leaves (B), the correct answer.

45. **B** The government spending multiplier equals $\dfrac{1}{(1-\text{MPC})}$. In this case, the multiplier equals $\dfrac{1}{0.80}$, or 5. Thus, 5 × \$400 billion = \$2 trillion increase in GDP. Choice (A) is incorrect because the multiplier would have to be 40 to get a \$2 trillion increase in GDP per \$50 billion increase in spending. Choice (C) is incorrect because the multiplier would have to be 4 to get a \$2 trillion increase from a \$500 billion increase in spending. Choice (D) is incorrect because it uses $\dfrac{1}{0.8}$ rather than $\dfrac{1}{(1-0.8)}$. Choice (E) is incorrect because the multiplier would have to be 0.25 to get a \$2 trillion increase in GDP from an \$8 trillion increase in government spending.

46. **D** The tax multiplier is: $\dfrac{-\text{MPC}}{\text{MPS}}$. In this case, it is $\dfrac{-0.8}{0.2} = -4$. So, for a \$1 trillion decrease, there will be a –1 trillion × –4 = \$4 trillion increase in GDP. Choices (A) and (B) are incorrect because they use an incorrect multiplier of $\dfrac{0.2}{0.8} = 0.25$. Choice (C) doesn't work because the tax decrease has a multiplier effect on GDP that will result in a greater than 1:1 increase in GDP. Choice (E) is incorrect because the tax multiplier is negative, as tax changes are inversely related with GDP.

47. **B** Expansionary policy leads to an appreciation of the domestic currency relative to foreign currencies. As a result, exports (X) decrease and imports (M) increase. Choice (B) is the correct answer because Net Exports (X – M) decrease, partially offsetting the effects of the expansionary policy. Choice (A) is incorrect because exports will decrease and imports will increase. You can also eliminate (C) and (D) because both imports and exports will change. Choice (E) is incorrect because exports and imports will change as a result of expansionary policy.

48. **A** Choice (A) is correct because if there is a change in relative income levels between countries, the country with the increasing income will increase the demand for the other country's products, and the other country's ability to buy those products. Choice (B) doesn't work because Country B's

currency will not decrease in value. Choices (C), (D), and (E) are incorrect because Country A's currency will not increase in value.

49. **C** After reviewing all answer choices, you should be able to eliminate (A) and (B) because the value of Japanese yen will increase. Since (D) and (E) both mention Japan's exports will be faster to increase in price, you can also eliminate those because Japanese products will be slower to increase in price. This leaves (C), the correct answer.

50. **A** Choices (B), (C), and (D) are all incorrect because the Canadian dollar will increase in value. Choice (E) also doesn't work because consumers will have high demand for the Canadian cars and will demand Canadian dollars to pay for the cars, which will increase the value of the Canadian dollar. Choice (A) is correct.

51. **C** Choices (A) and (D) are incorrect because depositors will demand more won. Eliminate (B) because the demand line will move to the right and the price will increase to $P_1$. Choice (E) is incorrect because savers will demand more won.

52. **B** Choice (A) is incorrect because a weaker currency will make a trade deficit smaller. Choices (C), (D), and (E) are incorrect because a weaker currency will decrease imports.

53. **A** Choices (B) and (C) are incorrect because it will take fewer units of that currency to buy a unit of another currency. Choices (D) and (E) are incorrect because when a currency appreciates, it becomes stronger.

54. **A** Choice (B) is incorrect because this describes a fixed exchange rate policy. You can also eliminate (C) because this describes a managed exchange rate policy. Choice (D) is incorrect because the exchange rate would change with demand in this situation. Lastly, (E) does not work because the demand curve is not negatively sloped. The correct answer is (A).

55. **A** Choice (B) is incorrect because the financial account balance is negative. Choices (C) and (D) are incorrect because the financial account balance includes asset ownership of individuals, businesses, and government. Choice (E) is incorrect because the financial account balance includes stocks, bonds, commodities, and other direct investments.

56. **E** The merchandise trade surplus or deficit is equal to the net value of exports plus the net value of imports, or the merchandise trade balance. Since it is negative, there is a merchandise trade deficit. Choice (A) is incorrect because the current-account balance includes services and other items. Choice (B) also does not work because the financial account balance includes only financial capital flows. You can eliminate (C) and (D) because services are not merchandise, leaving (E), the correct answer.

57. **A** Eliminate (B) because it describes the merchandise trade balance. Choice (C) is incorrect because it is the current-account balance. Choices (D) and (E) are also incorrect because they are blends of the merchandise trade balance and other items. The correct answer is (A).

58. **D**  The first thing you should realize is that (A) is incorrect because the value represents only merchandise. Choice (B) is only capital outflows, so that also does not work. Choice (C) is incorrect because it is only the financial account balance. Finally, (E) is incorrect because it is only the current-account balance. This leaves (D), the correct answer.

59. **E**  Choices (A), (B), (C), and (D) are all sources of economic growth, which shift the LRAS curve to the right or shift the PPC out. The only choice that works is (E) because a change in the exchange rate policy would not, on its own, spur economic growth.

60. **A**  Choices (B) and (E) are both incorrect because the relationship is inverse in the short run. Choices (C) and (D) are incorrect because the Phillips curve is vertical in the long run. You are left with (A), the correct answer.

# Section II: Free-Response

1.  A.  To enact expansionary fiscal policy, the Baselo government can increase government purchases. This has a direct effect on real GDP.

    or

    To enact expansionary fiscal policy, the Baselo government can decrease taxes. This will increase aggregate demand and boost real GDP.

    B.

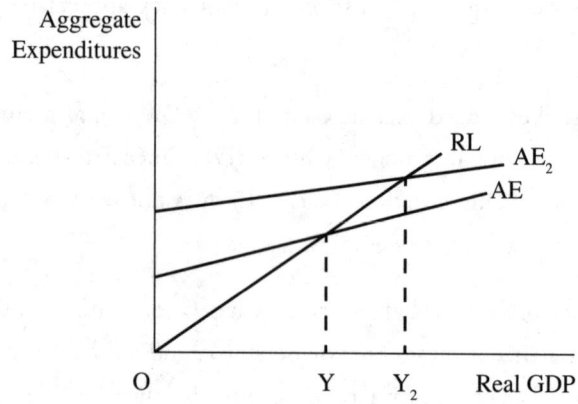

- RL is the 45° line along which AE = Real GDP

- An increase in government spending shifts the AE line up to $AE_2$.

- As a result, Y increases to $Y_2$.

    C.

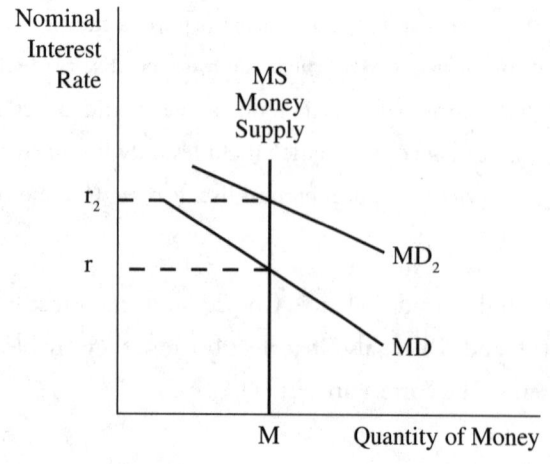

- With an increase in real GDP, the demand for money will increase, shifting the MD line to $MD_2$.

- The increase in demand for money will increase interest rates from r to $r_2$.

D. Government purchases are a part of total GDP. They are a part of autonomous expenditures. Therefore, the government spending multiplier is the same as the autonomous spending multiplier.

$$\text{Government spending multiplier} = \frac{1}{(1 - \text{MPC})} = \frac{1}{\text{MPS}}$$

E. The government spending multiplier is $\frac{1}{(1 - \text{MPC})}$. So, for Baselo it is

$$\frac{1}{(1 - 0.70)} = \frac{1}{(0.30)} = 3.33$$

For every dollar the government increases spending, the real GDP will increase by 3.33 dollars.

So, to achieve a $5 trillion increase in real GDP, Baselo must increase its expenditures by $x$:

$$x \times 3.33 = \$5 \text{ trillion}$$
$$x = \$1.5 \text{ trillion}$$

Baselo must increase its expenditures by $1.5 trillion, or $1,500 billion, to achieve a $5 trillion increase in real GDP.

F. The government tax multiplier is $\frac{-\text{MPC}}{\text{MPS}}$. So, for Baselo it is

$$\frac{-0.70}{0.30} = -2.33$$

For every dollar the government decreases taxes, the real GDP will increase by 2.33 dollars.

So, with a $1 trillion decrease in taxes, Baselo's real GDP will increase by $x$:

$$-\$1 \text{ trillion} \times -2.33 = x$$
$$\$2.33 \text{ trillion} = x$$

If Baselo decreases its taxes by $1 trillion, real GDP will increase by $2.33 trillion.

G. The balanced budget multiplier is 1.

So, the impact of a $1 trillion increase in government spending in Baselo is

$$\$1 \text{ trillion} \times 3.33 = \$3.33 \text{ trillion increase in GDP}$$

The impact of a $1 trillion increase in taxes in Baselo is

$$\$1 \text{ trillion} \times -2.33 = -\$2.33 \text{ trillion decrease in GDP}$$

The combined effect on real GDP is $3.33 − $2.33 = $1.0 trillion. This is no different from the initial change in G.

H. There are also indirect effects from expansionary fiscal policy. As the government increases expenditures, the demand for money will increase. This will drive up interest rates. Due to these higher interest rates, there will be a decrease in investments. The decrease in investments will decrease real GDP. However, this decrease in GDP will likely be smaller than the original increase in real GDP due to the increase in government expenditures. This is partial crowding out, which is illustrated by this formula:

$$G\uparrow \text{ or } T\downarrow \Rightarrow \ AD\uparrow \Rightarrow \ Y\uparrow \Rightarrow \ Md\uparrow \Rightarrow \ r\uparrow \Rightarrow \ I\downarrow \Rightarrow \ Y_2\downarrow \ \text{ where } Y_2 \text{ is higher than } Y$$

2.  A.  To enact contractionary monetary policy, the central bank can engage in open market operations to sell government bonds. This effectively removes money from circulation and will decrease the money supply.

or

To enact contractionary monetary policy, the central bank can raise the discount rate paid by banks to borrow from the central bank. This will make the banks less likely to borrow from the central bank when the banks' excess reserves do not satisfy their demand for loans. This will decrease the money supply.

B.

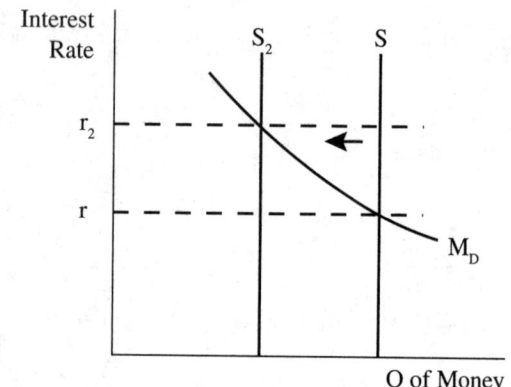

- The central bank can reduce the money supply and shift the S curve to the $S_2$ curve.
- As a result, nominal interest rates will increase from r to $r_2$.

C.

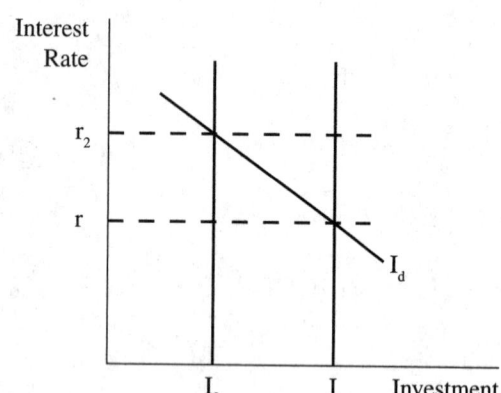

- As interest rates increase from r to $r_2$, investments will decrease from I to $I_2$.

D.

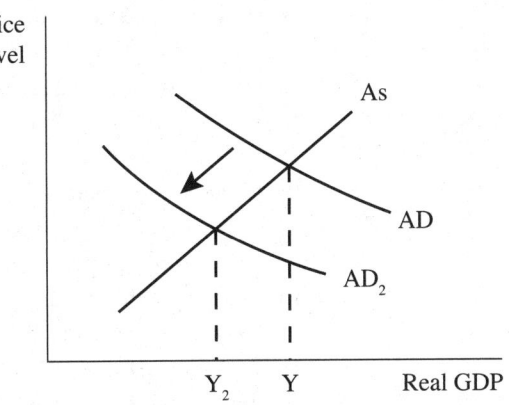

- As investments decrease, aggregate demand will decrease and shift from AD to AD₂.
- As a result, real GDP will decrease from Y to Y₂.

3. A. The money market depicts the supply of money in the short term, while the loanable funds market is solely concerned with real interest rates over the long term.

   B. The supply curve in the money market is vertical, while the supply curve in the loanable funds market is positively sloped. The reason is that the money market depicts the effect of the central bank increasing or decreasing the supply of money to lower or raise the prevailing interest rates. The central bank actions are illustrated by shifts in the vertical supply curve.

   The loanable funds market supply curve illustrates the sensitivity of loanable funds to changes in interest rates. As interest rates increase, the supply of loanable funds increases because households become more willing to forgo current consumption and make their money available to banks and borrowers.

   C.

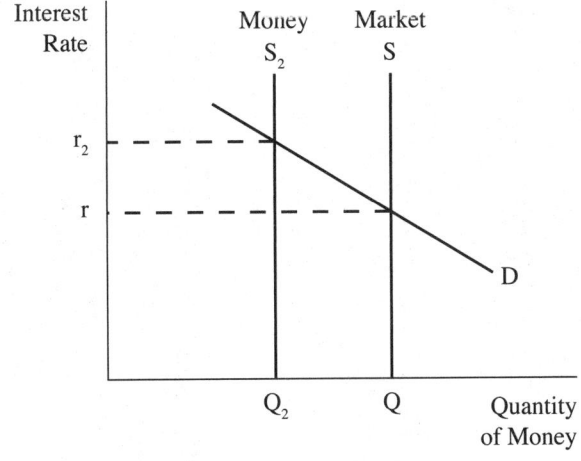

- As the government works to raise interest rates from r to r₂, the demand for money will decrease along the MD curve.
- This is a short-term adjustment to nominal interest rates.
- Consumers and businesses will be reluctant to borrow money at the new, higher interest rates.
- To match the decrease in demand, the supply of money will decrease, and the money supply curve will shift from S to S₂.

D.

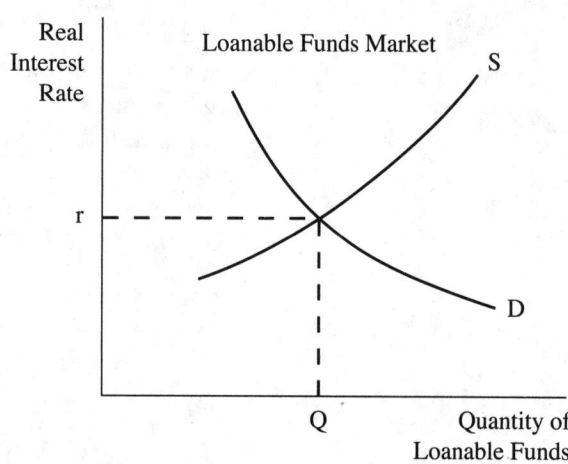

- In the loanable funds market, higher interest rates increase the supply of loanable funds. This is shown in the positively sloped S curve.
- As interest rates increase, households become willing to forgo consumption and put their money into savings, which can then be loaned out by banks to borrowers.
- In the long run, the only rate that matters is the real interest rate, as the markets adjust to changes in nominal interest rates.

# HOW TO SCORE YOUR PRACTICE TESTS

## Section I: Multiple-Choice

_____ × 1.66625 = _____
Number Correct                    Weighted
(out of 60)                       Section I Score
                                  (Do not round)

## Section II: Free-Response

Question 1   _____ × 2.50125 = _____
                  (out of 10)                (Do not round)

Question 2   _____ × 2.50125 = _____
                  (out of 5)                 (Do not round)

Question 3   _____ × 2.50125 = _____
                  (out of 5)                 (Do not round)

### AP Score Conversion Chart Macroeconomics

| Composite Score Range | AP Score |
|-----------------------|----------|
| 107–150               | 5        |
| 90–106                | 4        |
| 73–89                 | 3        |
| 56–72                 | 2        |
| 0–55                  | 1        |

Sum = _____
           Weighted
           Section II Score
           (Do not round)

## Composite Score

_____ + _____ = _____
    Weighted            Weighted          Composite Score
   Section I Score     Section II Score    (Round to nearest
                                            whole number)

_Note: This score sheet is to help you estimate your approximate score for the official exam, not your actual score._

# Appendix:
# Formula Sheets

Scan the QR code below and register your book to access the digital flashcards of these formula terms:

# Microeconomics

| | |
|---|---|
| **Allocative Efficiency Condition** | P = MC, or more precisely, Marginal Social Benefit (MSB) = Marginal Social Cost (MSC) |
| **Average Fixed Cost** | $AFC = \dfrac{\text{Total Fixed Cost (TFC)}}{\text{Quantity of Output (Q)}}$ |
| **Average Product** | $AFP = \dfrac{\text{Total Product}}{\text{Quantity of Input}}$ |
| **Average Profit** | $\text{Average Profit} = \dfrac{\text{Total Profit}}{\text{Quantity}}$ |
| **Average Revenue** | $\text{Average Revenue} = \dfrac{\text{Total Revenue}}{\text{Quantity}}$ |
| **Average Total Cost** | $ATC = \dfrac{\text{Total Cost (TC)}}{\text{Quantity of Output (Q)}}$ |
| **Average Variable Cost** | $AVC = \dfrac{\text{Total Variable Cost (TC)}}{\text{Quantity of Output (Q)}}$ |
| **Cross-Price Elasticity of Demand** | $\dfrac{\text{Percentage Change in Quantity Demanded of Good X}}{\text{Percentage Change in Price of Good Y}}$ |
| **Distributive Efficiency Condition** | $\dfrac{MU_F}{P_F} = \dfrac{MU_C}{P_C}$ |
| **Elasticity of Supply** | $\dfrac{\text{Percentage Change in Quantity Supplied}}{\text{Percentage Change in Price}}$<br><br>(Use the point or arc formula as indicated below for the price elasticity of demand, substituting the quantity supplied for the quantity demanded.) |
| **Factor of Production Hiring Rule: Hire Until** | MRP = MFC (in other books, MFC is sometimes called MRC) |

| | |
|---|---|
| **Gini Coefficient** | $$\dfrac{\text{shaded area}}{\text{area of triangle ABC}}$$ |
| **Marginal Cost** | $$MC = \dfrac{\Delta TC}{\Delta Q} = \dfrac{\Delta TVC}{\Delta Q}$$ |
| **Marginal Product of Labor** | $$MP_L = \dfrac{\Delta TP}{\Delta L}$$ |
| **Marginal Revenue** | $$MR = \dfrac{\Delta TR}{\Delta Q}$$ |
| **Marginal Revenue Product of Labor (MRP$_L$)** | $$MRP_L = MP_L \times P_{output}$$ |
| **Optimal Combination of Resources Condition** | $$\dfrac{MP_L}{w} = \dfrac{MP_K}{r}$$ |
| **Optimal Consumption Rule** | $$\dfrac{MU_X}{P_X} = \dfrac{MU_Y}{P_Y}$$ |

**Price Elasticity of Demand**

**Simple "Point" Formula**

$$\dfrac{\%\Delta Q_d}{\%\Delta P} = \dfrac{\dfrac{\Delta Q_d}{Q}}{\dfrac{\Delta P}{P}} = \dfrac{\dfrac{Q_{new} - Q_{old}}{Q_{old}}}{\dfrac{P_{new} - P_{old}}{P_{old}}}$$

**More Precise "Arc" Formula**

$$\dfrac{\dfrac{Q_{new} - Q_{old}}{\left(\dfrac{Q_{new} + Q_{old}}{2}\right)}}{\dfrac{P_{new} + P_{old}}{\left(\dfrac{P_{new} + P_{old}}{2}\right)}}$$

| Price for a Competitive Firm | $P = MR = AR$ |
|---|---|
| Production Efficiency Condition | $\dfrac{w}{r} = \dfrac{MP_L}{MP_K}$ or $\dfrac{MP_K}{r} = \dfrac{MP_L}{w}$ or $P = \min ATC$ |
| Profit | $Profit = TR - TC$ |
| Profit-Maximizing Output Level (if output should be produced at all), rule for finding | $MR = MC$ |
| Slope | $\dfrac{Rise}{Run}$ |
| Slope of the Total Product Curve | $\dfrac{Rise}{Run} = \dfrac{\text{Change in Total Product}}{\text{Change in the Number of Units of an Input}} = \text{Marginal Product}$ |
| Socially Optimal Level of Output | $MSB = MSC$ |
| Total Costs | Total Costs = Total Fixed Costs + Total Variable Costs, $TC = TFC + TVC$ |

## Macroeconomics

| Aggregate Expenditure in a Simple Model Without Government or Foreign Sectors | $AE = C + I$ |
|---|---|
| Allocative Efficiency Condition | $P = MC$, or more precisely, Marginal Social Benefit (MSB) = Marginal Social Cost (MSC) |
| Autonomous Spending Multiplier | $\text{Multiplier} = \dfrac{1}{1 - MPC} = \dfrac{1}{MPS}$ |
| Balanced Budget Multiplier | Balanced Budget Multiplier = $\dfrac{1}{1 - MPC} + \left( \dfrac{-MPC}{1 - MPC} \right) = \dfrac{1 - MPC}{1 - MPC} = 1$ |
| Bank's Reserve Ratio | $\text{Reserve Ratio} = \dfrac{\text{Bank Reserves}}{\text{Total Deposits}}$ |
| Budget Deficit | Budget Deficit = Federal Government Spending – Tax Collections (A negative deficit indicates a surplus.) |
| Financial Account Balance | Financial Account Balance = Foreign Purchases of Home Assets – Home Purchases of Foreign Assets |
| Consumer Price Index | $CPI = \dfrac{\text{Base Year Quantities} \times \text{Current Year Prices}}{\text{Base Year Quantities} \times \text{Base Year Prices}} \times 100$ |

| **Current-Account Balance** | Current-Account Balance = Trade Balance + Services Balance + Transfers |
|---|---|
| **Distributive Efficiency Condition** | $\dfrac{MU_F}{P_F} = \dfrac{MU_C}{P_C}$ |
| **Equation of Exchange** | $MV = PQ$ |
| **Gross Domestic Product** | $GDP = C + I + G + (X - M)$<br><br>$GDP = NI + \text{Depreciation} - \text{Subsidies} + \text{Net Income of Foreigners}$ |
| **Gross Domestic Product Deflator** | $GDP\ Deflator = \dfrac{\text{Current Year Quantities} \times \text{Current Year Prices}}{\text{Current Year Quantities} \times \text{Base Year Prices}} \times 100$ |
| **Income in a Simple Model Without Government or Foreign Sectors** | $Y = C + S$ |
| **Inflation Between Two Years** | Inflation Between Years Y and Z =<br><br>$\left[\dfrac{\text{CPI in Year Z}}{\text{CPI in Year Y}} - 1\right] \times 100$ |
| **Marginal Propensity to Consume** | $MPC = \dfrac{\text{Change in Consumption}}{\text{Change in Income}}$ |
| **Marginal Propensity to Save** | $MPS = \dfrac{\text{Change in Saving}}{\text{Change in Income}}$ |
| **Marginal Propensity to Save and Marginal Propensity to Consume are Complements** | $MPC + MPS = 1$ |
| **Merchandise Trade Balance** | Merchandise Trade Balance = Value of Merchandise Exports – Value of Merchandise Imports |
| **Nominal Interest Rate** | Nominal Interest Rate = Real Interest Rate + Anticipated Inflation |
| **Okun's Law** | % increase in unemployment above natural rate × 2 = % decrease in output (The 2 in the equation is an approximation.) |
| **Production Efficiency Condition** | $\dfrac{w}{r} = \dfrac{MP_L}{MP_K}$ |
| **Real GDP** | $\dfrac{\text{Nominal GDP}}{\text{CPI* for the same year as the nominal figure}} \times 100$<br><br>*CPI or GDP deflator |
| **Real Interest Rate** | Real Interest Rate = Nominal Interest Rate – Anticipated Inflation |

| Slope | $\dfrac{\text{Rise}}{\text{Run}}$ |
|---|---|
| Tax Multiplier | $\text{Tax Multiplier} = -\dfrac{\text{MPC}}{\text{MPS}}$ |
| Total Amount of Deposits Resulting from an Initial Deposit That Is Ultimately Held as Reserves | $\text{Simple Money (or Deposit) Multiplier} = \dfrac{1}{\text{Required Reserve Ratio}}$ |
| Unemployment Rate | $\dfrac{\text{Unemployed}}{\text{Labor Force}}$ |

Completely darken bubbles with a No. 2 pencil.  If you make a mistake, be sure to erase mark completely.  Erase all stray marks.

## 1. YOUR NAME:
(Print)  _____ Last _____ First _____ M.I.

SIGNATURE: _____  DATE: ___ / ___ / ___

HOME ADDRESS: _____
(Print)  Number and Street

_____
City _____ State _____ Zip Code

PHONE NO. : _____
(Print)

## 5. YOUR NAME

| First 4 letters of last name | | | | FIRST INIT | MID INIT |
|---|---|---|---|---|---|
| Ⓐ | Ⓐ | Ⓐ | Ⓐ | Ⓐ | Ⓐ |
| Ⓑ | Ⓑ | Ⓑ | Ⓑ | Ⓑ | Ⓑ |
| Ⓒ | Ⓒ | Ⓒ | Ⓒ | Ⓒ | Ⓒ |
| Ⓓ | Ⓓ | Ⓓ | Ⓓ | Ⓓ | Ⓓ |
| Ⓔ | Ⓔ | Ⓔ | Ⓔ | Ⓔ | Ⓔ |
| Ⓕ | Ⓕ | Ⓕ | Ⓕ | Ⓕ | Ⓕ |
| Ⓖ | Ⓖ | Ⓖ | Ⓖ | Ⓖ | Ⓖ |
| Ⓗ | Ⓗ | Ⓗ | Ⓗ | Ⓗ | Ⓗ |
| Ⓘ | Ⓘ | Ⓘ | Ⓘ | Ⓘ | Ⓘ |
| Ⓙ | Ⓙ | Ⓙ | Ⓙ | Ⓙ | Ⓙ |
| Ⓚ | Ⓚ | Ⓚ | Ⓚ | Ⓚ | Ⓚ |
| Ⓛ | Ⓛ | Ⓛ | Ⓛ | Ⓛ | Ⓛ |
| Ⓜ | Ⓜ | Ⓜ | Ⓜ | Ⓜ | Ⓜ |
| Ⓝ | Ⓝ | Ⓝ | Ⓝ | Ⓝ | Ⓝ |
| Ⓞ | Ⓞ | Ⓞ | Ⓞ | Ⓞ | Ⓞ |
| Ⓟ | Ⓟ | Ⓟ | Ⓟ | Ⓟ | Ⓟ |
| Ⓠ | Ⓠ | Ⓠ | Ⓠ | Ⓠ | Ⓠ |
| Ⓡ | Ⓡ | Ⓡ | Ⓡ | Ⓡ | Ⓡ |
| Ⓢ | Ⓢ | Ⓢ | Ⓢ | Ⓢ | Ⓢ |
| Ⓣ | Ⓣ | Ⓣ | Ⓣ | Ⓣ | Ⓣ |
| Ⓤ | Ⓤ | Ⓤ | Ⓤ | Ⓤ | Ⓤ |
| Ⓥ | Ⓥ | Ⓥ | Ⓥ | Ⓥ | Ⓥ |
| Ⓦ | Ⓦ | Ⓦ | Ⓦ | Ⓦ | Ⓦ |
| Ⓧ | Ⓧ | Ⓧ | Ⓧ | Ⓧ | Ⓧ |
| Ⓨ | Ⓨ | Ⓨ | Ⓨ | Ⓨ | Ⓨ |
| Ⓩ | Ⓩ | Ⓩ | Ⓩ | Ⓩ | Ⓩ |

IMPORTANT:  Please fill in these boxes exactly as shown on the back cover of your test book.

## 2. TEST FORM

## 3. TEST CODE

## 4. REGISTRATION NUMBER

| | | | | | | | | | | | |
|---|---|---|---|---|---|---|---|---|---|---|---|
| ⓪ | Ⓐ | ⓪ | ⓪ | ⓪ | ⓪ | ⓪ | ⓪ | ⓪ | ⓪ | ⓪ | ⓪ |
| ① | Ⓑ | ① | ① | ① | ① | ① | ① | ① | ① | ① | ① |
| ② | Ⓒ | ② | ② | ② | ② | ② | ② | ② | ② | ② | ② |
| ③ | Ⓓ | ③ | ③ | ③ | ③ | ③ | ③ | ③ | ③ | ③ | ③ |
| ④ | Ⓔ | ④ | ④ | ④ | ④ | ④ | ④ | ④ | ④ | ④ | ④ |
| ⑤ | Ⓕ | ⑤ | ⑤ | ⑤ | ⑤ | ⑤ | ⑤ | ⑤ | ⑤ | ⑤ | ⑤ |
| ⑥ | Ⓖ | ⑥ | ⑥ | ⑥ | ⑥ | ⑥ | ⑥ | ⑥ | ⑥ | ⑥ | ⑥ |
| ⑦ | | ⑦ | ⑦ | ⑦ | ⑦ | ⑦ | ⑦ | ⑦ | ⑦ | ⑦ | ⑦ |
| ⑧ | | ⑧ | ⑧ | ⑧ | ⑧ | ⑧ | ⑧ | ⑧ | ⑧ | ⑧ | ⑧ |
| ⑨ | | ⑨ | ⑨ | ⑨ | ⑨ | ⑨ | ⑨ | ⑨ | ⑨ | ⑨ | ⑨ |

## 6. DATE OF BIRTH

| Month | | Day | | Year | |
|---|---|---|---|---|---|
| ◯ JAN | | | | | |
| ◯ FEB | | | | | |
| ◯ MAR | ⓪ | ⓪ | ⓪ | ⓪ | |
| ◯ APR | ① | ① | ① | ① | |
| ◯ MAY | ② | ② | ② | ② | |
| ◯ JUN | ③ | ③ | ③ | ③ | |
| ◯ JUL | | ④ | ④ | ④ | |
| ◯ AUG | | ⑤ | ⑤ | ⑤ | |
| ◯ SEP | | ⑥ | ⑥ | ⑥ | |
| ◯ OCT | | ⑦ | ⑦ | ⑦ | |
| ◯ NOV | | ⑧ | ⑧ | ⑧ | |
| ◯ DEC | | ⑨ | ⑨ | ⑨ | |

The **Princeton** Review®

## Section ①

Start with number 1 for each new section.
If a section has fewer questions than answer spaces, leave the extra answer spaces blank.

1. Ⓐ Ⓑ Ⓒ Ⓓ Ⓔ
2. Ⓐ Ⓑ Ⓒ Ⓓ Ⓔ
3. Ⓐ Ⓑ Ⓒ Ⓓ Ⓔ
4. Ⓐ Ⓑ Ⓒ Ⓓ Ⓔ
5. Ⓐ Ⓑ Ⓒ Ⓓ Ⓔ
6. Ⓐ Ⓑ Ⓒ Ⓓ Ⓔ
7. Ⓐ Ⓑ Ⓒ Ⓓ Ⓔ
8. Ⓐ Ⓑ Ⓒ Ⓓ Ⓔ
9. Ⓐ Ⓑ Ⓒ Ⓓ Ⓔ
10. Ⓐ Ⓑ Ⓒ Ⓓ Ⓔ
11. Ⓐ Ⓑ Ⓒ Ⓓ Ⓔ
12. Ⓐ Ⓑ Ⓒ Ⓓ Ⓔ
13. Ⓐ Ⓑ Ⓒ Ⓓ Ⓔ
14. Ⓐ Ⓑ Ⓒ Ⓓ Ⓔ
15. Ⓐ Ⓑ Ⓒ Ⓓ Ⓔ

16. Ⓐ Ⓑ Ⓒ Ⓓ Ⓔ
17. Ⓐ Ⓑ Ⓒ Ⓓ Ⓔ
18. Ⓐ Ⓑ Ⓒ Ⓓ Ⓔ
19. Ⓐ Ⓑ Ⓒ Ⓓ Ⓔ
20. Ⓐ Ⓑ Ⓒ Ⓓ Ⓔ
21. Ⓐ Ⓑ Ⓒ Ⓓ Ⓔ
22. Ⓐ Ⓑ Ⓒ Ⓓ Ⓔ
23. Ⓐ Ⓑ Ⓒ Ⓓ Ⓔ
24. Ⓐ Ⓑ Ⓒ Ⓓ Ⓔ
25. Ⓐ Ⓑ Ⓒ Ⓓ Ⓔ
26. Ⓐ Ⓑ Ⓒ Ⓓ Ⓔ
27. Ⓐ Ⓑ Ⓒ Ⓓ Ⓔ
28. Ⓐ Ⓑ Ⓒ Ⓓ Ⓔ
29. Ⓐ Ⓑ Ⓒ Ⓓ Ⓔ
30. Ⓐ Ⓑ Ⓒ Ⓓ Ⓔ

31. Ⓐ Ⓑ Ⓒ Ⓓ Ⓔ
32. Ⓐ Ⓑ Ⓒ Ⓓ Ⓔ
33. Ⓐ Ⓑ Ⓒ Ⓓ Ⓔ
34. Ⓐ Ⓑ Ⓒ Ⓓ Ⓔ
35. Ⓐ Ⓑ Ⓒ Ⓓ Ⓔ
36. Ⓐ Ⓑ Ⓒ Ⓓ Ⓔ
37. Ⓐ Ⓑ Ⓒ Ⓓ Ⓔ
38. Ⓐ Ⓑ Ⓒ Ⓓ Ⓔ
39. Ⓐ Ⓑ Ⓒ Ⓓ Ⓔ
40. Ⓐ Ⓑ Ⓒ Ⓓ Ⓔ
41. Ⓐ Ⓑ Ⓒ Ⓓ Ⓔ
42. Ⓐ Ⓑ Ⓒ Ⓓ Ⓔ
43. Ⓐ Ⓑ Ⓒ Ⓓ Ⓔ
44. Ⓐ Ⓑ Ⓒ Ⓓ Ⓔ
45. Ⓐ Ⓑ Ⓒ Ⓓ Ⓔ

46. Ⓐ Ⓑ Ⓒ Ⓓ Ⓔ
47. Ⓐ Ⓑ Ⓒ Ⓓ Ⓔ
48. Ⓐ Ⓑ Ⓒ Ⓓ Ⓔ
49. Ⓐ Ⓑ Ⓒ Ⓓ Ⓔ
50. Ⓐ Ⓑ Ⓒ Ⓓ Ⓔ
51. Ⓐ Ⓑ Ⓒ Ⓓ Ⓔ
52. Ⓐ Ⓑ Ⓒ Ⓓ Ⓔ
53. Ⓐ Ⓑ Ⓒ Ⓓ Ⓔ
54. Ⓐ Ⓑ Ⓒ Ⓓ Ⓔ
55. Ⓐ Ⓑ Ⓒ Ⓓ Ⓔ
56. Ⓐ Ⓑ Ⓒ Ⓓ Ⓔ
57. Ⓐ Ⓑ Ⓒ Ⓓ Ⓔ
58. Ⓐ Ⓑ Ⓒ Ⓓ Ⓔ
59. Ⓐ Ⓑ Ⓒ Ⓓ Ⓔ
60. Ⓐ Ⓑ Ⓒ Ⓓ Ⓔ

**The Princeton Review®**

Completely darken bubbles with a No. 2 pencil. If you make a mistake, be sure to erase mark completely. Erase all stray marks.

**1. YOUR NAME:**
(Print) _____ Last _____ First _____ M.I. ___

SIGNATURE: _____ DATE: ___ / ___ / ___

HOME ADDRESS: _____
(Print) _____ Number and Street

_____ City _____ State _____ Zip Code

PHONE NO. : _____
(Print)

**IMPORTANT:** Please fill in these boxes exactly as shown on the back cover of your test book.

**2. TEST FORM**

**3. TEST CODE**

**4. REGISTRATION NUMBER**

**5. YOUR NAME**

| First 4 letters of last name | | | | FIRST INIT | MID INIT |
|---|---|---|---|---|---|

Test Code column has: 0, A / 1, B / 2, C / 3, D / 4, E / 5, F / 6, G / 7 / 8 / 9

Registration / name columns: 0–9 and A–Z bubbles

**6. DATE OF BIRTH**

| Month | Day | | Year | |
|---|---|---|---|---|
| ○ JAN | | | | |
| ○ FEB | | | | |
| ○ MAR | ⓪ ⓪ | ⓪ ⓪ | | |
| ○ APR | ① ① | ① ① | | |
| ○ MAY | ② ② | ② ② | | |
| ○ JUN | ③ ③ | ③ ③ | | |
| ○ JUL | ④ | ④ | | |
| ○ AUG | ⑤ | ⑤ | | |
| ○ SEP | ⑥ | ⑥ | | |
| ○ OCT | ⑦ | ⑦ | | |
| ○ NOV | ⑧ | ⑧ | | |
| ○ DEC | ⑨ | ⑨ | | |

**The Princeton Review®**

**Section 1**

Start with number 1 for each new section.
If a section has fewer questions than answer spaces, leave the extra answer spaces blank.

1. A B C D E
2. A B C D E
3. A B C D E
4. A B C D E
5. A B C D E
6. A B C D E
7. A B C D E
8. A B C D E
9. A B C D E
10. A B C D E
11. A B C D E
12. A B C D E
13. A B C D E
14. A B C D E
15. A B C D E

16. A B C D E
17. A B C D E
18. A B C D E
19. A B C D E
20. A B C D E
21. A B C D E
22. A B C D E
23. A B C D E
24. A B C D E
25. A B C D E
26. A B C D E
27. A B C D E
28. A B C D E
29. A B C D E
30. A B C D E

31. A B C D E
32. A B C D E
33. A B C D E
34. A B C D E
35. A B C D E
36. A B C D E
37. A B C D E
38. A B C D E
39. A B C D E
40. A B C D E
41. A B C D E
42. A B C D E
43. A B C D E
44. A B C D E
45. A B C D E

46. A B C D E
47. A B C D E
48. A B C D E
49. A B C D E
50. A B C D E
51. A B C D E
52. A B C D E
53. A B C D E
54. A B C D E
55. A B C D E
56. A B C D E
57. A B C D E
58. A B C D E
59. A B C D E
60. A B C D E